SPANISH POLICY
IN COLONIAL CHILE

SPANISH POLICY
IN COLONIAL CHILE

The Struggle for Social Justice, 1535-1700

EUGENE H. KORTH, S.J.

1968
STANFORD UNIVERSITY PRESS
STANFORD, CALIFORNIA

Stanford University Press
Stanford, California
© 1968 by the Board of Trustees of the
Leland Stanford Junior University
Printed in the United States of America
L.C. 68-26779

To those who believe in the dignity and rights of man

PREFACE

One of the most significant features of the Spanish conquest of America was the persistent effort by the Spanish Crown to protect the Indians of the New World against unjust aggression and exploitation. During the sixteenth century this effort became identified with the ideas and experiments of Bartolomé de las Casas, the Dominican friar and social theorist who gained lasting renown by his untiring defense of the rights of the Indians. Unfortunately, the controversies associated with his name have tended to obscure the broader outlines of the struggle and the achievements of less publicized men in other parts of Spain's huge American empire. The purpose of this book is to correct the imbalance to some extent by relating what happened in Chile during the years between 1535, when the first Europeans entered the territory, and 1700, when the Age of the Hapsburgs came to an end. The story deserves telling in its own right because of its intrinsic significance, but it is particularly appropriate at the present time, when questions of interracial amity and human rights are in the forefront of men's consciences.

As it materialized in Chile, the struggle for social justice was an integral part of a broader political-cultural-religious problem—the subjugation and conversion of the pagan Araucanians. The heroic resistance of these "Chilean Apaches" to white domination for more than three centuries has been the subject of much learned discussion in the past. Most of the writers who have treated this theme have sought an explanation for the bitter strife between the two races in the warlike character of the Araucanians, their love of liberty and independence, their political disunity, which made organized conquest almost impossible, their skill in adjusting to European military techniques, the paucity of Spanish arms in the region, the frequent changes in official policy and administration, and the isolated position of the colony. All of these factors undoubtedly constitute part of the answer, but they are not sufficient in themselves to explain the enduring quality of the Araucanian resistance. It is the thesis of this book that the principal cause of that resistance was the harsh treatment that the Indians experienced at the hands of the whites, many of whom looked upon the war as a convenient way of solving the labor problem and of acquiring slaves for their farms and haciendas.

An examination of the records supports this conclusion. It shows that the *encomenderos* (Spaniards who had Indians entrusted to them), aided frequently by unscrupulous or indifferent officials, selfishly ignored the royal decrees protecting the natives in order to profit from their labor. The tribute they exacted in the form of personal service resulted in a system of forced labor that quickly decimated the pacified tribes and led to the official enslavement of all "rebel" Indians. The *servicio personal*, with its attendant evils, was thus the strongest deterrent to interracial harmony and understanding.

That the Spaniards themselves recognized this fact is clear from numerous attempts at corrective legislation. The *tasas* (tribute assessments) that were issued on various occasions were tangible evidence of a desire to eliminate existing abuses. All of these measures failed because they conflicted with the interests of the encomenderos and lacked the support of the local bureaucracy, who in the final analysis controlled the machinery for effective enforcement.

Despite the abuses that prevailed, the lot of the Indians could have been worse. That it was not was due in great part to a number of ecclesiastical prelates, distinguished laymen, and religious leaders, who vigorously defended the principles of human dignity. Outstanding among them were Gil González de San Nicolás, a Dominican friar who publicly opposed the military conquest of Araucania on moral grounds; Bishops San Miguel, Medellín, and Humanzoro, whose constant agitation on behalf of the natives brought the Indians some measure of relief; Judge Hernando de Santillán and Governor Oñez de Loyola, two conscientious Crown officials who tried to introduce constructive reforms; and various members of the Society of Jesus who worked to establish a better social order under the progressive leadership of such men as Diego de Torres Bollo, Luis de Valdivia, and Diego de Rosales.

Considerable space is given in the narrative to the Jesuits' role in the struggle, for the Blackrobes were a controversial force in the colony almost from the time of their arrival in 1593. Their ideas on spiritual conquest, Indian slavery, compulsory service, and individual rights clashed with those of the civil and military authorities and aroused resentment among the landed proprietors and city merchants. This was particularly true of the campaign for fair labor practices that Torres Bollo initiated and of Luis de Valdivia's ill-starred program of defensive warfare. Because of the significance of these two experiments, each is the subject of a separate chapter. The murder of the Jesuit missionaries in Elicura, which was cited by Valdivia's critics as cardinal proof of the inherent weakness of his system, has been given like prominence in an attempt to correct some of the inaccuracies, false charges, and misinterpretations of earlier scholars, notably Diego Barros Arana, founder of the "liberal" school of Chilean historians of the nineteenth century, and Francisco Antonio Encina, the leading exponent of revisionist thinking among present-day writers in Chile.

The narrative as a whole has three main parts. The first chapter gives some background information regarding the doctrinal debates over Indian slavery and forced labor that developed in Spain and in America during the first half of the sixteenth century. Chapters Two, Three, and Four are concerned with the personalities and events that dominated the struggle for justice in Chile between Almagro's expedition of 1535 and the great Indian uprising of 1598, which seriously threatened to destroy the Spanish outposts in the Long Land. The activities of the Jesuits following their arrival in 1593 until the abrogation of Valdivia's system of peaceful penetration are discussed in Chapters Five, Six, Seven, and Eight. Chapter Nine traces social, political, and military developments that followed the resumption of offensive warfare in 1626 and culminated in the disastrous rebellion of 1655. Chapter Ten concentrates on events immediately preceding the emancipation decree of 1674 and the expedients that the colonists devised during the final quarter of the century to justify their evasion of the new legislation. Chapter Eleven concludes the story by emphasizing a number of factors, other than Indian slavery and personal service, that contributed to the complexity and longevity of the Araucanian conflict.

The year 1700 was chosen as the termination date for the study because it marks the end of what can be called the "aggressive" phase of the struggle for justice in Chile and the transition to a more settled period during which relations between Indians and whites changed perceptibly. As the text will explain, there were a number of reasons for this, but the most important one was the emergence of a mestizo laboring class, a product of the miscegenation of the preceding century. With the appearance of this new social and economic force, dependence on Indian labor began to decline and with it one of the basic causes of friction between the two races. This development was aided by the social reforms that Charles III introduced during the second half of the century, as a result of which the Indian's legal status was improved and the way was cleared for the final dissolution of the encomiendas and forced labor in 1791. Although the unpacified tribes south of the Biobío continued to hold out against foreign domination for another ninety years, they ceased to be a determining factor in the life of the country.

One final point. Although the Araucanian war figures prominently in this narrative, it is not the armed conflict itself that is of direct concern, but rather the legal-moral problems to which it gave rise. Readers who are looking for a military history of the war will have to seek it elsewhere.

The research that provided the initial impetus for this book was done in the manuscript section of the National Library in Santiago, Chile (Archivo Medina, Fondo Jesuítico, Archivo Vicuña Mackenna, Archivo Morla Vicuña) during a year's residence in that country on a Doherty Foundation Fellowship in the early 1950's. The private archives of the Colegio San Ignacio, the Jesuit "college" in Santiago, and of the archdiocese of Santiago provided additional information on a number of topics, particularly those dealing with Jesuit activities and the controversy over Luis de Valdivia's system of defensive warfare. The original research has since been supplemented with materials from the Pastells Collection in Spain, the Newberry Library in Chicago, the University of Texas Latin American Collection, and the historical archives of Marquette University.

A number of people have contributed, directly or indirectly, to the appearance of this book. To all of them I owe a sincere debt of thanks.

I am particularly grateful to the Henry L. and Grace Doherty Charitable Foundation for the financial support that made the basic research in Chile possible, and to Rev. John Amberg, S.J., director of Canisius House for writers in Evanston, Illinois, for allowing me to enjoy the hospitality of the House for an extended period in 1965 and 1966 while the manuscript was taking final form. Dr. Lewis Hanke first interested me in the problem of social justice in the Spanish American empire when I was a graduate student at the University of Texas in the 1950's. Sr. Ricardo Donoso, one-time director of the National Library in Santiago, Chile, and Sr. Guillermo Feliú-Cruz, curator of the Medina Collection in the same Library, graciously provided access to manuscript collections and made many useful observations on Spanish activities in Chile. My Jesuit friends at the Colegio San Ignacio in Santiago gave me much pertinent background material and facilitated my researches in the private and ecclesiastical archives of that city. Rev. Joseph P. Donnelly, S.J., my colleague at Marquette University, and Miss Della M. Flusche of Loyola University, Chicago, read the manuscript with a critical eye and made numerous helpful suggestions regarding its contents. Miss Flusche was also most assiduous in locating source material at the Newberry Library in Chicago and in checking bibliographical references and other data.

I owe special thanks to my brother, Rev. Francis N. Korth, S.J., Professor of Theology and Canon Law at Marquette University, for his expert assistance on points of church law and interpretation, and to Mrs. Anne Firth Murray of Stanford University Press for her careful editing of the manuscript and for many valuable suggestions that greatly improved the original narrative.

Universidad Católica de Salta   Eugene H. Korth, S.J.
Salta, Argentina

CONTENTS

SPANISH POLICY
IN COLONIAL CHILE

I

HISTORICAL AND DOCTRINAL BACKGROUND

THE DISCOVERY OF AMERICA was truly, as López de Gómara, the well-known Spanish chronicler of the sixteenth century, so aptly described it, "the greatest event since the creation of the world, with the exception of the incarnation and death of its Creator."[1] The conquest and settlement of a vast unknown continent not only paved the way for the release of tremendous physical and spiritual forces; it also brought into focus a number of critical socio-moral problems whose attempted solution embodied a notable intellectual advance. Prior to the pioneering expedition of Columbus, the legal and theological thinking of the Old World had been patterned on the principles incorporated in ancient Roman law and the teachings of the medieval Schoolmen. While admirably suited to dealing with the foibles and aspirations of a Christian and civilized society, these concepts proved inadequate when applied to the novel situations arising out of the forceful occupation of virgin territories in a pagan environment. Thus it was that the early decades of the Spanish conquest were characterized by a variety of dissenting voices. The validity of Spain's claim to the Indies, the justice of waging war against defenseless primitives, the moral obligation of Christianizing the infidels, the advantages and disadvantages of peaceful conquest, the rational nature of the aborigines, the possibility of Europeanizing them, the pros and cons of the *encomienda* system—these and many other issues of lesser import continually troubled the councils of the king and complicated the work of overseas empire. Some were settled by a salutary revision of time-honored precepts; others provided the bases for unscientific social experiments; and still others, such as the perennial problems of forced labor and Indian slavery, were never completely solved before the Spanish empire in America had ceased to exist.

Slavery was not a new institution in the Spanish experience. Its roots were deeply embedded in the Iberian past. The advent of Christianity in the first century had mitigated some of its effects, but had failed to eradicate it completely. It was too useful as a social and economic expedient to succumb readily to moral and religious pressures. The enslavement of prisoners captured in war was still a common practice in the sixteenth century. So, too, was the imposition of servitude as a penalty for crimes and unnatural vices. There were even theologians who maintained that the enslavement of infidels for spiritual reasons was justifiable, to say nothing of philosophers and would-be *pensadores* who confidently asserted, with a nod to Aristotle, that some men were by nature intended to be slaves. The intellectual climate of the time thus favored the acceptance of slavery in Spanish America.

The exigencies of frontier settlement provided additional rationalizations. The rapid geographical expansion of the conquest, the desire of the Crown to reward its agents at no cost to itself, the scarcity of European immigrants to till the soil and work the mines of the New World, the need for an abundant supply of cheap labor, and the availability of thousands of ignorant natives made the introduction of forced labor a foregone conclusion. The forms it most readily assumed were the encomienda and the *mita*.

The encomienda was one of several Spanish institutions that underwent significant modifications on being transferred to America. Originally an encomienda was a temporary grant of manorial rights and jurisdiction over reconquered territories that the Crown made to deserving individuals (*encomenderos*) as a reward for their services against the Moors. It included a number of special privileges, among them a lifelong title to the feudal services of peasants living on the land. As refined in the Indies, the encomienda referred regularly to grants of Indians rather than of lands. Such a grant obligated the encomendero to feed, clothe, protect, civilize, and Christianize the natives entrusted to his care; in exchange, he was given a right to their services and tribute. Although thought to be just at the time, the encomienda system was fraught with disastrous consequences for the Indians. Many encomenderos, prompted by the desire for quick, easy riches, overworked their charges in an effort to extract more and more wealth from the soil and the mines. Under such circumstances the encomienda frequently degenerated into a system of control that was hardly distinguishable from actual slavery.

The mita, originally proposed as an alternative to the encomienda, differed from the earlier institution in several important respects: (1) it was essentially a levy of workers for specific public or private projects; (2) the *mitayos* (mita workers) were to receive wages for their services; (3) the period of work (*demora*) was limited by law to a designated number of days per year; and (4) the labor contract did not establish a permanent relationship between employer and employee. This last difference was especially significant; it meant that the mita employer could afford to be less concerned with the physical well-being of the native Indians than the encomendero, whose personal fortunes were much more dependent on the continued good health and strength of his Indians.

Although the mita had the advantage over the encomienda of paying wages for the labor it exacted, its effects on the Indians were no less destructive. Thousands of them were systematically uprooted from their homes every year, at great cost to themselves and their families, in order to comply with their mita obligation. Many of these unfortunates, because they fell victim to accidents, diseases, or inhuman treatment, never returned. Particularly onerous was the mita service in the mines and factories (*obrajes*) of Peru, which became the subject of a famous confidential report to the Crown as late as 1749.[2] Conditions in other parts of the empire were often little better.

The historical origins of the encomienda and other forms of slave labor date from the earliest years of Spanish hegemony in the Caribbean. According to Las Casas, the first instance of forced labor in the overseas possessions occurred in 1496, while Christopher Columbus was governor of Hispaniola. The friar described the circumstances in these words:

> Either the Admiral before leaving for Castile in March, 1496, or else the Adelantado [Bartholomew Columbus] after the Admiral's departure, imposed upon certain tribal rulers and their people, in addition to the tribute they were required to pay, or perhaps as the main part of it (for I was unable to find out for sure regarding this point), the task of culti-

vating the fields of the Spanish pueblos. They and all their people were occupied in providing sustenance for the Spaniards and in performing other personal services. This was the origin of the pestilential system of *repartimientos* and encomiendas* which has devastated and consumed all the Indies.[3]

A further step in this direction was taken in 1499, when grants of land together with the services of the Indians living on them were made to Francisco Roldán and his rebellious followers in order to bring them to terms.[4] Thus precedents were established that provided a pretext for unscrupulous operators. During the regime of Francisco de Bobadilla, who succeeded Columbus as governor of Hispaniola in 1499, the exploitation of the aborigines became an open scandal.

Reports of the abuses and indignities that the Indians were experiencing at the hands of the Spaniards eventually aroused the humanitarian instincts of Queen Isabella, as is clear from the special instructions she gave to Nicolás de Ovando at the time of his appointment as governor of the Indies. On September 16, 1501, Ovando was directed to safeguard the freedom of the natives, to protect them from harm, and to refrain from levying taxes that were not demanded of other royal subjects. The Indians were to be excused from labor in the mines or on public works except in the interests of the Crown, in which case they were to receive a just wage for their services. Ovando diligently strove to carry out these instructions. He soon discovered, however, that wages held no attraction for the Indians. They simply refused to accept Spanish offers of work, and within a few months the colony was faced with disaster.

Confronted with this dilemma, Isabella abandoned the principle of freedom of choice for the Indians and authorized the application of

---

* The distinction between repartimiento and encomienda is not always clear in the documents of the period, especially during the early decades of the conquest when the two terms were used interchangeably to denote a division of lands or of Indians as a reward for services rendered. Repartimiento later became a more general term signifying the distribution of practically anything ranging all the way from lands and Indian services to household goods and taxes, whereas encomienda referred exclusively to allotments of Indians and never included title to the land. Among modern historians the tendency has been to equate repartimiento with the gangs of Indian workers who were temporarily assigned to work on public or private projects, frequently in localities far removed from their lands and villages and in conditions that were often extremely hard. To avoid confusion, this is the sense in which the term is used in this book also. In Peru and Chile this type of forced labor was known as the mita.

forced labor under conditions that she hoped would protect the natives against unrestrained exploitation. She outlined the terms of the new dispensation in a *cédula* of December 20, 1503, addressed to Ovando:

> Beginning with the day you receive my letter, you will compel the Indians to associate with the Christians on the island [Hispaniola], to work on their buildings, to collect and mine gold and other metals, and to till the fields and produce food for the Christian inhabitants of the island. You are to pay each one on the day he works the wage and maintenance you think he deserves ... and you are to order each *cacique* to assume charge of a certain number of these Indians so that they may be available for work whenever it is necessary. . . . The Indians are to perform these duties *as free people, for such they are, and not as slaves.* You must see to it that they are treated well, those who become Christians better than the rest, and not allow anyone to harm them or oppress them in any way.[5]

With the promulgation of this decree of 1503 the principle of forced labor—and indirectly, therefore, the encomienda system—which had been operative in the island almost from the beginning, received official sanction. It also gained the approval of respectable theologians and jurists, as Ferdinand II observed some years later:

> At the time the Queen and I decided that the Indians should serve the Christians as they now do, we first summoned a junta composed of all the members of our Council and of many other lawyers, theologians, and canonists, who, after examining the donation that the Sovereign Pontiff, Alexander VI, made to us of all the lands already discovered and to be discovered in those regions [the Indies], as well as the other legal and rational arguments that supported the proposed course of action, agreed, in the presence of the Archbishop of Seville and with his approval, that it was consonant with human and divine law to give the Indians in encomienda.[6]

That academicians in Spain supported the action did not mitigate its effects on the Indians. The decree of 1503 was a severe blow to the personal liberty of the natives, resulting as it did in their virtual enslavement. Nevertheless, it represented the first constructive legislation on the subject and prepared the way for more liberal enactments later. Despite the abuses that accompanied it, the system was so well suited to the conditions of life in America that it became one of the most enduring features of the Spanish regime in the New World, successfully resisting every effort to uproot it for almost three centuries.[7]

Isabella died on November 26, 1504. Her death marked an abrupt change in the Crown's attitude toward the Indians. Humanitarianism yielded to expediency, and during the next twelve years of her husband's regime as regent of the Indies the encomienda became firmly established. The royal contract that Ferdinand granted to Vicente Yáñez Pinzón on April 24, 1505, for the conquest of Puerto Rico included the permission to parcel out lands and Indians to his followers. During the same year the king also approved the repartimientos that Ovando established in Hispaniola, and made similar gifts of lands and natives to many of his favorites at court. Ovando vigorously protested that there were not enough Indians in the islands to satisfy the needs of the colonists, to say nothing of absentee landlords. The practice continued, however, and the Crown personally became one of the biggest encomenderos. With the passing of the years, the granting of encomiendas as a reward for successful conquests undertaken at private expense became an accepted custom.[8]

Although the conversion of the aborigines still provided a stimulus for the Crown's interest in the Americas, a more powerful motive was a desire for increased revenue to replenish depleted government coffers. Slaving expeditions to the Bahamas and the Pearl Coast set sail with increasing frequency and with royal approval. The king, it is true, stipulated that the victims of these forays were not to be treated as slaves, but were to be paid for their labor and accorded the same consideration as the natives of Hispaniola. In practice, however, this directive was forgotten. "Whatever vague rights the Indian population may have had were ignored on every occasion in which the fiscal interests of the Crown were involved."[9]

It was this exploitation of the Indians that finally aroused the opposition of the Dominicans in Hispaniola and forced the Crown to reexamine its Indian policy. Confronted with the evidence of abuses,[10] Ferdinand appointed a council of learned theologians and jurists to study the problem and devise a solution. The council began its work early in 1512 in the border town of Burgos, where the court was then staying. Among its members were two of the best minds in Spain at the time: the Dominican scholar Matías de Paz, a brilliant professor of theology at the University of Valladolid,[11] and Juan López de Palacios Rubios, who had distinguished himself as an outstanding lawyer and government adviser.[12]

Paz's views were cogently stated in his treatise *On the Dominion of the Kings of Spain over the Indians*, apparently written during the summer or winter of 1512 as a protest against his colleagues' approval of the system of forced labor in the colonies.[13] The treatise posed three questions that struck at the heart of the problem confronting the Crown. (1) Could the king govern the Indians with despotic power? (2) Could he continue to exercise political dominion over them? (3) Were Spaniards who had constrained Indians to work for them and treated them like slaves bound to make restitution?

After presenting a variety of arguments for and against each of these propositions, Paz concluded as follows. (1) Christian princes should not make war on infidels merely for the purpose of dominating them or enriching themselves, but only in order to spread the Faith. Christian princes could not, therefore, justly invade the territory of infidels who manifested a willingness to receive ministers of the gospel. Thus it was necessary, whenever possible, to urge the infidels to embrace Catholicism before initiating war against them.[14] (2) Unless the invaders acted in accordance with this principle, the Indians could justly take up arms against them; Indians captured under such circumstances could not legally be considered slaves unless they obstinately refused to obey the prince who had legitimately (by reason of his desire to spread the Faith) conquered them, or unless they refused to accept Christianity. Moreover, if after being captured they asked to be baptized, they had to be treated as free men. (3) Only by virtue of authority received from the Pope would it be lawful for the king to exercise political control over the Indians and retain them permanently under his sovereign jurisdiction. From this it followed that anyone who tyrannically oppressed the Indians after their conversion was obliged to make restitution for all the losses they had suffered. Even after their conversion, however, it would be within the Spaniards' rights to exact some services from the neophytes—even greater than those required of other Christians living in those parts, provided always that these demands were in conformity with the dictates of the Faith and of right reason—in order to help defray the costs involved in reaching those shores and in preserving peace and good government.[15]

Clearly, Paz was no rigid traditionalist in his approach to the Indian problem. He boldly disagreed with those many contemporaries who held that the natives of the New World were slaves by nature according to the Aristotelian dictum.[16] He likewise disagreed with those who classified the aborigines with other unbelievers (such as Jews, Turks, Saracens, and heretics) who had had an opportunity of investigating the doctrine of Christ but had rejected it. Since the Indians had never heard of the Catholic religion prior to the coming of the Spaniards, their infidelity was the result of ignorance rather than of positive rejection of the truth. Consequently, they belonged to the second class of infidels mentioned by St. Thomas, namely, those who either had never had the gospel preached to them or, having heard it, had forgotten it through no fault of their own.[17] This distinguishing circumstance, Paz asserted, demanded a revision of existing theological and juridical thinking if justice were to prevail.

Palacios Rubios, in his lengthy treatise *On the Islands of the Ocean Sea*,[18] expressed essentially the same conclusions as Paz. Like Paz, Palacios Rubios believed that the papal donation of 1493 was the sole basis for Spain's claim to the Indies. Also like Paz, he held that the Indians must be persuaded, not forced, to accept the Faith, and that those who mistreated them or used them as slaves were obliged to make restitution. So marked was his sympathy for the aborigines that it won the repeated praise of Las Casas,[19] even though the latter strongly opposed the Spanish jurist for upholding the theory of direct universal papal sovereignty in things temporal as well as spiritual.

This sympathy for the Indians was most apparent in Palacios' discussion of the complicated questions of legal slavery and property rights. His thesis—an attack on the ambitions of greedy *conquistadores* —provided doctrinal support for the Jesuit struggle against Indian slavery in Chile during the next century.

After first presenting Aristotle's views on natural slavery, Palacios Rubios went on to consider legal servitude. Since God had created all men free and equal, giving them power over the animal kingdom but not over their fellowmen, slavery, he observed, must be the result of human invention. Before the existence of written laws there was no distinction of freedom or right between human beings. It was war that had brought slavery into the world, and it was human law that had made captives the legal slaves of their conquerors.* Although slavery was a very ancient institution, it was nevertheless contrary to natural right. Furthermore, those not captured in war retained their liberty and did not lose it or their dominion over other things upon receiving baptism.[20] From these premises Palacios Rubios drew an important conclusion: Indian nobles who accepted the Faith not only retained their freedom, property, paternal power, and other rights they had enjoyed before their conversion, but also kept their rank as nobles. Consequently, they were exempt from paying tribute and performing personal services.[21]

Furthermore, the Indians were justified in defending themselves against the Spaniards until they had been made to understand their obligation of receiving missionaries and of recognizing the temporal and spiritual sovereignty of the Pope, who had granted jurisdiction over their territories to the Spanish monarchs. If, after proper deliberation, they decided not to accept the Faith, then the Spaniards could justly make war on them, seize their goods, and reduce their persons to slavery.[22] Assuredly this was not a pleasant alternative, but it represented the common doctrine of the time, and old beliefs die hard.

Palacios Rubios readily admitted that some of the Indians were evidently incapable of governing themselves. They could, therefore, be called slaves in the broad sense of the term, namely, persons born to serve and not to command. Nevertheless—and this is where the great Spanish jurist differed radically from Aristotle—they still retained their personal freedom and, being free, were not obliged to serve others or to perform tasks incompatible with the dignity of free men. For

---

* The reason was a humanitarian one: to prevent the wholesale destruction of human life. Had the victors not been permitted to derive some benefit from the captives, they would have killed them all. The end result of this arrangement was a new social class, that of "servers" or slaves. See Silvio Zavala and Agustín Millares Carlo, eds., *De las Islas del mar Océano por Juan López de Palacios Rubios; Del dominio de los reyes de España sobre los indios por Fray Matías de Paz* (Mexico: Fondo de Cultura Económica, 1954).

liberty, he noted, was a more precious possession than all the treasure in the world, and nothing was more vile and onerous than slavery. "If brute beasts strive with all their power to escape from a trap that ensnares them, is it strange that men, gifted with intelligence, obey the same instinctive law?"[23]

Palacios Rubios considered another touchy question in his treatise: did the Indians lose dominion over their property on being conquered by the Spaniards? The answer to this question paralleled the one he gave when discussing the problem of personal liberty: the Indians did not lose their dominion, since they were capable of exercising it and conversion to Christianity did not deprive them of it.[24] It would therefore be unjust for Christian princes to wage war against the Indians for the sole purpose of enriching themselves, and any Christians who participated in such a war were obliged to make restitution for damages inflicted. Moreover, Christians captured in the war became the slaves of those who captured them.[25] This final conclusion was a startling one. It was bound to arouse violent opposition, even in official circles.

How much influence the opinions of Paz and Palacios Rubios had on the deliberations at Burgos is debatable. That they must have had some seems clear from the more humane tenor of the new code that the council proposed. Promulgated on December 27, 1512, and considerably revised the following July,[26] the Laws of Burgos provided the basis for much of the Indian legislation of subsequent years.

The thirty-five ordinances related either to the conversion of the Indians, or to the personal services expected of them. All Indians were to be properly housed in villages close to the residences of their encomenderos, and their former settlements were to be destroyed in order to discourage the natives from returning to them. Churches were to be built in the new villages, and near the mines as well, to further the Indians' spiritual welfare. The encomendero was to provide religious instruction for his Indians, and those with fifty or more Indians were to instruct the brightest youth among them in reading, writing, and religion so that he in turn might teach the others.

The ordinances regulating Indian labor constituted what might rightly be called the first labor code in America. Harsh though they may seem, they nevertheless specified work conditions comparable to those that existed in Europe and the United States during the nineteenth century. One ordinance, for instance, forbade the use of Indians as carriers at the mines. Another stipulated that after five months in the mines Indians other than slaves were to have a forty-day rest period. Food was to be provided regularly, and on Sundays and feast days the diet was to include meat. Mine workers were entitled to a pound of meat or fish daily. Women more than four months pregnant were not to be sent to the mines, and they were to be allowed to nurse their offspring for three years. During this time they were to remain on the encomendero's estates and could be employed only in simple house-hold tasks (such as cooking, baking, and weeding) that would not endanger the infants' health. Each Indian was to receive a gold peso yearly for the purchase of clothing. The Indians were not allowed to change masters, nor could one encomendero take Indians belonging to another. The Spaniards were to be served only by their own Indians, and caciques were permitted a limited number of natives for their own personal service. The cacique and his family were also to receive better instruction and better clothing than ordinary Indians.[27]

The Laws of Burgos expressly forbade physical and verbal abuse of the natives. Indians who deserved to be punished for some offense were to be referred to inspectors appointed for that purpose by the governor or other royal officials. At least a third of the encomienda Indians were to be employed in the mines unless circumstances dictated an exception. Thus the encomenderos of La Sabana and Villanueva were permitted to employ their Indians in the manufacture of hammocks and cotton shirts, and in raising food for the community instead of sending them to the mines, because of the great distances involved. Occasionally, too, one encomendero was permitted to furnish workers for the mines and another to provide the food and other necessities that the workers required. In no circumstances, however, were encomienda Indians to be used for private commerce.

Included in the new code were provisions designed to ensure its observance. Two official inspectors were to be appointed for each vil-lage, to examine conditions in the settlements twice a year. Their conduct was to be officially reviewed (*residencia*) every two years. Conscientious service entitled them to receive Indians in encomienda in addition to any they might already possess. This reward was no small incentive to fidelity in carrying out their commission.

As originally promulgated in December 1512, the Laws of Burgos did not pose a serious threat to the economic stability of the colony, since they confirmed the principle of encomienda labor. The Clarification of July 1513, however, raised a storm of protest, for it introduced a number of modifications less favorable to the colonists' interests. Married women, for example, were released from the obligation of working in the mines or anywhere else unless—with their husbands' approval—they chose to do so. Instead, they were to work on their own farms or on those belonging to the Spaniards, in which case they were to be paid the current daily wage. Boys and girls under fourteen were to be employed for light labor only, were to be paid for their work, and were to learn trades if they wished. Nothing, moreover, was to interfere with their religious education. The Indians were to spend nine months of the year in the personal service of the Spaniards in order to prevent idleness and enable them to learn to live like Christians. During the remaining three months they could cultivate their own fields or hire themselves out for wages. These regulations were objectionable enough to the encomenderos, but even more displeasing was the proviso that Indians who responded to Christian training were to be given an even greater measure of independence and self-government. If enforced strictly, this ordinance could conceivably undermine the encomienda system and ruin the colonies. Obviously, the colonists argued, it had to be opposed.

And opposed it was, with the result that the Laws of Burgos had little direct effect on life in the Indies. Conditions failed to improve, and the encomienda problem remained an issue.[28] Additional impetus was given to the controversy by the rising prominence of Bartolomé de las Casas and the failure of the Jeronymite investigation.[29] In 1519 Fray Juan Quevedo, bishop of Darién, exasperated both sides with his vacillating views. In the presence of the king, Las Casas, and members of the Royal Council, Quevedo reverted to the Aristotelian dictum by openly declaring that the Indians were slaves by nature.[30] Later, for reasons known only to himself, he reversed his opinion. In a Latin treatise dedicated to his medical friend, the Licentiate Barrera, Quevedo argued that since the war against the Indians was not sanctioned by authority or a justifying cause, Indian captives could not properly be considered slaves. Furthermore, he maintained, the condition of slavery depended on three factors: (1) not only must the master surpass the slave in prudence and intelligence, but the slave must be wholly deficient in these qualities; (2) the master must be of as much utility to the slave as the slave to him; and (3) the slave could not be forced to serve by a private individual but only by the prince or some authorized public official. Since according to Quevedo the last two conditions were unfulfilled in Spanish America, it was wrong to consider the Indians slaves.

Quevedo undoubtedly meant well, but his logic was abominable. The whole force of Aristotle's position rested on the assumption that some men had been equipped with so little reasoning power that they seemed destined by nature for the service of others. In confining his attack to the second and third points, Quevedo implicitly accepted the first and thus destroyed the potential strength of his argument.

For all its shortcomings, however, Quevedo's argument reflected in a small degree the doctrinal evolution that accompanied the efforts of Spanish authorities to solve the Indian problem. Out of the maze of legal and theological reasonings and the clash of private opinions, there emerged new principles of international law and morality that were to have a lasting influence on the history of nations. In the formulation of these principles the contributions of Bartolomé de las Casas, Francisco de Vitoria, and Ginés de Sepúlveda were of considerable importance.

Few figures in the Spanish conquest of America have aroused such critical opinion as has the onetime encomendero turned friar Bartolomé de las Casas. Present-day scholars still differ regarding his merits as a historian,[31] but his stand on the Indian question is beyond dispute. Las Casas was first, last, and foremost a defender of the Indian against the whites, a tireless advocate of personal freedom against the harshness and oppression of the European. There were other such advocates, but he was the most outstanding for the singleness of his purpose. The vigor and intensity of his campaign and the emotional tactics he sometimes used aroused much opposition among his contemporaries. But these considerations should not be allowed to obscure the value of his work or the justice of his aims.

To speak of Las Casas only in terms of humanitarianism is to misunderstand the man and his age, for he was more than a social-minded altruist interested in extolling the virtues of the "noble savage." He was primarily a priest whose main interest was the welfare of souls. But he was also a Christian humanist who recognized a truth that others of his time were eager to forget: that even the lowliest of God's children is possessed of human dignity and human worth. To Aristotle's theory of natural slavery, he replied that "all the nations of the world are men," that there are not humans and subhumans within the same species. Either an individual creature is a man, endowed with an intellect and a will, no matter how retarded, or he is an animal. There is no *tertium quid*.[32]

In defending this position Las Casas used a variety of arguments— philosophical, theological, anthropological, historical, and personal— to prove that the Indians were rational creatures capable of being converted to Christianity by peaceful means. To this end he devoted much of his time and one of his principal polemics, the weighty and frequently idealistic *Apologética historia de las Indias*. Here, within the compass of some 870 folio pages filled with tortuous reasoning and copious annotations, Las Casas presented an overwhelming amount of information on Indian life and customs, with the aim of destroying the charges of irrationality and barbarism leveled against the natives.

Indeed, on the strength of numerous learned arguments, some of them decidedly bizarre, Las Casas confidently asserted that in some respects the American Indians were culturally superior to the Greeks and Romans, and even to the Spaniards themselves. They manifested, for example, a higher religious concept than the Greeks or Romans, since they honored their gods with more and nobler sacrifices.[33] Some tribes (the Mexicans) excelled them also in methods of training and educating their offspring.[34] Their marriage customs were reasonable and in conformity with natural and positive law.[35] In physical form the Indians were attractive and beautiful, and in matters of food and drink they displayed a laudable temperance.[36] The children were gracious, amiable, happy, and vivacious. Indian women were devout, energetic workers who, unlike many Christian matrons, did not balk at performing manual labor. Native handicrafts, and especially the imposing temples of Mexico and Peru, were visible proofs of native proficiency in the mechanical arts.[37] All these praiseworthy accomplishments were manifestations of a rational nature that was capable of further improvement by education.

Las Casas saw, to be sure, that some tribes were on a lower cultural level than others, but he was convinced that even the most backward were members of the human race—full members, not half members like Aristotle's natural slaves. It would be contrary to Divine Wisdom and the proper ordering of the universe, Las Casas maintained, for the Creator to have willed the existence of entire nations of unsocial, irrational beings "against the natural inclination of all the peoples of the world."[38] The only logical conclusion, therefore, was:

> All the nations of the world are men. . . . All of them are endowed with intellect and will. They all possess the five exterior senses and the four interior ones, and they react to the proper objects of each. They all take satisfaction in good and find enjoyment in happy and delightful things, and all of them deplore evil.[39]

Neither did Las Casas accept the idea of a static condition of barbarism from which there was no escape. All men could advance under the stimulus of proper instruction and doctrine:

> Just as uncultivated land produces only weeds and thorns yet has within itself the power to bring forth good and useful fruit when domesticated, so too all the peoples of the world, no matter how barbarous and cruel they may be, have the use of reason (if they are men) and, aided by proper instruction and especially by the doctrine of the Faith, will inevitably produce results which are reasonable proofs of their humanity.[40]

This same optimistic view of the Indians' nature occurs again later. After reviewing evidence drawn from ancient and modern times, Las Casas concluded:

> Thus we clearly see, by examples both ancient and modern, that no nation exists, no matter how rude, uncultured, barbarous, gross, or almost brutal its people might be, that cannot be persuaded and brought to a good order and way of life and made domestic, mild, and tractable, provided the method that is proper and natural to men is used, that is, love, and gentleness, and kindness.[41]

The method that is "proper and natural to men" was, of course, the one he had outlined earlier in his monumental work *Del único modo de atraer a todos los pueblos a la verdadera religión*, the orderly and peaceful preaching of the Gospel.[42]

In 1537, Pope Paul III intervened in the controversy over the nature of the American Indians with a ringing condemnation of those who "go about saying that the Indians of the West and of the South ought to be reduced to our service, as if they were brute beasts, under the pretext that they are incapable of receiving the Faith; and they actually do enslave them, grinding them down with such treatment as they scarcely use with their own beasts of burden." Then came the stirring pronouncement:

> Wherefore . . . wishing to provide a suitable remedy for these evils, We, by Our apostolic authority, do hereby determine and declare that, notwithstanding what may have been said in the past or what may be said in the future, the aforementioned Indians and all other peoples who may in the future come within the ken of Christians, even though they be infidels, are by no means to be deprived of their liberty or of their dominion over their property. Moreover, they may freely and licitly enjoy their dominion and liberty, and they are not to be reduced to slavery; and whatever has happened contrary to this declaration shall be null and void and have no binding force whatsoever.[43]

Unfortunately, this salutary pronouncement, like the Laws of Burgos before it, exerted no appreciable influence in the Indies. Papal authority proved impotent in the face of royal prerogative. In the following year, 1538, Charles V blandly declared that the bull had no binding force in the colonies, not because it championed the cause of the Indians, but because it had been sent to America without first receiving the *pase real*. The interests of the encomenderos were accordingly still secure.

While the intellectual world was still humming over the unexpected declaration of Paul III, a far more serious attack on the Spanish position in America was in the making. Ever since the papal bulls of Alexander VI in 1493, Spanish rulers and theoreticians had taken for granted the justification of their country's claim to priority in the Indies. Thus on September 14, 1519, when announcing the incorporation of the New World territories with those of Castile, the emperor Charles V confidently asserted: "By donation of the Holy and Apostolic See and by other just and legitimate titles, we are lord of the West Indies and of the islands and mainlands of the Ocean Sea already discovered and to be discovered."[44] Not until 1534, when reports reached Spain of Pizarro's cruelty to the natives of Peru, was there any significant questioning of Spain's claim to sovereignty in the Indies.

Among those deeply affected by the reports from Peru was the noted Dominican theologian Francisco de Vitoria. Writing in 1534 to a fellow Dominican in Seville, Miguel de Arcos, Vitoria expressed grave concern over Spanish mistreatment of the Andean natives. Three years later, at the conclusion of a series of lectures at the University of Salamanca on human sacrifices, he publicly attacked the justifying power of the papal donation in these memorable words: "Christian princes have no more authority over infidels by reason of papal authorization than they have without it."[45] In 1539 Vitoria substantiated this view in his celebrated *Relecciones de Indios y del derecho de la guerra*, two public lectures delivered at the University of Salamanca.[46]

In proposing a solution to the troublesome question of whether or not the Indians were true lords of their territories before the coming of the Spaniards, Vitoria reasoned as follows: if the barbarians lacked dominion over their possessions, it could only be because they were sinners, idiots, or infidels.[47] Ownership and dominion are natural rights based on the fact that man is a rational being endowed with intellect and will. Since sin does not deprive him of his nature, it cannot deprive him of the rights that flow from it. Similarly, only the exercise of those rights, not the rights themselves, is suspended because of insanity or inability to use intellectual powers. The Indians, moreover, were not idiots. The order that prevailed in their lives—properly governed towns, well-defined marriage customs, magistrates, lords, laws, professions, and industries—supposed and demanded the use of reason. Nor were the Indians strictly infidels; they possessed a kind of religion, and they were not deceived in matters that were evident to others also.[48]

God and nature, Vitoria continued, do not err in that which is indispensable for the species and the race. Reason, the highest and most essential perfection of man, would be useless if it remained inoperative. Irrationality—the basis of the "slave by nature" doctrine—would, therefore, be a reflection on divine wisdom and the natural order were it to exist in entire nations and tribes. Vitoria accordingly concluded that the dullness and stupidity claimed by some to be characteristic of the American Indians was mostly the result of faulty education, "since even among us we find many rustics who differ little from brute beasts."[49]

As for the argument that the Indians were slaves by nature because they lacked sufficient reason to govern themselves, Vitoria explained that Aristotle had not intended to imply that those who have little mental ability are naturally subject to the power of others, or that it is legal to seize the property of such persons and reduce them to slavery. On the contrary, his point was their need to submit to the authority of others, as sons submit to their fathers until they are of age.[50]

Although he favored this interpretation of Aristotle's theory, Vitoria did not reject the traditional view completely. This is clear from the concluding passages of his first Relección. After enumerating seven reasons why the Spaniards might legitimately exercise dominion over the Indians, he referred to another that, he stated, was personally unacceptable but that he dared not condemn entirely because it might have some validity. It was, in fact, almost the direct contrary of his earlier assertion about the nature of the Indians.

> These barbarians, even though they are not complete idiots, are, nevertheless, little different from madmen; thus they do not seem fit to establish and administer a legitimate republic within human and civil bounds. ... Because of this deplorable condition, some people say that it would be for the good of the barbarians if the Spanish princes were to take upon themselves the task of governing them ... so long as it was clear that the barbarians would profit from the arrangement. Such a course of action would not only be licit but even obligatory for our princes to assume if all the barbarians were really without reason, just as would be the case if they were all infants.[51]

In short, with adult barbarians whose reported mental incapacity was even more pronounced than that of children and cretins in other countries, the law of charity would provide the argument for intervention. Vitoria favored such action, but only on the condition that the overlordship be established strictly for the benefit of the barbarians and not for the profit of the Spaniards. He concluded with this surprising observation: "It should be noted also that something we considered previously might be of use in this connection, namely, that some people are slaves by nature. The barbarians indeed seem to belong to this category, and consequently they might be governed in part as slaves."[52]

Vitoria's apparent uncertainty regarding the mental capacity of the Indians was probably the result of his having no direct contact with them. In stating his opinion, he was more prudent than his contemporary Sepúlveda, who likewise had never set foot in America. Moreover, Vitoria did not accept the classical theory without reservations, as Sepúlveda seems to have done, but subjected it to critical scrutiny in the light of Christian beliefs. His interpretation differed widely from Aristotle's doctrine, in which charity played no part. With Vitoria, the Christian concept of brotherly love replaced the classical idea of a hierarchy of nature as the basic justification for establishing political dominion over less advanced peoples. This was Vitoria's principal contribution to the controversy over Indian slavery.

Since the papal bull of 1537 was not a dogmatic declaration, it did not prohibit the airing of contrary opinions. The controversy over Indian slavery continued to rage until it reached its boiling point at Valladolid in the famous debate of 1550–51 between the Dominican defender of the Indians, Bartolomé de las Casas, and the classical humanist Juan Ginés de Sepúlveda. The details of the incident do not concern us here.[53] Suffice it to say that the cause of the debate was Las Casas' opposition to the *Demócrates Secundus*, a treatise Sepúlveda had written some years earlier, at the behest of Cardinal García de Loaysa, to justify the Spanish method of conquest in America.[54] Among the arguments Sepúlveda had advanced in support of his thesis, and which he repeated in the Valladolid encounter, was one that proposed the crudity of the Indians as a legitimate excuse for conquering and enslaving them. In elegant Ciceronian diction, Sepúlveda tried to fit Aristotelian concepts to the American pattern.[55]

Sepúlveda made it abundantly clear that he considered the Indians vastly inferior to the Spaniards in every respect. He called them a barbarous and inhuman people, devoid of civil life, gentle customs, and the practice of virtue. They worshipped idols, indulged in human sacrifices, failed to observe the natural law, and oppressed the innocent.[56] Nothing would be more contrary to distributive justice than to grant equal rights and advantages to persons so inferior in virtue and merits.

Sepúlveda's apparent endorsement of the classical hierarchy of social gradations and his avowed efforts to justify the American conquest made him a popular figure in the eyes of many Spaniards. Conquistadores and imperialists alike hailed him as a brother, finding in his doctrine, as expressed in the *Demócrates Secundus* and the discussions at Valladolid, a rationalization for the past and carte blanche for the future.* But even though he supported the conquering of the Indians, he repeatedly stated that the overriding aim of such conquest was the greater good of the pagans and their gradual conversion to Christianity.[57] Dominion over the Indies had to be based on a program of "rectitude, justice, and piety" and must result in greater utility for the vanquished barbarians than for the Spaniards themselves.[58] On this point, Sepúlveda's argument was at variance with Aristotle's central theme that granted the greater benefit to the master.

Nowhere in his treatise did Sepúlveda deny that the Indians were human, albeit inferior to the Spaniards as children are inferior to adults and women to men.[59] Control over the Indians, he thought, ought to be exercised in the paternal spirit that is the truest sign of a well-ordered household, in which every member participates, in justice and affability, according to his station:

> I say that a good and just king who wishes to imitate such a father of families, as he has an obligation to do, ought to govern . . . these barbarians like servants who are free, with a kind of moderate control that combines the despotic with the paternal, and . . . treat them as becomes their condition in life and in accordance with the exigencies of the situation. And with the passing of time, after they have become more civilized and our control has produced in them a probity of conduct and the Christian religion, they must be treated with more freedom and liberality.[60]

* As a token of appreciation for his efforts against Las Casas at Valladolid, the *cabildo* (town council) of Mexico City resolved on February 8, 1554, to honor Sepúlveda with a gift of clothing and jewels valued at 200 pesos. Whether or not he ever received the present is unknown, but the action is indicative of the overseas response to his doctrine.

To enslave any but the most cruel, criminal, or obstinate Indians, according to Sepúlveda, would be not only unjust but futile and dangerous for the maintenance of Spanish control. He granted that Spaniards could exact just tribute in recompense for bringing civilization to the benighted savages, and that they could use Indians as servants to do light work. But his doctrine forbade tyrannical oppression and intolerable slavery. In a word, the Spaniards were to treat the Indians with genuine kindness, granting them the benefits of liberty in keeping with their natural status.[61]

The clash between Sepúlveda and Las Casas is a convenient note on which to close this review of doctrinal developments during the first half of the sixteenth century. The views expressed during this time did not put an end to the series of controversies and debates over the issue. The argument continued with variations in widely scattered parts of Hispanic America and especially on the Chilean frontier, where the issues at stake were an integral part of the recurrent campaigns against the indomitable Araucanians.

BEGINNINGS OF THE STRUGGLE
FOR JUSTICE IN CHILE

THE MOST DISTINCTIVE FEATURE of the Spanish conquest of Chile was the never-ending war with the Araucanians. In Chile alone of all the Spanish colonies in the New World the pattern of settlement was dramatically reversed. Instead of a quick military victory followed by a period of constructive advance, the Spaniards found themselves embroiled in a costly conflict that continued at intervals for more than two centuries and threatened at times to destroy them.* In the end the Araucanians admitted defeat, but only after setting an example of courage and resistance that is without parallel in the annals of the West.[1]

The reasons for this protracted struggle were many and varied. All the early chroniclers emphasize the warlike propensities of the Araucanians and their genius in adapting quickly to European methods of fighting. But other factors were equally important in prolonging the war. The guerrilla tactics of the Indians, their lack of political unity (necessitating a piecemeal reduction of the country),[2] their ingenuity

---

* In its entirety, the Araucanian struggle for independence lasted more than 300 years. It had its formal beginning in the first of the great Indian uprisings, which occurred in 1554 following the massacre of Pedro de Valdivia and his men at Tucapel, and it did not officially end until the Araucanians finally made peace with the independent Republic of Chile in 1881. The origin of the tribal name is disputed. According to Molina, an eighteenth-century Chilean naturalist, historian, and Jesuit, "they derive their appellation of Araucanians from the province of Arauco, which, though the smallest in their territory, has, like Holland, given its name to the whole nation, either from its having been the first to unite with the neighbouring provinces, or from having at some remote period reduced them under its dominion. This people, ever enthusiastically attached to their independence, pride themselves in being called *Auca*, which signifies frank or free, and those Spaniards, who had left the army in the Netherlands to serve in Chili, gave to this country the name of Araucanian Flanders, or the Invincible State." The Abbe Don J. Ignatius Molina, *The Geographical, Natural, and Civil History of Chili.* Translated from the original Italian with Notes from the Spanish and French versions by the English editor. (London 1809), II, 53–54.

in living off the land,[3] the rugged character of the terrain, the blundering inefficiency of many Spanish leaders, the numerous changes in administrative control, the lack of any coordinated overall military plan, the isolated position of the colony, the corruptness and independence of local bureaucrats, the flagrant disregard of royal decrees, the selfishness of vested interests, and the inferior quality of many Spanish troops. Not the least of the causes, however, was the fear of enslavement at the hands of the whites. The Araucanians were an agricultural, land-loving people. Reared in the traditions of tribal independence, they fiercely resented any curtailment of their freedom.[4] The Spaniards, for their part, were perhaps too reluctant to consider means of settlement other than the encomienda.[5] Their reluctance was understandable: the number of Europeans who ventured into Chile was always too small to care for the needs of the white population; without the assistance of native workers the Spanish outposts would surely have perished.[6] Nevertheless, the abuses that resulted from conscript labor and the encomienda were directly responsible for much of the misery and strife that developed. Some of the abuses were the logical offspring of the system itself; others could have been avoided by a conscientious application of such official prescripts as the Ordinances of Toledo (1528)[7] and the New Laws of 1542[8] concerning the proper treatment of the Indians. But in Chile, as elsewhere in Spanish America, Indian legislation was frequently a dead letter.*

The Ordinances of Toledo had explicitly stated that the Indians need not work as carriers against their will, even if they were paid. Certain exceptions were made for localities lacking roads and beasts of burden.[9] In no case, however, was the burden to exceed approximately two *arrobas* (fifty pounds).[10] The Spaniards were forbidden to keep encomienda Indians in their homes and haciendas as servants, nor could they require the Indians to work for them during the planting season. The prohibitions against slavery were to be enforced, and the natives

---

* Among other things, the New Laws defined the Indians as free persons and vassals of the Crown, forbade their enslavement under any pretext, prohibited the granting of new encomiendas, outlawed forced labor, ordered colonists guilty of mistreating their Indians to surrender them immediately, denied government officials, religious corporations, and individual ecclesiastics the privilege of possessing encomiendas, and required encomenderos to reside in the district of their encomiendas. Had these Laws been rigidly enforced, the encomienda system would soon have died out, and the colonists would have been left without the supply of cheap labor that was considered necessary for the continued existence and prosperity of the overseas empire.

were not to be removed from their homes for Spanish purposes even with their consent.[11] Typical fines for violations of these laws were one hundred pesos for the first offense, three hundred for the second, and loss of property for a third.

These regulations were openly violated by the Spaniards in Chile. Among the offenders was Diego de Almagro, the first of the conquistadores to attempt the conquest of the Long Land.[12] Incensed by the murder of three of his companions,[13] Almagro arbitrarily put to death several leading inhabitants of the district of Coquimbo, and gave the other natives of the area to his followers as personal slaves. Other outrages were committed by Almagro's men during the return march to Peru. Disappointed by their failure to find gold, they indulged in unrestricted plundering along the way, leaving behind them a trail of destruction. The captives they took, bound together by ropes and chains fastened around their necks, staggered along with the baggage of the army on their backs. Their only food was roasted corn, which they ate while on the march. Worn down by these hardships, many of the Indians sickened and died. To simplify the task of removing their bonds, the heads of the dead were lopped off, and the mutilated bodies were left lying in the dust, a grim testimony to the passing of the whites.[14]

The second entry of the Spaniards, under Pedro de Valdivia in 1540, gave promise of better relations between the two races, at least in the beginning. Valdivia came as a colonizer rather than a despoiler. Knowing that he was dealing with a proud and determined people, he endeavored to win their friendship with gifts and kindness, and sought to placate them by releasing prisoners taken in combat.[15] But he had his comrades to placate as well, following the precedent of Pizarro and Cortés.[16] In a proclamation dated January 12, 1544, he bestowed encomiendas on sixty of his followers, together with the privileges and obligations accompanying the grants.[17] In addition to generous tracts of land, the newly created encomenderos received exclusive title to the feudal services of large groups of Indians living in the vicinity of Santiago. It soon became apparent, however, that the governor had grossly overestimated the number of natives available for distribution. Consequently, on July 25, 1544, he issued a decree reducing the number of encomenderos from sixty to thirty-two.[18] The Indians pertaining to nineteen of the suppressed grants were redistributed among these thirty-two. Twelve additional caciques and their subjects who lived between the Maule and Itata rivers were included to increase the size of the grants. The remaining encomenderos were ordered to give back within fifteen days the Indians "deposited" with them earlier.[19]

The encomenderos who survived the shuffle were close friends of Valdivia and men who had distinguished themselves in the early campaigns. The others were mostly obscure soldiers whose loyalty Valdivia strove to retain by promising them encomiendas at a future date. Words, however, counted for little with such men; all their hopes of fortune were predicated on the early possession of a large number of Indians whose labor they could exploit to their own advantage. Many of them, poverty-stricken and embittered, conceived a profound hatred for Valdivia, which erupted two years later in a bitter attack upon his power and prestige. Instead of being a source of unity among the colonists in Chile, the encomienda thus became the focal point of internal jealousy and dissension.

The results for the Indians were much more serious. Encouraged by their remoteness from Spain, the encomenderos confidently ignored the Crown's instructions regarding Indian labor. As Gil González de San Nicolás, a Dominican friar who was partial to the natives, reported at a later date:

> The holders of encomiendas in Chile benefit continually from the personal service of all the Indians of their encomiendas, children as well as adults. The treatment they give them is much worse than that accorded to slaves, since they compel the Indians to travel distances of twenty and thirty leagues, carrying their own food as well as other burdens which they are forced to transport ceaselessly from one place to another in the interest of their masters.[20]

Hernando de Santillán, *oidor* (judge) of the audiencia of Lima, who lived in Chile for some time, agreed with González. In his tour of the colony (1558–59) he noticed that one of the encomenderos' most profitable enterprises was "driving droves of Indians laden with merchandise and other gainful objects from Santiago to Valparaíso, a distance of some fifteen leagues over a very bad road." No wages were paid for this work. The Indians were regarded as little better than beasts of burden, and some of them were literally worked to death.[21]

The *cabildo* of Santiago made periodic gestures toward regulating these abuses, but its efforts were halfhearted and ineffectual. Thus one of its resolutions threatened violators of the carrier laws with a fine of fifty pesos and confiscation of all goods under transportation. This penalty was later judged too severe and reduced to a fine of ten pesos for the cargo and one blanket for the Indian porter. Failure to provide the blanket meant an added fine of ten pesos.[22]

In the use of Indians as domestic servants—a direct violation of the king's will—Valdivia himself erred as is clear from a document of November 1552: "I entrust to you [Juan Jufré] for the time being the cacique named Tipitureo, together with all his leading Indians and subjects who formerly belonged to my chief lieutenant, Captain Francisco de Villagra. . . . Of the Indians of the aforementioned Tipitureo you are to give twenty young males as servitors to Captain Francisco de Villagra."[23]

Another common practice was for encomenderos to hire their Indians out to others, contrary to a royal cédula of 1529 that forbade "encomenderos and other persons to rent or offer Indians of their encomiendas to any person whatsoever under pain of forfeiting the said Indians and one half of their property."[24] Valdivia's own wife, Doña Marina Ortiz de Gaete, to mention only one offender, openly disobeyed this decree not once but many times, as her last will and testament shows:

> Likewise, I declare that Juan de Azocar, a resident of this city [Santiago], has eleven Indians of my encomienda, whom he hired for one year in exchange for 100 pesos of good gold, 100 fanegas of wheat, 50 fanegas of corn or its equivalent, 50 fanegas of barley, and 20 rams, of which last he has given me 10. I order that the matter be investigated and that all of the above be collected from the said Juan de Azocar.
>
> Likewise, I declare that Francisco de Riberos has rented the services of sixteen Indians of my encomienda in the current year of 1589. I order that the question of wages and rent be examined and that the amount due be collected from him.[25]

The Ordinances of Toledo had forbidden the Spaniards to move the Indians from one place to another, even with their consent. A later cédula signed in Talavera in 1541 repeated the injunction, adding that natives were not to be transferred from warm to cold climates, or vice versa, because of adverse effects on their health.[26] The colonists, however, ignored these directions. As a preliminary to laying the foundations of Santiago, they systematically cleared the area of all the resident Indians. The natives accepted the destruction of their villages with apparent resignation and departed peacefully from the scene. Seven months later they returned in force, attacked the Spanish settlement, burned it, and would have wiped out the European population but for the Spanish cavalry and the aid of the Spaniards' Indian allies.

Surely no historian would question the justice of the Indians' attack. They had been deprived of their lands and homes without compensation, and were merely trying to recover what was rightfully theirs. Their claim was implicitly recognized by the cabildo of Santiago some years later. In its session of August 4, 1553, the cabildo granted the lands of Quinamba to Pedro Gómez de Don Benito for his Indians of Quilicura "as recompense for the lands taken from them at the time of the founding of Santiago."[27]

The documents of the period show many other instances of forced evacuation of the Indians from their homes. On March 8, 1545, Valdivia endorsed the practice in the following terms:

> For the time being I deposit with you, Rodrigo de Araya, the caciques named Pillinarengo and Birocuspa, together with all their subjects, as well as the chief named Tinguimangui and his brother Gualtimilla, with all of their subjects; likewise the other chief named Guaupilla, whose home is in this valley of Mapocho, all of whose lands were taken away from them and given over to the service of the *vecinos* [Spanish householders] of this city [Santiago].[28]

Another example is provided by the testimony of Diego García de Cáceres, Francisco Martínez, Francisco Rubio, and Juan de Ardila, witnesses in a law suit that the royal officials of Santiago brought against Pedro de Miranda and Alonso de Córdoba in 1561. The case involved the title to various encomiendas of Indians in the valley of Quillota.

In the examination, two questions that referred directly to the matter of moving Indians were answered in the affirmative:

> 3. [Did] they know that Alonso de Córdoba, at the time mentioned, had and possessed (by virtue of the title of encomienda he had received in the name of His Majesty) the caciques Alonso, Baltazarillo, and Guandarongo together with their subjects, ... that the aforementioned Alonso and Baltazarillo had their lands and residences in the [valley of the] Mapocho [River], and that they were driven away from there in order to make room for the founding of the city of Santiago?
> 4. [Did] they know that Pedro Gómez de Don Benito, at the time mentioned, had the caciques Don Hurtado and Comparavando together with their Indians (by reason of the title of encomienda he had received in the name of His Majesty) and that the aforementioned caciques lived in the [valley of the] Mapocho and were moved away from there to the valley of Chile?[29]

Among the other encomenderos who were guilty of similar offenses were some of the most prominent members of colonial society. Francisco de Aguirre, a leading conquistador, transported some of his encomienda Indians from Santiago to La Serena for work in the gold mines.[30] Captain Pedro de Lisperguer, husband of Doña Agueda Flores, transferred the Puelches (trans-Andean Indians) of his encomienda in northern Patagonia to his *estancias* in Putagan and Cauquenes in Chile.[31] Later, all these Indians, the Puelches as well as those of Putagan and Cauquenes, were removed to the estancia of Peñaflor, where their descendants were still living at the turn of the eighteenth century.[32] Similar examples could be cited for practically every decade of the colonial era.

Another violation of the Crown's will was the granting of encomiendas to individual ecclesiastics and to religious houses. In recognition of personal services and in payment of a financial loan, Pedro de Valdivia awarded large encomiendas of Indians to a cleric named Rodrigo González (who was confirmed in their possession by later governors), and made a similar grant to Juan Lobo, also a cleric. Valdivia publicly admitted that such awards were contrary to the established regulations. In a writ of encomienda in favor of García de Villalón, dated November 19, 1548, he said:

Insofar as His Majesty has ordered in one of his royal decrees that prelates, churches, hospitals, and monasteries may not possess encomiendas of Indians, and since in conformity with this decree it is necessary to deprive the convent of Our Lady Help of Christians, in the city of Santiago, of the cacique Llangallave and his subjects whom I deposited with it for the service of the church and convent, I hereby entrust to you [García de Villalón] the aforesaid chief and his people.[33]

Although he admitted that his action was illegal, Valdivia favored the cleric González with the best encomiendas in the conquered territory, and he continued to do so until his tragic death in Tucapel during the Indian uprising of 1553.[34]

In Chile as in other parts of Spanish America, the lot of the Indians in the mines was especially hard. Valdivia had hoped that the establishment of encomiendas would stimulate interest in agricultural development. The colonists, however, had other plans, namely, to acquire a quick fortune and live a life of ease. Agriculture was needed to feed the colony, but it was the white or yellow metal that made men wealthy and opened the door to social distinction.

In the search for gold and silver, no holds were barred. Encomenderos sought to capitalize on their Indians' labor by using them without respite in the backbreaking work of the *lavaderos de oro* (placer mines).[35] Valdivia encouraged this interest in mining because one of his first concerns as governor of the colony had been to erase the stigma of poverty that Almagro's men had attached to the land. He himself assigned to the historically productive mines of Malgamalga, slightly north of modern Valparaíso, several hundred Indians he had brought from Peru.[36] Knowledge of the mines, which in earlier times had supplied the gold that the *mapuches* (Chilean natives) used for tribute payments to their Inca overlords, had come to the Spaniards through Michimalongo, cacique of Aconcagua, who offered the information in exchange for his freedom after being captured by Rodrigo de Quiroga, one of Valdivia's lieutenants.[37] The wealth the Spaniards found in Malgamalga had an enormously heartening effect on the whole colony. Pedro Mariño de Lovera, a contemporary chronicler of the period, recorded the delight of the conquistadores on seeing the gold:

They began to act as if the gold were already in their pockets. . . . The only thing they thought about was whether there would be enough sacks and bags in the country to enable them to carry off so much treasure; and they thereupon started to put on airs like rich people, thinking that in a short time they would be able to return to Spain to establish a family estate or even an earldom and castles of gold, commencing from then to construct them out of air.[38]

At first women were excluded from working in the mines, but after the rebellion of the cacique Michimalongo in 1541[39] Valdivia reversed this policy, and thereafter women were regularly employed along with men in the gold diggings. Their presence led to numerous abuses, but it was the general spirit of brutality prevailing in the mining districts that aroused the most criticism and complaints. Fray Francisco de Victoria, a Dominican friar, summed up the situation in a letter from Lima to the Council of the Indies, dated January 10, 1553:

From the reports of two persons recently arrived from Chile . . . it is evident that Christian principles and charity are completely lacking in that colony, and the abominations that occur there cry out to heaven for vengeance. All the encomenderos send their Indians—men, women, and children—to the mines to work without giving them any opportunity to rest, or any more food than a daily ration of maize during the eight months of the year that they labor there. The Indian who fails to produce the required amount of gold is beaten with clubs and whips. And if any Indian conceals a single grain of gold, he is punished by having his ears and nose cut off.[40]

Rodrigo de Quiroga, one of Valdivia's lieutenants, was a typical encomendero in this respect. He is reported to have employed six hundred Indians of his encomienda, half of them women and all ranging from fifteen to twenty-five years of age, in the mines for eight months at a time, to the notable detriment of their health. The chronicler adds that Quiroga would have kept them at work for the entire year had not the streams dried up during the autumn months and made it impossible to pan the gold.[41]

Not all the encomenderos viewed their Indians simply as slaves or laborers. Men like Bartolomé Flores, Francisco Hernández Gallego, and the elder Alonso de Córdoba treated them as human beings. Flores, who was married to Doña Elvira de Talagante, a daughter of the cacique of Talagante, left all his property to a child who resulted from this union, Doña Agueda Flores.[42] But men with unselfish motives were few during the early decades of the conquest.

Under the twin pressure of scandalous abuses of the Indians and periodic goadings from across the Atlantic, individual viceroys and governors of the colony made sporadic efforts to lighten the native's burden. The upshot of this intermittent concern was a series of *tasas* (tribute assessments) designed to free the Indians from the grasp of the encomenderos. The most important of these early reform measures was the so-called Tasa de Santillán.

When García Hurtado de Mendoza was named governor of Chile in 1557 by his father, the Marquis of Cañete (then viceroy of Peru),* he was given as adviser and chief justice of the realm one of the oidores of the audiencia of Lima, the talented licentiate Hernando de Santillán y Figueroa.[43] In addition to his ordinary duties as counselor to the governor, Santillán was charged with ending the practices that had enslaved the Indians. It was a formidable assignment that needed both patience and tact.

While stopping in La Serena en route to Santiago, the capital of the colony, Santillán had an opportunity to judge for himself the actual state of affairs. He soon observed that the Indians were "worn out from working for their masters, who employed them indiscriminately—men, women, and children—in working the mines, carrying heavy burdens, and performing various personal services that left them no time for rest and relaxation."[44] Stirred by their condition, Santillán immediately took steps to remedy the situation. He promulgated the royal decrees that prohibited the use of Indians as beasts of burden; he forbade the encomenderos to employ more than a fifth of their natives in the lavaderos de oro, and ordered them to pay the miners a weekly salary of one-sixth of the ore they extracted.[45] Reliable men were to be assigned to the mines as *alcaldes* (judicial and administrative officials) to protect the workers against mistreatment. Draft animals, supplied at the

* Since Chile was a dependent province of the viceroyalty of Peru, the governors of the colony often received their initial appointment from the viceroy.

encomendero's own expense, were to replace female porters for carrying supplies to the mines. Each Indian worker was to receive sufficient food daily to maintain his health, a ration of meat three times a week, and a supply of clothes if he needed them. The encomendero was forbidden to demand any additional tribute from his Indians, or to intervene in their disputes except as a disinterested judge. He was to make a sincere effort to treat his workers with kindness and understanding, and on no account was he to force them to work on Sundays or on feast days. Rather, he was to make sure that those who were Christians attended Mass faithfully and complied with their other religious obligations.[46]

In line with the repeated instructions of the Crown, Santillán set free all the yanaconas attached to encomiendas, noting that if they voluntarily consented to work in the mines, their Spanish employers would have to provide them with food, implements, and a salary amounting to one-fourth of the product of their labor.[47] Before leaving La Serena he announced his decisions in seventy-nine ordinances that left no doubt of his intentions.

Upon arriving in Santiago Santillán found that conditions in the central valley were even worse than in La Serena, and he promptly ordered enforcement of the royal cédulas concerning Indian porters. To eliminate the need for human carriers, he arranged for the domestication of more than two hundred horses and oxen and the manufacture of as many pack saddles; before long, well-equipped animals were available for freight service out of Santiago. Next, Santillán turned his attention to a more difficult aspect of the Indian problem: the regulation of personal service in the districts under Spanish control. The kings of Spain had repeatedly forbidden compulsory personal service as a form of tax, and had instructed Crown officials to devise a moderate tribute, payable in agricultural or handicraft products rather than labor,[48] that would leave the Indians sufficient resources for their own needs. Owing mainly to the disquieting influence of the Araucanian war, the royal directions had remained inoperative in Chile, with the result, Santillán reported, that the native women preferred to let their offspring die rather than see them seized later for service in the mines.[49]

The economics of Araucanian life made a satisfactory settlement of this problem difficult; except for the ore they coaxed from the mines the Indians had no ready capital for taxes. Their crops were too small, their herds too few, their pottery, weaving, and basket-making industries too unproductive to make payment in kind feasible. The only remaining alternative was the illegal personal service. The dilemma confronting Santillán was not an easy one. If he abolished personal service, he would arouse the wrath of the encomenderos; if he sanctioned it, he would offend the Crown.

Fortunately for all concerned, Santillán was a prudent and practical man. For several months he studied the situation, visiting the holdings of the big encomenderos around Santiago[50] and talking with both Spaniards and Indians. Eventually he summed up his conclusions in the prudent ordinances that bear his name. Santillán realized from the start that the abolition of personal service would mean the ruination of the colony and would result in serious disturbances. He accordingly limited himself to introducing only a partial reform, one that restricted but did not abolish personal service. Nor did he attempt to suppress the encomiendas themselves, since experience in other parts of the empire had indicated strongly that such a move could lead to revolution.*

Many of the provisions of the Tasa de Santillán were concerned with regulating labor conditions in the mines and estancias of Santiago and La Serena, along the lines of a modified mita system.[51] The caciques of the various repartimientos were ordered to supply one worker for the mines for every six subjects under their jurisdiction. Women and persons under eighteen and over fifty were exempt, and the workers chosen were to be employed in the mines nearest to their home villages. To protect the miners from being overworked, a rotation of labor was also prescribed: mitayos assigned to digging were to be changed every two months, those occupied in washing the ore, every six months at the most. If an Indian were included in one mita, he could not be assigned to the next, or the employer would be fined five hundred pesos per person for each violation. In addition to food and tools, the mitayos were to receive a sixth part of the gold they mined, with which to buy clothes, sheep, and useful articles. The encomendero was entitled to the remaining five-sixths, to compensate him for feeding the workers, supplying their tools, providing them with instruction in Christian doc-

---

* There was a revolution in Peru in 1544 following the passage of the New Laws of 1542, and near-revolutions in New Spain, Guatemala, and New Granada during the same decade.

trine, paying the salaries of servants on the hacienda, and so forth. Division of the profits was to take place regularly on the last Saturday of each month.[52]

To provide mitayos for the encomendero's fields and estancias, the cacique had to assign one man for every five of his subjects. The encomendero, in turn, had to supply food, tools, and pay that varied according to the type of work done. Mitayos who helped in sowing the crops, for instance, were to receive a complete set of cotton clothes. Those who worked during the harvest season were to be given a *manta* (blanket). Teamsters, shepherds, cultivators of vineyards, and male house servants were entitled to a suit of clothing every year plus two pigs and a goat. Female house servants were to receive two outfits of cotton clothes yearly.

An encomendero who planted flax could have it harvested and spun by the Indians in exchange for half of the finished product. The other half went to the encomendero to reimburse him for the cost of furnishing the looms and other necessary equipment. The original contract and the division of goods were to be witnessed by the *justicia mayor* (chief justice), and both the cacique and the encomendero were to keep records of the transaction.[53]

In keeping with the provisions of the tasa, the Indians were obliged to perform only that work required of them as tribute.[54] The encomenderos, in turn, had to provide the Indians with religious instruction, to allow them time for rest and relaxation on Sundays, to care for their health and physical well-being, to aid them in times of sickness, and to supply them with grain if they needed it.[55] Any encomendero found guilty of violating the prescriptions, either by employing the mitayos in tasks other than those specified or by sending them to work in more distant mines, was deprived for one year of the rent and services of his Indians for a first offense, and of his repartimiento for a second.[56]

After completing his work in Santiago, Santillán moved south to Concepción in the spring of 1558, where he intended to perform an identical service for the vecinos of the frontier settlements. He began by visiting the encomiendas to compile a register of Indian vassals. An Araucanian uprising that had broken out shortly before his arrival prevented the completion of this survey, so Santillán decided to issue a general ordinance applicable to Concepción, La Imperial, Cañete,

Valdivia, Osorno, and Villarrica.[57] The document was modeled on the Santiago tasa, differing mainly in the number of mitayos permitted to work in the placer mines; probably because the southern provinces were more thickly populated with Indians than the northern areas, Santillán allowed one out of every five mapuches to be assigned to the mines, instead of one in six. In determining how many Indians actually constituted this one-fifth proportion, the word of the caciques and leading natives was to be accepted.[58]

Several interesting provisions illustrate the thoroughness of Santillán's proposed solution. For every ten men sent to the mines, the cacique had to supply one native woman to serve as cook. Two mitayos were included in each group of workers to keep the camp supplied with water and firewood. Each mitayo was to have a daily ration of grain, corn, or frijoles plus fish, salt, and chili. Miners were also to receive meat three times a week.[59]

The demora, or permissible period for working the mines, was to last from December 1 to the end of July.[60] A vecino who violated these limits was to be deprived of his encomienda Indians and their tribute for one year for the first offense; a repetition meant permanent deprivation. Other culprits were subject to fines of five hundred gold pesos payable to the royal exchequer for a first offense, and one thousand pesos for a second.[61] No vecino could send his Indians to mine gold in the territory of another pueblo, but only in territories of which he was a resident and then only in the mines closest to that pueblo. Failure to observe these restrictions entailed loss of all the gold mined.[62] The encomenderos had to provide adequate housing for the workers living at the mines, as well as religious instruction by a cleric or a qualified layman.[63]

With one-fifth of the mitayos in the mines, only another fifth could be employed in other labor for the encomenderos at any one time; violation would cost the employer twenty pesos for each person thus illegally employed. Other fines included five hundred pesos for making natives work at jobs away from their own villages during the planting or harvesting season, one hundred pesos for hiring out the services of encomienda Indians, and one thousand pesos (or a hundred lashes for penurious offenders) for using Indians as carriers.[64]

Two other provisions are of interest. One specified that any person having a native girl working for him was obliged to provide her with a dowry after four years of service, if she was of marriageable age. He was also bound either to give her a separate dwelling place when she married or to send her home with her husband to her own people. Disregard of these measures carried a fine of two hundred pesos and deprivation of the right to similar service in the future. The other provision stated that all natives of Peru were to be allowed to return home; anyone who hindered them was to be fined five hundred pesos.[65]

Before he could finish his ordinance for the southern districts, Santillán became involved in a series of disagreements with Governor Hurtado de Mendoza that caused him to return to Peru without receiving any official instructions to do so.[66] One of his last acts before sailing from Valparaíso was to complete the tasa for the border settlements, which was issued on June 4, 1559.[67]

In his report to the audiencia of Lima concerning his activities in Chile, Santillán stressed the necessity of official confirmation of the measures he had initiated. Otherwise, he declared, the encomenderos would take advantage of his absence to ignore the decrees:

> The disordered greed and blindness of heart they display in thinking and believing that it is all right for them to exploit the Indians as if they were slaves are so widespread in that land . . . that they have no scruples whatsoever in disregarding the aforementioned regulations or any others enacted in favor of the Indians. Nor do they hesitate to use deceit in undermining the efforts of those who strive to enforce the regulations, which they have found and still find all sorts of subtle ways to evade. As a result, the only effective means of enforcing the regulations is to apply rigorous and severe penalties that will put the fear of the law into these rascals and make them realize that justice is vigilant.[68]

The members of the audiencia, however, were either not sufficiently impressed with the need for such action or not sufficiently interested in the fate of the Chilean natives to heed Santillán. Undismayed by their lack of cooperation, he directed his plea to the Council of the Indies itself in a letter of March 18, 1560.[69]

To make sure that the Indians would receive and profit from the gold due them for their work in the mines, Santillán had stipulated that each year the cabildos and justicias mayores of Santiago and La Serena were independently to appoint two trustworthy men to serve as purchasing agents for the Indians of those districts, to spend their gold judiciously on clothes, woolen blankets, cattle, sheep, and other necessary items.[70] The purchases were to be made with the knowledge and approval of the encomendero and the curate in charge of the encomienda. The herds thus acquired were to be entrusted legally[71] to the encomendero, who had to render a periodic account of their numbers to the Indian owners.

Hoping to foil the encomenderos' efforts to avoid paying the Indians their share of gold and the royal *quinto* (mineral tax) assessed by the Crown, Santillán ordered that all mined gold be turned over immediately to the local mints, and he forbade the Spaniards to use unminted gold as a species of exchange among themselves. Merchants could accept gold dust from the Indians only for purchases costing less than ten pesos.[72] Another measure aimed at providing greater personal freedom for the Indians allowed the use of Negroes in the gold mines, and permitted the Indians to pan gold for themselves. If crops were planted in partnership with their encomendero, he had to arrange for the plowing of the fields and had to reimburse the Indians with one-third of the harvest.[73]

Despite these precautions, violations occurred as Santillán had feared. In his letter to the Council of the Indies he recounted a number of such transgressions. Juan Jufré and several other encomenderos employed Indians in the textile mills without paying them, and Juan Bautista Pastene and his associates did the same in their ships'-rigging factory. Other encomenderos, disregarding the laws on employing natives outside of their own territory, sent Indians to work in the newly discovered mines of Choapa and Convalbalá, situated some sixty leagues from Santiago and in a very different climate.[74] Unless the Council intervened, Santillán predicted, such violations would become standard practice.

The Council proved more cooperative and farsighted than the audiencia of Lima. It quickly endorsed Santillán's legislation, and commanded the new governor of Chile, Francisco de Villagra,[75] to put the ordinances into effect and to punish violators severely. The Council further appointed a commission composed of Villagra, the bishop of

Santiago, and two members of religious congregations to report on the advantages and disadvantages of a faithful execution of the decrees. In an additional effort to help the Indians, the Council authorized the governor to require the encomenderos to employ Negroes in the mines, a prescription that was never carried out, for as Francisco de Galvez, one of the royal accountants, noted in one of his reports: "In this realm [of Chile] there is no traffic in [Negro] slaves; nor do they command much of a price because the people here are so poor."[76] Nevertheless, he admitted that the experiment was worth trying, and recommended that fifty Negroes be sent to Chile together with mining tools and farm equipment.

Had Santillán's ordinances been diligently applied, they might have made a striking contribution to the freedom of the Indians and the general prosperity of the colony. In the mines of Quilacoya, near Concepción, where the ordinances were actually put into practice for a time, the Indians responded favorably and production increased. More than a million pesos of gold were shipped to Peru during the first year of the experiment. Quilacoya was a unique case, however, with no counterpart elsewhere in Chile.[77]

Unfortunately, not only the Spaniards but also most of the mapuches ignored the ordinances. Ill-equipped as the Araucanians were for appreciating the advantages of such legislation and inclined as they were to a carefree type of existence, many of them preferred to remain independent rather than take up the settled regime of miners and farmhands. Others fled into the mountains, and still others formed guerrilla bands and preyed on the Spanish settlements. The Spaniards, for their part, saw the ordinances as an effort to deprive them of their "just and natural rights," and accordingly evaded them, in which course they were encouraged by the bad example of certain governors and the connivance of corrupt local officials. As a result, neither Santillán's ordinances nor the vigorous injunctions emanating from Spain succeeded in mitigating the evils of personal service in the encomiendas. The efforts of succeeding generations were no more successful. The encomiendas of yanaconas proved particularly durable, continuing to exist until the end of the eighteenth century with little or no change.

What to Santillán was obvious, the encomenderos would not concede: that the failure of local officials to enforce the laws protecting the natives was one of the principal reasons for the perennial strife between Spaniards and Araucanians. As Diego de Rosales, a seventeenth-century observer of events in Chile, put it: "What man would not despair upon seeing his wife torn from his arms? What man would not willingly expose himself to any danger in order to defend his offspring, especially when he sees them being led away and sold into slavery?"[78] If decades of bloodshed and war characterized the establishment of Spanish hegemony in Chile, the Spaniards had only themselves to blame.

Santillán's tasa failed to achieve its primary objective, the abolition of abuses afflicting the natives, not because it was wrongheaded but because it was too revolutionary for its time. It offended too many vested interests to win the support needed to make it work, that of the encomenderos and the local politicians. Nevertheless, it was the most significant social and political experiment attempted in Chile during the sixteenth century. In retrospect, its various provisions, aimed as they were at giving the natives a certain amount of economic independence and the necessary stimulus to improve their social and economic status, were not only fundamentally just but wise. If the reforms had succeeded, the history of Chile would have been different. That they failed was not the fault of Hernando de Santillán, or of the courageous men who followed in his path.

FRAY GIL GONZALEZ AND DEFENSIVE WAR

WHILE HERNANDO DE SANTILLÁN was attempting to curb the abuses of personal service, another of García Hurtado de Mendoza's advisers was exerting his influence in a different direction for a similar purpose. Gil González de San Nicolás was a Dominican friar of strong convictions, whose ceaseless defense of the Indians made his name anathema to many of his contemporaries. A native of Ávila[1] in Old Castile, González came to America at an early age and quickly won recognition in Lima as a defender of the rights of the Indians. No doubt this was what prompted Domingo de Santo Tomás, the provincial of the Dominicans in Peru, to assign him to Chile in 1552 as protector of the natives and vicar general.[2] Five years elapsed, however, before González was able to set sail for the south. Perhaps the infrequency of communications between Chile and Peru, as well as the disturbed state of affairs in the southern province, contributed to the delay. Perhaps, too, González's superiors deemed it more convenient to await the departure of the newly appointed governor, García Hurtado de Mendoza. In any event, Fray Gil joined Mendoza's entourage and with Luis de Cháves, and Hernando de Aguayo, the first Dominicans to come to Chile, landed at Coquimbo in 1557, charged with establishing a convent of the Order in Santiago.[3]

Gil González de San Nicolás was a colorful, generous person with a strong sense of justice, a man of solid virtue and ardent faith, an indefatigable minister of religion who was capable of doing great things, but like many other defenders of right, he failed to understand the necessity of sometimes tempering zeal with common sense. As a religious, his conduct was irreproachable; as a political adviser, it was frequently reprehensible. Convinced of the rectitude of his own position, González did not hesitate to speak out boldly. Governor Mendoza, for his part, was extremely reluctant to hear, much less to accept, criticisms of his actions. Only twenty-two and determined to make a name for himself in pacifying the Araucanians, he did not intend to allow any interference with his plans.[4] González was equally determined to prevent any injustices during the coming campaigns. Under the circumstances, a clash of wills was inevitable.

On arriving in La Serena, the principal town in northern Chile, Mendoza revealed that one of the basic considerations in his strategy to gain firm control of the country was to multiply the number of Spanish settlements; he planned to found a pueblo of Spaniards in the valley of Quillota, in the northern jurisdiction of Santiago,[5] perhaps with the concomitant aim of increasing the output of the nearby mines of Malgamalga.[6] Much to his surprise, the resident officials of La Serena unanimously opposed the idea, pointing out that the surrounding territory was in no danger of an Indian rebellion. Such a move, they contended, would only serve to divide military forces that could be used to better advantage elsewhere. On this occasion, at least, Mendoza swallowed his pride and desisted,[7] but he did not abandon the original idea. Instead of acquainting himself first with the condition and resources of Santiago, the governor planned to bypass that area and go directly to Concepción. Oña in his *Arauco domado* and some of Hurtado de Mendoza's biographers suggest tenuously that the reason for his decision was that Mendoza wished to shield his troops from the softening influences of the capital. Santillán hinted at a more plausible reason when he wrote in his report to the audiencia of Lima that "after the removal of Villagra and Aguirre, I went with Governor García de Mendoza *to rebuild and repopulate* the city of Concepción."[8] Whatever the reason may have been, the plan must surely have been unpopular, for there was no urgent need to go south at that particular time. Good military judgment, in fact, advised against it. Winter had already set in, and the winter of 1557 was a very severe one. Torrential rains in the south made impossible any extensive campaigns or attempts to rebuild Concepción, Angol, and the forts of Arauco, Purén, and Tucapel, which had been destroyed during the Indian uprising of 1553–57. The appearance of new Spanish forces on the frontier could only alert the enemy to future reprisals, causing them to hide their supplies and not plant new crops, in hopes of preventing the Spaniards' looting. The rank and file in the army would have to suffer not only inclement weather, but also possible hunger, since supply lines from Santiago were dependent on roads and rivers that frequently were impassable in the winter. Even the Indians would undertake no important excursions during this season; in any case, the death of Lautaro, their foremost leader,[9] had left them more disorganized than usual and they would need considerable time to regroup their forces for a new offensive.

Such considerations must have given the governor pause. Certainly his adviser Fray González urged him not only to pass the winter of 1557 in Santiago working to free the Indians from their obligatory service to the encomenderos but also to dispatch a messenger immediately to the rebellious southern provinces to make peace with the Araucanians. González offered to serve as ambassador, with the understanding that Mendoza would accept whatever agreement he could make with the rebels. Not until an offer of peace had been made did he think it would be prudent for the governor to visit the frontier.

These proposals, so contrary to the ordinary Spaniard's conception of how to handle an obdurate enemy, met with considerable support from the military personnel, but for a different reason. It was not concern for the mapuches that prompted their cooperation, but fear of the lengthy ocean voyage from Coquimbo to Concepción during the stormy winter season.

The Franciscan missionary Juan Gallegos, who was another of Mendoza's advisers,* had no such misgivings. He supported the governor unconditionally, taking a stand directly opposed to that of González.[10] In a sermon delivered in the church at La Serena on Pentecost Sunday,

---

* Three ecclesiastics served as advisers to the governor in addition to the lawyer Santillán. The third member of the trio was a secular priest, Antonio de Vallejo, whom the archbishop of Lima had named visitor general of the church in Chile. Vallejo was a prudent man, an enemy of discord, and blessed with a more tranquil temperament than either González or Gallegos, neither of whom complained of his conduct in the disputes that followed, leading one to suspect that he did not attempt to moderate their conduct, even though as the ranking cleric in the party he would have been justified in doing so. About the character of Fray Juan Gallegos we know very little, but events show that, like González, he was a quick-tempered man, who frequently acted on the spur of the moment and was prompt to condemn an opponent who contradicted him. Since González says nothing against him personally when reporting their bitter polemics, we must conclude that he, too, was a worthy and virtuous priest.

he defended the thesis that "there are times when the Gospel must be preached with tongues of fire, that is to say, with flaming guns." He thus implied, Fray González indignantly commented, that the war against the Araucanians was just.[11] The issues were clear, the forces were joined, and the struggle had begun.

Encouraged by the pronouncements of Gallegos, Governor Mendoza disregarded the opinions of Fray González and the military and weighed anchor for Concepción on June 21, 1557.[12] With him went one hundred and eighty foot soldiers, less than half of the reinforcements that he had brought with him from Peru.[13] The remainder, composed of cavalry units, were ordered to proceed overland to Santiago and from there to Concepción.

González, who saw in the governor's decision a criticism of his position, claimed that the rebuff he suffered was due to his bad relations with Santillán, who held the important position of deputy governor and principal legal adviser to Mendoza. It seems improbable that Santillán's disapproval would have made much difference to the governor; nevertheless he and González rarely agreed on any question pertaining to the war.

After a nerve-racking voyage, the weary fleet finally dropped anchor at Quiriquina, an off-coast island near Concepción. Mendoza's determination to disembark and prepare fortifications made it clear that the governor intended to continue the war against the rebels *"a sangre y fuego,"* with blood and fire. González reproached his superior privately for this decision,[14] reminding him that by royal order the *requerimiento* (a document urging the natives to accept Spanish suzerainty) had to be read to the Indians before hostilities could be initiated. Mendoza countered by summoning the two friars, González and Gallegos, to a meeting to discuss the matter,[15] perhaps as a subtle precaution against the rigors of a future residencia.* More probably, however, Mendoza merely hoped to quiet González's objections by confronting him with Gallegos' approval of his policy. The conference turned out to be even stormier than the ocean voyage.

---

* The residencia was a judicial inquiry to which all public officials, from the viceroy down to the ordinary town alcaldes, had to submit upon the conclusion of their term of office. As the colonial period advanced, evasions of this requirement became rather common.

In stating his reasons for opposing the governor's course of action, Fray González did not content himself with vague generalizations in defense of the Indians. He hit at the very heart of the matter by attacking the legality of the action itself, basing his argument on the instructions that the king's Council had issued in 1513 for the regulation of future *entradas* (entries into new territories for the purpose of conquest).[16] According to these instructions, the governor was legally bound to offer the Araucanians an opportunity to accept peaceful coexistence before making war on them.[17]

Governor Mendoza's reply might have been that such preliminaries were farcical and useless, but this would have reflected unfavorably upon the Crown. Instead he argued that if he were to attack the rebels quickly and force them to surrender before they had an opportunity to unite and strengthen themselves, unnecessary bloodshed would be averted. Fray Gallegos, agreeing with Mendoza, even asserted that the greatest Dominican of them all, St. Thomas Aquinas, held the same view in his treatise *On Fraternal Correction*! The effect of this verbal bombshell was summed up vividly by Fray González when he said: "The meeting ended in shouts, and that was its only result."

The disappointing outcome of the conference did not, however, silence González, who continued to deplore what he called the aberrations of his religious rival and the unfortunate attitude of the governor. Before long González learned that Mendoza was preparing to cross to the mainland from the island. Once again González warned him that he would be guilty of a "grave offense against God," since he would be provoking the Indians to resistance and thus exposing them to the danger of dying in their infidelity. He insisted that the governor's reason for the move did not hold, since the Indians had already had plenty of time to prepare their forces while the Spaniards had been on the island. He urged waiting for the arrival of the cavalry from Santiago, whereupon the governor could more effectively take the field and frighten the Indians off with an impressive display of strength. When Mendoza replied that the lack of provisions on Quiriquina made the move necessary, the friar retorted that, since the governor had made the initial mistake of coming to the place, he ought to put up with the inconvenience for a while longer until reinforcements came.

Realizing that his reasoning had not impressed the governor, the

friar requested permission to go to Santiago. Mendoza refused, probably fearing that González would stir up public opinion against him
there; it would be safer to keep him in the camp, even though he was
a source of continual friction. There was, too, the possibility that word
of the rupture might reach the ears of the viceroy, his father, and of the
oidores in Lima, who held González in high esteem and who would be
inclined to side with the Dominican when judging the matter.[18] González now decided to change his tactics. Throwing caution aside, he
began to denounce the governor's conduct publicly before the whole
army. As one historian of the period has aptly remarked with reference
to a later similar incident: "This was going too far. It was tantamount
to advocating rebellion openly to an army that was in the field. It was
carrying indiscretion to the point of fanaticism."[19]

Clearly such resentments and recriminations had to reach a climax
before long. After the crossing to the mainland, Fray González requested the governor to let him try to persuade the Indians to come
to terms with the Spaniards. But because Fray Gallegos opposed the
idea the permission was refused. The Dominican's reaction was characteristic. He commenced to criticize the governor anew for leaving
Quiriquina. Mendoza was sorely vexed. So, too, was Fray Gallegos,
who is reported to have shouted on one occasion: "If the governor
sinned in crossing over to the mainland, then Jesus Christ sinned in
becoming man!" With tempers at such a pitch, it was futile to hope
for any reasoned compromise.

A series of disturbing incidents now occurred to heighten the tension.
One day an Indian appeared before the temporary stockade indicating
that he wanted to talk of peace. Some of the Spaniards, including Santillán and Fray Gallegos, urged that he be taken prisoner as a spy.
Fray González energetically counseled a different approach. If every
messenger of the enemy were considered a spy, he argued, this would
be equivalent to a declaration of war. Even if the man were a spy, he
continued, it would be wiser to act as if he were not, to treat him well,
allow him to examine the fort and its resources, and send him back to
his people with conciliatory words and feelings of fear and respect for
the Spaniards. Then, Fray Gil believed, he would advise his comrades
to lay down their arms. Mendoza, however, thought that his forces
were too weak to run the risk of allowing the enemy to acquire any

firsthand information regarding their strength. Consequently he commanded that the Indian be put in chains.

The wisdom of Mendoza's decision became clear a week later on August 25, when the Araucanians attacked the fort, wounding thirty Spaniards and killing two. González made light of the incident in a subsequent letter to the Council of the Indies: "Finally, some harmless Indians attacked the fort, and the soldiers killed as many of them as they could, without regretting the fact that they were sending them to hell. On the contrary, one of the soldiers remarked that shooting Indians was the best sport in the world." While it is reported that the action did not resemble a pitched battle, and Mendoza himself and numerous other witnesses called it a *reencuentro* or *guazábara* (encounter or skirmish), terms commonly used to denote a clash of limited size and importance, it was, nonetheless, a more serious engagement than the words of Fray González would imply.

This affront to his judgment led Fray González to ascend the pulpit in a final all-out effort to convert the governor. He harangued the rank and file daily, absolving them of obedience to their commanders, and inciting them to revolt. The governor and any soldier who willingly participated in the entrada, he warned, would be guilty of mortal sin and bound to make full restitution for all the damage he inflicted. Not only in speech but also in writing, he expanded on the reasons for his stand and on the policy that ought to be adopted in dealing with the insurgents.

The camp's reactions to these warnings and denunciations revealed conflicting loyalties. Most of the military, as well as the governor, were incensed, because many of them hoped to use the war as a means of gaining such advantages as encomiendas of Indians. There were others, however, who responded more favorably, and who offered to make restitution for whatever injuries they had caused. Although these offers were proportionately few, the fact that they were made by people who were highly respected rendered them more significant. Some obscure soldiers, too, disgruntled with the way the campaign was being handled, were eager to make the Dominican's views their own.

Mendoza displayed amazing moderation and tact in dealing with this new problem; instead of charging the friar with sedition, he decided to ship him off to Santiago. Since González had requested permission earlier to visit the capital, he could hardly refuse to leave now. Fray Gallegos proved to be less diplomatic. From the pulpit he declared that the war was legal, saying that even Thomas Aquinas would agree on that. Gallegos painted visions of an exalted crusade, a war so holy that if there were no professional soldiers to do the fighting, he and his Franciscan brethren would eagerly assume the responsibility.

Fray González, not to be cowed, promptly challenged his adversary, proposing that each of them prepare a signed statement of his own views, but Fray Gallegos disdainfully rejected the challenge. Thus the debate descended to personalities once more, with Santillán, who participated in the proceedings, lashing out at González, so the latter complained, "with insulting language." Some of the soldiers, too, evidently had had their fill of the Dominican's intransigence and heartily wished that he would leave. González, nonetheless, obstinately delayed his departure until Mendoza broke camp and headed south into Araucanian territory, destroying the crops of the natives as he advanced.

The question naturally arises at this point: what was Antonio de Vallejo, the third of Mendoza's ecclesiastical advisers, doing while all this quarreling was going on? Vallejo must have been moderate and discreet for González merely remarked, without reproach, that "his whole concern was to side with the governor and not only to approve of what he did, but to act as his confessor." This speaks well of Vallejo's prudence and patience, which must have been considerable in the midst of the heated denunciations and pointed accusations.

Fray González arrived in Santiago firmly resolved to return to Peru, but he had not yet fulfilled the commission to found a convent of the Order in Chile, and the interest of the people of Santiago in the project convinced him that the capital would be a logical choice for it. His confidence was not misplaced, for material support was quickly forthcoming. The lieutenant governor, Pedro de Mesa, purchased in the king's name some old houses belonging to Santiago de Azócar[20] and on November 16, 1557, deeded them to Fray González, who took possession of the property on the same day.[21] Eight days later Bartolomé Flores donated a small farm on the north bank of the Mapocho River, which had formerly belonged to Pedro Gómez de las Montañas.[22] The following year, on August 22, Rodrigo de Quiroga and his wife, Doña Inés Suárez, transferred to the Dominicans the administration of the hermitage of Our Lady of Montserrat, which they had erected on the summit of Cerro Blanco, together with the lands that Pedro de Valdivia had granted to that institution. At the same time they established a chaplaincy in the hermitage in favor of the Order.[23] These gifts assured the new house of financial security.

Events progressed smoothly until the Lenten season of 1558, when Santillán and Fray Gallegos arrived in the capital. Their appearance was the signal for a renewal of differences. Without waiting for his opponents to take the initiative, Fray González moved to the attack, repeating his earlier charges. "Seeing," he wrote later, "that the people were already assembled and that the time was ripe, I commenced preaching to them that they were obliged to make restitution to the Indians for past grievances and instructed them on how they were to act in the future."[24] Fray Gallegos did not hesitate to resume the debate either. He spoke for the conquistadores and the economic interests in the colony, and he was supported in his views by the local authorities and especially by Santillán. González, in opposition, defended the rights, the possessions, and the lives of the Indians.

In his sermons Fray Gallegos not only denied that the conquistadores were obliged to make restitution but declared that the onus of reparation was wholly the Indians'. Not only must they accept the losses they had suffered, but they must reimburse the Spaniards for the cost of the military expeditions sent against them! It was a startling thought anticipating by centuries the philosophy of the Treaty of Versailles after World War I.

The controversy quickly broadened in scope to include other issues, notably the obligation of instructing the Indians in the Faith and the legality of obligatory personal service. Fray Gil maintained that unless the encomenderos provided their Indians with a thorough religious training, they were not entitled to profit from their labor. Fray Gallegos insisted that all that was necessary was one Indian youth who could recite the Pater Noster. The dispute over personal service must have been especially distasteful to Santillán, who was at the time engaged in determining the labor tribute that the natives owed their masters; he had already decided to moderate the tribute rather than to abolish it, as González urged.

The tenacity of González's defense of the rights and freedom of the mapuches produced such a storm of vilification, particularly among civil officials and certain ecclesiastics, that it threatened not only his reputation for sound orthodoxy but also the existence of the monastery he had founded. "Feeling against me became so strong," he informed the Council of the Indies, "that they began to persecute me with deeds."[25] On purely doctrinal grounds, however, the Dominican was secure against the accusations of those who opposed him. What, then, must have been the glee of his adversaries when they discovered an occasion for discrediting him? González had declared that a certain financial agreement involving two of the colonists was not usurious. Fray Gallegos noisily insisted that it was, and that the victim was a poor, maltreated citizen. The case was submitted to the judgment of the courts, and Santillán, urged on, so González claimed, by his Franciscan associate, decided in favor of the "victim." González protested the court's interpretation, but Santillán simply issued a statement to the effect that the Dominican friar did not know what he was talking about.

This was not the last or the greatest of the public humiliations. Before the controversy had ended, Fray González was summarily excommunicated by the vicar general of Santiago, Martín del Caz, for his part in a dispute over the publication of a papal bull. The matter was quickly settled and the excommunication rescinded, but the experience was a severe test of the friar's humility.[26]

The anti-González faction, apparently not satisfied with mere character assassination, went a step further by trying to suppress the monastery that González had founded. At their urgings, Santiago de Azócar, the original owner of the structures, demanded repossession of them. Santillán granted his petition and declared invalid the transfer of property previously effected by Pedro de Mesa. Fray González hastened to comply but, fortunately for him and his Order, a group of wealthy citizens of Santiago who were partial to the Dominicans succeeded in buying up Azócar's claim for two thousand two hundred pesos, thus temporarily checkmating the strategy of the friar's persecutors.[27]

Shortly thereafter, on August 26, 1558, Santillán convoked the cabildo of Santiago and pressured its members into annulling the grant of land to the hermitage of Montserrat on the grounds that the land belonged to the Indians of Rodrigo de Araya's encomienda,[28] and that it was not fitting to give such a fertile part of the Mapocho valley to ecclesiastical establishments, thus diminishing the total amount of land and water available for farming.[29] This action, if allowed to stand, would deprive the Dominicans of a valuable source of revenue and would likewise nullify the chaplaincy that Rodrigo de Quiroga and his wife had founded at Montserrat in favor of the religious. González immediately directed an appeal to the audiencia in Lima and left Chile at the first opportunity to defend in person the interests of his Order.[30] On March 13, 1559, the audiencia handed down a judgment favoring the Dominicans.[31] Heartened by the audiencia's decision, González resolved to return to Chile without delay, but Viceroy Mendoza, fearing that Fray Gil's presence there would lead to further disturbances, forced him to stay in Lima. Finally the fall from power of Andrés Hurtado de Mendoza and his son, García Hurtado de Mendoza, opened the way for his return south, and by early January 1560 he was back in Santiago.

The future looked bright for the defender of the mapuches. Francisco de Villagra, who had gone to Lima to testify at the residencia of the two Mendozas, had been appointed governor of Chile in place of García Hurtado de Mendoza, but it was not until June 1561 that he arrived in Santiago to take up his duties.

The appointment of Villagra, who had been a close friend in Lima, was welcome news to Fray González. Villagra's known dislike of his predecessor, Mendoza, led González to conclude that the new governor would willingly support his campaign for justice in dealing with the natives.[32] When Villagra arrived in Santiago, Fray Gil besieged him "with eloquence and sound reasons" to convince him that the enemy must be brought under the dominion of the king "by peaceful means and kind treatment and by teaching them the principles of Christianity."[33] Villagra appeared to be convinced, and when he departed for the southern frontier in October 1561, he took Fray Gil with him as official adviser and ordered his captains to treat the Indians well.[34]

When the army arrived at Cañete, the center of Araucanian resistance, in the province of Tucapel, Fray González received a rude shock, for Villagra allowed his captains to engage in numerous forays into enemy territory without first attempting to reduce the rebels by peaceful means. Bitterly disillusioned, he lost no time in making his views known throughout the camp, publicly denouncing the soldiers for killing the Indians, threatening them with eternal damnation, and warning them that they would have to make restitution for the damages they inflicted. He declared that the Indians were justly resisting the Spaniards because they were defending their homes, their liberty, and their possessions against unlawful invasion. His pronouncements had such force and conviction, reported one of Villagra's officers, that they made a great impression on the minds of his hearers.[35] He spared no one, not even Villagra himself. On one occasion, while the governor was chatting with some soldiers who had used their lances to good effect in a skirmish, the friar interrupted to inform them bluntly that their crimes would send them to hell. Military obedience and discipline meant little to Fray González when moral values were at stake. But they did make a difference to the troops, who were thus faced with a disturbing dilemma: if they disobeyed the commands of their leaders, they would be court-martialed; if they obeyed them, they would run the risk of eternal damnation.

Thus Fray González once again succeeded in throwing the camp into an uproar with his sermons and seditious counsels. Villagra, a man who detested extreme measures, shrank from the task of reprimanding the friar. Advanced age and infirmities had weakened him and left him in no condition to deal vigorously with the misconduct of his friends or to pursue the war to a successful conclusion.[36]

While the turmoil was at its height, Juan de Herrera, one of Villagra's lieutenants, came up with a proposal calculated to ease the minds of the soldiers and satisfy Fray González. It was a legal process for justifying the war against the Araucanians. Herrera began by summoning the Araucanians to trial. No defendants appeared, of course, nor were any expected, since the summons was merely a concession to legal formalities; Herrera then announced that the Indians were guilty of rebellion and enumerated their offenses. They had, he stated, professed allegiance to the king of Spain in the beginning and had agreed to live in peace with the Spaniards and to receive Christianity. Later, they had rebelled against their sovereign's authority, putting to death more than seven hundred Spaniards and impeding the spread of the

Gospel and the practice of religion among the baptized. Therefore, they deserved to be punished.[37]

To forestall any criticism of his tactics and to demonstrate his willingness to allow the accused every opportunity for defense, Herrera next called upon the protectors of the Indians, and especially Fray Gil González, to present their arguments in defense of the natives.[38] What was González to do? What answer could he make to Herrera's charges? It was true that occasionally the Indians had come to terms with the Spaniards, that many of them had accepted baptism, and that many of them had also reverted to arms. He could argue that the Araucanians had been forced to accept terms and that they had been justified in trying to protect themselves against the Spaniards who abused them. But the burden of proof lay with him and not with Herrera. He would have to substantiate his claims to the satisfaction of the court, and what chance would he have before such a judge and such a jury? So he contented himself with replying that "neither the king, nor Herrera in his name, was capable of judging the matter fairly because they were not certain of the facts."[39] Herrera disregarded the implication, continued the trial, and demanded the deaths of the defendants and the forfeiture of their property, ordering that the verdict be made known to the culprits and to their protectors. After the period for appeals had passed without any being submitted, he commanded that the sentence be carried out.

Herrera decided to execute the sentence personally. Backed up by a detachment of two hundred armed men captained by an officer of his own choice, Herrera moved out to arrest and punish the offenders, arguing that the Indians were going about killing and pillaging in all directions.[40] The war against the Araucanians had now been formally "legalized!" The provisions of the requerimiento had been fulfilled!

This extraordinary trial instituted against an entire nation, and the sentence of death handed down by a field commander, added an unexpected fillip to the military operations against the Araucanians, but it did not prevent the Spanish defeat at Catiray nor the evacuation of the frontier town of Cañete. Nor did it save Herrera from future embarrassment. He later admitted to the Council of the Indies that upon returning to Peru in 1562 no priest would give him sacramental absolution until after the leading theologians and civil officials in Lima had studied the transactions of the trial and declared it legal.[41]

Herrera's intervention caused González to lose face in the eyes of the troops and to suspend his defense of the Indians temporarily. For this reason or because of the resentment his sermons had aroused, he decided to return to Santiago, where he at once resumed his activities, to the dismay of many leading citizens who started a bitter campaign of their own against the friar. One of the most vehement was the distinguished conquistador Alonso de Escobar, who paid for his opposition by being subjected to a brief investigation on the charge of heresy by the ecclesiastical authorities in Santiago. He was later freed of the charge but not before undergoing twenty days of searching examination.[42] Public indignation reached such a point that Antonio de Molina,[43] vicar general of Santiago, tried to pressure González into leaving the country. Although desirous of helping the Indians, Molina realized that little progress would be made as long as González was present to stir up resentment. He accordingly requested Juan Jufré, the lieutenant governor, to arrest Fray Gil on a charge of heresy (a common stratagem of the time for silencing troublemakers); but Jufré, knowing that González was a friend of Governor Villagra, tactfully refused to do so. The cabildo of Santiago likewise refrained from interfering in the matter. Molina then acted on his own authority, publishing a decree of excommunication against González, placing the city under interdict, and ordering ecclesiastical services to cease. González hit back by persuading the Guardian of the convent of San Francisco to excommunicate Molina in turn and order his imprisonment. Jufré put his men at the disposal of the Franciscan superior, and Molina was interned for several days in the convent of Santo Domingo.

The Guardian of San Francisco reiterated his excommunication of Molina on January 25, 1563, and ordered him to make a public retraction from the pulpit of all his accusations against Fray González. Molina ignored these injunctions, took refuge in the convent of La Merced, and caused to be posted on the door of the church still another decree of excommunication directed against twenty-five persons, including the Guardian of San Francisco, Fray Gil, the bishop-elect, Rodrigo González, and the lieutenant governor, Juan Jufré.

In the midst of these proceedings, the Father Guardian issued a second order for the arrest of Molina, who was forcibly removed from his refuge in La Merced to the convent of San Francisco. From there he was taken under guard to the home of the Licentiate Fernando

Bravo de Villalba, where he remained incommunicado until his friends engineered his escape. Again he sought asylum in La Merced and again was forcibly removed by the public authorities, this time to the residence of the *alguacil mayor* (chief constable) Alonso de Córdoba. When several of his friends—Juan Godinez, Juan Bautista Pastene, and Pedro Gómez de don Benito—came forward with assurances of proper confinement for the prisoner, Molina regained his freedom and escaped to Callao in Peru. Some months later Fray González followed, and, like Molina, began composing memorials to the audiencia of Lima and the king justifying his role in the unseemly episode.[44]

Nothing positive resulted from this incident, but it is worthy of note that on January 22, 1564, Molina addressed a letter to the king from Peru in which he informed His Majesty that in Chile "the authorities are guilty of using great force on the natives, subjecting them to in-humanities unknown among people however barbarous they may be and however ignorant of God."[45] Despite the incident of 1563, Molina and González were of one mind as far as the exploitation of the Chilean natives was concerned.

The return to Peru in 1563 marked the end of Fray Gil's career in the colony but not the end of his lively interest in the welfare of the mapuches.[46] Like the other great Dominican of his time, Las Casas, he continued to draw the attention of authorities to the problems that existed. Toward the end of 1563 he composed a sobering account of the sufferings of the mapuches that, in content and tone, closely re-sembled the *Brevísima relación de la destrucción de las Indias*, which Las Casas had published a decade earlier in 1552.[47] In this account, intended primarily for the enlightenment of his religious superiors in Spain, González singled out the bad treatment that the Indians re-ceived from the whites as the principal cause of the war. Speaking of the cruelties practiced by the colonists, he said:

> They take the Indian women and men whom they capture in the war and feed them to the dogs without first killing them. They frequently do this just for the sport of watching such an inhuman struggle. They kill as many boys and girls, women, and old men as they encounter. And if some Indians kill a Spaniard for some reason or other, the army im-mediately retaliates by slaying all the inhabitants of that particular pueblo

or district on the grounds that they are all guilty. In addition to all this they commit horrible murders, destroy crops, and burn villages and dwellings. If the natives are trapped inside their homes, the Spaniards bar the doors so they cannot escape, and they burn them alive. In short, they are at present perpetrating all the cruelties that have appeared in the Indies since their discovery.[48]

That abuses existed is incontrovertible; that they existed on the scale and measure that González implied is not correct. If what he said had been literally true, no Indians would have survived to be enslaved or employed. His account must accordingly be judged for what it really was—a misguided attempt to effect a cure through shock treatment.

González spared no one in his catalogue of delinquencies; even the ecclesiastics were accused of complicity, and of grave negligence in their pastoral duties because they baptized the Indians "without giving them any instruction whatsoever in our holy Christian faith." His most scathing denunciations, however, were reserved for the encomenderos, who, he maintained, were guilty of not only exploiting the physical strength of the natives, but also defrauding them of their personal goods. "In a word," he concluded, "the Indians experience no relief whatsoever from the time they are born until the day they die."[49]

Although González had left Chile, the issues he had raised were not forgotten. Civil and ecclesiastical authorities continued to wrestle with the problems.[50] Particularly noteworthy was the inquiry sponsored by Bartolomé Rodrigo González Marmolejo, first bishop of Santiago and one of the founders of the *iglesia chilena*.[51]

González Marmolejo was determined to put an end to the controversies stirred up by Fray Gil González. Shortly after taking possession of his see on July 17, 1563,[52] he therefore summoned a council of theologians to discuss, orally and in writing, the essential issues underlying the war: (1) Is there any justification for the war? (2) If there is, how should the war be waged and how should the Indians be treated? (3) What obligations do the encomenderos have toward the natives of their encomiendas? The answers to these questions would, it was hoped, provide confessors with a practical guide for dealing with penitents who had deprived the Indians of their rights and possessions.

No known documents give the names of all the theologians who participated in the council, but Francisco de Paredes, the archdeacon of Santiago, was definitely one of the group, since his accounts are the major source of information on the subject. Others who must have submitted opinions were Agustín de Cisneros, vicar general of the diocese; Melchor Calderón, treasurer of the cathedral church in Santiago; Francisco Jiménez, canon of the cathedral and nephew of the bishop; and other leading members of the religious and secular clergy in the city.[53]

The opinion the bishop finally adopted was that of the archdeacon Francisco de Paredes.[54] His *parecer* (opinion) revealed a firm grasp of the subject and demonstrated his dexterity in arguing a case. By concentrating on the legality of the war, he adroitly sidestepped the question of whether or not the Indians were justified in resisting the Spaniards. For a man of Paredes' intellectual agility it was easy to prove that the Spaniards were in the right. Since the governor of Chile exercised legitimate authority because his appointment came from the Crown, only two additional conditions had to be verified, Paredes maintained, in order to justify aggression: a just cause and a justifiable end.

Proving the existence of a just cause presented no difficulty. For more than twenty years, Paredes pointed out, the Spaniards had been in possession of a large part of Chile; therefore a body of rights and privileges had developed already. There were, for instance, many baptized Indians in the rebel provinces. True, experience had shown that the natives frequently accepted baptism simply for reasons of convenience, and apostatized with equal alacrity later on when it suited them to do so. But there were also many Indians who were sincere Christians, and it was a common occurrence for dying natives to request the sacrament. Another consideration was that there were many Spanish soldiers and women of low social position who had married Indians and had established their homes in the rebellious provinces. There were, too, thousands of encomienda Indians and yanaconas who were Christians and who lived in enemy territory. Separated as they were from their religious brethren, they were without spiritual ministrations of any kind. Finally, the very lands in the provinces of Arauco and Tucapel (the center of the native uprising) that were now in the hands of the enemy had been peacefully possessed and cultivated by the Spaniards for many years before. Since everyone had admitted their rights to the lands for a long time, they ought not to be dispossessed of them.*

After presenting these general considerations, Paredes concluded that the Indians had a dual obligation to permit the preaching of the Gospel and the administration of the sacraments to Christians living in their territories, and to give up the lands that they had taken away from the Spaniards.

It would clearly be futile, however, to petition the Indians to allow missionaries to cross the frontier or to permit Christians to seek spiritual aid from the faithful in Spanish territory, for it was clear that the rebels opposed the practice of Christianity. But if the Araucanians acted so unreasonably in matters of religion, they would surely be far less amenable to the suggestion that they surrender territory. The only solution, therefore, was a recourse to arms, not only to win respect for the rights of the Christians and to protect them against the tyranny of the infidels, but also to recover the lands belonging to the Spaniards. In other words, the war against the Araucanians was not only just but obligatory.

Although Paredes did not hesitate to pronounce the war justifiable on religious and economic grounds, he did recognize a possible moral objection: would not the damages, grievances, and outrages that armed conflict invariably entailed be sufficient in themselves to make the war unjust? His answer was in the negative. Since the Indians had freely accepted the dominion of the Spanish Crown (an assumption the Araucanians would have denied heatedly), they were obliged to act like other royal subjects when seeking redress for injuries sustained. Instead of rebelling, they should have appealed to the courts. By failing to do so, he argued, they had in effect invited the war. (His reasoning was reminiscent of the opinions of Sepúlveda during the first half of the century.)

Paredes was honest enough to acknowledge that, although armed rebellion by the Indians could not be justified, the civil authorities had an urgent obligation to end the abuses that gave the rebels legitimate

---

* Paredes ignored the fact that the Araucanians could have advanced the same argument as a justification for opposing the Spaniards.

reasons for complaint. By treating well the Indians who made peace and especially by eliminating the inequities of personal service, the Spaniards could gradually convince the Araucanians of the advantages of peaceful coexistence with the whites, for good treatment of the pacified tribes would take away from their warring compatriots every reason for continuing the rebellion. Paredes emphasized also the need to promise the Indians that they would not be punished for past offenses, such as the death of Pedro de Valdivia, Pedro de Villagra, and others. They were to be given all manner of assurances that "they would be heard, that justice would be meted out to those who had injured them, and that from now on no one would be allowed to do them any harm." If after all these demonstrations of peace and goodwill they still refused to lay down their arms and permit the unobstructed preaching of the Gospel, then the Spaniards could justly make war upon them.[55]

Thus did Francisco de Paredes attempt to solve the problem of racial antipathies and social inequities in Chile. The acceptance of his ideas by Bishop González Marmolejo was a tacit rejection of the principles of defensive warfare of Fray Gil González de San Nicolás. The climate of opinion in the Long Land was not yet propitious for a large-scale experiment in peaceful penetration, for the old concepts of political hegemony and racial superiority were still too strong in the minds of too many. Not until the arrival of a black-robed missionary extraordinary, Luis de Valdivia, did defensive warfare become for a time the official policy of the Spanish government.

BISHOPS AND GOVERNORS, PRO AND CON

GONZÁLEZ MARMOLEJO'S ENDORSEMENT of Paredes' argument for offensive warfare was his sole contribution to the issue of interracial justice, but it was an important one. It effectively nullified the efforts of Fray Gil González and provided the colonial authorities with a justification for exterminating or enslaving the Araucanians. Had the bishop lived longer his views might have changed, but within a few months the aged prelate was in his grave.[1] With his death the episcopal see of Santiago remained vacant until 1570 when the new bishop, Fray Fernando de Barrionuevo of the Order of Friars Minor, arrived.[2]

During the interval, however, significant events were occurring elsewhere in the colony that were to have repercussions in the conflict between Spaniards and Indians. On March 22, 1563, Pope Paul IV created a second episcopal see in Chile, that of La Imperial; he named as its first prelate the eminent Franciscan friar Antonio de San Miguel.[3] The new bishop, one of the first Franciscans to come to Peru, had distinguished himself by his learned preaching and his solicitude for the poor. While he was Guardian of the convent in Cuzco, he initiated a successful drive for the founding of a hospital, by collecting, with the help of the corregidor Garcilaso de la Vega, more than 34,000 ducats during the opening days of the drive. The provincial chapter of the Order, which met in Lima in October 1562, recognized his administrative talents by electing him provincial of the Peruvian province, a position he filled with outstanding zeal and capability.[4]

Contrary to the king's wishes, San Miguel refused to take possession of his see until the pontifical bulls confirming the appointment were in his hands.[5] This meant a delay of several years, since the originals were lost in transit and duplicates did not reach Lima until 1568, when San

Miguel accepted episcopal consecration; shortly thereafter he left for Chile.[6]

He found his diocese in a deplorable condition, sections of it desolated by the wars, its few priests overburdened by the spiritual demands of the resident Spaniards and native converts. The Indians under his jurisdiction had been reduced to a level of veritable slavery; bowed down as they were by excessive labor, they had little inclination to embrace a religion that appeared to be completely associated with the conqueror. With characteristic energy and determination, San Miguel set about improving the situation. Instead of restricting his efforts to a more complete enforcement of the ordinances of Santillán, he began lobbying for an unqualified abolition of personal service as the best means of ending the Araucanian struggle.[7] The audiencia of Chile (established as the supreme governing authority by a decree of Philip II on August 27, 1565) finally yielded to his appeals and directed two of its members to visit the colony with a view to moderating the labor tribute demanded of the natives.[8] Egas Venegas was to investigate conditions in the southern encomiendas, while Torres de Vera y Aragón was assigned to Santiago and La Serena.

The audiencia's reluctance to order the investigation might have presaged negligible results, but the two officials displayed an impartiality and thoroughness in their work that surprised even San Miguel. Writing to Philip II on October 24, 1571, he praised the manner in which Venegas had executed his commission, saying: "I was present in La Imperial when he made his *visita,* and it seemed to me that he did things in an orderly fashion and was desirous of doing good to the Indians and of providing them with some relief."[9]

The praise was well merited. The fines Venegas imposed on the encomenderos of only two towns, La Imperial and Valdivia, totaled more than 150,000 pesos, and some say this was a conservative estimate.[10] Torres de Vera was equally conscientious in conducting his investigation. According to an account of services compiled in Santiago in 1576,

> he left Concepción in the dead of winter and personally visited the Indian pueblos to instruct the natives concerning the tribute and to procure good treatment for them. He travelled over poor roads to encomiendas situated

in remote and dangerous places, thus performing a great service to Your Majesty. He devoted an entire year to this visita during the course of which he became very ill and almost died. Moreover, he spent more than six thousand pesos of his own money to carry out the assignment.[11]

The fines that Venegas and Torres de Vera levied must have worried the encomenderos at first, but characteristically the landed proprietors brought pressure to bear on the audiencia, and not only succeeded in having the investigations cut short, but escaped without paying a peso.[12] The end result of the visita was expressed in a letter that a later governor of the colony García Oñez de Loyola wrote to the king in 1598, in which he stated flatly that the encomenderos "carried their appeal to the audiencia and, although two years passed after the appeal, the audiencia took no action against them, and conditions remained as before just as if no visita had been made."[13]

The audiencia's failure to deal firmly with the encomenderos was a severe blow to San Miguel's hopes. Disgusted with their lack of cooperation, he advised the king in a letter of June 27, 1570, to suppress the tribunal because it was accomplishing nothing for the pacification of the country.[14] The audiencia's reluctance to act was understandable, however; because of the endless war, the colonial authorities were forced to depend more and more on the assistance of the local *hacendados* (property owners) for necessary supplies. The encomenderos capitalized on this need to promote their own interests at the expense of justice and royal legislation.

The audiencia's failure prompted San Miguel to turn to the pulpit to impress the Spaniards with the seriousness of their offenses against the Indians. His hard-hitting sermons met with far more success than had his political lobbying. In 1573, for example, one of the wealthier vecinos of La Imperial, Pedro Olmos de Aguilera, who held an encomienda of approximately ten to twelve thousand Indians, founded seven churches and a hospital for the benefit of his Indians.[15] Diego de Gaete, a resident of Osorno, bequeathed twenty-seven thousand pesos to the three thousand Indians of his encomienda as recompense for injuries sustained while in his service.[16] Miguel de Velazco, Gabriel de Villagra, Baltazar Rodríguez, Rodrigo de Hoces, Andrés Martínez de Santa Ana, and Luis Barba likewise showed a change of heart by endowing chaplaincies and engaging in other pious works. According to a public document issued in August 1573, another encomendero, Hernando de San Martín, constructed two churches for the benefit of the natives of his encomienda.[17]

The greatest triumph, however, was yet to come. In response to San Miguel's repeated urgings, Philip II signed a decree in Madrid on July 17, 1572, that commanded the audiencia of Chile to revise the tribute schedule for the diocese of La Imperial "in conformity with the cédulas and provisions that we have issued for the taxing of the Indians."[18] Another cédula of the same date empowered the bishop of La Imperial to deliver the decree to the audiencia and to impress on the members the need for its early execution. The prelate was also to inform the king of how the civil authorities complied with the royal orders.[19]

The provisions to which the king referred were those that absolutely prohibited compulsory personal service. Part of a cédula issued in 1563, is characteristic:

> Obligatory personal service shall not be countenanced in the future. Rather, the Indians who have been entrusted to private individuals, as well as those who have been placed in the Crown's care, are to pay their tribute with money or other specie according to the amount required of them. The rest are permitted to work as free men, and if any one of them wishes to serve the Spaniards it must be of his own free will and not in any other manner.[20]

The language of the decrees was clear. The audiencia's compliance was not. Of course, the oidores were in a difficult position: they dared not offend the encomenderos for fear of losing their support, yet if they failed to act they would be disobeying the Crown. So like all good politicians the judges decided to compromise by solemnly appointing two high-ranking ecclesiastics—Fray Juan de Vega, provincial of the Franciscans in Chile, and Fray Lope de la Fuente, vicar-provincial of the Dominicans—to continue the investigation begun by Venegas. But they stripped them of all effective authority, for theirs was to be a tour of inspection, nothing more. They were not permitted to impose any fines whatsoever on their own initiative.[21]

The two friars dutifully visited the frontier towns of Angol, La Imperial, Valdivia, and Osorno and submitted a report on what they considered an equitable tax for the mapuches. There the matter ended. The audiencia was unwilling to sacrifice the support of the encomenderos by enacting a measure opposed to their economic interests. Thus they suspended indefinitely the promulgation of the tasa that the king had ordered.[22] As Bishop San Miguel indignantly informed Philip II on October 26, 1575:

> The oidores have fulfilled their obligations to all concerned: to Your Highness by issuing a decree providing for a new tasa, and to the encomenderos by countermanding it. Personal service continues unrestricted. The Indians suffer much mistreatment, and I do not understand how we can expect those who are at war to accept a peace that is really a heavy, insufferable yoke.[23]

While Bishop San Miguel was loudly deploring the audiencia's shortcomings, a change in government was already in the making. By a decree dated in San Lorenzo on July 31, 1573, Philip II abolished the short-lived audiencia of Chile and elevated Rodrigo de Quiroga, who had served as lieutenant under both Valdivia and Hurtado de Mendoza, to the political leadership of the colony.[24] News of the appointment reached Santiago some fifteen months later, and on January 26, 1575, Quiroga took the oath of office.

Unlike Bishop San Miguel, the new governor was a firm believer in obligatory personal service. Writing to the king in 1577 he enumerated his reasons:

> With regard to taxing the Indians of this kingdom, I have informed Your Majesty in a previous communication that the war and the pacification of the country in which I am engaged are a serious obstacle to its realization. These Indians are a disunited people and so bestial in their habits that they do not live together in pueblos or according to the dictates of natural law. They have no system of justice or any kind of political life. They possess no haciendas, nor do they raise herds in sufficient numbers to support themselves and to pay taxes. Thus it is fitting that the tribute be a form of personal service . . . so that they might acquire the capacity and the enlightenment of Christians.[25]

Acting on this conviction, Quiroga consistently neglected to obey a royal directive of August 5, 1577, which enjoined the enactment of a new tasa for the diocese of La Imperial.[26] That he was himself a fairly wealthy encomendero may have had something to do with this policy; however, he did take steps to ensure a better observance of the regulations that Santillán had promulgated for the protection of Indians assigned to work in the mines. Thus at the beginning of 1577 and again in 1580 he named Diego Vásquez de Padilla alcalde of the mines of Choapa, Quillota, Curaoma, and Alamillo as well as of those near Espíritu Santo and La Serena.[27] Similarly, on March 19, 1579, he appointed Juan Bohón, son of the founder of La Serena, alcalde mayor of the mines within the jurisdictions of Santiago and La Serena, directing him to "inspect the labor gangs in the mines to find out whether the ordinances that provided for their good treatment were being observed."[28]

This concern for the pacified Indians living in territory under Spanish control did not extend to the warring tribes in Araucania. Quiroga was a firm believer in the use of force to solve unrest, and he accordingly set out for the southern frontier on January 8, 1577, determined to subdue the Araucanians once and for all. With him went an imposing detachment of four hundred Spaniards and fifteen hundred Indian auxiliaries.

The plan Quiroga intended to follow in pacifying the frontier called for penetration into enemy territory, the execution of prominent chiefs, the forced deportation of prisoners of war, and their reduction to slavery in the gold mines of the north. These strategies were not unusual in the sixteenth century, but Quiroga's plan had an additional feature: the captured rebels were to be "disabled" in order to minimize the chances of escape. Had the Araucanians been aware of what this implied, it is doubtful whether any of them would have surrendered, for "disablement" left the victims permanently maimed. With a chisel or sharp machete, a foot was hacked off around the ankle, after which the mutilated stump was thrust into a cauldron of boiling tallow to stop the bleeding. The wonder is that any of the victims were expected to survive.[29]

Cruel though it was, the plan had the support of Francisco de Toledo, the viceroy of Peru, who was more interested in ways of financing and terminating the war than in the means used to achieve these ends. The official announcement of Quiroga's appointment as commander in chief of the Chilean forces on March 6, 1574, expressly authorized him to transfer six or seven hundred prisoners of war to the province of Coquimbo where, "after securing them against flight by disabling one of their legs, they might work in the gold mines and produce the means of financing the war more easily and of paying the soldiers with less vexation and bother to His Majesty's vassals."[30]

Whether or not the plan also had the known approval of Philip II is open to debate. Quiroga claimed that it did. Writing to the viceroy on January 26, 1578, he stated that:

> Following the instructions Your Excellency gave me when appointing me general of this realm, I have worked toward the banishment of these re-bellious Indians, because by exiling them and making *mitimaes* out of them this kingdom will be pacified much more quickly. His Majesty approved this course of action in a cédula that he sent me authorizing me to do what I think best in the case.[31]

That Quiroga recognized the need for some such extrinsic justification is shown by the steps he took to ease the consciences of his men and to forestall the reproaches of the clergy. In a tactic reminiscent of Juan de Herrera, he instituted legal proceedings against the rebellious Araucanians, summoned them to trial, appointed a prosecutor to plead their case, tried them in absentia, and then condemned them to death for the crime of insurrection against established authority. Commutation of the death sentence to physical mutilation and labor in the mines completed the travesty. Gregorio Sánchez, the commissioner whom Quiroga put in charge of the expatriated prisoners, described their arrival in La Serena in a report submitted to Viceroy Toledo on March 25, 1578:

> When the deportees arrived at this city some of them tried to escape, but they were recaptured and six or seven of them were hanged while the feet of about five hundred others were cut off; and although some people are of the opinion that these mutilated creatures can be of use in the mines, they are actually good for nothing except for work in gardens and on farms.[32]

Approval of the type of treatment described above would seem to contradict the humanitarian policy of the Spanish Crown, referred to earlier. But some explanation can be found in the fact that there was a profound difference between the Crown's attitude toward conquered and unconquered natives. The Spanish rulers issued many laws and decrees to aid and protect conquered Indians, but toward unconquered Indians they displayed less clemency, condoning at times outright barbarism. But the sixteenth century was not shocked by the presence of barbarism and cruelty; nor were such practices confined to Spain and the Spanish possessions in America: criminals in England, France, Germany, and other parts of the civilized world were legally subject to maiming that was as horrendous as anything applied to the Araucanians. And though the crude and extreme barbarism of the sixteenth century must shock us all today, it could be argued that the more refined practices of recent times are no less cruel.

As for the colonists in Chile, they were as assiduous in obeying the decrees of the monarchs that sanctioned the use of violence against the mapuches as they were in disobeying those that sought to safeguard the rights of the natives. Thus, for example, they never accepted the abolition of obligatory personal service regardless of how obedient their encomienda Indians were and regardless of the fact that its abolition had been commanded in scores of official decrees. Had it not been for the persevering efforts of such men as Diego de Medellín, it is doubtful that any protracted attempt would ever have been made to alleviate the status of the Chilean Indians.

Diego de Medellín was a native of old Medellín in Extremadura, Spain. Born in 1496, he entered the Franciscan Order in the province of Salamanca and went to Peru during the early period of its conquest. In Lima, where he gained repute as a clergyman and a teacher of philosophy, theology, and jurisprudence,[33] he was elected Guardian of the Franciscan convent and later provincial of the Order in Peru. Philip II presented his name for the bishopric of Santiago in 1573 as a successor to Bishop Barrionuevo, who had died two years earlier. Pope Gregory XIII raised him to the purple on June 28, 1574,[34] and on February 27 of the following year the king issued a decree instructing the authorities in Santiago to receive him as head of the church in that city. He arrived in Chile around the middle of 1576,[35] and was consecrated bishop in 1577 by San Miguel in the diocesan town of La Imperial.

At the time of his consecration Medellín was already an old man of eighty-one, but his advanced age did not noticeably hinder him in the performance of his duties. The diocese of Santiago, he quickly discovered, was in a state of profound confusion after the brief tenures of the first two prelates.* The intervening six years that the see had been vacant had occasioned evils that Barrionuevo's short incumbency had not erased.

The new bishop began his administration with an official tour of the diocese. Even prior to his consecration as bishop, Medellín had written to the king about the necessity of a new tasa and of gathering the natives into pueblos where they could receive proper training and spiritual care and be less dependent on the whims of the encomenderos.[36] On the tour he saw that "all the male and female Indians living on the haciendas, the old as well as the young of both sexes, and even the blind and the crippled, were occupied in working for the encomenderos and were treated worse than savages." The encomenderos treated them as beasts of burden and indulged in carnal excesses with the native women.[37] Even the protectors of the Indians (whom Medellín appropriately called *destructores*), who had been appointed to safeguard the Indians' rights, took advantage of their position to conspire with the encomenderos for wholesale exploitation. As a result there were some Indians who had spent more than thirty years working in the mines without receiving a single *real*† for their labor. Unless the Crown took a firm stand in the matter, Medellín warned, nothing would be accomplished "because here neither bishops nor preachers are powerful enough to force a remedy."[38]

The chances of a reform were slim, however, as long as Rodrigo de Quiroga remained governor of Chile. But the fates were kind to the mapuches at last. Worn out by the rigors of years of combat, Quiroga died on February 25, 1580, after designating his son-in-law, Martín Ruiz de Gamboa, to be his successor.[39]

Hoping to stimulate cooperation on the part of the new administra-

---

* González Marmolejo had governed the diocese for slightly more than a year and Barrioneuvo for eighteen months. Medellín's ability to bring order out of chaos made him the first real organizer of the diocese.

† The *real* was a Spanish coin equal to thirty-four *maravedís* (the coin of least value in the system, worth about one-sixth of a cent).

tor, Bishop Medellín had recourse to a scheme that San Miguel had adopted some years before in La Imperial. During the Lenten season of 1580 he instructed his clergy to refuse sacramental absolution to any encomendero who did not present a signed document from the bishop authorizing confession to be heard. To receive this permit the bearer had to sign a petition to the governor requesting him to issue a new tasa for the diocese, "since a refusal to sign the petition would be a certain indication that they were not properly disposed to receive absolution."[40] The prelate had judged the religious temper of his flock well. Practically all of the encomenderos signed the petition, albeit with considerable reluctance and grumbling.

As for Gamboa, there was no need to stir him to action; he wanted very much to obtain royal confirmation of his provisional appointment, so he seized the opportunity of currying favor with the king by carrying out the decrees concerning native labor.[41] In May 1580, he promulgated the Tasa de Gamboa, a document that one modern historian has described as the outstanding piece of social legislation in Chile during the sixteenth century.[42] The evaluation by Francisco Encina, a present-day protagonist of the revisionist approach to Chilean history, is the exact opposite:

> Gamboa's tasa plunged the natives into the most shocking physical and moral degradation without producing any compensations whatsoever. The Araucanian war necessitated sacrifices of the hardest kind and cost hundreds of thousands of lives, but it gave rise to the character, discipline, endurance, and courage that typified the Chilean people in the nineteenth century. Gamboa's system of tribute, on the other hand, engendered nothing more than the idleness, covetousness, and corruption of officials and ecclesiastics that undermined the culture and prosperity that the union of Spanish intelligence and native strength had created in Chile.[43]

The new tasa abolished obligatory personal service by substituting a monetary and produce tax. Each tributary Indian in the diocese of Santiago was obliged to pay his encomendero a yearly tribute of seven gold pesos, two of which were earmarked for general expenses and the salaries of curates, corregidores, and other officials. He also had to contribute two pesos' worth of wheat, corn, barley, fish, fowl, or sheep thus bringing the total yearly tax up to nine pesos. The tax in the jurisdiction of La Imperial was limited to seven pesos yearly, and the Indians of that diocese were free to substitute for the monetary tribute personal labor, evaluated according to a predetermined wage scale. The long rainy season in the south, which reduced the number of working days in the year, explained the lower rate in that area.[44] Four corregidores were appointed to supervise the tribute collection, to protect the natives against the encomenderos, and to guard against the reestablishment of compulsory personal service.[45] The tasa also stipulated that in the future the Indians were to live together in pueblos, which the encomenderos were forbidden to enter.[46]

The abolition of forced labor was a triumph for the ecclesiastics over the landed proprietors whose anger rose in proportion to the temporary benefits resulting from the tasa.[47] Having been forced to request it, they were now resolved to revoke it. They hoped at first that the Indians would prove negligent,[48] but the natives continued to pay their taxes regularly and to enjoy their newfound liberty. As the governor reported to Philip II, "this tasa was so odious to most of the vecinos, especially since it placed corregidores in the native villages to protect the Indians and to keep out the Spaniards, that some began to complain that I had caused the ruination of the colony by depriving them of their means of support."[49]

Seeing their profits diminishing, the encomenderos enlisted the support of the cabildo of Santiago who responded favorably on November 11, 1580, by sending Juan de Escobedo and Francisco de Irarrázaval as procurators to Peru in the hope of persuading the audiencia of Lima to abolish the tasa.[50] Their most promising assistance, however, came from a wholly unexpected source, from the prior of the monastery of St. Dominic in Santiago, Fray Bernardo de Becerril.[51] Convinced that the tasa was against the best interests of the colony, Becerril dispatched one of his subjects, Fray Cristóbal Núñez, to Lima for the purpose of interceding with the viceroy for its revocation, but they both realized that a direct attack on a measure supported by leading ecclesiastics and the Crown would be futile. Thus they decided to pose as friends of the Indians and to claim that the tasa was so prejudicial to the economic welfare of the natives that they themselves were clamoring for its repeal. What the viceroy ought to do, they urged, was to restore the ordinances of Santillán, which had provided the Indians with the means of becoming economically independent. Gamboa's system, they argued, was depriving the mapuches of their meager resources and of every incentive for bettering themselves. Moreover it had been devised by men who were newcomers to Chile and grossly inexperienced in the affairs of the colony.[52] After submitting his argument, Núñez realized that he had been guilty of a very important omission: he had included nothing that would discredit the bishop and clergy of Santiago, the most enthusiastic partisans of the tasa. Therefore he presented the viceroy with a second document which caricatured the bishop of Santiago as a half-demented prelate and the rest of the clergy as ignorant ministers. He complained of the many mestizos Bishop Medellín had admitted to the priesthood, and suggested that all the curacies in the diocese be declared vacant, since they had been filled independently of the privileges included in the *patronato real.*[53]

Fray Núñez's arguments, as well as those of the two civilian procurators, Irarrázaval and Mercado (who had replaced Escobedo in April 1581), made little impression on the audiencia of Lima, which refused to exercise any initiative in the matter, contenting itself with referring the case to the Council of the Indies.[54] This was not too displeasing to the encomenderos, for they had reason to think that the Council's decision would not be entirely unfavorable. While the appeal to the audiencia of Lima was hanging fire, the encomenderos had enlisted the assistance of Ramiriañez Bravo de Saravia, who was passing through Peru en route to Spain on personal business. Ramiriañez was the son of Melchor Bravo de Saravia who, while president of the defunct audiencia of Chile, had presented him with the rich encomienda formerly held by Villagra. Ramiriañez had been deprived of this grant by Governor Gamboa and had undertaken the journey to Spain to defend his claim at the royal court. His dislike for Gamboa made him a natural advocate for the encomenderos, so Irarrázaval and Mercado pressed him to plead their cause before the Council of the Indies if an appropriate occasion should arise. Apparently it never did, or else Ramiriañez proved to be ineffective, for the Council discreetly never came to an agreement about Gamboa's troublesome tasa.

Nevertheless, some action was taken: Gamboa's failure to gain a decisive victory over the Araucanians stirred the king to dispatch a new military expedition to Chile, one supposedly capable of pacifying the rebellious provinces completely. As head of the expedition he chose a veteran of numerous campaigns, Alonso de Sotomayor, to whom he entrusted the governorship of Chile and the successful termination of the war.[55] Ramiriañez capitalized on Sotomayor's presence in Spain to draw him over to the side of the encomenderos; long before his arrival in Chile, Sotomayor had already resolved to undo as much of Gamboa's work as possible.

The new governor reached Santiago on September 22, 1583, to the warm greetings of the populace, who saw him as a harbinger of the long-awaited peace. Realizing that he could not bring the war in Araucania to an end without the cooperation of the hacendados, Sotomayor was prepared to make whatever concessions might be necessary to win their assistance. In a letter of December 22, 1583, he accordingly informed the king that he had decided to levy a new tax that would be a compromise between that of Gamboa and that of Santillán.[56] Before implementing his plan, Sotomayor solicited opinions and reports from representative Spaniards in the capital. Two of the replies—by the Franciscan provincial, Fray Cristóbal de Ravaneda, and the prior of the Dominican convent, Fray Bernardo de Becerril—agreed that Gamboa's tasa ought to be revoked. Fray Ravaneda was particularly opposed to monetary tribute as a tax, because the encomenderos could easily overtax their Indians illegally; he argued that the labor tribute, performed a little at a time, was actually less onerous even though the Indians ended up by doing more work than was legally required.[57]

Strengthened by the backing of these two influential friars, Sotomayor felt justified in executing his plans despite the opposition of Bishops Medellín and San Miguel. He proceeded slowly, limiting himself at first to abolishing the office of corregidor established by Gamboa and reducing the monetary tribute by two pesos. Later, however, he also suppressed most of the other provisions of Gamboa's tasa, and reinstated forced labor as the regular form of Indian tax.[58] He likewise appointed administrators for the Indian villages whose salaries consisted of a fourth of the grain and herds that the natives raised. The encomenderos were allowed to share in these administrative responsibilities, a privilege they apparently fully utilized, since Sotomayor's successor García Oñez de Loyola found it necessary to strip them of their authority "because of the damage resulting to the natives.

This kind of system," Loyola informed the king, "amounts to real slavery for the Indians because they derive no benefit from their lands ... which are all mortgaged to the encomendero. Consequently they keep on sinking further and further into debt ... thus the system serves only to make them work unprofitably their whole life long."[59]

Although there was considerable truth in the dismal picture that Loyola painted, it would be unfair to blame Sotomayor for all of it. The abuses that resulted from compulsory service were not so much the fault of the governors as of the lesser functionaries who winked at the crimes and cruelties of the landed proprietors. There is, moreover, evidence to show that Sotomayor did have some regard for the well-being of the mapuches. He was personally instrumental in securing the appointment of more than twenty-five clerics to the rural *doctrinas** in the diocese of Santiago.[60] He selected trustworthy men to serve as alcaldes in the mining districts and to act as official protectors of the natives. Prior to his arrival in Santiago the governor had named his brother, Luis de Sotomayor, protector general of all the Indians in the colony. Some years later, on March 10, 1589, he appointed Martín de Zamora administrator general and defender of the natives in the province of Santiago. Francisco de Soto, who had been active in the Araucanian war since the days of Pedro de Villagra, served three terms as alcalde of the mines.[61] More important still was the post of visitor general of the mines, which Sotomayor established on July 29, 1588. Its first incumbent, Gregorio Sánchez, had the right to preside at the residencia of retiring alcaldes, punish offenses against the Indians, impose penalties on natives who transgressed the law, and arrest military deserters.[62] The punishments meted out to Indian offenders were surprisingly mild for the times: paternal correction, the stocks, and prison sentences.[63]

The motivating force behind these measures was economic rather than humanistic, for Sotomayor, who was primarily interested in the profitable operation of the mines, knew that the physical health of the native workers was essential. In line with his objective he organized two mining districts—one in the valley of Quillota and the other in the valley of Choapa, the principal gold producing centers in the juris-

---

* A doctrina was a parish of recently converted Indians that did not yet have a resident pastor or curate.

diction of Santiago at that period—and put two corregidores in charge of the areas: Baltasar de Reinoso in Quillota and Juan de Tapia in Choapa. Reinoso received his appointment on January 23, 1590, and Tapia his on February 7 of the same year. Reinoso's jurisdiction was over the entire valley of Quillota, stretching six leagues in all directions from the mines to the sea and extending along the coast from Concón to Valparaíso. His yearly salary was two hundred gold pesos, half paid by the encomenderos who supplied the workers, and the other half by the Indians who had to work outside of the regular mining season to meet their obligation. Tapia's area of control embraced the valley of Choapa and a territory extending six leagues in all directions from the *asiento* (mining district); his salary was four hundred pesos a year. The corregidores had authority both judicial and administrative: as judges they were empowered to punish any crimes by or against the Indians; as administrators they were to provide for the education and welfare of the natives, to increase the output of the mines, and to further explorations for new sources of mineral wealth.[64]

Sotomayor's restoration of personal service had once again shifted the advantage in the seasaw struggle between *indigenistas* and *anti-indigenistas* to the side of the encomenderos, at least for a time. But the governor's inability to subdue the Araucanians,* coupled with his secret marriage (contrary to the express order of the Crown) to Doña Isabel de Zárate, daughter of Francisco de Irarrázaval and Lorenza de Zárate, turned the king against him and led to his downfall. Martín García Oñez de Loyola, a close relative of Ignatius de Loyola founder of the Jesuits and a nephew of Viceroy Francisco de Toledo of Peru, replaced him as governor of Chile on September 18, 1591.†

Of all the officials who governed Chile during the sixteenth century

---

* Several factors contributed to Sotomayor's failure, among them the recall to Spain of the troops intended for Chile, the limited resources of the encomenderos, and Sotomayor's ferocity toward the enemy. When his brother, Luis de Sotomayor, failed to win a decisive victory in the campaign of 1583, the governor decided to take the field personally in the following year. To intimidate the Araucanians and force them to come to terms, he ordered that the hands and noses of many prisoners be cut off before they returned home, for he thought that their appearance would frighten the others into submission. Instead it filled them with a desire for revenge and further resistance.

† In 1568 Toledo had brought Oñez de Loyola to Lima as captain of his guard, though he was only nineteen years of age. While in Peru, Loyola married Beatriz Sapay Coya, a rich Inca princess.

none showed a more lively interest in the welfare of the mapuches than García Oñez de Loyola. He not only subscribed to the social principles of Bishops Medellín and San Miguel, but also strove earnestly to advance their programs. Although he made no attempt to abolish forced labor, it was solely because he believed he did not have the authority to alter the system.[65] In matters concerning the government of the Indians, however, he had no such scruples. He replaced Sotomayor's functionaries with corregidores, alcaldes de minas, and similar officials of his own choosing, commanding them "diligently to procure the good treatment of the Indians and their training in the Faith . . . allowing no one to use force against them or to do them any harm."[66] Likewise, Lesmes de Agurto, who became administrator general and protector of the Indians on February 23, 1593, was cautioned to safeguard Indian interests and see that the encomenderos paid the yanaconas for their services. Oñez de Loyola also appointed Matías Carreno administrator of the pueblos and mines of Peumo and Colchagua on June 7, 1593, and designated Luis Abad administrator of the encomiendas of Gaspar de la Barrera in Colina and of Tomás Durán in Lampa on June 6 of the same year.[67]

These measures were, of course, distasteful to the encomenderos, who looked with disfavor on any official who dared to challenge their traditional system of exploitation. But their displeasure reached an all-time high when the governor undertook to put an end to the deportation of slaves from the frontier settlements to points beyond the Maule River. Traffic in Indian slaves was not new in the colony. When Pedro de Valdivia, the conqueror of Chile, decided to send Jerónimo de Alderete to Spain to secure for him the governorship of the colony and other royal favors, he sold his natives to help finance the journey. Alderete did the same with his encomienda Indians. Since the sale of pacified natives was legally prohibited, Valdivia and Alderete explained that they had not actually sold the Indians but had merely loaned them to other Spaniards for personal considerations. The money they had received—over 30,000 pesos—was not really payment but simply a private donation "for the support of the realm."[68]

Valdivia's example encouraged other conquistadores; thus the decimation of the northern tribes plus the constant need for workers quickly resulted in the forced migration of thousands of southern natives from their homes. The district of Arauco became a regular clearinghouse for the deportation of slaves to the mines and encomiendas of Santiago, La Serena, and Peru. It was the tribes who had accepted fealty to Spain who suffered most in this traffic, for peaceful Indians were easier to capture. As Gabriel de Zelada, oidor of the second audiencia of Chile, informed the king on a later occasion, "many more Indians from the pacified provinces have been seized and sold into slavery than have rebels captured in the war, albeit very unjustly and contrary to the will and express commands and laws of Your Majesty."[69]

The commerce in Indian slaves had already reached scandalous proportions by the time Oñez de Loyola assumed office in 1591. Fray Agustín de Cisneros, who succeeded San Miguel as bishop of La Imperial, described one aspect of the situation in the following words:

This war is the cause of many injuries and offenses against God, our Lord, for the principal occupation of the soldiers when they are not engaged in military campaigns is to visit the towns that lie between here and the Strait [namely, Angol, Villarrica, Valdivia and Osorno] for the purpose of hunting down Indians, both male and female, for their personal service. And even if two or three are all that a man needs, he does not hesitate to capture eight or ten or more if the opportunity arises. And it frequently happens that they leave the husband alone and take his wife and vice versa. Others seize young boys and girls, stealing them away from their parents. Many soldiers, too, carry off female Indians for immoral purposes.[70]

The words of Governor Oñez de Loyola corroborated those of Bishop Cisneros: "Another reason for the decimation of these aborigines," he informed the king in 1598, "is the wholesale exportation of Indians of both sexes, including boys and girls, from the diocese of La Imperial to that of Santiago where the climate is considerably different."[71] In their desire for profit, the Spanish merchants boldly traded in human flesh, scouring the backwoods and the fields of the frontier towns in their search for victims whom they straightway dispatched to the port of Valdivia for transferral north.

[The victims] arrived at the port of Santiago [Valparaíso] crowded into hulls in a fashion that resembled Negro slavers. Not infrequently, too, mothers of families were forcibly separated from their husbands and off-spring and sent into exile with the rest. So excessive was this nefarious trade that slaves were sold publicly in exchange for clothes, horses, coats of arms, and other items. And the residents of these towns [Osorno, Valdivia, Angol, Concepción, and Villarrica] made presents of slaves to their friends and acquaintances in Santiago. All in all the situation was truly deplorable.[72]

Appalled by his countrymen's indifference, Oñez de Loyola resorted to his legislative power to halt the practice: by a decree of November 17, 1593, he declared illegal the sale of Indians brought from the south for service as workers in the northern mines. Some months later, on March 5, 1594, he explicitly forbade the captains, corregidores, and justicias of the frontier towns and forts, as well as their successors, to "transport or alienate from these realms, in any manner whatsoever, any Indian, regardless of whether he be a rebel or not."[73] As a warning to those concerned, he commanded Francisco de Galdámez, one of the erring captains, to return to Villarrica all the Indians that he had transported from there, or pay a fine of five hundred gold pesos.[74] About four months later he issued a supplementary decree that threatened severe penalties against anyone guilty of transporting natives from Arauco to Peru, Santiago, or La Serena.[75] These decrees had no appreciable effect, however, save that of uniting the encomenderos solidly against the governor. The hacendados simply applied their old tactic of refusing to provide the government with any military or financial aid against the Araucanians as long as Oñez de Loyola remained in office. In fairness to the encomenderos it must be admitted that the resources of the colony had been seriously strained by the recurring demands of previous administrations. The encomenderos' refusal to make additional sacrifices without some assurance of a return on their investment may be reprehensible, but it is understandable. Their short-sightedness reaped its own reward in the Indian uprising of 1598, which devastated the entire southern frontier and marked the beginning of one of the bloodiest stages of the war. On December 23, 1598, a party of three hundred Indians from Purén, one of the Araucanian provinces, surprised and virtually annihilated some thirty-five Spaniards under Governor Oñez de Loyola in the valley of Curalaba.[76] Only two Spaniards survived the ambush—a cleric named Bartolomé Pérez, whom the Araucanians held prisoner for two years, and a soldier, Bernardo de Pereda, who was left for dead at the site of the massacre. According to their custom, the Indians decapitated Oñez de Loyola's body, taking the head as a trophy of their victory. Nine years later, in February 1608, they surrendered it to Governor Alonso García Ramón as a pledge of their future fidelity.[77]

With the uprising of 1598 as a bloody background, the stage was set for the appearance of Luis de Valdivia and his blackrobed associates, who led the campaign for human rights in the succeeding century.

THE BLACKROBES TAKE A HAND

WITH FEELINGS OF GRATITUDE and relief the passengers and crew of the *San Francisco Javier* disembarked at Coquimbo on March 20, 1593,[1] for the voyage from Callao had been long and dangerous, and the feel of solid ground was vastly reassuring.[2] As soon as they had landed the weary travelers made their way on foot to the town of La Serena, some two and a half leagues from the harbor; there they visited the church of San Francisco and gave thanks to the Almighty for delivering them safely from the perils of the sea.[3] In the party were seven Jesuits, the vanguard of one of the most influential religious organizations to establish a foothold in colonial Chile.

The arrival of the Jesuits fulfilled a long-standing request of civil and ecclesiastical authorities in Chile who had been impressed by the work of the padres in Peru as educators of youth and defenders of the Indians. As early as 1571 Bishop Barrionuevo of Santiago had endeavored to secure a contingent of Blackrobes for his diocese.[4] In line with Barrionuevo's attempt, the viceroy of Peru, Don Lope García de Castro, had persuaded Philip II to petition Francis Borgia, third General of the Order, to send more missionaries to Peru. Borgia complied with the request, but since the viceroy was more concerned about the spiritual needs of Peru than of Chile, none of the new recruits were allowed to go south. Manpower limitations and concern for other areas dissuaded the Jesuit superiors in Lima also from accepting the Chilean invitation. In his first letters to the General in Rome, for instance, Father Juan de Atienzo, who became superior of the Peruvian province in 1585, referred to Chile as a mission territory that had been offered to the Society for many years. Although he judged it a fruitful field for missionary labors, he considered the wants of the Spaniards in

Tucumán and Quito more urgent.[5] Despite these disappointments, the Chileans continued their appeals, relying on the assistance of Bishop Medellín, the governors of the colony, and the cabildo of Santiago to achieve their end.[6] The Jesuits in Peru supported these efforts by instructing their procurator in Spain, Father Juan Ramón, to solicit the king's permission to open a house of the Order in Chile.[7] Philip II, ever alert to opportunities to foster the spread of Christianity, issued a series of instructions in September and October 1590, in which he granted Ramón and seven companions the *pase real* (royal approval) for entering Chile, and ordered the treasurer of the Council of the Indies, Antonio de Cartagena, to underwrite the costs of the expedition.[8]

Armed with these documents, Ramón hastened back to Lima, eager to begin the long-awaited mission. But the provincial of Peru, Father Sebastián de la Parra,[9] judging it more prudent to staff the new mission with men acquainted with the rigors of the frontier and skilled in working with the Indians, appointed Baltazar de Piñas to head the expedition and gave him a free hand in choosing his companions.[10] It was a reasonable move. Through his experience as procurator general to Rome and provincial of the Peruvian province, Piñas had acquired an intimate knowledge of the talents and potentialities of its members. His prudence and sound judgment had been amply demonstrated when he introduced the Order into the kingdoms of Cerdeña and Quito. In short, he was a qualified leader for a difficult pioneering enterprise in spite of his advanced age.[11] Among those Piñas selected as associates were Luis de Valdivia, who was to gain lasting fame as the "Las Casas of Chile"; Hernando de Aguilera and Juan de Olivares, natives of Chile, who were familiar with the temperament and language of the Araucanians; Luis de Estella and Gabriel de Vega, men of deep spirituality and outstanding intellectual endowments; and the temporal coadjutors, Miguel Teleña and Fabian Martínez, whose mechanical abilities made them especially valuable in a frontier environment.

Equipped with the *carta de obediencia* (a credential from their provincial)[12] and the authorization of the Holy Office in Lima, the party of seven Blackrobes set out from Callao on February 9, 1593, en route to Valparaíso.[13] Stormy weather damaged the *San Francisco Javier* to such an extent that its captain decided to stop at Coquimbo for necessary repairs before continuing to Valparaíso. During the interval, the Jesuits lodged in some abandoned houses in La Serena that were reputed to be haunted. Before occupying their temporary quarters they took the precaution of exorcising the dwellings with the prescribed rites, whereupon the noises and apparitions popularly associated with the structures ceased, and the missionaries' stock among the people rose appreciably.[14] The zeal they displayed in preaching to the Spaniards and Indians, each in their own tongue,* in hearing confessions, and helping to reform public morals was so effective that when the time came to resume their journey the residents of La Serena begged them to remain.[15] Failing in this, they insisted that the Jesuits travel to Santiago by land to avoid further dangers on the sea, and they themselves provided the mounts for the journey.[16]

As news of their approach reached the capital, enthusiastic preparations were made to receive them. The Dominican friars were particularly generous, even delegating one of their members to meet the travelers at La Ligua, a town lying some twenty-six leagues north of Santiago, and to escort them to the convent in Santiago. The party arrived at the capital on April 12, entering at a very early hour in order to avoid the effusive demonstration that had been prepared.[17] They stayed in the Dominican monastery for more than a month, until arrangements could be made for an establishment of their own.[18] On the Sunday following their arrival in Santiago (Easter Sunday), Father Piñas preached to a capacity congregation in the cathedral. After giving a brief account of the Order's history and institute, he offered himself and his companions for the service of the people—Spaniards, Indians, and Negroes—declaring that they sought no material recompense but only the greater glory of God. He concluded by announcing that they had not yet decided on a fixed residence because they wished to be free to travel wherever their presence might be useful, especially into the territory of the Araucanians, whose conversion was the principal reason for their coming.[19] While Piñas was outlining the group's plans to the Spaniards in the cathedral, Aguilera was doing the same for

---

* Since the province of La Serena had formerly been under the control of the Incas, the language of Cuzco was a common idiom among the natives. Several of the Jesuits were familiar with it because of their years spent in Peru.

the Indians in the church of Santo Domingo. Speaking to them in their own language, he emphasized that the Jesuits had come to work for the spiritual and temporal welfare of the natives, and he invited them to attend the instructions in Christian doctrine on subsequent Sundays and feast days. The prospect of hearing sermons in their native tongue — a new experience for them — so delighted the Indians that many eagerly assisted at the services on the days appointed.[20]

The possibility that the Jesuits might decide on some other locale for their first residence produced a flurry of activity in the capital. The citizens were determined to keep the newcomers in Santiago, so with the approval of the civil and ecclesiastical authorities they immediately opened a drive for funds to purchase a living place for the community. The drive netted 3,916 pesos, most of which went to the acquisition of two houses on a corner of the plaza where the National Congress now stands. They were the property of Martín Ruiz de Gamboa and had been built by the former governor Rodrigo de Quiroga, Gamboa's father-in-law. Though valued at 10,000 pesos, they were obtained for 3,600 due to the decline in real estate values occasioned by the Araucanian war.[21] Under the expert direction of Brother Teleña, rather extensive alterations were carried out to suit the building to the purposes of a religious community: a cloister, a small chapel, and living quarters for the members had to be arranged. The cabildo of Santiago contributed an additional 450 pesos for furnishings. Within six weeks most of the remodeling was finished, and the Blackrobes were ready to operate as an independent religious establishment.[22]

While still residing in the Dominican monastery, the new arrivals began to apply themselves earnestly to the works of the ministry. The task of catechizing the Indians fell to Luis de Valdivia, who had shown a facility for learning native languages and a talent for dealing with the Indians.[23] Gabriel de la Vega performed a like service for the *morenos* (half-breeds), both slaves and freedmen. Luis de Estella devoted much time to the instruction of children, while Piñas, Olivares, and Aguilera dedicated themselves particularly to the service of the Spaniards. All assiduously administered the sacraments, heard confessions, visited the sick and those in prison, and collected alms for the needy. It is reported that as a result of their efforts, many Spaniards who had been at odds with each other settled their differences, others were persuaded to give up their mistresses and concubines or to make restitution for ill-gotten gains, and some of them even became members of religious Orders and congregations.[24]

During the first two years of their sojourn in Chile the Jesuits seem to have concentrated on Santiago and its environs, since no mention of missionary excursions is made in the records. Toward the end of 1595, however, a spirit of greater initiative became evident. Earlier that year Luis de Valdivia had succeeded Piñas as superior of the community in Santiago,[25] and he looked eagerly toward Araucania, where thousands of infidels awaited the message of Christianity. His aspirations coincided with those of Governor Oñez de Loyola, who, mindful of the political advantages of a peaceful penetration of the Araucanian stronghold, invited the Jesuits to send representatives into the area. Valdivia readily accepted the invitation, and assigned two of his best men— Gabriel de la Vega and Hernando de Aguilera—to the project.[26] The choice of Aguilera was particularly appropriate in view of the importance attached to the undertaking. He was a native of Concepción and had a complete command of the Araucanian idiom, speaking it as one who had known it from childhood.[27] This accomplishment won for him the immediate respect of the Indians who regarded linguistic eloquence as a mark of superiority.[28] The government's use of Jesuit aid to pacify the Araucanians was one of the most significant developments during Valdivia's term as rector in Santiago. Though the later political and social repercussions of this move were far-reaching in their effects, there is no reason to suppose that this first excursion into enemy territory was anything but a spiritual mission entirely free of political overtones as far as the Fathers themselves were concerned.

The two missionaries left Santiago on November 1, 1595, intending to rendezvous with the governor in Penco (near present Concepción) before crossing the frontier into Arauco. With characteristic energy they visited the scattered Spanish and Indian settlements along the way, pausing in each of them to instruct the Christians and to confer the consolations of religion. Upon reaching Penco they were met by the governor who accompanied them to the other side of the Biobío River for a conference with the principal caciques of Arauco. In his address to the Indians, Oñez de Loyola outlined the purpose of the missionaries' visit, praised the lofty character of their aims, and urged the natives to accept their words and "reasonable counsels."

Know well that these priests are very different in their conduct and customs from other Spaniards. They seek neither gold nor silver nor any temporal gain. Their sole desire is to promote everywhere the glory of God our Lord, and to win souls for heaven, lifting them up out of their ignorance and drawing them to a knowledge of the Creator. By keeping them in your lands you will acquire some of the strongest defenders of your liberty, who will ever be solicitous of your comfort and well-being, and who will treat with the governors and justices of the country for this purpose.[29]

Encouraged by this promising beginning, the padres devoted almost a year to the provinces south of the Biobío, spreading the Gospel, and reclaiming sinners. They also ministered to the Spaniards and converts in Cañete, Concepción, Valdivia, Osorno, Villarrica, Angol, Santa Cruz de Oñez, and Chiloé. Although this first experiment produced little in the way of conversions among the infidels, it did prove that the natives were interested in learning about Catholicism in their own tongue. Moreover, it demonstrated both the absurdity of trying to convert the Indians through the medium of missionaries who did not understand or speak their language, and the necessity of preparing future ministers in this respect.[30] This lesson was not wasted on the bishop of La Imperial, Agustín Cisneros. Shortly thereafter he issued a decree ordering all the pastors in his diocese to explain the catechism to the Indians in the Araucanian language.[31] How many of them were able to comply with this instruction is unknown.

More important from the Spaniards' point of view was the help they received from the missionaries in settling their consciences. Aguilera noted that the frontier troops and vecinos were greatly confused about whether the war against the Araucanians was just or unjust, or what their obligations were to the natives whom they had been treating as slaves. There were very few learned men on the frontier who knew the legal and moral principles involved and to whom the colonists could turn for advice when doubts arose. "All of this difficulty," he stated, "was cleared up in our conferences with the vecinos regarding the obligation of restitution, and so forth.... In our sermons to the soldiers we outlined in general the principles they ought to follow in dealing with the Indians." Just what these principles were Aguilera did not say. He merely added that "we were greatly guided in this matter by the opinions of Father Luis de Valdivia who had solved similar cases of conscience in Santiago."[32] The reference to restitution, however, would indicate that the padres felt that the Indians had been treated unjustly.

The field reports that Vega and Aguilera sent back to Valdivia in Santiago stimulated him to participate personally in the work. He ordered the missionaries to return to Penco, promising to join them there as soon as business in the capital permitted. The reunion took place toward the end of 1596. After receiving detailed accounts from both of his subordinates and discussing the method to be followed in evangelizing the natives, Valdivia set out, accompanied by Father Aguilera and Brother Teleña, in the hope that his presence among the Araucanians would help to curb their animosities toward the whites and allay the rumors of impending disaster that had begun to circulate along the frontier. For seven months the little group toiled among the natives, catechizing, baptizing, and assisting at marriages. But it soon became apparent to Valdivia and his aides that unless the Spaniards curbed their greed and lightened the burdens on the yanaconas, the frontier would flame with rebellion. Sensing the rising tide of hostility, the Jesuits called upon the border encomenderos to make up for past injuries and moderate their treatment of the Indians, but their advice went unheeded. The Spaniards were blind to the dangers that threatened, and their hardheadedness paved the way for their destruction. Before the end of 1598, the southern frontier had erupted in a devastating conflagration of rapine and death that resulted in the annihilation of several forts and towns,* the massacre of scores of whites, and the temporary suspension of Spanish control in the area. Property damage amounted to millions of pesos.[33]

Still reeling from the initial shock of the disaster, the Spaniards in Santiago began laying plans for a counteroffensive. The ferocity and extent of the uprising convinced even the most conservative among them that the Araucanians understood only the language of armed con-

---

* Santa Cruz de Oñez, Valdivia, Angol, La Imperial, Villarrica, Cañete, and Osorno.

quest. Oñez de Loyola's offers of peaceful coexistence had ended cata-strophically. What peaceful means could not accomplish, the rigors of wholesale enslavement might be able to achieve. Thus reasoned Mel-chor Calderón, a resident of Chile since 1555 and treasurer of the ca-thedral church in Santiago. A man who had enjoyed a record of friendly relations with the Indians, Calderón spoke before a packed gathering of clergy, civil officials, and military spokesmen, presenting a thought-ful "Treatise on the Importance and Utility of Enslaving the Rebel-lious Indians of Chile."[34] With tears in his eyes and deep expressions of sympathy for the victims of the massacres, Calderón placed his pro-posal in the hands of the Jesuit superior Luis de Valdivia, asking him to read it aloud. Valdivia acquiesced. When he had finished, "all who were present unanimously agreed on informing the viceroy that it was their opinion that the Indians captured in the war could justly be en-slaved."[35]

The judgment expressed on this occasion was a natural reaction to many years of frustration in dealing with the Araucanians. But how could Valdivia, a man already recognized by his contemporaries as a defender of the mapuches, subscribe to a measure that would result in their degradation? An answer can be found in a close examination of the document, which shows nothing vindictive in Calderón's proposal; he sincerely believed that slavery was a last resort, the only means of containing the Araucanians, halting their destructive actions, and bring-ing peace to a war-wracked land.[36] With restraint and fairmindedness, he presented the arguments justifying his conclusion as well as those favoring the Araucanians. This willingness to see both sides of the question and to submit his views to the judgment of others was un-doubtedly one of the considerations that persuaded Valdivia to support the proposal. The Jesuit superior was almost certainly one of the "learned persons of Santiago" whom Calderón had consulted while preparing his tract;[37] surely the decision to submit the proposal for evaluation by moralists in Lima seems to indicate the presence of a moderating influence. It was a decision Valdivia could encourage be-cause he knew that the Jesuit theologians in Lima would be among the *letrados* (learned men) the viceroy would consult.

Before discussing the actual proposal, Calderón enumerated four advantages that would result from its acceptance. First, the experience of forty-six years had shown that neither the resources of the Crown nor those of the colonists were sufficient to bring the war to a successful conclusion, for most of the soldiers who served in the war had no interest in their jobs, recompenses were few, and life on the frontier was totally unattractive. This state of affairs discouraged newcomers to the colony, many of whom sought to escape from Chile at the earliest opportunity. All this would be changed if the Crown were to permit the enslavement of the rebels. "It is certain," Calderón asserted, "that if these Indians were awarded as slaves many people from outside the realm would willingly come here to procure slaves, and the need of forcing them to come would vanish. Those who are already here would voluntarily assist the war effort in order to secure servants for their farms, haciendas, and residences."[38] The royal treasury would also profit since the slaves taken in the name of His Majesty could be employed in the mines, thus increasing the flow of revenue into the exchequer. Most important of all, the war would soon come to an end, for once the rebels realized that they were paying for it with their own lives and those of their wives and children, they would quickly agree to peace on any terms. Second, the Spaniards' Indian allies would benefit because the supply of slave labor would relieve them of the burden of serving the encomenderos. The *chinas* and *mallenas* (servant girls) could remain at home; now more than a third of them were regularly being drafted from their native pueblos to work for the whites. The Indian population would increase because more of the women would have a chance to marry, something denied them while they were working for the Europeans. As a result of this prohibition, Calderón observed, many of them had lived as concubines for lengthy periods and had failed to receive Christian instruction because their masters had forbidden them to attend religious services for fear they would use the opportunity to contract marriage.[39] Third, the colony as a whole would profit, for yanaconas who were freed from personal service could secure employment as carpenters, blacksmiths, tailors, teamsters, farmers, and fishermen, "of which we have great need at the present time." The Indians would readily apply themselves to these trades, Calderón stated, especially if they were permitted to use copper money in their transactions with the Spaniards. Last, enslavement would be of advantage to the rebels themselves since they would profit spiritually from receiving instruction in the Faith.[40]

Calderón next proceeded to the main point of his presentation: is it just to enslave the rebels? He considered first the motives in favor of enslavement and then the objections that the Araucanians could reasonably advance against these contentions.

The first part of his argument is characterized not so much by cogency as by a readiness to admit the existence of previous abuses. Granted, said Calderón, that in the beginning of the conquest of Chile the Spaniards had committed many injustices against the natives "contrary to the will of His Sovereign Majesty"; nevertheless, these same Indians had later accepted obedience to the king, not only once but many times, and manifested their acceptance by paying tribute. The king, in turn, had watched over them as a Christian ruler, providing them with ministers of the Gospel, governors, and other officials to protect and instruct them. Therefore, by recognizing the king as their rightful lord, their rebellion against him was most unjust. Nor did the king forfeit his dominion over them simply because the grievances they had suffered had caused them to rebel. The contrary would be true only if His Majesty had failed to take steps to satisfy their complaints and provide them with the resources of justice. The record showed, however, that he had taken all necessary precautions to insure their welfare. He had appointed the oidor Santillán to work out a system of equitable taxation and to pacify the country, and García Hurtado de Mendoza had sincerely tried to translate that tasa into actuality. And how had the Araucanians responded to these overtures? With an open rebellion, refusing to pay the tribute to which the king was entitled.

Furthermore, even though there may have been abuses while other governors were in power, none such occurred while Oñez de Loyola administered the colony. Seldom had the mapuches benefited more, Calderón claimed, from the actions of a public official.

Those whom he captured in the war he liberated and sent back to their provinces, offering them exemption from paying tribute and personal service for many years. He supplied them with tools belonging to His Majesty for the work of plowing and digging; he distributed knives, hatchets, wine, food, and clothing among them. As a result of these acts of confidence and kindness many tribes surrendered themselves peacefully to the Spaniards. He also punished severely any offense against the natives, sending inspectors into the mines, *obrajes* [factories], and *chacras* [small farms] to prevent any abuses. All this good treatment he offered the rebels through their own interpreters and caciques. . . . Accordingly, there is no injury they can cite as an excuse for persevering in this rebellion.[41]

As a matter of fact, the partiality that Oñez de Loyola displayed toward the natives, Calderón continued, was such that "one of the most persistent complaints against him was the great love he had for those who had come to terms with the Spaniards."[42]

The king had shown his concern for the Indians in other ways, too. Through his representative, the governor, he had recently dispatched members of the Society of Jesus to preach to the rebels in their own language. They had visited the provinces of Arauco and Millapoa, where they had met with the infidel chiefs to assure them of the Crown's friendship. In Purén, another of the insurgent provinces, the superior of the local Jesuits, Luis de Valdivia, had participated in a conference with one of their captains, explaining to him the king's interest in their salvation and offering them "all good treatment." Despite these offers the Araucanians had revolted. If Scripture allowed rulers to make war on those who rejected their just dominion, surely the king of Spain could do the same with these rebellious subjects. Scripture also sanctioned the war David undertook against the king of Damascus because of the aid the latter had given against him to the ruler of Saba. On this score, too, the Araucanians deserved punishment, for they had in the past joined forces with the English pirates against the Spaniards and had given no guarantees that they would not do it again.[43] Calderón admitted, however, that the natives' "unreasonable desire for liberty" had been just as influential as any other factor in driving them to rebellion.[44]

The effect of the war on civic life in Chile further justified enslaving the rebels, Calderón argued. The Spaniards had suffered many injuries at the hands of the Araucanians, not the least of which were the murders of two governors (Pedro de Valdivia and García Oñez de Loyola), several priests, and hundreds of Spanish soldiers. In addition to this, the rebels had slaughtered hundreds of Indian allies, destroyed homes and villages, impeded commerce, obstructed traffic on the royal roads, and inflicted so much damage on Spanish encomenderos and property owners that many of the vecinos were reduced to poverty. The troops, too, were suffering, manning the frontier without pay in an effort to ward off enemy attacks. Thus to recruit sufficient military personnel in Chile itself was difficult, with the result that the army was riddled with foreign mercenaries, many of whom were inept.[45] All of this reflected unfavorably on the realm. But the government had to pursue the war, for a hands-off policy would solve nothing; the rebels would merely interpret it as a sign of weakness and an invitation to perpetrate still more mischief.* Since the Spaniards were in Chile to stay, the war had to be solved, and slavery was the only practical solution. As the "last avenue to peace" it was morally permissible. Since the Araucanians killed every Spaniard who fell into their hands,[46] the Spaniards were certainly justified in punishing the enemy with a lesser evil, namely, slavery.

From the standpoint of religion, Calderón noted, there were additional reasons for adopting this policy. There were many baptized persons among the Araucanians whom the rebels were molesting in their practice of the Faith and inciting to insurrection. The king had the right, as well as the duty, to assist and protect the faithful. Furthermore, the rebel caciques were preventing missionaries from entering their territories and converting their subjects. Finally, the numerous crimes of the insurgents—the murders, the destruction of property, the profanation of sacred objects, the cannibalism, and so forth—all these could rightfully be punished with enslavement, and Calderón cited numerous examples from civil and criminal law to prove this contention. If the king had acted justly when sentencing the Moors of Granada to slavery for their crimes, he could assuredly do the same with these aborigines who had been guilty of equally grave offenses against the moral and civil code.[47]

After enumerating the reasons for his proposal, Calderón considered at some length the arguments that might reasonably be presented in defense of the Araucanians. This spirit of openmindedness was rather unusual among the Spaniards in Chile, most of whom took it for granted that the natives were in the wrong, but Calderón admitted that the rebels had "very probable arguments" on their side, some of them rather difficult to refute.[48]

---

* Since this same objection was one of the principal arguments later leveled against Luis de Valdivia's theory of defensive warfare, it is interesting to see its inclusion here in a proposal that he himself endorsed. However, as we will note later, Valdivia's theory included more than a passive, hands-off attitude.

The rebels could argue, for example, that they had originally sworn obedience to the Crown out of fear. What the conquistadores were seeking was wealth, and to acquire it they abused the mapuches, stole their wives and children, demanded excessive tribute, and treated them like beasts of burden. The thing the conquerors least remembered was their duty to Christianize. Instead, they used religion as a wedge for gaining the goodwill of the Indians and then capitalizing on it to secure laborers for the mines and personal service. Since these evils were the result of professing fealty to the king, and since the king was not adequately protecting the victims, they were justified in rejecting his sovereignty.

Another legitimate complaint of the Indians could be the vacillating policies of the Spanish government. An instance in point was the Tasa de Santillán, which fell into disuse after the departure of Santillán and the recall of Governor Hurtado de Mendoza. Conditions reverted to their former state, for it had been evident all along that the Spaniards were more concerned with their own interests than those of the Indians. No one could deny, for example, that Governor Oñez de Loyola had treated the natives kindly, but he had been forced to do so because he lacked sufficient military resources to act otherwise. The record proved only too well that when the army was strong, violence and oppression were the order of the day. The harshness the encomenderos displayed in the mines and encomiendas was no incentive for coming to terms. No law, human or divine, obliged people to endure such cruelty passively.

In the final analysis, the natives could argue, it was precisely this inhumanity that vitiated the Spanish cause. The so-called crimes of the rebels were nothing more than a legitimate defense of their land and their personal liberty, a form of vengeance for the many evils they had suffered at the hands of the Spaniards. Unlike the Moriscos, who had not been subjected to onerous laws, the Araucanians were justified in their rebellion. Whatever the Spaniards might claim, as long as they continued their nefarious practices, any attempt to enslave the insurgents would be unjust.[49]

Calderón concluded with a brief rebuttal to these objections that added little to what he had already said. He refused to admit that the king could be held responsible for the existing abuses, steadfastly maintaining that the Crown had sincerely tried to correct them by every available means. The evils perpetrated by the first conquistadores had already been "aptly punished," he added, "because those who are the poorest in the colony today are none other than the descendants of the original conquerors." If the Araucanians persisted in their rebellion, the Spaniards would have no alternative but to make war on them, "not only as rebels, but as enemies of God and religion, whose desire it is to wipe out all Christians." Equity demanded, therefore, that their crimes be punished with enslavement for a period of twelve years.[50]

The request for quick action on the Calderón proposal did not meet with much success in Lima. Before formulating a reply, the viceroy submitted the issue to the judgment of the archbishop of Lima, Reginaldo de Lizárraga, and other leading ecclesiastics of the city, who were asked to give their answers to the following questions:

1. Is the king justified in making war on vassals who have rejected his authority without the shedding of blood, in order to bring them back again under his jurisdiction?

2. Is the king justified in making war on vassals in order to punish them for abandoning the Faith, provided they have done so without rejecting his authority?

3. Is the king justified in making war on rebellious vassals and apostates who have attacked his loyal subjects?

4. Is the king justified in making war on people who have never accepted Christianity or who have never been subjected to his dominion, but who have attacked his subjects?[51]

Archbishop Lizárraga replied affirmatively to all of these questions in a parecer dated in Lima on July 16, 1599.[52] He justified the war against the Araucanians, citing the authority of Francisco de Vitoria and of other theologians, canonists, and learned men in Spain and Peru. Neither his predecessor in the archbishopric, Jerónimo de Loaysa, nor members of the religious Orders in Lima had ever denounced the war from the pulpits, he observed, which they would certainly have done had they considered it unjust.[53] (Lizárraga seems to have disregarded entirely the objections of Fray Gil González de San Nicolás.) Moreover, when Governor Alonso de Sotomayor expressed doubts about the justice of the conflict, the king's own confessor, the most holy and learned Fray Diego de Cháves, had assured him that there were no grounds for doubt, advising him to carry out the royal precepts without fear or scruple.

Furthermore, the king was obliged under pain of mortal sin to maintain the settlements of Chillán, Concepción, Angol, Villarrica, Valdivia, Osorno, and Chiloé, which were already established among the Araucanians, and to supply them with missionaries for the spiritual comfort of the resident Spaniards and Christian natives. This was the opinion of all the learned men of Spain whom Emperor Charles V had consulted when debating the wisdom of withdrawing from the Indies "because of the many scruples he was experiencing." Consequently, since the king was bound to send missionaries into those parts, and since the Indians were impeding their entry, it was just to take up arms against them.[54]

Lizárraga's remaining arguments concerned the safety of the realm; the rebels not only tried to incite their pacified countrymen to rebellion but also dispatched subversives to Santiago, Quillota, and Coquimbo to persuade the Christian Indians in those districts to rebel. These enemy agents, when captured, confessed that "they had been carrying on this treacherous activity for six years, and if they had not been discovered the peaceful and Christian Indians living along the Maule River in the jurisdiction of Santiago would have rebelled. And the same would have happened with those who are neutral."[55] Less insidious, but nonetheless dangerous, was the case of some fifteen hundred baptized yanaconas who had gone over to the rebels, subsequently inflicting damages on the white settlers and their Indian allies; it was just for the king to demand that they return and, if they refused, to make war on them. Finally, Lizárraga noted, it seemed not only lawful but mandatory to "expel the Indians of Purén, Tucapel, Arauco, and the island of Mocha from their lands with all the rigors of war" in order to prevent their assisting the English and becoming converts to Protestantism. If the English were to gain control of the Chilean coast, the Spanish empire in Chile, Peru, Mexico, and Tierra Firme would be greatly endangered. For these and other reasons, which he refrained from mentioning, the archbishop pronounced the war against the Araucanians to be "most just."[56]

He was less convinced about enslaving captured rebels. "Since slav-ery is one of the worst misfortunes that can befall a free human being ... I refuse to say that they should be given into slavery or that the penalties of just war or of the *jus gentium* that applies in war between Christians and infidels should be used against them."[57] He suggested, instead, that the following criteria be adopted: Christian Indians who deserted to the enemy and participated actively in the rebellion should become the "property" of the soldiers who captured them and be bound to them as servants for the rest of their lives. The captors could loan or hire them out to others, but not sell them. If the viceroy considered this form of punishment too moderate, he should first consult the king before declaring them slaves, either permanently or temporarily, and the final decision regarding enslavement should be left to His Maj-esty.[58] Lizárraga's acceptance of the Crown's competence shows that he did not consider enslavement morally wrong. Lizárraga advocated this course of action in order to avoid the difficulties of restitution if the viceroy were to allow the captives to be sold, and the king were later to nullify the transactions. He added that if some other course seemed more suitable he would willingly accept it.[59] The pacified In-dians of La Imperial, Villarrica, and Toltén, who had been goaded into joining the recent uprising, should be treated *"piadosamente"* (merci-fully) because this was the first offense for many of them. The best policy would be to punish the most guilty and to pardon the rest; thus they would come to understand "how great is the Christian piety of the Spaniards."[60]

The moderate character of Lizárraga's parecer won the support of the three major religious Orders in Peru: the Jesuits, Franciscans, and Dominicans. Encouraged by this unanimity, the new governor of Chile, Alonso de Ribera Figueroa y Zambrano,[61] decided that he could safely do what Lizárraga had warned the viceroy against doing: sanc-tion the enslavement of the rebel Araucanians until such a time as the king or the Council of the Indies were to determine otherwise. One of Ribera's contemporaries, Domingo de Eraso, had serious doubts about this measure, as he explained in his "Papel sobre la esclavitud de los indios de Chile."[62] Although this document is, for the most part, a summary of the points contained in Calderón's tract, Eraso suggested several reasons for *not* enslaving the rebels. Enslavement, he argued, would not advance the commonweal but would result in the depopulation of the frontier, for many men, spurred by greed, would deport the Araucanians to other countries, thus depriving Chile of the native labor needed for its maintenance and conservation. Slavery would also be an injustice for the innocent, especially the women and children, as well as for unborn generations who would be consigned to perpetual servitude. Eraso suggested that the leaders of the rebellion be enslaved for their lifetimes, and the less guilty for a limited period; for this reason he advised that the culprits be confined to the limits of Santiago and La Serena for the term of their sentence. Under no circumstances should they be sent to Peru, where they would be a constant source of disturbance for the pacified natives of that region. His greatest objection to enslavement, however, was that the policy itself would evoke a dangerous reaction. "So great is the love that the Araucanians have for their land," he pointed out, "and so great is their courage and valor, that once they realize that the Spaniards plan to enslave them and deport them to far-off places, they will never surrender. Even the most cowardly among them will fight to the end, and the women and children will take up arms to defend themselves also, preferring to die than to submit to slavery." It was for this reason that the viceroy of Peru, Luis de Velasco, and the audiencia of Lima had refused to declare the Indians slaves on prior occasions despite the many petitions that came to them from Chile.[63]

The doubtful legality of Ribera's action moved the authorities in Santiago to step up their agitation for a formal declaration from the Crown. Therefore when the Augustinian friar Juan de Vascones visited Madrid as a representative of the cabildo of Santiago, he took with him a petition justifying the war against the Araucanians and urging the king to condemn the rebels to slavery. The nine reasons Vascones outlined in support of his thesis contained little new doctrine, for it was clear from the concluding words of his argument that he considered the outrages of the Araucanians a more potent reason for their enslavement than any theological or philosophical argument:

> If this matter be examined thoroughly it will become clear that neither in the case of the Negroes of Guinea, who are commonly considered slaves, nor in that of any other tribe of Indians, no matter how fierce or

malicious they have been, nor in that of the Moriscos of Granada, against whom this same sentence [of slavery] was invoked, do there concur so many just causes and crimes of the enemy as is true of this terrible people; for which reason they ought to be condemned as slaves.[64]

Vascones added that although there was a decree of Emperor Charles V forbidding the enslavement of any Indian, it ought not to apply to the natives in Chile, because at the time the decree was issued the affairs of the colony were not in the same state as they were by 1600, nor had the barbarians committed the atrocities to which he had referred. "It is perfectly evident," he remarked, "that if that same decree were to be issued at the present time, the Indians of Chile would be excluded from its provisions."[65]

What was evident to Vascones was not equally evident to the authorities in Spain. A royal order of August 16, 1604, informed the governor of Chile that the friar was returning to the colony with a thousand soldiers; but no definite permission to enslave the Araucanians was given on this occasion.[66] The continued disasters of the war and the failure of successive governors to turn the tide in favor of the Spaniards finally induced the Council of the Indies to present a memorial to the king on November 13, 1607, advising him to accede to the repeated demands from Chile. Philip III reluctantly consented. By a royal cédula dated in Ventosilla on May 26, 1608, he commanded that all male Indians over ten and a half years of age and all females over nine and a half years old captured in the war were to be the slaves of those who captured them. All the younger captives were to be removed from the rebellious provinces and entrusted to persons who would "instruct them in the Faith, as was done with the Moriscos of the kingdom of Granada."[67]

Thus ended another phase in the struggle for social justice in Chile. As a solution to the Araucanian problem, the decree of 1608 was a colossal failure. It satisfied only the soldiers, who looked upon it as an excuse to enrich themselves at the expense of the Indians.[68] Within a few years the Crown was forced to retract its pronouncement and to resort to other means of pacifying the Araucanians. Events, meanwhile, were building to a climax on another front and turning the spotlight of public attention on the Jesuits in Santiago.

TORRES BOLLO'S CAMPAIGN AGAINST
SLAVE LABOR

THE YEAR 1608 was a trying one for the Jesuits in Chile. An outburst of popular indignation threatened for a time to engulf the community in Santiago and to undo much of the success that the Order had enjoyed in the capital for more than a decade. The cause of this unexpected tumult was an apparently innocuous decision affecting the internal administration of the Jesuit college in Santiago. That institution had long been the possessor of some twenty *indios de servicio* (Indian slaves) whom a generous benefactor had donated to the college shortly after its foundation.[1] The presence of these Indians was a source of constant reproach for Diego de Torres Bollo, first provincial of the province of Paraguay (founded in 1604) of which Chile was a part. Before admonishing others for their lack of Christian charity and justice, Diego de Torres knew that the Jesuits would have to purge their own house of racial inequalities.

The provincial's determination was the product of considerable soul-searching following a chance encounter with a Portuguese hidalgo at the Spanish court. In 1602, while visiting Spain as procurator of the Peruvian province, Torres had met Juan de Salazar, a native-born Portuguese layman who had migrated to America and settled in Tucumán, Argentina.[2] Salazar had been shocked by the distressing conditions of the Indian slaves in Tucumán and resolved to do something to help them. He had journeyed to Spain at his own expense to intercede personally for their liberation, and he was there when Torres passed through the country on his way to Rome. The Jesuit soon became a Salazar supporter, encouraging him to persevere in his endeavors regardless of difficulties or delays. He also arranged a meeting between Salazar and the "most influential ecclesiastics of the court" to enlist their aid in the project. But the question hung fire until March 27, 1606, when the king finally resolved to revive the moribund audiencia of Chile as the most practical means of resolving the problem of Indian servitude in that area. (The president of the audiencia of Charcas, Alonso Maldonado de Torres, was commissioned to visit the provinces of Tucumán, Río de la Plata, and Paraguay for the same purpose.)[3] Three years were to elapse, however, before the audiencia began to function. In the interval, events moved to a climax with startling rapidity.

On the eve of setting out to inspect his province in 1607, Torres received a letter from the General of the Order, Claude Aquaviva, ordering the abolition of obligatory personal service in the Colegio Máximo of Santiago. Realizing the volatile nature of the situation, Aquaviva assumed that the provincial would proceed slowly in the matter, as he himself cautioned in a later communication:

> Your Reverence should under no circumstances allow the Indians of our houses freedom to go wherever they wish, because, aside from the fact that this might arouse some disturbance in the realm and indignation against the Order, it would not be good for the Indians themselves, who would be leaving us for other Spaniards who would not treat them as well. Consequently we think it best that the Indians assigned to our care be treated with such justice in regard to salaries, maintenance, and alleviation of all their spiritual and corporal necessities, that they will recognize the advantage of working for us, and the Spaniards will receive an example of how they ought to deal with their Indians.[4]

Unfortunately this advice arrived too late to have any effect, and Torres was forced to decide for himself the best method of carrying out his superior's instructions. Acting with more alacrity than Aquaviva had anticipated, but with some prudence, Torres summoned a meeting of the most learned Jesuits then in Lima to advise him on the morality of the servicio personal. Among those who participated in the conference were Estevan Páez, the provincial of Peru; Rodrigo de Cabredo, rector of the University of San Pablo in Lima; Juan Sebastián de la Parra, former provincial of Peru; Francisco Coello, a doctor of civil and canon law, *asesor* (adviser) to two viceroys and an oidor of the audiencia of Lima; Juan Pérez Menacho, *catedrático de prima* (senior professor) at the University of San Pablo; Luis de Valdivia, Diego Álvarez de Paz, Juan Perlin, Juan de Alva, Andrés Hernández, Juan Domínguez, Diego González Holguin, and Pedro del Castillo.[5] The question that the conferees were asked was whether the servicio personal was unjust or not. Several previous *consultas*, Torres observed, had held that it was. Archbishop Loaysa's junta had unanimously agreed that the system was unjust, Fray Gil González de San Nicolás had denounced it in a treatise written in 1559, the Augustinians in Lima as well as the Franciscans in Paraguay had reached a similar conclusion in 1598, and their views were corroborated by those of the Dominicans, Franciscans, and Jesuits whom Viceroy Velasco had consulted shortly thereafter. In view of these decisions, Torres asked, what was the mind of the present gathering on the subject? Their answer was unequivocal. The servicio personal was evidently unjust and should, therefore, be abolished in all Jesuit houses as the General had commanded.[6]

Although Torres no longer had any doubts, he continued gathering additional pareceres. The Jesuits in Potosí endorsed the opinion of those in Lima, as did the Dominicans in Chuquisaca. The Blackrobes in Tucumán heartily applauded the Lima declaration, adding that if the Fathers in Lima had had the same experience as those in Tucumán, they would have urged their views with even greater emphasis, "because the servicio personal that prevails in this province has been the ruination of the Indians and the reason the infidel natives resist conversion. It also explains why the consciences of the Spaniards who profit from the system and those of the governors who sanction it are so grievously burdened."[7]

On arriving in Chile, Torres presided over the first provincial congregation of the Order held in Santiago in April 1608, at which he enlisted the aid of the delegates in determining how the servicio personal in the Jesuit houses could be abolished "to the greater glory of God, the good of the Indians, the edification of seculars, and the economic advantage" of the houses concerned.[8] What was to be done with the Indians attached to the residences in Tucumán, for instance, where the Order possessed no haciendas and the natives had to be employed in petty household chores making them more of a liability than an asset to the Jesuit community? Would it not be advisable, perhaps, to adopt the policy practiced in Peru, where the viceroys commuted the tribute of certain yanaconas into services performed for the benefit of the Jesuits? These services, Torres explained, were limited to one week's labor every month, in exchange for which the Indians received fields for cultivation, a yearly supply of clothing, and their meals while on the job. "If they freely desire to work for us during the rest of the month," Torres informed the assembled Fathers, "we give them their meals and a daily wage, the same as they would receive anywhere else, and we have the same regard for them as for our regular domestics, particularly when they are ill."[9] This arrangement, he contended, was surely fairer than anything the Indians of Chile had yet experienced.

After debating the problem from every aspect, the delegates to the provincial congregation passed a resolution on April 28, 1608, outlining the reasons why the servicio personal involved injustices and "why we cannot make use of it even if the king were not to forbid it, as he does by his royal decrees."

> The first of these injustices is the fact that it imposes perpetual servitude on free men, and deprives them of control over their liberty and their offspring. . . . The second is the failure to pay them a just wage such as other laborers in the republic receive for the same kind of work. This wage ought to be sufficient to support the worker and his family in moderate circumstances and to allow them to save something for old age. The salary the Indians receive at present does not come up to this standard. . . . The third injustice consists in overworking them.[10]

Embodied in the resolution were a number of suggestions for remedying the injustices already noted, the most important of which had to do with a just wage. The Fathers of the provincial congregation recommended that each skilled worker receive forty *patacones'** worth of dry goods yearly, including cotton and woolen clothing, shoes, blankets, and uncut cloth. The salary of unskilled workers was set at twenty-five patacones to be paid in the same fashion, and employees in domestic service were to receive free meals also. Unmarried workers would receive part of their salary in coin. Each worker was entitled to woolen cloth for children's garments, a pair of oxen, a plot of ground

* A *patacón* was a silver coin weighing an ounce and worth approximately one peso.

on which to raise foodstuffs for his family, and leisure time in which to work his fields properly. Furthermore, all workers were to receive cooked meat on feast days and jerked beef at other times during the year, as well as two cartloads of firewood per annum. Bonuses for superior workers were to be awarded at the discretion of the local Jesuit superior. An employee at the age of fifty was to retire and receive an allowance of food, clothing, and grain. Widows and disabled workers were to receive the same pension. Bachelors were to be allowed to marry the women of their choice, "as has been the custom up to now, and as all those who have the care of Indians are obliged to do." Any employee who wished to visit relatives outside of Santiago for two or three days would be permitted to do so, provided he could be trusted not to break his contract or be guilty of any other moral offenses. The official protector of the Indians was to be present when salaries were paid twice a year on December 25 and on the feast of St. John, and all accounts and new labor contracts for the coming year were to be settled during the Christmas season.

As a guarantee against overworking the Indians, the resolution suggested a working day from sunrise to sunset,* with rest periods at meal times and time off for prescribed spiritual devotions in the morning. Instructions in Christian doctrine were assigned for Mondays, Wednesdays, and Fridays after the conclusion of the day's work, and all employees were to be encouraged to go to confession and communion regularly, avoid drunkenness and other vices, live like Christians, and treat their wives well. Special benefits—hospitalization, medical care, and food—were to go to the sick. Women were to work only in times of urgent need, and then were to be paid fairly. Children under twenty were to help their parents or learn a trade. These provisions were to be observed until such time as the king or his ministers ordered something better.[11]

These and related recommendations formed the basis of the ordinances Torres promulgated publicly on June 19, 1608.[12] In stating the reasons for his action, Torres paid tribute to the numerous royal decrees and to the opinions of "all the learned men of Spain and the

---

* This may sound excessive today, but it should be remembered that even child laborers in the mines and sweatshops of nineteenth-century England and the United States commonly worked longer hours.

Indies" that condemned obligatory personal service as an evil institution. Noting that "it has been the cause of the war and of the punishments that God, our Lord, has visited upon this realm, and that these punishments will not cease as long as the servicio personal and the afflictions of the Indians do not cease," he deemed it necessary to set an example for the Spaniards of Chile by freeing the Indians of the Colegio Máximo of Santiago of all their obligations as compulsory servants. He then outlined the main features of this private reform, emphasizing the points described above. Torres explained that any Indian attached to the Jesuit college in Santiago who did not wish to accept the conditions outlined in the ordinances could freely have recourse to the justicia real (royal judge), who would dispose of him as he saw fit. Those who accepted the conditions and later changed their minds had the same freedom of recourse after their year's contract had expired.

Evidence of the difference in legal status between yanaconas and unpacified Araucanians is contained in a concluding paragraph of Torres' pronouncement. Speaking of the natives captured in the war, he said:

> With respect to the prisoners of war assigned to us by the governors, we have no further obligation than that of feeding and clothing them well. The work demanded of them shall be moderate, and the care exercised in catechizing them and Christianizing them shall be very great. We are also obliged to treat their infirmities and see that they marry. Their women shall be supplied with dresses and woolen cloth for clothing their children. They shall be given a ration of food, just as the yanaconas are, and they and the other workers shall be buried from our churches. The Fathers shall say Masses for them, and shall baptize all adult infidels at least when they are in danger of death. Their infants shall be baptized along with the children of other servants. They are on no account to be considered slaves, but are to receive the same treatment as the other yanaconas.

The provisions of the ordinances, made retroactive to the beginning of May 1608, were explained to the assembled Indians by the Jesuit interpreter Martín de Aranda in the presence of Juan de Ugalda, the alcalde of Santiago, Juan Venegas, the protector of the Indians, and Miguel Jerónimo Venegas, a notary public. All the Indians but one expressed willingness to accept the labor contract. The exception was an Indian who wished to return to his native province; permission was granted, and he was given a gift of clothing and a blanket. The alcalde then gave his approval to the contract, which was accordingly signed and witnessed by the attendant officials.

The reaction to the reform was immediate and intense. The encomenderos were quick to realize the revolutionary implications of the ordinances, for the frank condemnation of compulsory service, the acceptance of the ideas of a family wage, social security, old-age pensions, labor bonuses, health benefits, and accident insurance were an attack on the economic credo to which the propertied class adhered. To understand more completely the depth of their resentment, it is sufficient to observe that the social principles embodied in the ordinances anticipated the teachings contained in Pius XI's encyclical *Quadragesimo Anno* of 1931. As Amunátegui Solar remarked: "If the reader did not know the date of the document's promulgation he would confuse it with some modern legislation on social security and insurance."[13] And although Encina is correct in pointing out the similarities between the ordinances of Diego de Torres and the tasa of Hernando de Santillán,[14] he fails to note that Torres' plan included an outright rejection of forced labor that was promptly related to action; Santillán's did not. This point alone suffices to give the Jesuit legislation a social significance that the Tasa de Santillán lacked.

The encomenderos appreciated this point only too well. Complaints and murmurings against the Jesuits began to be heard on all sides. Many Spaniards who had previously befriended the padres broke off relations with them, while others accused them of failing to understand economic affairs and the colony's need of the servicio personal, and of fearfully seeing dangers where none existed. Their attempt to change a system of such long standing was seen by many (but not all) as nothing less than a capricious and censurable innovation.[15]

Disturbing though the outcries were, they failed to shake Torres' conviction that what he had done was right. The seriousness of the situation, however, demanded a public defense, so Torres appealed to the authorities in Peru for notarized copies of the pareceres that the theologians and legalists of Lima had submitted in the past in favor of Indian liberty. He also procured a copy of Philip III's cédula of

November 24, 1601, which forbade the encomenderos to make use of the servicio personal under penalty of forfeiting their encomiendas.[16] He likewise requested written opinions from two of the most learned theologians then in Lima: the Jesuit Juan Pérez Menacho and the Augustinian Tomás Ximénez, a former professor of theology at the most celebrated universities in Spain and Rome. Ximénez's prestige was so great that the president of the audiencia of Chuquisaca, Alonso Maldonado de Torres, had commissioned him to write a treatise on the servicio personal, which he later eulogized as one of the most profound and substantial contributions to the literature on the subject. Ximénez immediately made a summary of the treatise, which he was preparing for the press, and forwarded it to Torres. When all the documents had been gathered, Torres assembled them in the form of a manifesto that he made public throughout Chile and the adjacent provinces. In the conclusion attached to the declaration he stated:

> These are the opinions that have been offered on this point. In opposition to them there is only fear or false private interest, while in support of them there is the service of God, obedience to our king, the fulfillment of his decrees and commands, the satisfaction of our consciences and the hope of salvation, concern for our true interests and for the welfare of the unfortunate Indians to whom we owe much, their conversion to Christianity, the improvement of the commonweal, which could hardly be in a worse condition than it is now, and the cessation of the war that has lasted so many years without hope of a successful conclusion unless it be by means such as this.[17]

Wishing to impress the citizens of Santiago with the moral aspects of the case, Torres devoted one of his public sermons to a discussion of the subject, addressing an audience that included the bishop of Santiago, Fray Juan Pérez de Espinosa, the Licentiate and later oidor of the audiencia of Chile, Juan Cajal, the resident encomenderos of the capital, and other leading vecinos. With his accustomed clarity and moderation, he spoke of the injustices of the servicio personal, the moral obligation of the encomenderos, and the error of those who defended the system by saying that the king approved it. Not only did His Majesty not approve it, Torres exclaimed, but he explicitly forbade it, as was only proper since he was not lord of the liberty of his vassals, but only a just creditor to whom tribute was due. It was this tribute, and not control over the freedom of his subjects, that the king had transferred to the encomenderos.

The Jesuit's reasoning must have been persuasive, for Bishop Espinosa and the Licentiate Cajal publicly added their signatures to the manifesto, as did a junta of the most prominent theologians of Santiago, who unanimously declared that the servicio personal was unjust, tyrannical, and contrary to law.[18] Many of the local encomenderos professed a change of heart and approached Torres for guidance in the matter. He advised them to send a petition to the governor of the colony, Alonso García Ramón,[19] urging speedy enforcement of the royal decrees forbidding forced labor. This they did, submitting with the petition a copy of the manifesto Torres had prepared.[20]

Despite this display of public opinion, García Ramón refused to act on such an explosive issue by himself, preferring to wait for the reestablishment of the royal audiencia before intervening personally in the controversy.[21] The governor's reluctance lent impetus to the campaign against the Jesuits, stimulating various powerful men in the capital and some of the encomenderos who had earlier applauded Torres' declarations to join the opposition. Not content with personal insults against the Blackrobes, they now began to vilify them as enemies of the realm, disturbers of the peace, and instigators of sedition. Animosity reached such a pitch that the future of the Order in Chile was temporarily threatened, but at the height of the crisis Bishop Espinosa and two members of the Dominican convent in Santiago rose in defense of the Jesuits and succeeded in mitigating some of the feeling against them. Nature also lent a hand, when the Río Mapocho flooded in 1609, resulting in the deaths of several people and property damage estimated at more than 100,000 ducats; public attention turned to more material problems affording time for tempers to cool. Finally, the installation of the long-awaited audiencia of Chile in September of that year gave additional promise of calmer days to come.[22]

As mentioned earlier, the audiencia had been charged with the unpleasant task of putting an end to the servicio personal. Public opinion was still very much divided, and the chances of reconciling the opposing factions seemed slim. On one side were the indigenists headed by the bishop of Santiago, Pérez de Espinosa, and composed mainly of Jesuits and a few encomenderos who had accepted the teachings of Diego de Torres. The anti-indigenists included the governor, García Ramón, and most of the encomenderos, under the leadership of the secular cabildo of Santiago. Even among the oidores of the audiencia there was division. Juan Cajal campaigned vigorously for a fulfillment of the decree of 1601, while his colleague Talaverano Gallegos, who had held the post of deputy governor since 1604, opposed its execution with equal zeal. Before making its decision, the audiencia convened a meeting of civil and ecclesiastical authorities and of leading citizens of Santiago. Since the meeting was concerned with one of the most significant political and social decisions in the colony's history, the halls were crowded. The bishop of Santiago, the superiors of the numerous religious houses, members of both the civil and ecclesiastical cabildos, the protector of the Indians, leading encomenderos, and other influential residents of the capital were in attendance. The conference had many of the characteristics of a political convention, but it lacked the smoke-filled back room where problems are worked out. Despite the energy of the participants, the meeting was a failure. No agreement was reached, and perhaps none was possible. Spaniards in Chile were not particularly noted for their ability to compromise in politics, and the audiencia had to be satisfied with an airing of opposing views. Having listened to the arguments of both factions, it now proceeded to state its verdict.

Fortunately the legal instrument containing this decision has been preserved.[23] A rather remarkable example of Spanish casuistry, the document explains in sonorous phrases how the governor had informed the audiencia of the petition that Father Torres and his party had submitted urging the abolition of personal service, and how the oidores had studiously collected the opinions of all the responsible elements in Santiago in an effort to reach a just decision, and had conscientiously reviewed all previous decrees, ordinances, and tasas pertaining to the subject (although, they noted, they were unable to find the text of the Tasa de Santillán).[24] One point had emerged from this investigation, namely, that it was impossible to apply the same legislation to the many different classes of Indians in Chile whose legal status varied considerably. Some were residents of pacified areas, others belonged to dismembered encomiendas; some were captives taken in the war during Quiroga's administration and sentenced to serve as miti-maes for ten years; others had been taken prisoner and declared slaves when Ribera was governor, and still others (rebel Araucanians) had been enslaved by a recent decree of the king.[25] Because of these complications the audiencia thought it best to adopt the resolution that the president of the tribunal and the governor of the colony, Alonso García Ramón, had proposed: that, since the Indians objected most to being separated from their families and seeing their wives and children working for the Spaniards, the servicio personal of single and married women, as well as of boys under eighteen years of age, should be abolished.* The audiencia tempered this decision, however, by authorizing voluntary labor for women and children, with the proviso that wives obtain the permission of their husbands, and children that of their mothers. Annual contracts, renewable for additional one-year periods and witnessed by the protector of the Indians or the judge of the locality, were required and were to stipulate the employee's salary and the employer's obligation to care for him in times of sickness. The workers had the right to change employers after the contracts had expired. This arrangement, judged by the audiencia to be advantageous to both the natives and the Spaniards, "who at such great cost have sustained and continue to sustain the realm," was signed by Alonso García Ramón, Luis Merlo de la Fuente, Hernando Talaverano, Juan Cajal, and Gabriel de Celada. It was dated September 28, 1609.[26]

Despite the concessions of the decision, it was another triumph for the encomenderos. The king's ministers had straddled the fence to appease the clerical group without antagonizing the landed proprietors. The contracts and guarantees concerning women and children reflected Jesuit influence, but did not attack the basic problem, for as long as obligatory service remained in effect for adult males, the concessions would have no more than a nuisance value. There is little reason for supposing that the audiencia intended anything more than that. Their failure to implement the king's orders by devising some kind of legislation that would have guaranteed freedom of contract to all Indians living peacefully under the law is a clue to their personal convictions

---

* Eighteen was taken as the cutoff point because it was "the age at which they are obliged to begin paying tribute in conformity with the ordinances of His Majesty."

in the matter. So, too, is the omission of any assigned penalties for violations of the ordinance. Laws that lack teeth are ineffective laws, and the audiencia must have realized this.

Nevertheless, the judges took the precaution of justifying their action to higher authorities. As Celada reported to the king in explaining his reasons for signing the document, "the natives of the district of Santiago are so few in number that they do not suffice for the work of tilling the soil and raising herds,* both of which are essential to the economic prosperity of the country."[27] The argument that freedom of contract and a living wage were incompatible with economic prosperity was not borne out by the Jesuit experience. Even critics of the Order admit that the Jesuit haciendas, which depended primarily on Indian labor, represented some of the most productive real estate in the colony. Much of this prosperity was the result of intelligent management and of the advanced agricultural techniques that the Jesuits imported from Europe.† But much of it was also due to the favorable conditions of work on the Order's estates and the satisfaction the Indians found in their jobs. As a result, productivity remained high and there were none of the labor problems that plagued the encomenderos. The Indians were so eager to work for the padres that the cabildo of Santiago eventually had to appeal to the Crown for assistance in stemming the migration of native workers from the encomiendas, Indian pueblos, and government obrajes to the colleges and haciendas of the Order.[28] This migration suggests that the freedom of the Indian workers on Jesuit land was not "illusory," as some critics have asserted.[29] Had the encomenderos adopted a similar policy they might not have felt a need for the servicio personal and decrees on slavery to achieve and maintain their long-range prosperity.[30]

Torres Bollo's campaign against personal service achieved its most striking results not in Chile but in the lands directly east of the cordillera. In his capacity as adviser to Francisco Alfaro,[31] oidor of the audiencia of Charcas, who had been appointed visitor of the provinces

---

* It is interesting to note that Celada did not refer to the need for Indian labor in the mines; perhaps he feared that unpleasant memories in the royal mind might be awakened.

† They were among the first, for instance, to use irrigation on an extensive scale. Remains of one of their famous irrigation canals can still be seen in the neighborhood of Calera del Tango, the summer residence of the Jesuit community of the Colegio San Ignacio in Santiago.

of Tucumán, Paraguay, and Río de la Plata in place of Maldonado de Torres, Torres Bollo played a decisive role in formulating the Ordinances of Alfaro outlawing obligatory personal service in those areas.[32] The ordinances were signed in San Miguel de Tucumán on January 19, 1612. Attached to the text were the approbations given by the bishop of Tucumán, the governors of Chile and Tucumán, the Franciscans and the Jesuits. The Jesuit approval, signed by Diego de Torres, Luis de Leiva, Diego de Boroa, and Horacio Monelli, included these words:

> We have examined the ordinances and find them to be completely justified and drawn up with a notable understanding of the affairs and needs of all the provinces. . . . And I, the aforementioned provincial [Diego de Torres], certify that the principal points of these ordinances . . . are in perfect conformity with what the most learned and prudent Fathers of this province of Paraguay have held and desired for the salvation and prosperity of the Indians and Spaniards of this land.[33]

It was not to be expected that the encomenderos would submit to the ordinances without a struggle. They immediately dispatched representatives to argue the case before the audiencia of Charcas and, when these tactics failed, they carried the appeal directly to the Council of the Indies in Spain.[34] After several years of dilatory litigation the Council gave its decision on October 10, 1618. Except for some minor modifications, it endorsed Alfaro's legislation and ordered it to be enforced everywhere in the provinces of Tucumán and Paraguay.[35] The last hope of the encomenderos in those areas had been crushed. Though abuses still existed, rooting them out became easier. The Ordinances of Alfaro did not remedy all the evils, but they did provide the Indian with a better way of life.

In Chile, too, the government began to display a firmer attitude toward the encomenderos. In a way, this was not surprising, for the new viceroy of Peru, the Prince of Esquilache, was a close friend of the Jesuits and sympathetic to their teachings and aims.[36] He made his position clear when appointing Lope de Ulloa y Lemos to the post of governor of Chile on November 23, 1617, [37] with explicit instructions to suppress obligatory personal service and replace it with a monetary tax. Ulloa disembarked in Concepción on January 12, 1618.[38] He apparently spent several weeks on the frontier before proceeding to the capital, for Hernando Machado, *fiscal* (attorney general) of the royal audiencia, reported to the king some two months later that "the servicio personal of this realm has not yet been abolished, although it is so inhumane and such a weight upon our consciences. I am diligently pursuing the matter with the viceroy who informs me that General Lope de Ulloa carries orders to that effect."[39] Once arrived in Santiago, Ulloa lost no time in attacking the problem. After taking the oath of office in the presence of the cabildo, he announced the plans for abolishing personal service,[40] a declaration that caused a stir among the assembled officials whose interests were closely allied with those of the encomenderos. The cabildo accordingly decided on April 23 that Andrés de Toro Mazote, the deputy corregidor of Santiago, as well as the alcaldes ordinarios and the procurator general of the town, Francisco Rodríguez del Manzano y Ovalle, should acquaint the governor with the disadvantages of a monetary tax. When Ulloa learned of their intention, he requested that the size of the delegation be reduced. The cabildo acquiesced, designating two of its members, Jufré del Aguila and Rodríguez del Manzano, to meet with the governor and discuss the judicial and extrajudicial aspects of the problem.[41]

The discussion changed nothing, for Ulloa was determined to carry out the viceroy's orders and did so by issuing a writ suppressing compulsory personal service in favor of tribute in money or kind. The cabildo appealed the writ (the enactment of which was therefore suspended) and called upon its sister corporations in Chillán and Concepción for support. Since funds were not available for sending a representative to Lima, the cabildo had recourse to public subscriptions to raise the necessary money. A *cabildo abierto* (open town meeting) of August 28 entrusted the task of securing contributions from the encomenderos to the alcaldes ordinarios of Santiago under the direction of Captain Diego de Godoy and Andrés de Fuenzalida. Another group headed by Captain Juan de León and the *alférez* (standard bearer) Gonzalo Ferreira were assigned the job of canvassing the local merchants. The corregidores of the diocese of Santiago were later authorized to solicit contributions from residents of their jurisdictions also. Ten days later, on September 7, the cabildo appointed Pedro Lisperguer y Flores procurator general of Santiago, placing at his disposal some four thousand pesos to cover the costs of the journey to Lima and the execution of his commission.[42] Within a month Lisperguer was on his way. The choice of Lisperguer as spokesman was shrewd, for he was at that time one of the colony's leading citizens and had performed outstanding public service under Governor García Ramón. His wife was Doña Florencia Velasco y Solórzano, a daughter of the Licenciate Pedro Álvarez de Solórzano, a member of the royal audiencia of Chile. The descendants of this union formed one of the most distinguished families in Chile. Lisperguer's social and political standing thus made him particularly suitable for pleading the cabildo's case before the officials in Lima.[43]

The authorities in Peru, however, refused to be stampeded into a decision, and months dragged by without progress. Finally, in October 1619, Lisperguer reported to Santiago that the case was at last under discussion, and the prospect of defeating the proposed legislation was good.[44] This news aroused the advocates of the tasa to prompt action. Luis de Valdivia quickly took ship for Lima during November of the same year to see what he could do to thwart Lisperguer's mission.[45] Before leaving Chile he secured Governor Ulloa's promise to enforce strictly the decrees against Indian slavery, obligatory personal service, and war against the Araucanians.[46] Valdivia's representations in Lima proved decisive. After conferring with the viceroy for four months, he persuaded him to "come to a decision regarding the tasa and ordinances regulating the service of the Indians of the realm, regarding which he [Valdivia] had submitted written recommendations that were discussed in the various juntas that the viceroy held on the subject."[47] The decision, decidedly favorable, assumed legal form in the lengthy and detailed instructions known as the Tasa de Esquilache that the viceroy signed on March 28, 1620.[48]

Valdivia left for Spain shortly thereafter to report to the king and to secure confirmation of the new tasa. Esquilache meanwhile had the ordinances printed in Lima and forwarded to the governor of Chile for promulgation. In an extensive report to the cabildo of Santiago, presented in person on December 11, 1620, Lisperguer advised the town fathers to accept the ordinances.[49] It was a bitter pill to swallow, but since it was evident that further appeals were out of the question for the time being the cabildo had little choice in the matter. The ordinances were duly published in Concepción on February 14, 1621, by Cristóbal de la Cerda y Sotomayor, *oidor decano* (senior judge) of the royal audiencia, whom Ulloa had appointed interim governor on November 24, 1620, in one of his last acts before his death.[50] In the preamble to the document Viceroy Esquilache summarized the precautions he had taken in preparing the tasa, adding that he had discussed the subject fully with men whose advice he valued. Among these advisers Luis de Valdivia must surely have been numbered.

As had been expected, the new legislation abolished compulsory personal service for all Indians except those over eighteen years of age who had been captured in the war during the two years between the publication of the slavery decree of 1608* and the beginning of Valdivia's system of defensive warfare, which is described in the next chapter. (Even these Indians were freed from personal service if their captors were unable to produce legal proof that they had been captured during the stipulated period.) Nevertheless, the abolition was more nominal than real because the Indians were, in effect, forced to pay their tribute out of what they earned by working for the Spaniards. The tasa, however, did cut down on the amount of work required and forbade the enslavement of all Indians. It also abolished forced labor in the mines, a significant accomplishment emphasizing the shift that had occurred in the economic base of the country in the period between the Tasa de Gamboa in 1580, which had been primarily concerned with labor in the mines, and the Tasa de Esquilache in 1621, when agriculture had replaced mining as the most important industry in the colony.†

For purposes of tribute payment the Indians were categorized according to the geographical areas in which they lived. Adult males between eighteen and fifty years of age residing in the jurisdictions of La Serena, Santiago, Chillán, and Concepción were required to pay an annual tribute of ten and a half pesos, of which eight pesos were earmarked for the encomendero, one and a half pesos for the doctrina, and half a peso each for the protector of the Indians and the corregidor of the district. Natives living in the provinces of Cuyo (Mendoza, San Juan, and San Luis) were required to pay ten pesos in tribute each

---

* The decree of 1608 was not officially promulgated in Chile until August 1610. Valdivia's program of peaceful conquest became official state policy on March 29, 1612.

† By 1621, only the *lavaderos* of Quillota and Andacollo were still in operation.

year, while those in Chiloé had to pay only nine and a half pesos because of the greater poverty of that region. Wages, also set in terms of
location, were expressed as money but made payable in kind because
of the scarcity of coined currency. The daily wage of farm workers in
the jurisdictions of La Serena, Santiago, Chillán, and Concepción was
set at one and a half reales plus meals. In the provinces of Cuyo the rate
was one and a fourth reales plus meals, while in Chiloé it was one and
a fourth reales without meals. After deduction of the tribute to the
encomendero, doctrina, corregidor, and protector, the worker received
the remainder of his salary in clothes, grain, livestock, cloth and other
items, the value of which was determined by the local justice of the
peace. Natives living south of the frontier in Araucania and peaceful
mapuches in the Spanish settlements along the Biobío River were put
under Crown control. If any of them chose voluntarily to work for the
Spaniards they were to receive a daily wage of at least one and a half
reales.

A modified version of the mita system was another feature of the
tasa. Only one-third of the members of an encomienda were obliged
to serve as mitayos each year for a nine-month period consisting of
twenty-three working days per month. During the remaining three
months of the year they were free to work in their own fields. The
two-thirds not engaged in mita service were allowed to work as they
pleased and could hire out their services to other Spaniards if they chose
to do so. Mitayos, however, could not be employed in any other labor
than that of the farms without express consent of the governor. If the
Indians lived only a short distance from the haciendas of their encomenderos, the governor could order all the members of the encomienda to serve as mitayos in the same year, but when this happened
the term of service was to be only three months for each group instead
of nine. The mitayos' work supplied all the tribute for that encomienda,
but each mitayo also had to work without pay for fifteen days each
year to compensate the encomendero for the cost of caring for the sick
members of the encomienda. After all the deductions were made, the
mitayos received take-home pay for only twenty-four days, amounting
to thirty-six reales in income for nine months' work. The figures were
proportionately lower, of course, in the provinces of Cuyo and Chiloé.

Women and children were excused from mita service but could hire out as paid laborers. Indian carpenters, blacksmiths, tailors, shoe-makers, and so forth were also excused from the mita. (This was a significant provision, since it indicated that an appreciable number of natives were capable of practicing a trade, thus countering the argu-ment that forced labor was defensible because the Indians were in-capable of improving their barbarous condition and learning to live and work as free, civilized people.) Artisans had the choice of paying trib-ute in money or the products of their craft and had, moreover, the right to live in the Spanish settlements. Apprentices, however, were subject to mita duty, but as soon as they had earned enough money to pay their taxes they could return to their regular jobs. Their salary while serving as mitayos was half a real a day more than that paid to non-skilled mitayos.

Inquilinos (Indians and mestizos living voluntarily on the haciendas of the Spaniards) had to work on the estate for one hundred and sixty days a year, for a daily wage of one real, a plot of ground plus seeds of vegetables and cereals, and tools and animals necessary for cultivating the land. Their wives and children were exempt from service of any kind. Domestic servants and those attached to the army were to be treated as free persons, and were not obligated to pay tribute as the other Indians were. The owner of the house had to feed them, provide them with sleeping quarters, take care of them if they became ill, provide a set of clothes for children under thirteen, and pay annual salaries of thirteen patacones to men over eighteen, sixteen pesos to women over eighteen, and twelve pesos to those between thirteen and eighteen. Payment regularly took the form of garments made in Chile or cloth imported from Quito. Female servants were permitted to marry and live with their husbands after completing their current annual con-tracts. *Patrones* (employers) were forbidden to hire out their domes-tics to other Spaniards under pain of forfeiting their services.

The ordinances also included measures to safeguard morality and promote observance of religious duties. For example, unmarried In-dian women serving at the military garrisons in Arauco and Yumbel were to be housed in separate barracks to reduce the possibility of con-cubinage and to protect them against molestation by the troops. To enforce these regulations, the corregidores were to visit the native families each year to hear complaints and to approve the next year's contracts. Servants who presented proof of mistreatment by their masters were to be given their freedom.

An ominous recommendation of the tasa was that the encomenderos purchase Negro slaves to serve as farm hands, industrial workers, and household domestics as a precaution against possible abolition of the encomiendas. This suggestion may have been prompted by the Crown's approval of the Ordinances of Alfaro, which foreshadowed the disintegration of the encomiendas of the Río de la Plata and Paraguay.

In many respects, the Tasa de Esquilache was a promising step forward. It prohibited the enslavement of the Indians; it abolished forced labor in the mines; it limited the amount of obligatory work by the Indians; it forced the holders of encomiendas to allow the mapuches to live in pueblos; and it empowered the corregidores to free all natives mistreated by their employers. It is not surprising, then, either that the encomenderos objected vehemently when Cristóbal de la Cerda tried to enforce the tasa, or that they again tried their formula of refusing to support the war in an effort to thwart the government. They adamantly refused to cooperate with any measure that involved surrendering any of their control over the physical resources of their encomienda workers. As Barros Arana observed: "This labor [of the Indians] provided them with much more revenue than they would have gained from any kind of tribute, no matter how heavy it might have been."[51] As always, the argument rationalizing their stand was that without the labor of the Indians the agricultural and industrial life of the colony would weaken and die. The mapuches, the argument continued, were still too savage to be trusted with freedom of choice.

Pedro Osores de Ulloa, who at almost eighty years of age succeeded Cerda as governor of the colony on April 22, 1622, made his opinion of the tasa clear in the *auto* (edict) that he issued on December 8 of that year when he declared that "this Ordinance seems to be wholly ineffective ... due to the lack of any habits of work among the Indians, and their lack of interest in making money. The only thing they desire is to get drunk and to indulge their vices."[52] The governor cited with evident exaggeration many other examples of sloth and instability by the natives to prove that without obligatory service they would be of no use to the encomenderos or themselves. Convinced that forced labor was the only feasible means of persuading the mapuches to do any work, Osores de Ulloa invoked his authority as governor to introduce what he considered necessary changes into the viceroy's legislation. He rescinded the prohibition against forced labor in the *lavaderos,* forbade Indian boys to learn mechanical trades without the governor's permission, obliged all artisans to serve in the mita, increased the number of Indians who could be assigned to guarding herds, allowed the encomenderos to employ mitayos and yanaconas in other than farm work, levied a tax of four reales per day on native artisans in the towns, forbade Indians living on haciendas to hire out to neighboring proprietors, and so forth. In line with his conviction that the Indians were incapable of caring for their own property, he appointed Spanish administrators for the native villages and obliged the Indians to support them.[53] In short, he effectively nullified most of the advantages of the original tasa.

The encomenderos, of course, were delighted by Osores de Ulloa's revisions; but most surprising was the favorable reception given them by many of the leading ecclesiastics in Santiago. Eighteen signed their names to a pronouncement of December 10, 1622, stating that the governor's provisions coincided perfectly with the needs of the colony. The signers included Bishop Juan de la Fuente Loarte of Santiago, the provincials of the Franciscans, Dominicans, Augustinians, and Mercedarians, as well as other prominent members of these Orders.[54] The names of the Jesuits were conspicuously absent. Absent also was the approval of the royal audiencia whose members refrained from endorsing the governor's action "because of the law suits that would arise therefrom and of which they would have to be the judges." The audiencia's stand proved to be decisive, for Osores de Ulloa promptly suspended enactment of his edict and of the viceroy's tasa until higher authorities expressed their will in the matter.[55]

The king's opinion was already in the mails. In a cédula dated July 17, 1622, Philip IV approved Esquilache's tasa but with important reservations, some favoring the mapuches and some not. The most important for the future of the Indians were those that reduced the amount of yearly tribute by two pesos in the jurisdictions of La Serena, Santiago, Chillán, and Concepción, with proportionate adjustments for the provinces of Cuyo and Chiloé,[56] and those that condemned to slavery all Indians over fourteen years of age who attacked the Spaniards. This included women and female children, but they were to be placed under the authority of the governor and the audiencia, while males could be sold as legal slaves, inside or beyond the borders of Chile.[57]

The cédula of 1622 was a blow to Jesuit hopes for better relations between the Spaniards and the Araucanians. Coupled with the subsequent decree of April 13, 1625, which put an end to Valdivia's system of defensive warfare, it temporarily eclipsed the principles of social justice for which the padres had fought for more than two decades. But these principles lived on, emerging with increasing vigor during future crises, and achieving their most compelling expression in the revolutionary struggle for national independence almost two centuries later. Thus the early efforts of the Jesuits were significant, and what was said of Diego de Torres Bollo could with truth be said of all the Blackrobes whose names became synonymous with the achievement of justice for the Indians: "Had he accomplished nothing else in life than to inaugurate this admirable work [the Ordinances of Alfaro], he would justly merit the respect of the entire world as one of the outstanding benefactors of humanity."[58]

VALDIVIA INTRODUCES DEFENSIVE WAR

No ACCOUNT OF THE STRUGGLE for justice in Chile would be complete without reference to Luis de Valdivia's controversial system of defensive warfare.[1] Like Las Casas before him, Valdivia was a firm believer in the efficacy of peaceful conquest as a means of overcoming the resistance of pagan aborigines and of extending Spanish rule in America. And like Las Casas he put his ideas to a practical test, with much the same result.*

For years the Spanish government had tried to pacify the Araucanians by force of arms, but by the end of the sixteenth century the cost to the Crown in terms of men, money, supplies, border maintenance, and defense had already assumed formidable proportions, with little to show for the investment. Something was clearly wrong, and the new viceroy of Peru, Gaspar de Zúñiga y Acevedo, was given the job of uncovering the source of the trouble and of doing something about it.[2]

Zúñiga approached the problem with caution, first enlisting the aid of expert opinion in determining the underlying causes of the prolonged Indian resistance. Having been informed by his predecessor, Luis de Velasco, of the talks he had had with Luis de Valdivia regarding Indian grievances, Zúñiga instructed the Jesuit to prepare a review of the subject.[3] The conclusions Valdivia submitted coincided with those of other *periti* (experts) the viceroy had consulted:[4] that the servicio personal was the principal cause of native disaffection and that its abolition was essential to the cessation of hostilities.

Zúñiga accepted this view and promptly convened still another junta

---

* In 1537 Las Casas and a group of co-religionists attempted to subdue by peaceful means alone the barbarous inhabitants of Tuzutlán province in Guatemala. The experiment was successful for a number of years but finally ended in disaster.

to devise a solution.[5] The result was a series of guarantees to provide the basis for new peace talks, including a general amnesty for past offenses, the abolition of obligatory personal service, a more moderate form of tribute, immediate and complete abolition of service in the mines, restrictions on the use of women and children as household servants, and revocation of the decrees of previous governors that had in effect enslaved the rebels and permitted their sale and deportation. All such slaves would be set free, including the three hundred who had been sent to Peru. To lighten the blow for the landed proprietors, the abolition of compulsory service was to take place over a period of two years during which time the Indians would continue to work for their current masters, and efforts would be made to supply the colony with Negro slaves as replacements. During the transitional period the Indians would be treated as mitayos rather than as encomienda workers and would receive the salary fixed by law for their labor. Indians formerly assigned to the mines would alternate with the other natives in the mitas.[6] A logical corollary to these peace terms was the granting of pardon to the mapuches for past uprisings.

Agreement on these guarantees disposed of one problem. But another weighty one still remained: how could the rebels be convinced of the government's sincerity? They had suffered too many disillusionments in the past to believe future promises. The authorities decided that the situation required a goodwill ambassador whom the natives could trust, someone whose word they would accept as proof of the government's good faith. From the viceroy's point of view, Luis de Valdivia appeared to be an excellent choice. Thoroughly familiar with affairs in the colony, he spoke the language of the aborigines and was sympathetic to them. The Araucanians knew and respected him, and there was every reason to suppose that they would listen to his words and follow his suggestions. Thus when García Ramón departed for Chile on February 1, 1605, to take over the reins of government there, Valdivia went with him. In his portfolio were letters from the viceroy of Peru and the king of Spain outlining the conditions for permanent peace between the Araucanians and the whites.

Immediately on arrival in Chile,[7] Valdivia began publicizing the peace terms. For nine months he traveled among the rebels, instructing them in the faith and holding frequent conferences with their leading *toquis* (war chiefs). The Indians received him well, listened to his proposals, and were willing to accept them. Progress seemed possible. But Governor García Ramón, who had no intention of pacifying the Araucanians with diplomatic phraseology, had an army at his command and intended to use it.[8] Once free of the conciliatory atmosphere of the viceroy's juntas, he lost no time in asserting his real views.[9] Instead of enforcing his superior's wishes, he abetted the encomenderos in exploiting the natives, even going so far as to issue licenses for the transportation of slaves to Peru.[10]

The governor's about-face came as a shock to Valdivia. The bright prospects of peace began to fade as the Araucanians found difficulty in reconciling their belief in the king's sincerity with the conduct of his political representatives. "The king," they told Valdivia, "is very good, and his commands are just. But your captains and governors do not obey his will, and consequently there is no justice for the Indians. Back up your promises with good works. Keep your word in a manner that we can see. After having dealt with you for so many years we are no longer inclined to believe what we hear but only what we see."[11]

Valdivia had to admit that the complaints were justified. The peaceful Indians, he informed the Council of the Indies, were subjected to more personal service now than formerly. Many former mitayos in the mines were now serving as yanaconas on the estates of the Spaniards. Large numbers of natives, including many who were already at peace with the whites, were being sold into slavery in Peru in complete disregard of His Majesty's orders, "the observance of which is necessary if we wish to justify our position."[12] Disenchanted completely by the governor's actions, Valdivia requested permission to return to Peru, but the viceroy urged him to remain in Chile in the hope that his presence would calm the Araucanians. The Jesuit obeyed for a time, but by the summer of 1606, he was back in Lima, having spent fourteen months in fruitless negotiations among the aborigines.[13]

The failure of Valdivia's diplomatic mission set the stage for the next act in the evolution of defensive warfare as an instrument of official policy. The credit for this development belongs to Juan de Villela, oidor of the audiencia of Lima, who had been asesor under Viceroy Velasco. Villela's plan of 1607 differed from Valdivia's later proposal only in its rejection of the use of force to quell actual uprisings.

Briefly, it called for the establishment of a string of forts along the Biobío River, the sole function of which would be defensive: to protect the frontier against hostile attacks and to keep the border closed to enterprising vecinos. The only Spaniards permitted to venture beyond the line would be emissaries of the Faith. Thus by a combination of vigilance and peaceful penetration Villela hoped to accomplish what military aggression had failed to achieve for more than fifty years—the conquest and pacification of Araucania.

Villela's plan captured the imagination of the viceroy's advisers, including Valdivia, who supported the proposal with so much vigor and enthusiasm and labored for its realization with such tenacity that the identity of its true author has been obscured.* Extrinsic circumstances also contributed to this historical oversight, for while the plan was still in the blueprint stage, Villela was promoted to the presidency of the audiencia of Guadalajara in New Spain, and he left Lima before being able to translate his ideas into action. Ignored, too, by most critics was the role of the viceroy of Peru, Juan de Mendoza y Luna, Marquis of Montes Claros, in the proceedings. Yet without his favorable intervention it is unlikely that defensive warfare would ever have become a reality in Chile, for it was Mendoza who sent Valdivia to Spain to argue for its acceptance, and it was he who made the final decision regarding its enforcement. But opponents of the system conveniently forgot these facts. They needed a target for their wrath and the Jesuit served admirably. There was less danger in victimizing a Blackrobe than in vilifying a prominent government official.

The pattern of the struggle was clear from the start. Political officials in Chile were sure to oppose any scheme that savored of peaceful conquest. When García Ramón learned of Mendoza's pacific intentions he straightway dispatched his personal secretary, Lorenzo de Salto, to Spain to request additional troops and to lobby against the project. The viceroy countered with an agent of his own, Luis de Valdivia, who was to acquaint the king with Mendoza's views and answer any objections that Salto might raise.

The exact date of Valdivia's arrival in Spain is unknown, but he probably reached Seville by the end of September or the beginning of Octo-

---

* The germ of the theory could be said to have been contained in the preachings of Fray Gil González de San Nicolás in the 1560's.

ber 1609.[14] Lozano records that in his first audience with the king, Valdivia succeeded in persuading the monarch of the utility of the viceroy's recommendations.[15] Whether or not this statement is entirely accurate, there is no doubt that Philip III and the Council of the Indies were eager to hear any proposal that offered a possible solution to the Indian problem, and particularly one that relieved the constant drain on government resources. Anything would be better than the existing stalemate, and there was always the chance that the plan might succeed.

In a lengthy memorial addressed to the king, Valdivia explained the deficiencies of armed conquest, the advantages of defensive tactics,[16] and the practical impossibility of subjugating the Araucanians by force of arms. For one thing, the distances involved were too great: enemy territory, which extended over an area of one hundred leagues from north to south, had been penetrated by the Spaniards to a depth of only forty leagues in the preceding fifty-eight years, and even this modest gain had not been completely consolidated. At the same rate, it would take another hundred years to bring the entire hinterland under control. Thus some observers had suggested that the country be reduced piecemeal by constructing a continually advancing network of forts, but if seven or eight forts were necessary to control an area of only twelve leagues in Arauco, Tucapel, and Catiray, how many more would be needed for the rest of the territory? And where would the Crown find the money and men to carry out such a costly and extensive project? The same objections argued against the establishment of new towns beyond the frontier. Where would Spaniards in sufficient numbers be found to build and populate the settlements? Few wanted to risk their lives in such a perilous undertaking, the cost of garrisoning the towns would be prohibitive, and the failure of similar outposts in Arauco showed that the idea was premature.

What about a program of extermination? García Ramón and other governors had attempted such a method, and the Indians had retaliated by adopting the same tactics and killing off the whites. Annihilating the Araucanians was not only impossible but even suicidal in a sense, for the Indians acted as a buffer against hostile foreigners who might otherwise gain a foothold in southern Chile and menace the entire Spanish empire along the Pacific coast.

The suggestion that Indian auxiliaries be used against the rebels—on the assumption that the native allies would be more cruel than the Spaniards and thus the rebels would be more easily persuaded to make peace—was not convincing, Valdivia observed. Pacified Indians could not be expected to make war on their tribal friends and relatives, even in exchange for freedom and perpetual exemption from obligatory labor and tribute, for favors extended to one group would constitute an injustice to others, and dissension would result. There was also the possibility that if a thousand Indians were considered more feared adversaries than a thousand Spaniards, they might conceivably turn on the Europeans themselves once they were united and supplied with arms.

After dealing with alternative proposals, Valdivia outlined the plan that he and Viceroy Mendoza favored: defensive warfare resulting in peaceful conquest. The plan included cessation of all offensive operations against the rebels, establishment of the Biobío as a dividing line between Araucanians and whites, fortification of the line with military garrisons and towns,[17] and the use of missionaries to convert the rebels and persuade them to live at peace with the Spaniards. While this proselytizing was going on, the existing outposts south of the Biobío would be maintained lest their abandonment be interpreted by the enemy as a sign of Spanish weakness. Their maintenance would provide a first line of defense for the frontier, would hopefully discourage the hostiles from going on the warpath, and would provide more immediate protection for missionaries. As the pacification of the country became a reality, the outposts could gradually be abandoned. "From everything that has been said in this treatise," Valdivia concluded, "it is clear that there is no room for choice concerning the prosecution of the war in Chile. The strategy to be adopted must be practical, justifiable, and possessed of greater advantages than disadvantages, qualities lacking in the present method of conducting the war, but included in the viceroy's proposal."[18]

Philip III, favorably impressed with the memorial, referred it to the Council of the Indies, which immediately appointed a special *junta de guerra* (committee on war) to study the plan as well as Lorenzo de Salto's counterproposals. The deliberations lasted through almost all of 1610,* but it was apparent from the first which side would win, for the prospect of pacifying the Indians by converting them to the Faith satisfied the Christian instincts of Philip III. The hope of doing so without vast expenditures of money and blood appealed to the junta's members. Salto had requested numerous troops,[19] while Valdivia wanted only a few reinforcements for the army in Chile. Predictably, as early as February 18, 1610, just six weeks after beginning its discussions, the junta had already recorded its approval of defensive warfare as a Crown policy. Part of an official memorandum of that date stated: "It seems that defensive warfare ought to be tried for a period of three or four years, placing particular emphasis on the good treatment of the peaceful Indians and the fulfillment of His Majesty's orders regarding the abolition of personal service."[20]

After settling this important point, the junta turned to a consideration of the means to be employed. Should the governor of Chile or a special agent of the king direct the experiment? If an agent, how much authority should he have? Should he be independent of the governor? Should he be a layman or an ecclesiastic, and if a churchman were chosen, what special dignity, if any, should he receive? These were knotty problems for men who were inexperienced in the affairs of the colony; though they did their best, their solutions were inadequate, as events were to prove.

Only one man—Luis de Valdivia—seemed to the junta fully qualified to take charge of the experiment. His enthusiasm for the plan, the dexterity with which he defended its utility, his intimate knowledge of the Araucanians, and the viceroy's confidence in his judgment all contributed to their thinking. But the junta knew from past experience that an unfriendly governor or bishop could hamstring a project by refusing to cooperate. Therefore, freedom of action was imperative. In the political sphere, Valdivia could be made independent by placing him directly under the viceroy's control. Freedom from local ecclesiastical control posed a more difficult problem. The episcopal see of Concepción† had recently become vacant, and, after consultation with the

---

* The first meeting was on January 2, the last on December 9.
† Diocesan headquarters were officially transferred from La Imperial to Concepción on February 7, 1603.

king, the Pope had designated the bishop of Santiago, Juan Pérez de Espinosa, as temporary administrator of the diocese. The junta, therefore, in its report to the king naively recommended that Valdivia be consecrated bishop of Concepción.[21] In doing so it ignored the rule that Jesuits are forbidden to accept episcopal honors unless commanded to do so by the Pope. It also ignored the objections that Valdivia's superiors were certain to raise.

On April 27, 1610, the General of the Order, Claude Aquaviva, wrote to the provincial of Toledo, Bartholomé Pérez: "We understand that arrangements are being made secretly at court to give Father Luis de Valdivia a bishopric in Peru [Chile was part of the viceroyalty of Peru] on the grounds that this dignity will aid him in carrying out the task His Majesty has assigned him in the kingdom of Chile. We shall not fail to take the necessary steps here in Rome to block this effort."[22] Aquaviva advised the provincial to do the same in Spain "by pointing out to the gentlemen concerned, and even to the king if necessary," not only how contrary such a dignity would be to the Order's constitutions and what a harmful precedent it would establish for the future, but also that, as far as His Majesty's service was concerned, Valdivia would be able to participate more effectively in the Chilean venture as a simple religious than as the administrator of an episcopal see. Aquaviva sent similar instructions to Valdivia on the same day, ordering him to oppose the measure personally on the ground that it would hinder execution of the king's aims, emphasizing that it would deprive him of the mobility that the founder of the Society of Jesus had envisaged when legislating against the acceptance of prelacies by his subjects.[23] The Jesuit authorities in Madrid quickly made their protests known to the junta. Their representations must have been successful, for in a reply to a letter of Valdivia on June 22 Aquaviva remarked: "With reference to the episcopacy, I need only say that we rejoice that the subject has been dropped. You will be able to accomplish far more for the service of God and His Majesty in the business of Chile as a simple missionary."[24]

The idea may have been dropped temporarily, but it was not forgotten. It came up again for serious consideration in a meeting of the junta on June 2, 1610. A letter from the viceroy of Peru, which reached Spain some time later, also strengthened the junta's determination:

"Regarding the other affairs of Chile, it would help very much if there were some prelate who knows the Indians, who loves them and is zealous for their welfare, and who could assist the governor in these matters. The opinion I have of Father Luis de Valdivia is such that I would be happy to see him as bishop of La Imperial [Concepción], even though this dignity is contrary to his humility and the constitutions of his Order. Your Majesty will decide what is most conducive to your service."[25]

Although he preferred that Valdivia receive episcopal consecration so that his independence would be assured, the king recognized the obstacles that stood in the way. He accordingly prepared a letter addressed to the bishop of Santiago, Juan Pérez de Espinosa, recommending that he ease his already heavy burdens as bishop of the diocese of Santiago, by entrusting the administration of the sister diocese of Concepción to Valdivia. If, however, the bishop found it inadvisable to do so, he was to make whatever arrangements he judged best.[26]

Valdivia objected strongly to allowing Pérez de Espinosa, who was no friend of the Jesuits, the final say in the matter. He was sure that the prelate would try to curtail his efforts in one way or another. "I find myself obliged to go [to Chile] in obedience to the king, whose letter I received yesterday. For many reasons I find it difficult to do so as long as I am subordinated to the bishop, especially since he is very unfriendly to the Society.... On the other hand, my religious profession obliges me to refuse the episcopacy, and my superiors are insisting on its refusal. It is imperative to find some appropriate means whereby I shall avoid failing in my duty to the king, to my Order, and to my superiors, and they shall be spared the embarrassment of sending me on a journey of four thousand leagues in a bewildered state of mind. The dangers and trials that I shall have to face from without are sufficient in themselves without afflicting me with more difficulties from within."[27]

Valdivia himself suggested the "appropriate means" in a letter to one of the clerics at the royal court.[28] "Let him [the king] request the Holy See to entrust the government [of the diocese of Concepción] to Father Valdivia for whatever period of time His Majesty deems convenient for the pacification of Chile ... investing him with the powers of a bishop so that he might carry out His Majesty's commands

for the pacification and conversion of the kingdom of Chile."²⁹ A letter
he wrote to Pedro de Ledesma, secretary of the Council of the Indies,
on November 28, 1610, clarifies why these "powers of a bishop" would
not conflict with his religious profession. The authority he had in mind
was that which was occasionally conferred on Jesuit missionaries in
Japan and other foreign lands—that of a vicar general. The General
of the Order, he assured the secretary, would not object to this arrangement. He stated emphatically, however, that he desired neither this
authority nor the episcopacy: "I declare before God our Lord, whom
I call upon as my witness, that as far as I am personally concerned, I
would prefer to remain here in Spain."³⁰

Valdivia's reasons for urging this unusual form of ecclesiastical independence are set forth at length in a memorial to the king that he
drew up at this time. If, he wrote, the bishop of Santiago were not disposed to transfer to him the administration of the diocese of Concepción, he would have no authority to make decisions in ecclesiastical affairs pertaining to the peaceful conquest of Araucania, a strictly missionary territory. As things now stood, whatever authority he might
receive from the bishop of Santiago would be delegated authority,
which he would not be able to subdelegate. Yet power to subdelegate
would be absolutely indispensable on the frontier because of the great
distances between mission stations. Moreover, were Bishop Pérez de
Espinosa to die before his arrival in Chile, he would be unable to exercise any jurisdiction whatsoever, and the whole enterprise would be
delayed.³¹

Valdivia's suggestions did not substantially alter the thinking of
the junta, who, no doubt influenced by the viceroy's expressed predilection, continued to debate the propriety of elevating the Jesuit to
the episcopal rank. In a final vote of December 9, 1610, three of the
seven members opposed the measure, while the other four favored
petitioning the Pope and the General of the Jesuits to sanction it. In
their recommendation to the king they wrote: "It appears that it would
contribute very much to the service of Your Majesty and the success of
the project under consideration if Father Valdivia were made bishop
of La Imperial [Concepción], as the viceroy suggests, and if Your
Majesty were to acquaint His Holiness and the General of the Order
with the notable advantages accruing therefrom, so that a matter of

such great value to the service of God and the public may be brought to a successful close. . . . For we understand that the statutes of the Order do not exclude having Jesuit bishops in pagan territories as an aid to the conversion of the infidels."[32]

Philip III rejected the majority opinion of the junta and ordered instead that the views of the minority group be adopted and that the bishop of Santiago be directed to turn over the administration of the diocese of Concepción to Valdivia in the capacity of vicar general.[33]

So much for the ecclesiastical authority Valdivia received. What about his political jurisdiction? According to Lozano, the king appointed Valdivia *visitador general* (official inspector) of Chile, an appointment that was tantamount to making him the temporary superior of all Crown officials in the colony.[34] But the records show that Valdivia received his political authority later, from the viceroy of Peru in the king's name,[35] for the king and the Council of the Indies had decided to refer the question of defensive warfare to the viceroy's judgment. It was in Lima, then, and not in Madrid that Valdivia received his commission as visitador general of Chile.

He also received special faculties from his religious superiors, but historians have differed about the nature of the authority they conferred. Rosales states that Valdivia came to Chile with the title of vice-provincial.[36] Lozano asserts that Valdivia was made vice-provincial of the missions he was to establish in Araucania,[37] and supports this deduction with the contents of a letter from the General of the Order, Claude Aquaviva, to the provincial of Paraguay, Diego de Torres Bollo, even though the term "vice-provincial" does not appear in the letter. Enrich reports more convincingly that Aquaviva exempted Valdivia from the jurisdiction of the regular provincial, Torres Bollo, and made his companions immediately subject to him.[38] None of these authors had access to all the documents on the subject, but Astrain, who had the opportunity to examine the original manuscripts in the Jesuit archives in Rome, has succeeded in explaining the discrepancies. His investigations indicate that while in Spain Valdivia had petitioned the General for complete independence of the Jesuit authorities in America, a request summarily rejected by Aquaviva in his letter to Valdivia dated April 27, 1610: "Your Reverence will readily understand that your request to be made independent of the superiors over there [in Paraguay and Peru] and immediately dependent upon us here in Rome is not conformable to our type of government and would establish a most harmful precedent in the Society, something that I am sure you, as a good religious, do not desire."[39] Three months later, Aquaviva urged Valdivia to observe the usual subordination to local superiors and to consult their opinion on the duties of his office: "In order to preserve the necessary subordination, while you are in Chile you will treat of these matters with the provincial of Paraguay. But since it will be necessary to arrange the details of the project with the viceroy of Peru, while you are still in Lima you will defer to the judgment of the provincial of Peru."[40] That Valdivia was not happy with these arrangements can be deduced from the fact that Aquaviva was forced to repeat his instructions a third time on February 28, 1612: "The order that you must observe in carrying out your commission is to consult the provincial of Lima or his locum tenens concerning matters that come up for discussion there, and to follow his counsel completely. Matters requiring no decision in Lima should be discussed with the provincial of Chile, to whom you should show the proper subordination, as a result of which God will be more propitious to the work you are doing."[41]

Developments in Lima and the opinions of certain Jesuits in Peru caused Aquaviva to modify his stand later, allowing Valdivia a limited measure of jurisdictional independence. He communicated this decision to the padre in a letter of February 26, 1613:

> We believe that Your Reverence ought to have control of the disposition of your companions . . . and of the work assigned to them without being dependent in any way on the provincial of the province in things concerning the mission, and much less upon the provincial of Lima, except when it is advisable to consult with him on matters that may contribute to the happy outcome of what you are seeking. But in case you find it useful to replace one of your subjects with a member of one of the houses of this province or of Lima, or especially of the College of San Miguel in Santiago (in which you have no authority whatsoever, as neither in other houses of the province, but only in the residences that you have newly established) . . . you must inform the provincial or the rector concerned and come to an agreement with him as befits good brethren.[42]

An examination of these documents reveals clearly the nature of the authority Valdivia received from the General in Rome. He was not appointed vice-provincial of Chile, but only an independent superior of the three missions that he established in Araucania. He definitely did not receive jurisdiction over the Jesuit college in Santiago nor over any other house of the Order in Chile. And since the letter cited above was not written until the end of February 1613, when Valdivia had already spent almost a year in Chile, he could not have left Peru with any title or office of vice-provincial.[43] He did, however, have more independence than most local Jesuit superiors, and as visitor general for the Crown, vicar general of the diocese of Concepción, and independent superior of the Jesuit missions in Araucania he was a leading figure in the colony.

Despite the powers he possessed, Valdivia was still worried, for even though as visitor general he outranked the governor of Chile, García Ramón had vehemently opposed defensive warfare and was not likely to defer graciously to Valdivia's temporary superiority. Thinking that it would be safer to forestall probable complications by replacing García Ramón with a more friendly administrator, Valdivia made such a suggestion to the king and the Council of the Indies,[44] and Philip III issued a decree removing García Ramón and appointing Alonso de Ribera, who had held the position previously from 1602 to 1607. At that time he had displayed marked military and administrative abilities, but he had fallen into disfavor by marrying while in office and had been demoted to the governorship of Tucumán.[45] His fairmindedness plus the fact that he was related through marriage to a fellow Jesuit convinced Valdivia that Ribera would be an easier man to work with, but events were to prove otherwise. Ironically, the opposition that Valdivia had feared from Bishop Pérez de Espinosa never materialized, while Ribera became the cause of numerous tribulations.

Having arranged the governorship to his satisfaction, Valdivia left for Peru early in 1611 with ten other Jesuits who were to assist him in the work of pacifying the Araucanians. The group included two temporal coadjutors, Estevan de la Madrid and Blas Hernández, and eight priests—Juan de Fuenzalida, who had had previous experience in Chile, Juan Bautista de Prada, Mateo de Montes, Rodrigo Vásquez,

Gaspar Sobrino, Agustín de Villaza, Vicente Modolell, and Pedro Fonella. (Three of these men—Vásquez, Sobrino, and Modolell— later became vice-provincials of Chile.) The king had entrusted final responsibility for the project to Viceroy Mendoza, who was not one to take such commitments lightly. Hopes for a prompt beginning of the experiment fell when he summoned a council of twenty men to review all the pros and cons of the proposal. During the deliberations that followed, the Chilean encomenderos made a final desperate attempt to sabotage the plan, and by exerting their influence in the local cabildos they secured the appointment of Jerónimo Hinojosa, a Dominican friar, as procurator to Lima. But Hinojosa never had a chance. By the time he reached Lima, the viceroy's council had unanimously approved defensive warfare.[46] Realizing the futility of the situation, Hinojosa decided to refrain from pushing his commission, but the viceroy insisted that he be given a hearing. He therefore recalled the council and reopened the case, but after listening to Hinojosa's arguments and examining his documents, the council concluded that there was no reason for reversing its decision. Hinojosa himself "prudently replied that if all those in Chile had been present at the meeting they would have been convinced just as he was by so many compelling reasons."[47]

Hinojosa's capitulation removed the last obstacle to the initiation of the system of peaceful conquest, which was made official state policy on March 29, 1612. In a series of decrees, Mendoza ordered the cessation of offensive warfare in favor of peaceful penetration by the Jesuit missionaries under Valdivia, whom he appointed visitor general of Chile.[48] The governor and the audiencia of Chile were reminded that they had no jurisdiction over the Jesuit but were to cooperate with him in every way. As visitor general Valdivia was to secure the abolition of compulsory personal service and the introduction of a pecuniary tax. The frontier forts of Angol and Paicaví were to be abandoned, but not those at Cayugano, Yumbel, Santa Fe, Nacimiento, San Jerónimo, Monterrey, and Arauco.* The Biobío River was designated as the frontier, and military personnel were forbidden to cross the line for private purposes under penalty of death, in the case of ordinary soldiers, and loss of rank or command plus the burden of serving for three

* The first three were north of the Biobío River, the others south of it.

years without pay, in the case of officers. Illicit unions between the Spanish troops and native women were likewise forbidden, as was the trading that the officers of the forts and the encampments frequently carried on with the Indians.[49]

The viceroy extended pardon to the rebels for their past crimes on condition that they did not again take up arms against the Crown. He promised that the military would not molest them in their own territory. Natives living in the *reducciones de paz* (villages inhabited by pacified Indians) would not be assigned to encomiendas or be obliged to work in the gold mines. The Indians, for their part, had to surrender all Christian captives, and those who lived in the reducciones had to obey the Jesuit missionaries or other religious who were charged with their conversion. More important from the standpoint of the Indians was the provision that suspended the slavery decree of 1608 for the duration of defensive war, and prohibited the sale outside of Chile of hostiles who had been captured in the war up to that time.[50]

These regulations were sure to stir up ill feeling among the encomenderos, but whatever the outcome might be the die was now cast. The viceroy had done his part. The rest was now in the hands of Providence —and of Luis de Valdivia.

Valdivia and his companions disembarked in Concepción on May 13, 1612. He immediately paid his respects to the *ayuntamiento* (town council) of the city and presented the credentials and dispatches he had received from Viceroy Mendoza. He also communicated these dispatches by messenger to the governor and the audiencia in Santiago, as well as to Pedro Cortés and Núñez de Pineda, the commanders in charge of the frontier forces.[51]

On May 21, he left Concepción to begin negotiations with the Araucanians. His haste in visiting the rebels before consulting with the governor or the audiencia of Chile has been interpreted by some scholars as proof of his high-handed methods. The Jesuit historian Astrain reflects this in commenting on Valdivia's conduct: "Already in this way of acting there is something we cannot approve. There were in Santiago at the time the governor, Alonso de Ribera, the audiencia, and the bishop, Espinosa, who was supposed to hand over to Valdivia the ecclesiastical administration of La Imperial [Concepción]. It was to these persons, who were the supreme authorities in Chile, and not to the ayuntamiento of Concepción, that Father Valdivia should have presented his credentials."[52]

On the face of it this criticism seems valid. However, there was another circumstance that neither Astrain nor other historians have stopped to consider. The Indian situation had again reached a critical stage by the time Valdivia and his band arrived in Chile. Three months earlier, at the beginning of February 1612, the natives of Arauco, Tucapel, and Catiray had killed twenty Spanish soldiers in an uprising. The outbreak was the initial blow in a projected insurrection of all the tribes between the Biobío and Maule rivers, and there was danger that the discord would spread to the pacified Indians farther north,[53] in repetition of the disaster of 1598. Valdivia states that it was the seriousness of this crisis, and not any disrespect for the authorities in Santiago, that prompted him to set out immediately for the Indian country. In a letter of September 30, 1612, he says:

> In order to forestall and smother this fire [of rebellion] that was burning stronger all the time, six days after my arrival I left the Fathers of the Society whom I had brought with me from Spain in the city [Concepción], and set out for the rebel provinces of Arauco and Tucapel. The road was very dangerous because it was here that the aforementioned Spaniards were killed during this rebellion, and no one travelled it without an escort of at least a company of cavalry.[54]

It could be argued that Valdivia nevertheless was guilty of disobedience to his religious superiors by not first consulting with the provincial of Chile as the General had ordered him to do, but the crisis was real and threatening, and Valdivia could legitimately have assumed that the provincial would have approved of his action if there had been time to consult him. Assumptions of this kind are not contrary to Jesuit obedience.

Valdivia's first meetings with the rebel chieftains confirmed the wisdom of prompt action. On arriving at the Spanish fort in Arauco, he sent out messengers to the neighboring tribes with news of his coming and a summons to a council. Included among the messengers were five Araucanians who had been transported as slaves to Lima and later freed by Viceroy Mendoza. Valdivia had brought them back with him to Chile to aid him in convincing their countrymen of the sincerity of the king's offers.[55] The rebel response to Valdivia's invitation must have been embarrassing to the Spaniards in Concepción who had strongly opposed the plan,[56] for within three weeks the messengers returned with representatives of numerous rebellious tribes. After conferring with the padre, they all agreed to lay down their arms and to settle peacefully in their own territories.[57]

Shortly thereafter four caciques from Catiray arrived to invite the missionary to a *parlamento* (peace conference) of five hundred Indians in Mancu.[58] Since the natives objected to having a military escort accompany the Blackrobe, Valdivia returned with them attended by only one soldier, one servant, and one half-breed interpreter. The conference was a huge success. The missionary addressed the assemblage for three hours, explaining the nature of the king's offers and insisting on the Crown's sincerity. On one point only did the negotiations threaten to break down: the Indians, experienced in the ways of the Spaniards, demanded some proof of the king's sincerity and asked that the Spaniards abandon the fort they had built in that vicinity. Since this was a military matter, Valdivia offered to relay the request to the governor, but certain chiefs threatened to break up the conference then and there, and the interpreter, fearing for his life, urged the missionary to grant the request. The Jesuit did so, considering the matter of secondary importance because the forts south of the Biobío were to be abandoned later on anyway. Valdivia remained with the Indians that night, since Caranipaque, the principal toqui, and thirty other caciques had expressed a desire to accompany him to Concepción to see the governor. The Spaniards in Concepción received them well and feasted them for two weeks until they departed again for their homes.[59]

Valdivia's success evoked tremendous official rejoicing in Santiago. Church bells chimed, Te Deums were sung, and Bishop Pérez de Espinosa celebrated a solemn Mass of thanksgiving in the presence of the audiencia, the secular and ecclesiastical cabildos, and a throng of joyful worshippers. Within a period of a few short weeks the entire frontier from Concepción to the cordillera, from the Maule to the Biobío, had been pacified without the loss of a single Spanish life, and the outlook for the future looked bright. Only the encomenderos found little to applaud in the proceedings. Peace with the Indians meant the end of slave hunts and the slave trade, and of cheap labor. For the time being, however, there was nothing they could do but accept the situation and hope for a change.

The frontier remained quiet during the cold winter months of 1612, and Valdivia utilized the opportunity to tour the diocese of Concepción. It was a wholesome move, for abuses were rampant—many of the priests did not know Latin, others neglected their native converts, the cathedral was falling apart, the holy oils were lacking—but Valdivia's efforts to correct the situation were stifled by conflicting authorities. "This diocese of Concepción," he informed his provincial, Diego de Torres, "has seven superiors! One is the bishop of Santiago, who is its ecclesiastical head; another is the ecclesiastical cabildo of Santiago to whom he has given its government; a third is myself, whom they call administrator and superior judge; a fourth is the *provisor* (ecclesiastical judge) and vicar general of Concepción; a fifth is the provisor and vicar general of Santiago; and now the provisor here in Concepción wishes to appoint someone else in his place, saying that he has the authority to do so. Besides all these, there is a visitor whom the bishop [of Santiago] has sent. So altogether there are seven superiors, an arrangement that is an unintelligible monstrosity."[60]

So confusing was this labyrinth of overlapping jurisdictions that Valdivia judged it more expedient to resign his office as administrator of the diocese and devote himself to the main purpose of his stay in Chile: the establishment of new missions and the permanent pacification of Araucania. The winter season, however, was not very suitable for this purpose, for traveling was difficult and dangerous. Nevertheless, he dispatched emissaries in all directions to acquaint even the most distant tribes with the king's offer of a cessation of hostilities. Some of the tribes responded favorably by sending representatives to Concepción,[61] but others, especially those living farther south, adamantly refused to lay down their arms and continued to stir up trouble among the pacified tribes living in the neighborhood of the Spanish forts. Particularly irritating to the Spanish garrisons were the raids engineered by a rebel caudillo named Tureulipe. Emboldened by the passivity of the royal forces, who had been ordered to refrain from aggressive action, Tureulipe brashly attacked the fort in Arauco. Much to his surprise, the Spaniards promptly counterattacked and succeeded in capturing him and sending him off to Concepción, where the governor, recognizing his value as a political pawn, insisted on keeping him in prison.

Similar raids by other guerrilla bands convinced many of the Spaniards that defensive warfare was merely a dream. Valdivia, however, continued to believe in the sincerity of the natives and the peaceful desires of most of the Araucanians, but he nevertheless took steps against future recriminations. Around the middle of September 1612, he arranged for a notary public to take down the sworn testimony of qualified witnesses in Concepción, army officers for the most part, who attested to the merit of the missionary's work during the preceding four months.[62] Some weeks later a fellow Jesuit, Francisco de Arevalo, caused another document of the same kind to be drawn up in Santiago in defense of Valdivia's services in pacifying the realm.[63] Such documents, though undoubtedly slanted in favor of Valdivia, nevertheless proved that others in the colony also favored peaceful conquest.[64]

Having fortified himself with legal precautions, Valdivia once more turned his attention to the work of pacification. Up until this time the messengers he had employed had all failed to inspire the confidence of Governor Ribera, who wanted to use some of his own men for the purpose. The difficulty lay in finding Spaniards who were willing to risk their lives in such a perilous assignment. The capture of Tureulipe was considered an advantage in this connection, for the hostiles were unlikely to harm the king's men as long as their leader remained a prisoner. Encouraged by this thought, Pedro Meléndez, a sergeant in the army, volunteered to serve as Ribera's agent among the rebels and set out for enemy country on September 18, 1612.

Among the chiefs whom Meléndez contacted was Anganamón, one of the fiercest warriors of Purén and a close relative of Tureulipe. With a view to securing the release of his kinsman, Anganamón readily agreed to discuss terms and sent messengers to Valdivia to that effect. The Jesuit was elated, for he had talked with Tureulipe and was convinced of his desire for peace. Tureulipe had even proposed to act as mediator between the Spaniards and his own people in exchange for his freedom. Although Ribera and some of his military advisers opposed the move, toward the end of October Valdivia left Concepción with Tureulipe to begin negotiations with Anganamón at the fort in Paicaví.*

Anganamón arrived at the fort on November 10 with a large retinue of Indians from Purén. Prisoners, including Tureulipe, were exchanged, the peace pipe was smoked, and the natives agreed to lay down their arms. They pointed out, however, that the pacification of the region would be incomplete unless the tribes in Imperial and Villarrica followed their example; Anganamón, moreover, volunteered to secure their approval, but when Valdivia offered to send some missionaries along to assist in the work, the chieftain demurred, saying that he wished to prove his friendship by his own unaided efforts. The padre, seeing no reason to doubt his word, headed back in the direction of Arauco to rejoin the governor at the Spanish fort, and after tarrying there for several days the entire party set out once again for Paicaví on November 26 to conclude negotiations.

While still on the road to Paicaví the group met a native runner who brought news that threatened to destroy the promising alliance with Anganamón. Ribera's agent, Pedro Meléndez, seems to have been the protagonist in the sorry affair. While visiting Anganamón's village in the interests of peace, he had become enamored of one of the toqui's wives, a Spanish captive named María de Jorquera. He had persuaded her and two of Anganamón's native consorts to seek refuge among the Spaniards, and while Anganamón was engaged in pacifying his neighbors, they took advantage of his absence to flee to Paicaví with two of Anganamón's daughters whom Meléndez coveted as personal servants. Anganamón's anger on learning of the treachery knew no bounds. He hastened to the fort and passionately demanded the return of his women, but the Spaniards refused to surrender them on religious grounds, for the Spanish woman, they argued, was already a Christian, and the others desired baptism. As Christians they could not practice the polygamy common among the Araucanians. The chief would, therefore, have to be satisfied with the return of his daughters and with whichever one of the women he might choose for his lawful wife. Anganamón did not, of course, appreciate these fine distinctions of

---

* Situated on the north bank of the Paicaví River a short distance from the sea, this fort was the southernmost Spanish outpost along the coast.

moral theology that were contrary to tribal custom. He was interested only in recovering his property.

The situation was still uncertain when Ribera and Valdivia arrived in Paicaví for the conference with the hostiles. For several days not a single rebel visited the fort. During the interval, Anganamón's wives repeatedly warned the Spaniards against having any further dealings with their deceitful husband or the rest of the enemy. Finally, on November 7, at three o'clock in the afternoon, a large party of Indians appeared at the fort, dressed in peaceful regalia and headed by a septuagenerian named Utablame who prided himself on having fought against sixteen Spanish governors. Shortly after their arrival the parlamento began. Utablame frankly admitted that he would never yield to the force of arms, but since the terms of the proffered peace seemed reasonable he was willing to accept them and give his friendship to the Spaniards. The other caciques spoke in like manner, and as an earnest of their sincerity, they asked that some Jesuit missionaries be sent to their people. They also requested the Spaniards to demolish the fort in Paicaví as part of the agreement.

The request for missionaries met with protests from many of the Spaniards who considered it a trick. The failure of Anganamón, Tureulipe, Pelantaru, Ainavilu, and other leading war chiefs to participate in the conference seemed to bode ill for any Spaniards who entered their territory. Ribera, too, urged Valdivia to refuse the petition,[65] but the Jesuit felt that a display of trust in the good faith of the rebels would be a proper foundation for lasting peace. After spending the night in prayer he decided to accept the invitation. The Indians, for their part, promised to watch over the missionaries, to assist them in their work, and to do for them whatever they could.[66] Valdivia assigned three of his companions—Horacio Vecchi, Martín Aranda Valdivia, and the temporal coadjutor Diego de Montalbán—to return with the chiefs to their tribes. That same afternoon, December 8, the demolition of the fort began. On the following morning the Indians departed for their homes in Elicura, a region nestled among the western foothills of the coastal range.

For the first few days everything went well. The report that Aranda and Vecchi sent back to the governor on December 10 was full of hope for the success of their mission:

The contentment that all the natives display on seeing us among them is unbelievable and inexplicable. One of their scouts tells us that the whole countryside is well-disposed, and that there is no Indian of any standing who opposes this peace and the pacification of the land, for they are all now convinced that the Spaniards are not planning any deceitful move as they had feared. Tomorrow we shall finish sending messengers throughout the land. All of them have sworn to sacrifice their lives in helping us achieve our goal. Everything is progressing very nicely, and we hope in the Lord that it will terminate successfully.[67]

By the afternoon of December 13 the travelers had reached the shores of Lake Llanalhue, where they passed the night in easy slumber.

But catastrophe both bloody and swift struck. On the morning of December 14, around nine o'clock, Anganamón and his followers swooped down on the camp and massacred its members in a barbarous fashion. Valdivia records the death of the three Jesuits in a few brief, descriptive lines:

Father Horacio received a lance wound in his neck, two cuts from an axe over his right ear, another in his side, and two lance thrusts in his back. Father Aranda, my cousin, they beat with clubs, crushing his entire skull and breaking every bone in his body. Brother Diego de Montalbán, a coadjutor novice of two months, whom I received into the Society here, suffered a fractured skull from the clubbing and received six lance wounds and one from an axe in his neck.[68]

Thus died the first Jesuit martyrs of Chile who sacrificed their lives in defense of the moral law and for the sake of peace in Araucania. Defensive warfare never fully recovered from the tragedy of their deaths, for with virtuous indignation the encomenderos cited the episode as proof of the futility of peaceful conquest. The massacre in Elicura, they claimed, demonstrated clearly that the Araucanians did not want peace and that war was the only feasible alternative. There were many others in the colony who held the same opinion.

ELICURA AND AFTER

IN DETERMINING THE SIGNIFICANCE of the Elicura incident, it is of paramount importance to know whether the missionaries were killed because of their association with defensive warfare, or because of Anganamón's desire for revenge. Valdivia's critics hold that only the first of these alternatives is historically tenable. The massacre, they assert, was part of a widespread plot to annihilate the whites and to lure the military away from the forts and expose the frontier to a deadly assault.[1] The altercation over Anganamón's wives provided the plotters with a perfect cover for their nefarious designs. What could seem more harmless than a private vendetta? As long as the colonists viewed the incident in this light, they would not be unduly upset and thus put on their guard. This explains why so many of the tribes pretended to accept the king's proposals of peace, and why the inhabitants of Elicura disclaimed any complicity in the crime. The demonstrations of friendship were meant to deceive the Spaniards and insure their entry into the trap.[2]

The plan did not succeed, the theory maintains, because of the wisdom and insight of Governor Ribera, who refused to send the army in pursuit of the culprits as Valdivia suggested. The attempt to interpret the disaster in terms of private vengeance is seen by some as a clever ruse by Valdivia and his associates to escape responsibility for the massacre and to conceal the flaws in their system of defensive warfare. Fearful lest the king begin to question the efficacy of peaceful conquest, they hoped to gloss over the true cause of the debacle and avoid the humiliation of having to scrap their plans.[3]

If this theory is correct, then the charges of misrepresentation and falsification that Valdivia's critics occasionally have leveled against him are measurably strengthened. For if the Jesuit deliberately manipulated the facts in this instance, might he not have done so on other occasions also? The present discussion thus involves not only an exercise in historical analysis, but also an evaluation of the veracity of a man who is highly esteemed by the Chilean people.

The basis for the charge of falsifying evidence appeared originally in Valdivia's letter of December 24, 1612, to the Jesuit provincial. Speaking of the events immediately preceding the murder of his brethren, he stated unreservedly:

> On the sixth day [after their departure from the fort in Paicaví], namely, on Friday, December 14, at nine o'clock in the morning, there arrived a troop of one hundred Indians from Pellaguén under the command of Anganamón, who spoke with the Fathers and demanded from them the release of his women. Father Horacio Vecchi replied by explaining that it was impossible to sanction their return because they were Christians, and the law of our God forbade a man to have more than one wife. They could, however, give back one of his daughters who was still a pagan. Anganamón, *furious because the Fathers had such a law and enforced it,* struck them, and the Indians stripped them of their garments prior to killing them.[4]

The same explanation occurs again in a report to the king two months later. In straightforward language, Valdivia recorded the circumstances of the incident. After describing the arrival of the missionaries in Elicura and the great satisfaction they experienced among the natives, he continued:

> Messages reached them from Pellaguén inviting them to visit [the province of] Purén. The caciques of Elicura, however, refused to let them go because of the promise they had given [to watch over the missionaries and to protect them]. In view of this refusal, Anganamón and Tureulipe came to Elicura with one hundred of their warriors. Maddened by the Fathers' failure to bring back his wives and daughters (whom he had lost through his own evil ways), Anganamón diabolically ordered them to be slain.[5]

That this account of the tragedy was acceptable to Valdivia's confreres is apparent from several independent sources. For example,

Father Pedro Torrelas, one of the Jesuits in Chile at the time, concluded his description of the massacre with these words:

> All of us are deeply grieved by such great treachery; but on the other hand, we also derive much spiritual consolation from their sacrifice and are inspired to lay down our lives in a similar undertaking. And surely, Father, there is no mission in these lands that offers more opportunities to do so, thanks to the obstinacy with which these Indians cling to their vices of drunkenness and polygamy. Knowing that the ministers of the Gospel, or, more correctly, the law of God, forbids indulgence in these vices, they have no use for the guardians of religion.[6]

Valdivia's provincial, Diego de Torres, viewed the incident in a similar light. The death of the missionaries, he informed the General of the Order, was "a joyous and most glorious end." Far from being discouraged over the misfortune, he found in it a source of consolation, for the martyrdom of the three religious, he noted, would encourage other Blackrobes to follow in their footsteps and would serve to convince the Araucanians of the king's desire for lasting peace. Once they realized that the entire nation was not going to be punished for the crimes of a few, they would readily accept the royal offers. The massacre did not, therefore, undermine the effectiveness of peaceful conquest, "for in no other year have the Spaniards suffered fewer reverses and fewer deaths, excepting only those of these blessed Fathers and Brother . . . nor in all of the four preceding years were so many men and women rescued from captivity as in the one just passed." Surely these and other significant gains justified the system Valdivia had introduced.[7]

The same line of reasoning runs through the memorial Father Gaspar Sobrino presented to the king in 1614, in which he took pains to show that the death of his fellow religious was not a result of peaceful conquest. Had hatred of the whites been the motive, the murderers would surely have spared their own countrymen. As it was, some Elicureans lost their lives in trying to protect the padres, while others became the captives of the slayers.[8] Sobrino might well have added that the Elicureans were the first to set out in pursuit of the culprits, that they stationed a guard of honor at the scene of the crime, and that they helped bring in the bodies of the victims when Governor Ribera refused to act in the matter.[9]

Why the Elicureans should have assumed the role of good Samaritans and why so many of them were themselves either killed or captured by Anganamón's band is hard to understand if the massacre was part of a general conspiracy. Equally difficult to understand, on that supposition, is the failure of the murderers to decapitate their victims and use the gruesome trophies as the recognized summons to united hostile action. Yet the bodies of the missionaries were left intact, as Torres recorded with manifest surprise: "They did not cut off their heads as is the custom among them." He attributed this oversight to "the singular providence of the Almighty, who did not wish to deprive us of such precious relics."[10] This unusual detail of the incident is ignored by those who postulate a native conspiracy.

Similarly, no satisfactory answer has yet been given to another objection that Sobrino originally expressed in his memorial. If Anganamón had already decided to kill the Jesuits prior to the dispute over his wives, then why did he refuse the offer of missionaries that Valdivia had made at their earlier meeting? If his protestations of loyalty at that time were feigned, would he not have welcomed the opportunity to get the religious into his power? As it happened, he made no attempt to exploit the offer. Consequently, it seems logical to conclude, with Sobrino, that the death of the missionaries was "purely accidental and had no intrinsic connection with the program of defensive warfare. It was not the result of the aforesaid system, and cannot be used as an argument against it."[11]

The seventeenth-century Jesuit historian Diego de Rosales arrived at the same conclusion in his treatise on defensive warfare, a work of more than one hundred and fifty printed pages that is one of the best detailed treatments of the subject available.[12] Rosales' account of the incidents preceding the massacre leaves no doubt as to its cause. Referring to Anganamón's role in pacifying the natives, he cited the testimony of Francisco Almendras, an officer in the Spanish army, who had spent many years as a captive among the Araucanians. Almendras was present at the parlamento in which Anganamón explained the peace proposals, and witnessed the eagerness with which the hostiles agreed to accept the royal offers. Rosales wrote that it was the Spaniards' refusal to release his wives that changed the cacique's attitude; the warlike Araucanian received their decision "with much anger and disgust, *and from that time on* he resolved to seek revenge, to disturb the peace, and to kill the padres if they came to evangelize."[13]

The accuracy of this statement is confirmed by another independent testimony, that of Francisco Núñez de Pineda y Bascuñán, a Spanish soldier who had also been a captive of the Araucanians. In a conversation with him in 1629, Anganamón disclosed that the reason for the assassinations was the perfidy of Meléndez, which was an insult to his honor. Had the Spaniards punished the offender as he deserved, all would have been well, but their failure to do so was a sign of their insincerity. He therefore determined to exact his own retribution.

> Shortly after my [Anganamón's] return [from Paicaví] I learned of the arrival in Elicura of two missionaries of the Company of Jesus, sent there by that same priest [Valdivia] who had deceived me.[14] Wishing to convince my in-laws of my personal grief [over the loss of my women] and to allay their suspicions,[15] as well as to gain some revenge for so heinous a crime, I gathered some two hundred of my friends and neighbors, went to the place where the padres were staying, and caused them to be killed like ravenous dogs. Judge for yourself whether or not I was justified in doing so in view of the insults to which I have referred.[16]

Núñez de Pineda adds that he doubted the veracity of this tale until he had a chance to investigate it personally following his release from captivity. After discussing the matter with "certain mature and trustworthy persons," he finally concluded that everything Anganamón had told him was true. His conviction failed to impress Barros Arana, who dismissed the account as a figment of Núñez de Pineda's imagination.[17] Though some parts of Pineda y Bascuñán's *Cautiverio feliz* do contain rhetorical embellishments, the incidents described are not necessarily historically false (and many are supported by evidence from other sources), for Núñez de Pineda had nothing to gain from fabricating lies. Barros Arana himself admits that there was some truth to the traditional opinion that revenge was the sole cause of the missionaries' deaths.

Several decades after the massacre in Elicura the ecclesiastical authorities in Concepción and Santiago began an investigation into the circumstances surrounding the death of the Jesuits, to ascertain whether the missionaries had sacrificed their lives in defense of the Faith and in so doing deserved to be honored as saints of the Church.[18] The two investigations ran consecutively and covered a period of several months in 1665. The one held in Concepción lasted from January to March and involved eighteen witnesses, while that conducted in Santiago took the depositions of eight witnesses between June and September. The testimony of these witnesses was recorded under oath and later forwarded to the Holy See.[19] All the witnesses agreed that the reason for the massacre was the zeal with which the missionaries upheld the law of God. One of them, Father Juan de Alvarez, was more explicit. He declared that it was the refusal of the governor and Father Valdivia to surrender the toqui's women "because they were Christians" that provoked the attack. "And for this reason the aforesaid cacique, Anganamón, became very indignant. He returned to his province [Purén], gathered a large band of followers, and invaded Elicura, killing the natives of that district because they had been responsible for bringing the religious into their lands. Then he went in search of the padres themselves and found them in the act of preparing for Mass." Anganamón angrily confronted the religious, demanding that they give back his wives, but the padres insisted that this was impossible unless he first renounced polygamy, since any other arrangement would be a serious offense against the moral law. "And because they defended this truth, the cacique and his followers slew them."[20] Alvarez added that Father Juan de Toledo, "a priest of singular virtue," would back up his assertions. Many Spaniards who had been captives of the Indians, he declared, had told Toledo repeatedly that the missionaries had died because of their zeal in preaching the Faith. Similar testimonies were given by Pedro de Castillo, a soldier in the king's army in 1612,[21] General Mieres y Arce, Captain Jiménez Lobillo, General Santiago Tesillo, Sergeant Meneses, and several other representatives of the military establishment. The testimony of these "hostile" witnesses is especially significant, for as army men they could more logically be expected to favor the Indian conspiracy theory.

The same can be said with reasonable assurance of the testimony of the Araucanian chieftains who appeared before the investigators in Concepción. Gullipangue, Anganamón's successor in the tribal hierarchy, had witnessed his predecessor's reaction to the doctrine of monogamous marriage. Anganamón was so enraged by this teaching, Guillipangue asserted, that "he went with his followers to seek out [the missionaries] in order to kill them as well as those who had received the Faith of Jesus Christ. And he did as he had planned."[22]

Of even greater weight is the statement made by Llancagueni, a cacique of Elicura, one of the few Elicureans present at the massacre who survived to tell the tale.

> Because two of his wives had fled to the Spaniards and had received baptism, Anganamón came to take them back. When the Spaniards refused to let them go he became angry and coming with a large retinue of warriors to Elicura, the territory of this witness, he killed all the Christians. Then he went in search of the padres who were preparing to say Mass. He assailed them with insults, calling them liars and preachers of lies who wished to prevent him from having many wives, and saying that they must die. . . . They tried to placate him by offering him payment as was the custom, but this also he refused. . . . After having confessed each other [they were put to death]. . . . This declarer hid himself to avoid being killed, and in this manner he escaped.[23]

The reliability of the evidence of the witnesses is accepted by two secular historians of the period, Córdoba y Figueroa and Carvallo y Goyeneche. The former errs in stating that Anganamón was a Christian, but the rest of his narrative agrees substantially with the accounts already cited. "Father Aranda," he wrote, "tried to appease [Anganamón's] wrath by explaining that the reason for their coming into his country was to preach the gospel, and that they were willing to compensate him with appropriate indemnities for the loss of his women. He exhorted him with apostolic fervor to live like a Catholic, since he was a Christian. Anganamón was too enraged to take notice of what was said . . . and he commanded them to be put to death as they were preparing to say Mass."[24] Carvallo y Goyeneche gives some additional interesting details:

> "Realizing that they were not going to give up his wives because they were Christians, [Anganamón] began to utter blasphemies against the law that deprived him of them, and against the padres who supported it. Having

been informed of their presence in Elicura, he armed two hundred of his
Indians and set out for that locality by hidden paths, determined to kill
all of its inhabitants because they had allowed representatives of a religion
that condemned polygamy to enter into their territory. . . . Hearing the
clamor of the enemy's cavalry, Father Aranda went out to face Anganna-
món who assaulted the padre with angry words . . . Father Aranda endeavored to calm the cacique and persuade him to become a Christian so
that he would be qualified to marry the woman he loved most. . . . He
offered to pay Anganamón whatever he stipulated as a recompense for
the loss of his wives, as was customary among the Araucanians. But
Anganamón began to blaspheme . . . and to shout *"lape, lape,"* which
means "Let them die! Let them die!" Whereupon his warriors approached the Jesuit and ran him through with their spears. Turculpi, one
of the caciques of Elicura, tried to save Father Vecchi's life by pulling
him up across the saddle of his horse. When Anganamón noticed this he
put spurs to his own mount and, overtaking them he personally killed
them on the spot, shouting: "Death to all these liars. Do not leave a single
one of them alive." He also slew almost all the inhabitants of that place,
and carried off ninety-two women captives. . . . These he took with him
to Purén, where, garbed in the sacred vestments [of the missionaries],
he celebrated his barbarous victory with the usual drunken orgies."[25]

The consistency of the participants in the ecclesiastical enquiries in
citing Anganamón's rage over the loss of his wives as the reason for
his actions confirms the theory that personal vengeance rather than any
clandestine political plot was the cause of the murders. Since it might
be objected,[26] however, that this interpretation is based on nothing
more reliable than the hearsay evidence of interested parties, it is profitable to examine more closely the credibility of these people.

Seventeen of the twenty-six persons who testified in the Concepción
and Santiago investigations were eyewitnesses to some of the events
they recounted. One, the cacique Llancagueni, was directly involved
in the disaster. Twelve were soldiers, inclined to be more skeptical in
their judgments than civilians. Ten were priests. Three were Araucanians. Only one was a woman, and she was the wife of a former army
captain. In other words, these witnesses were such that their testimony
cannot be discarded as prattle; it was the studied conviction of responsible citizens who had no reason to perjure themselves (for it must

be remembered that the statements they made were delivered under oath). In any case, who could have profited from falsifying evidence on this occasion? Surely not the witnesses themselves. The Jesuit Order would not have gained, for the good name of the Society would inevitably have suffered from such misrepresentations. Not the murdered victims either, for canonizations based on falsehoods have never succeeded. The collective testimony and other documentary evidence suggests only one valid conclusion: that the Elicura massacre was not part of a sinister plot to wipe out the Spaniards but was the frustrated gesture of a revengeful barbarian who smarted over a personal grievance.

This was clearly the conclusion of the public authorities in Santiago and Concepción also. In a letter of March 2, 1665, the cabildo of Concepción requested His Holiness Pope Alexander VII to accept the findings of the ecclesiastical tribunal as a reason for instituting canonization proceedings. "It is evident from this investigation," the cabildo wrote, "how much they deserve to be declared martyrs, for it is a common belief in the entire realm that they died in defense of the Faith while preaching the gospel to the infidel natives in Elicura."[27] The investigations of 1665 are thus a key consideration in the Elicura controversy, for they argue strongly that the death of the missionaries was not the result of peaceful conquest.

Public opinion in 1613, however, unlike that of a half century later, was not as dispassionate in its judgment of the incident. The murder of the missionaries had unpleasant repercussions throughout the colony. Despite the penalties leveled against the detractors of defensive warfare,[28] opposition to the system became increasingly vocal. But, as even Barros Arana admits, the Elicura episode was not the only cause for this disquiet. "There was in it something much less commendable than a zealous regard for the good of the realm."[29] This less commendable something was the selfish hostility of the encomenderos whose interests were endangered by peaceful conquest. In order to impress the Araucanians with the Crown's sincerity, the viceroy of Peru had decreed the abolition of compulsory personal service as a concomitant of defensive warfare. The encomenderos had evaded identical measures before, thanks to the cooperation of liberal-minded officials. But now they were faced with a different situation. Luis de Valdivia was no disinterested civil servant but a powerful, determined ecclesiastic whose prevailing interest was the welfare of the mapuches. More than that, he was the chosen agent of the Crown, with the backing of the king as well as the viceroy of Peru. As visitor general of the colony he was politically superior to both the audiencia and the governor. His word was law in anything that pertained to peaceful penetration. Already he had laid the foundation for sweeping reforms in the encomiendas and Indian pueblos of the southern provinces. Unless Valdivia could be stopped, unless defensive warfare could be discredited, the encomenderos knew that they were faced with ruin. The abolition of personal service meant the end of easy profits and of a lucrative slave trade, losses that the hacendados were unwilling to accept. The slaughter of the missionaries offered them a way out of their predicament; if they could turn the incident against Valdivia, the system of defensive warfare might soon be rescinded by the Crown.

The months immediately following the triple murder were a period of intensified activity in both camps. Notaries public spent much of their time recording statements of army officers, government flunkies, local politicians, and influential vecinos who hastened to tell the Crown of the disastrous consequences of defensive warfare and of the urgent necessity of suspending the system or of modifying the ordinances on personal service. The cabildos of Santiago, Concepción, and La Serena sided with the encomenderos by commissioning Fray Pedro de Sosa, Guardian of the Franciscan convent in Santiago, to protect their interests in Madrid. Sosa was also instructed to ask for military reinforcements to help reestablish Spanish prestige among the Araucanians, and to urge the Crown to continue paying the salaries of colonial troops until the complete pacification of Chile was a reality.[30] Sosa departed for Spain at the end of April 1613, with Pedro Cortés de Monroy, a military veteran of fifty-six years' experience in Chile, whom Governor Ribera had chosen to present the army's side in the fight against Valdivia.[31]

Both Valdivia and the Jesuit provincial Diego de Torres did their best to expose the unreasonableness of the attacks, Torres reminding Ribera that the murders were the work of one man's vengeance and would have occurred regardless of the political policy in force at the time. Even now, despite the adverse happenings in Elicura, the frontier was at peace and more and more Indians were laying down their weapons.[32] Valdivia expressed the same thought, and attributed the opposition of the military cabal to their fondness for the profitable slave hunts, which had been banned under the rules of defensive warfare.[33]

The reasoning of the two Jesuits convinced no one who did not want to be convinced. A group of eleven army captains countered with a memorial addressed to the king in which they heatedly insisted that unless the Crown authorized a resumption of active campaigning against the rebels the lives of the Spaniards would be in mortal danger and the whole colony would be threatened with economic disaster.[34]

Discouraging as the opposition of the governor and the military was, understandably more disheartening was that of the local clergy, led by Fray Pedro de Sosa, who pungently satirized the idea of peaceful conquest before the audiencia and other leading citizens of Santiago.[35] The Jesuit provincial promptly requested an explanation of Fray Sosa's philippic from the Father Visitor of the Franciscans in Chile. The judges of the audiencia also expressed their displeasure by ordering the friar to avoid the subject in future sermons. After a few months of official sparring, the Franciscan superior forbade Sosa under pain of excommunication to disgrace the pulpit with further polemics. Sosa interpreted the injunction literally. "Although he did not again refer to the subject in his sermons," an anonymous account of the incident reports, "he continued to speak of it in public and defended his views with great fortitude" until he left for Spain in April 1613.[36]

Governor Ribera's approval of the cabildos' action in naming Fray Pedro de Sosa procurator to Spain was largely responsible for widening the rift that had begun to appear between him and Valdivia following the latter's return to Chile. Even though Ribera owed his appointment to Valdivia, he resented deferring to a cleric in political matters. Furthermore, his military instincts balked at the idea of peaceful conquest; like most military strategists, he believed in armed force as the best way of putting an end to the Indian problem. The Elicura fiasco and the predatory raids that enemy guerrillas were making on the pacified tribes in Catiray and Arauco seemed to support this opinion. At all events, they afforded him a pretext for resuming the offensive.

Without waiting for approval from Lima, Ribera proceeded to invade Purén, the nucleus of armed resistance, with a sizeable force of Spaniards and Indian allies. He crossed the frontier on February 23, 1613, and advanced to Purén, where he inflicted heavy losses on the enemy by destroying large stores of provisions, burning many *ranchos* (small farms), killing some Indians, and capturing fifty women and children in addition to a number of horses.[37]

Ribera was jubilant; the entrada, he informed the king on April 17, had put new life into the troops who had grown very lackadaisical. It had also disheartened the enemy by showing them that the government still had power to punish their excesses, something they had begun to doubt because of Valdivia's insistence on peaceful means. The damages, he boasted, would have been greater still had the rebels decided to make a fight of it as they used to do in times past. The Spaniards, for their part, lost only one man who had foolishly wandered off by himself to pick grapes and had fallen into an ambush.[38]

Valdivia's qualified approval of the entrada points up a facet of his thinking that most historians have neglected. Defensive warfare, as he conceived it, was not something purely passive. It was a dynamic force that made ample provision for an expanding frontier and the use of military power when occasion demanded. He said as much in a letter to the king on February 20, 1613, a few days before the beginning of the invasion: "The experience of the past eight months proves that the system of defensive warfare Your Majesty has decreed is an effective one if it is applied with the necessary latitude that the defense of the colony requires. This means that we must not only oppose the enemy when they come to attack us in our own backyard, but we must also impede and discourage them from uniting against us." He accordingly suggested that Purén, the focal point of rebel intrigue, be made a part of the Spanish frontier, and that a fort be established there and another along the coast in Paicaví. If this were done the core of enemy resistance would be smashed, and "all the Indians who desire peace will seek the protection of these forts." These Indians could then be gathered into pueblos and taught how to defend themselves against future enemy attacks.[39] The whole tenor of the letter proves that Valdivia did not, as Barros Arana charges, "authorize the abolition of defensive warfare."[40] His approval of Ribera's action on this occasion was prompted by the need to defend the Indian allies in Araucania from continued depredations. This is clear from a report he submitted to the king in the following year. Referring to the inroads Ribera had made, Valdivia said: "The excuse the governor gives for making these entradas is his desire to repair the damages that the enemy has inflicted on the frontier tribes in Arauco and Catiray. . . . Those [who desire the abolition of defensive warfare] say that the only way we can protect our native allies and repair the harm they endure at the hands of the enemy is by making war. This is a manifest deception. Your Majesty's method [of warfare] includes the means of repairing these losses without violating the provisions of the system, namely, by bringing the friendly frontier tribes under the protection of our forces."[41]

Ribera's complacency over the success of his military tactics was soon shattered. On February 24, one day after the start of the initial campaign, his messengers had arrived in Lima with his report to Viceroy Mendoza of the Elicura debacle. Greatly upset by the news, Mendoza angrily reproached Ribera for his part in the proceedings, seeing in it a deliberate effort to discredit the experiment in peaceful conquest. If the governor had been convinced of the future treachery of the Araucanians, he should have taken steps to forestall it. He should not have dismantled the fort in Paicaví nor allowed the missionaries to depart without retaining some of the caciques as hostages for their safety. His failure to take such steps gave substance to the suspicion the Marquis had entertained from the beginning, namely, that Ribera wanted a continuance of offensive warfare. The stratagem would not succeed, however. "As long as I am in charge of the government of this realm," the viceroy declared, "there will be no change in this regard."[42]

Ribera replied by recalling the extensive powers Valdivia had received from the Crown, implying thereby that the responsiblity for the misfortune lay with him. His arguments carried no weight with the viceroy, who continued to support the Jesuit unreservedly. Ribera, in turn, became increasingly critical of Valdivia, accusing him of excessive credulity in his dealings with the hostiles. To prevent further blunders, he informed the king, "I have reassumed the authority that belongs to me for the exercise of my office, and I shall not surrender it to the padre in the future unless it contributes to Your Majesty's service in a way that will enable me to give a good account of my obligations."[43] In short, Ribera was defying Valdivia's authority as visitor general of Chile.

By the beginning of 1614 the rupture between Ribera and Valdivia was complete. The two men avoided each other as much as possible, preferring to handle necessary business by correspondence, and mutual recriminations became more and more bitter. Ribera, determined to enforce his own ideas, openly violated Valdivia's instructions by authorizing excursions into enemy territory, forbidding the Jesuits to work among the hostiles, and allowing the enslavement of natives caught with arms in their possession.[44] There was little that Valdivia could do to counteract these measures except refer the matter to the Crown for judgment. Early in 1614 his close friend and fellow missionary Father Gaspar Sobrino embarked for Spain to present his defense of Valdivia's experiment and to acquaint the king with conditions in Chile.

The controversy now shifted to Madrid, where Ribera's adherents, Fray Pedro de Sosa and Pedro Cortés, were lobbying for the abolition of defensive warfare; but their efforts were nullified by the arrival of Sobrino whose memorial of 1614 was a masterly defense of peaceful conquest.[45] Though the efficacy of this method of pacifying the Araucanians, he assured the king, was indisputable, it was not surprising that some people were still unconvinced, for the system had not yet received a fair trial. It had been in effect for only a short time, and even during that time it had not received the full support that the king had commanded. Furthermore, the Indians looked with suspicion on the Spaniards when they came bearing gifts and offers of peace, for the experience of more than seventy years had taught them that such advances were frequently the prelude to attacks on their liberty and welfare. Only time, patience, and understanding would make them change their minds.

Despite these handicaps, the system had already produced outstanding results. The rebellious provinces of Arauco, Tucapel, and Catiray had come to terms with the Spaniards following the capitulation of two thousand warriors. The governor attributed this success to the army, but a comparison of conditions showed his claim to be groundless.

Before the advent of defensive warfare the frontier had been in a state of bloody unrest. Fear of the Indians had paralyzed the inhabitants of Concepción and Chillán and even those in Santiago, eighty leagues away. Communications between Concepción and the garrison at San Pedro, two leagues farther south, were limited to infrequent night dispatches because of the danger of daytime travel. Thus when Valdivia and Sobrino had set out for San Pedro, two companies of cavalry had accompanied them "because the way was so perilous." Following the publication of the king's offers, however, within six weeks Sobrino had been able to make the same journey by himself without fear of attack, and Valdivia had traveled all the way from San Pedro to the fort in Catiray with only two Spanish companions, "a trip that a regiment of four hundred soldiers would have hesitated to undertake a short time before." No armed force had been used, yet the results achieved surpassed anything accomplished in a comparable period during the preceding seventy years of oppression and strife. "Neither Governor Alonso de Ribera, with his extensive military experience and ability, nor any of his predecessors had succeeded in persuading two thousand Araucanians to lay down their arms in favor of peace despite the severe losses they had inflicted on the natives in full-scale campaigns."[46] What military prowess had failed to accomplish, peaceful conquest had made a reality. Ribera himself had admitted this earlier before his mind had become poisoned against Valdivia's experiment.[47]

The pacification of large areas of Araucania was not the only benefit resulting from defensive warfare. Several Spaniards, including Don Alonso de Quesada, Sergeant Juan de Torres, Francisco Fernández, a Dominican friar, and three women had been rescued from captivity during the early months of the experiment, something that had not been accomplished during four years of all-out fighting. Furthermore, commerce between the two nations, one of the king's objectives in approving the system, had increased with the introduction of friendly treatment for the natives.

Most important of all was the advance of Christianity among the Araucanians. In fourteen months more than seven hundred had received baptism, and over three hundred had been married in the Church. "Besides this, when I left Arauco on the first day of Lent 1614, more than fifty native catechumens were receiving instructions daily in our church, something that had never happened before among recently pacified Indians in Chile during seventy years of offensive warfare."[48]

A further consideration was the fact that only one Spaniard had died as a result of this experiment,* and that the only damages suffered were those inflicted on the Indian allies. Even these losses ceased as soon as the friendly Indians were gathered into villages under the protection of the Spanish forts. Since the system was obviously proving successful, what reason was there, Sobrino asked, for a change in policy?

Sobrino then went on to discuss Ribera's support of the project during its early stages, quoting at length from the governor's letters, which showed that he had recognized the merits of the new form of pacification. Writing to a Jesuit acquaintance, Father Juan de Fuenzalida, on August 1, 1612, Ribera had announced his intention of enforcing the system rigidly regardless of the protests of those who condemned "this common good because of their deplorable self-interest." One month later he had informed the same correspondent that "those who oppose [this experiment] are not motivated by zeal nor military science, but only by passion mixed with envy and other things that I refrain from mentioning. Their outcries do not disturb me."[49] Similarly, when certain religious in Santiago ventured to denounce the system publicly from the pulpit, Ribera warned the religious superiors to instruct their subjects to give support to the measure, "for anything to the contrary would displease His Majesty very much." The undertaking, he assured them, was based on such sound reasons that "those of us who are familiar with it are convinced of its suitability. The good results that we continue to experience have impressed all the officials and soldiers who are able to view the effects from close at hand. . . . And I assure Your Paternity that the course we are now following does not involve any danger. Rather it offers great promise of accomplishing the ends which we desire."[50]

To Diego de Torres, the Jesuit provincial, the governor wrote on August 31, 1612: "I am not the least bit upset over the activities of people in this town [Concepción] who criticize this type of war with so little justification and so little knowledge of military affairs. For

---

* This one was a victim of the Indian ambush during Ribera's march to Purén in February 1614. Sobrino did not consider the murder of the missionaries a consequence of defensive war.

military science is not their profession, nor do they understand what is really meant by offensive and defensive war."[51] Ribera went on to state that the program was well planned and that those who opposed it were afraid that this new method of conquest would result in the abolition of forced labor and the enactment of other measures designed to improve the lot of the Indians.[52]

Economic considerations did not, however, provide the full explanation of this irritating split in public opinion. Some people, the governor noted, opposed the system simply because of their antagonism to the Jesuits; had the king entrusted the program's execution to others, these malcontents would have been enthusiastic supporters. As it was, they were "maliciously trying to discredit the whole undertaking." But, "as far as I am concerned," Ribera stated, "this opposition is sheer nonsense. The king's orders must be carried out, regardless of who suffers in the process, and the evil intentions of these scoundrels must be blocked."[53]

Strange words, indeed, when one compares them with the text of the governor's letter to Valdivia on February 9, 1614, following his unauthorized resumption of offensive warfare: "Your Paternity may hold this for certain, that if the methods you favor had not been introduced here, the country would be in a much better condition and might even be entirely pacified. It is this program of peaceful conquest that keeps the colony in such a sorry state. As long as it remains in effect conditions will not improve. On the contrary, they will daily grow worse. It is impossible that anyone who considers the situation dispassionately will not arrive at the same conclusion."[54]

Sobrino confessed that he did not understand the reason for Ribera's change of heart. It could not be due to a lack of familiarity with the state of affairs in Chile for he had served an earlier term as governor of the colony. Nor could it be the result of military ineptitude or of ignorance of the ways of the hostiles. The history of fourteen months of defensive warfare could not easily justify a loss of confidence in the system either. Whatever may have been the cause of his sudden volteface, one thing was certain: Ribera no longer had any intention of enforcing the king's decrees regarding the pacification of Araucania. The most important of these decrees, the one abolishing personal service, had been ignored. So, too, had the one forbidding the army to engage in *malocas* (slave hunts) across the border. At least four such excursions had taken place during the first fourteen months of defensive warfare. "It should be noted," Sobrino wrote, "that the alleged purpose of these malocas was to compensate our Indian allies for the manpower losses they had suffered at the hands of the enemy. I hereby inform Your Majesty—and I speak as an eyewitness—that not a single captured Indian was turned over to our friends. On the contrary, some of them were assigned to various military officials, while others were auctioned off for eighty and one hundred reales, depending on their physical condition." Consequently, apart from the fact that these entradas were clearly against the king's orders, not even their ostensible purpose had been achieved; thus they accomplished nothing but to rearouse the soldiers' greed for slaves and to disturb the peace. These slave hunts also violated another royal decree granting liberty to all Indians captured after the establishment of defensive war. "This is an injustice that demands an immediate remedy," Sobrino urged, "especially since these malocas were not necessary for the defense of the colony, and only succeeded in stirring up the Indians and in defeating Your Majesty's aims." Finally, the royal order that none of the rebels who accepted the peace proposals was to be given in encomienda had been violated by Ribera in Catiray. As long as such conditions prevailed, Sobrino predicted, defensive warfare was doomed to failure, not because of intrinsic weaknesses but because of a lack of official cooperation.[55]

Sobrino's eloquent defense of the system, plus the viceroy's evident distrust of the opposing faction, convinced the legislators and the king that a policy change would be inadvisable.[56] In a series of decrees issued from Burgos on November 21, 1615, Philip III reiterated his approval of defensive warfare and ordered it to be enforced with all the authority at his command.[57] The governor of Chile was reminded in strong terms of his subordinate role in the enterprise. Only Valdivia and his religious associates were to have complete charge, only they could hold conferences with the hostiles in the future, and only Valdivia could appoint interpreters. Ribera was to respect and enforce all concessions that Valdivia made to the Indians, and he was to allow as many religious as the Jesuit judged prudent to work among the unpacified tribes. Valdivia was also authorized to establish mission stations wherever he thought necessary. The viceroy of Peru was instructed to appoint a new visitor general whose duty it would be to guarantee the observance of these regulations and to set free all rebels who had been captured and enslaved during the last few years.

Slave hunts into hostile territory were strictly forbidden. Punitive expeditions could be undertaken only for the purpose of rescuing captives and punishing enemy invaders. In the future all prisoners of war were to be kept in jail until they could be exchanged for Spaniards who had fallen into the hands of the rebels. The pacified natives of Aracuo, Catiray, Elicura, and Paicaví were to receive a regular salary for their work. In short, Ribera was to confine his activities to guarding the frontier and allow Valdivia to take care of all other relations with the Araucanians.[58]

These royal injunctions were a complete vindication of Valdivia's conduct. The only reproof that the Jesuit received from the king was a mild admonition urging him to live in harmony with the governor.[59] Valdivia's ideas had won a singular triumph in the council halls of Spain. Defensive warfare had carried the day.

In a sense, Ribera was more fortunate than the rest of the anti-Valdivia faction. Unconfirmed news of the king's intentions reached Chile early in 1616 following the arrival in Peru of a new viceroy, Don Francisco de Borja y Aragón, Prince of Esquilache, who assumed control in December 1615. But the full import of Philip III's decision was not known in the colony until the arrival in March 1617, of the royal cédula of January 3, 1616. By that time Ribera was already dead. Worn out by a strenuous career and debilitating infirmities, the governor had breathed his last on March 9, 1617, shortly before the arrival of the official decree.[60] His death was a fitting climax to the first phase of the controversy over peaceful conquest.

Valdivia, finding himself freed of the man whose opposition had been like an albatross around his neck, wrote to the king a few days later: "Your governor Alonso de Ribera passed away on the ninth day of this present month of March 1617. His death will put an end to the multitude of reports and relations opposing the resolutions of Your Majesty, and to the extraordinary diligence he practiced in securing the support of the cabildos, religious Orders, and army officers for his views."[61]

Ribera's demise and the resolute cooperation of the new viceroy facilitated for a time the execution of Valdivia's mission. The Prince of Esquilache needed no prodding from Madrid to throw the full weight of his office behind the program. As a blood relative of Francisco de Borja, Duke of Gandia and third General of the Society of Jesus, his sympathies were with the Jesuits. Luis Merlo de la Fuente, one-time governor of Chile and judge at the time of the audiencia of Lima, cited this family connection as the main reason for Esquilache's unwavering support of the Jesuits in Chile. Speaking of his own efforts to change official policy, the oidor said:

> I urged the viceroy many times . . . to convene a junta composed of Father Gaspar Sobrino and of all those whom he considered most inclined to his views, in order that the situation might be thoroughly investigated and the most useful decision be taken. And although the viceroy assured me frequently that he would do so, he never did . . . mainly because of the extraordinary influence that [the Jesuits] had with him on account of the memory of Father Francisco de Borja.[62]

Esquilache made his views known promptly to the acting governor of Chile, Fernando Talaverano Gallegos,[63] ordering him to carry out the royal decrees to the letter and threatening to take over the appointment of army officials personally if he displayed any laxity in following the orders. At the same time he informed Gallegos that he was appointing Hernando Machado, fiscal of the audiencia of Lima, visitor general of the colony, an appointment possibly prompted by Valdivia's superiors who had never completely approved of Valdivia's political authority in the position.[64]

Gallegos was willing to follow the viceroy's lead, for he was an old man and had had his fill of political intrigue. Moreover, he learned the wisdom of refraining from any expression of doubt about peaceful conquest, when shortly after taking office he ventured to acquaint the viceroy with the dissatisfaction that the latest royal dispatches had evoked in Chile. In reply, the viceroy rebuked him for failing to "chastise those who do not respect the commands of the king," adding that "unless this situation is remedied I shall personally assume full control of the colony, and I shall assign all offices in the army to persons who will aid and advance the regulations His Majesty has issued with such great prudence and after mature investigation.... Your Excellency ought not to weary yourself," Esquilache warned Gallegos, "with writing reports that are contrary to peace and defensive war, and least of all with making suggestions that are inimical to what Father Luis [de Valdivia] prescribes in this matter."[65] It is not surprising, therefore, that in the ten months during which he supervised the destinies of the colony, Gallegos carefully abstained from interfering with Valdivia in any way. The Jesuit reciprocated by pushing forward the work of pacification with renewed vigor. With the governor he visited the isolated frontier forts, released the Indians imprisoned in them, and after baptizing many of them allowed them to return to their homes as advocates of goodwill among their people. More and more tribes sued for peace, ignoring for the time being the guerrilla activities of Anganamón, Tureulipe, and others who continued to vent their animosity in recurrent raids on the Spanish outposts. While Valdivia was engaged in visiting the forts, Hernando Machado was making his presence felt. Faithful to the instructions he had received from the viceroy, he freed some six hundred Indians whom the Spaniards had captured in illegal malocas during the preceding five years.[66] When the cabildo of Concepción expressed disapproval of the action, Machado promptly silenced them with the threat of imprisonment if they refused to quiet down. Thus by the end of 1617 Valdivia's position in the colony was stronger than ever.

His status was further enhanced by the arrival on January 12, 1618, of the new governor of Chile, Don Lope de Ulloa y Lemos, who brought with him four weighty letters from the Prince of Esquilache.[67] The first of these urged the audiencia of Santiago to abolish the servicio personal of the Indians.[68] The second, to Valdivia, approved his measures "for the defense and security of the realm," praised him for his unselfish devotion to duty, and urged him to continue his efforts for the total suppression of slave labor. The viceroy also announced his intention of writing to all the provincials of religious Orders in Chile to guarantee their unqualified support of peaceful conquest.[69] The remaining two documents reminded the bishop of Santiago and the military officials to adhere strictly to the decisions of the king and to assist Father Valdivia in securing the abolition of compulsory service.[70] As the contents of these letters indicate, the Jesuit's triumph over his critics could not have been more complete.

The second phase of the experiment in peaceful conquest came to an abrupt end in November 1619, when Valdivia suddenly decided to return to Spain. His abrupt departure has been a source of perplexity for some historians. Barros Arana, for instance, frankly confessed that he could find no explanation for this development: "This journey [to Spain] at a time when the Father Visitor was at the height of his power and when his system was in full-blown operation, without, however, producing the results expected of it, seems to lack reason and is truly inexplicable."[71]

Actually, there was nothing very mysterious about the Jesuit's decision to leave Chile. It was the product of a bitter disagreement between him and the new provincial of Paraguay, Pedro de Oñate. On more than one occasion Valdivia's adversaries had accused him of immoral deeds. None of these charges had ever been proved and some had been retracted,[72] but their very existence drew the attention of superiors to his conduct. Zealous of the Order's good reputation, the new provincial closely scrutinized the missionary's actions and discovered some possible indiscretions (such as the placing of a hand on the head of a distressed female Indian while trying to console her), which might provide ammunition for scandalmongers. It seems certain that Oñate never suspected Valdivia of anything more serious than this, but his handling of the situation left room for doubt. He sternly reprimanded his subject, admonishing him to avoid such mistakes in the future, and reinforced his warning with ecclesiastical censures. Valdivia's reaction was characteristic. His sense of justice had been bruised, he found it difficult to submit any longer to the direction of a superior whom he suspected of unwarranted antipathy, and so he decided to leave.[73] Saying that he wanted to inform the viceroy and the king of the state of affairs in Chile, he asked for and received permission from the provincial to proceed to Lima and Madrid; then he hurriedly left the colony, never to return.[74]

Valdivia's departure was another turning point in the fitful struggle for the peaceful conquest of Araucania. Although he left behind him a group of coreligionists imbued with the same spirit and principles that had moved him, none of them attained the political stature that made his role in the history of defensive warfare so unique. Without that advantage they were handicapped in combating abuses in a system that the propertied classes openly condemned. Philip III died on March 31, 1621, and was succeeded by his son, Philip IV, who displayed far less generosity in his provisions for the Indians. Although he lent his support to a revised version of Esquilache's tasa, he emasculated it by legalizing the enslavement of rebel Araucanians. From this point on, the course to a final suspension of defensive warfare was short and straight. Less than three years later, on April 13, 1625, Philip IV issued the decree that put an end to Valdivia's dream.[75] The royal cédula reached Santiago on January 24, 1626. On the following day Governor Fernández de Córdoba ordered it to be published throughout the realm.[76] Defensive warfare was legally dead.

THE TURBULENT MIDDLE YEARS

WITH THE DEPARTURE of Luis de Valdivia in 1619 the Indians of Chile lost their most powerful intercessor, but the loss brought to the fore other Jesuits who were excellently qualified to continue his work, and to continue it without the political rivalries and power plays that had accompanied his efforts. Gaspar Sobrino, Francisco de Astorga, Juan de Moscoso, and Francisco de Vargas were the nucleus of a group that quietly kept alive the ideals for which Valdivia had striven. Outstanding among them was Diego de Rosales, a man of many talents, who may be considered Valdivia's successor in the struggle for Indian justice. Rosales inspired confidence and scorned self-praise; he combined erudition, executive ability, and tact with a remarkable skill for working with people. Under his thoughtful leadership the Jesuits in Chile performed some of their greatest work in the seventeenth century.

Rosales was born in Madrid in 1603,[1] to Don Jerónimo de Rosales and Doña Juana Baptista de Montoya, who belonged to the most select stratum of Spanish nobility.[2] As a young man, he gave promise of a brilliant career. His family background and personal attainments assured him of success in almost any field, but the young hidalgo aspired to something more durable than worldly acclaim. After receiving his degree from the university of Alcalá, he exchanged his scholar's robes for the simpler garb of a Jesuit scholastic.[3] By the mid-1620's Rosales was in Lima, where he completed his studies for the priesthood and was ordained.[4] When Vicente Modolell, rector of the Jesuit college in Santiago, visited Lima in 1629 Rosales asked for and received permission to return with him to Chile. Before the end of that year he had been appointed superior of the mission in Arauco.

The next thirty years of his life were spent almost entirely among the Indians. Building on the foundations Valdivia had laid, Rosales traveled from one end of Araucania to another, converting and instructing the heathen. The majority of the inhabitants of Arauco, Boroa, Purén, Tucapel, and Labapié accepted the Faith under his guidance.[5] His sympathy for the natives, his command of their language,[6] and his interest in their physical and spiritual welfare made a lasting impression on the Indians who regarded him as one of their own.

The Indians' need for a protector was greater than ever in the middle decades of the seventeenth century. Brutality and greed stalked the frontier following the abandonment of peaceful conquest. The decree of April 13, 1625, had been the signal for a concentrated assault on the native population, for, although the king had authorized the enslavement of rebels only, his subjects on the outskirts of empire were not overly concerned about this restriction. The supplementary license to attack the Indians "in the manner that was customary before the establishment of defensive warfare"[7] provided them with all the legal justification they needed. The prospect of booty served as an incentive to keep conscript soldiers from deserting, but unfortunately the only booty to be had in Araucania was the Araucanians themselves. It was regrettable that the pacified natives were easier to catch than their less docile relatives. But as everybody knew, war was full of hardships, and a soldier was entitled to take what he could, especially when he was underpaid. Furthermore, so the arguments went, the Indians had only themselves to blame for their current predicament, for they should not have resisted the Spaniards in the first place. Just how this reasoning applied to the pacified tribes was never made clear.

The renewal of offensive hostilities thus became a screen for an extensive commerce in Indian slaves. Hundreds of victims were seized in malocas and shipped off to Peru, where they commanded better prices than on the Chilean market. The greed for *piezas*, as the victims of the malocas were contemptuously called, affected commoner and hidalgo alike, including even the governor himself. Luis Fernández de Córdoba y Arce, who ruled Chile from 1625 to 1629, gleefully informed the king on one occasion that he had captured more than two hundred and fifty Indians during his campaign in the province of Imperial in 1627, and had killed or captured over two thousand five hundred more in the territories of Yumbel and Arauco.[8] The deportation of piezas eventually assumed such proportions that the king had to step in to forbid the practice anew.[9] The decision seems to have been prompted by the vociferous objections of the Chilean hacendados, for the supply of encomienda Indians had decreased so alarmingly in the northern provinces as a result of epidemics, desertions, and cruelties that the vecinos in Santiago had begun to import workers from the province of Cuyo across the Andes. The abuses that followed aroused the wrath of the bishop of Santiago, Francisco de Salcedo, whose protests finally persuaded the Crown to stop the traffic.[10] These actions, while good in themselves, provided the Indians with scant relief. Although the number of slaves sent to Peru diminished temporarily, the slave trade itself continued to flourish, the only difference being that now it was diverted more directly into local channels.

The unauthorized practice of selling friendly natives as slaves under the guise of having captured them in war, led to the revival of a brutal expedient, that of branding all captured rebels to identify them as legal slaves.[11] If the government hoped by this means to protect the pacified tribes from indiscriminate raiding, it was sadly disappointed. The military simply branded all Indians who fell into their hands—pacified and unpacified alike, irrespective of age or sex—and sold them freely as bona fide slaves.

Hoping to remedy the situation before it got completely out of hand, Governor Fernández de Córdoba finally issued an edict forbidding the branding of any rebel who had not been presented to the authorities within three months after his capture so that his name could be entered in the official register as a certified slave. He also established severe penalties for the branding of Indians who were neither rebels nor slaves, and sought to clamp down on the clandestine transportation of slaves to Peru by assigning a fine of five hundred pesos and loss of the slaves for each violation.[12] But despite these enactments, the abuses in the slave trade went on. Too many people, including too many government functionaries and politicians, were profiting from the trade to be concerned about cleaning up the mess.

The profiteering had to end sooner or later. And end it did. Some of the more sober-minded citizens in the colony, appalled at the viciousness, decided to act. The fight began in earnest shortly after Francisco Lazo de la Vega became governor of Chile in 1629.[13] The Jesuits, led by two of their most persuasive apologists, Juan de Alvis, ex-rector of the Colegio Máximo in Santiago, and Diego de Rosales, a close friend and unofficial adviser of the governor, threw the full weight of their learning and prestige into the movement.[14]

The controversy that ensued centered almost exclusively on the issue of the legality of branding slaves. This was the real crux of the problem, for the king had already taken a stand against the enslavement of pacified natives and the sale of legal slaves outside the colony. If the moralists could show that branding was illegal and impractical and that it ought to be condemned, the case would be closed.

In preparing their brief in favor of abolition, the Jesuits relied on moral, legal, and pragmatic arguments. They first attacked the practice on doctrinal grounds: God had created man in His own image and likeness; it was not moral, therefore, to disfigure any part of the human composite, which had been dignified in so noble a manner.[15] They next cited a royal decree of 1532, giving their position a legal foundation: when the branding of slaves had been discussed at that time, Charles V had prohibited the practice; since this prohibition had not been revoked by subsequent decrees, its effect was still binding. The Jesuits' final argument turned out to be the most compelling: the branding of captured rebels, they observed, had begun to boomerang, for instead of tamely bowing to the mutilation inflicted on their tribesmen, the hostiles had stolen a page out of the Spaniards' book and were administering the same treatment to all white soldiers who fell into their hands. A measure that produced such objectionable results was clearly impractical and, consequently, ought to be abolished.[16]

After diligently examining these and other reasons that the indigenistas advanced, the viceroy of Peru, the Count of Chinchón, called on the governor and the audiencia of Chile to explain why they tolerated such a practice. In its reply the audiencia humbly admitted that the branding of rebels was a violation of the royal decree of 1532, but added that circumstances had seemed to justify the action, especially since it was an approved custom in many other countries. However, seeing that the practice was destroying all hope of peace and was causing the natives to seek revenge, the members of the audiencia, including its fiscal,[17] were now convinced that there should be no further branding of slaves.

The governor of Chile, Lazo de la Vega, took a different stand. As a soldier he favored harsh measures when dealing with an enemy, and saw no reason to change the practice. He maintained that the decree of 1532 did not apply to Chile because it had been issued before the Spaniards entered the territory. Moreover, it had apparently been designed to protect Indians who were peaceful and legally free. Since the Araucanians did not fit into this category, the decree did not cover them. Furthermore, if the king were to forbid the branding of rebels, the natives would interpret his action as a reversion to defensive warfare, and would attribute it to fear rather than mercy. The decision would likewise mean loss for the army, for unless the soldiers had some way of identifying their piezas, they would be unable to recover them if they fled. The practice of branding captives should, therefore be continued.[18]

After discussing the question thoroughly with his advisers and other "men of conscience,"[19] the viceroy decided to leave the final decision to someone else. He accordingly referred the matter to the authorities in Spain, together with his suggestion that the branding of slaves be modified to allow it to be done only on the hands. This solution would satisfy the military by making it possible for them to identify and recover fugitives, and it also would satisfy the indigenistas who objected to the disfiguring of a man's countenance.[20] The viceroy, a good politician, knew how to compromise in a difficult situation.

Four members of the king's junta de guerra — the Marquis of Fuentes, the Marquis of Castrofuerte, the Count of Humanes, and Bartolomé de Anaya—voted for the proposal unconditionally, while four others—Felipe de Silva, Hernando de Villaseñor, Diego de Cárdenes, and Lorenzo Ramírez de Prado—opposed it. De Silva and Ramírez, however, were willing to allow branding on the hand in the case of prisoners who had escaped and were recaptured. The remaining member of the junta, the Count of Castrello, straddled the fence; without committing himself either way, he advised passing the buck back to the viceroy on the score that he was in a better position to know all the pros and cons of the case.[21] This was precisely what that official had been trying to avoid. Philip IV's thinking on the subject was expressed in one brief sentence scrawled at the bottom of the junta's report: "Since the vote [of the junta] is not conclusive, I think it best that the matter be referred back to the viceroy, as the Count of Castrello suggests, together with the reasons that determined the voting."[22]

A few days later, Philip IV dispatched a decree to the Count of Chinchón in which he authorized him either to approve the existing practice of branding slaves on the face, to permit branding on the hands only, or to prohibit branding entirely except on the hands of fugitive slaves who had been recaptured. Another decree containing a summary of these instructions was sent at the same time to the governor of Chile urging him to cooperate with the viceroy in the matter and to enforce the decision wih diligence.[23]

The result of this lengthy debate, characterized by the typical reluctance of high officials to assume responsibility, was the effective abolition of the brutal custom. Influenced, perhaps, by the thinking of Diego de Torres, who had served for a time as his private confessor, the Count of Chinchón decided to outlaw the branding of Indians entirely.[24] It was in its own way a significant decision for it not only cleared the way for a possible rapprochement between Indians and whites, but it also underlined the role that public opinion could play in the achievement of social reform. Had it not been for the determined efforts of a few private citizens in Santiago, it is doubtful whether the demand for reform would ever have been heard.

Lazo de la Vega's tenure as governor of Chile (1629–39) was marked by another event of some importance: the promulgation of another tasa. Like its predecessors, Lazo's tasa potentially could reduce the irritation between Indians and whites, and like its predecessors, it remained largely inoperative.[25]

As mentioned in a previous chapter, Philip IV had introduced a number of significant changes into Viceroy Esquilache's tasa before approving it in 1622. Although most of these revisions were definitely favorable to Spanish interests in the colony, the encomenderos obstinately refused to abide by the new regulations, and with the cooperation of sympathetic local officials they managed to emasculate the reform completely. Governor Fernández de Córdoba blandly informed the king on February 1, 1627, that conditions in Chile made it impossible to enforce the objectionable provisions, and that he was suspending them until His Majesty's counselors could devise something more appropriate.[26] The presence in the colony of a new visitor general, Cristóbal de la Cerda, whom the viceroy of Peru had appointed to investigate the situation in Chile, did not produce any change. In its session of August 19, 1628, the cabildo of Santiago passed a resolution urging the visitor to enforce the tasa in the districts he inspected, but they did so without any fear because they were certain that "it would be impossible to iron out the difficulties that the measure involved." In other words, the cabildo did not object to his trying because they knew in advance that he would be unable to accomplish anything.[27]

The governor's announcement caused quite a furor in Madrid when it arrived, for Esquilache's tasa had been the first in a series of such measures to receive royal confirmation and to be incorporated into the codex of laws for the Indies; disregard of its provisions was consequently a much more serious offense than it had been with respect to previous tasas, and one more directly calculated to arouse the king's displeasure. Whether or not this actually happened is a matter of conjecture, but the fact is that Philip IV suddenly reversed his earlier position and on April 14, 1633, signed a decree abolishing the servicio personal "wherever and in whatever form it existed" in Chile.[28] The Indians were not excused from paying tribute, but the tribute was to take the form of money or fruits of the land rather than physical labor. The composition of the tasa was left to the discretion of the governor who was to recruit the aid of experienced ecclesiastics, crown officials, and other periti to work out the necessary details. The new legislation was to become effective within six months after the receipt of the royal decree.

Philip's decision, implying as it did a radical change in the economic system of the colony, led to such a "monstrosity of opinions"[29] that the execution of the tasa seemed entirely hopeless. After examining dozens of conflicting pareceres, Lazo sought the advice of the audiencia as to whether or not he should attempt to implement the decree of April 14.[30] The opinion of that tribunal was divided. Pedro Machado de Cháves was in favor of implementation "because of the numerous evils that the Indians suffer and because the royal tasa of 1622 was not being enforced except in things prejudicial to the natives." Adaro y Samartín thought that the decree ought to be respected in its entirety "except for the provisions regarding the congregation of natives into pueblos, and the payment of tribute in money or kind." He advised that no definite action be taken until the king had a chance to reexamine the matter and to prescribe something else. Since these two points constituted the essence of the king's command, Adaro y Samartín was, for all practical purposes, voting against it. Cristóbal de la Cerda favored the abolition of personal service but felt that "since the principal purpose of the decree was to assist the Indians in the profitable enjoyment of their freedom, it would be contrary to their liberty to force them to live in reductions against their will or to oblige them to pay taxes in kind instead of in physical labor if they preferred the latter." He therefore recommended that Indians who wished to remain on the haciendas of the Spaniards or who wished to continue paying the labor tax be allowed to do so. Otherwise the aim of the decree would be frustrated and the same inconveniences would follow from this tasa as from previous ones.[31]

The cabildo of Santiago finally decided to get into the act also. In its session of March 10, 1635, the cabildo appointed a commission composed of two army alcaldes, two former corregidores (Diego González Montero and Diego Jaraquemada), Captains Juan Ortiz de Urbina and Andrés de Fuenzalida, and the Licentiate Caspar de Lillo to study the possibility of a new tasa and submit a report to the governor.[32] In another session two weeks later the town fathers instructed the procurator general of Santiago, Juan Rudolfo Lisperguer y Solórzano, to inform the governor that in their opinion it would be more useful to collect the tribute in the form of labor and to allow the Indians to reside on the estates of the encomenderos instead of forcing them to congregate into villages.[33] Lisperguer carried out his instructions without delay. A few days later he presented the governor with a summary of the cabildo's views, which that official promptly passed on to the fiscal of the audiencia, Pedro Machado de Cháves, for consideration.

Machado was equally diligent in preparing his report. Early the following month, on April 6, he issued a lengthy statement in which he reviewed the effectiveness of the earlier tasas and concluded by recommending the immediate enactment of the royal decree of April 14, 1633, exempting the Indians from forced labor.

> Your Excellency [he assured the governor] ought to carry out this decree because it is most just and is founded on natural law, both human and divine. No theologian approves of free men being made to serve others

for the space of a lifetime against their will, without being free to work for others, or to learn trades, or to relax with their families, or to acquire property of their own . . . [none of which is possible to the natives of this realm] who are constantly employed in some occupation or other all year long without enjoying any liberty to do as they please with the time that remains after they have paid the labor tribute.[34]

Machado's reasoning convinced Lazo de la Vega. Ten days later, on April 16, 1635, he promulgated the ordinances that bear his name.[35]

The new legislation consisted of sixteen articles, none of which made any provision for slaves captured in the war. It declared the servicio personal abolished for all Indians regardless of whether they were living in native reductions or on property belonging to private citizens. They were in the future to be treated as all other vassals of the king, but they still had to pay tribute to their encomenderos, either in money or in kind (grain, livestock, poultry, lentils, anise seed, and so forth). Payments were to be made yearly during March and in the presence of the proper authorities, namely, the curate and the protector of the Indians in the case of natives attached to encomiendas, or the curate and the administrator of the village for those living in reductions. The corregidores were given the job of fixing a just price for the products offered in payment of the tax. Although forced labor was prohibited as a form of tax, the Indians could, nevertheless, pay their tribute with manual work if they voluntarily chose to do so and informed the corregidor of their intention.[36] They were also free to choose to live either in the native pueblos or on the farms and haciendas of the Spaniards. A native was permitted to hire out his services to employers whose property lay within four leagues of the Indian's home, but he was urged to work for his own encomendero until he had paid off the required tribute and had earned his share of the salaries of the protector, corregidor, and *doctrinero* (catechist).

In drawing up the provisions of the tasa the governor was careful to specify the exact payment the natives were to receive for a day's work, as well as the form the salaries were to take. The wage scale was set at two reales a day payable once every month in the presence of a corregidor, curate, protector of the Indians, or notary public. One third of the monthly salary had to be paid in coin, one patacón of which was handed over to the worker and the rest entrusted to the protector who credited it to the individual's account. This was an attempt to keep the Indians from squandering their income and to protect them from being swindled by unscrupulous operators. The remaining two-thirds of the salary could be paid in clothes for the worker and his family.

Lazo's ordinances also reiterated the long-standing custom of requiring the natives to perform certain public services, such as guarding herds, taming horses for use in the war, building bridges, and acting as messengers for the delivery of official communications, except in the case of the inhabitants of the Melipilla district who, instead, helped out in the royal textile factories located in that area and for this were entitled to the usual daily wage.

The governor also approved the employment of Indians in the copper and gold mines and foundries of La Serena, provided the natives voluntarily agreed to do the work. The reason for this exception to the general rule of forbidding Indians to work in the mines was largely physical and geographical. La Serena was located in an area where the scarcity of rain made it impossible to engage in agriculture. The town was dependent on the mines for its existence, and on the labor of the Indians for the operation of the mines. If the mines were to close down, the area would soon be depopulated, something the governor wanted to avoid.

Included in the ordinances were several provisions designed to protect the mapuches against the cruelty and oppression of the encomenderos. Thus the Spaniards were ordered to treat their employees as free persons and vassals of the Crown, "without abusing or punishing them in any way, ... and without forcing them to work on Sundays, on feast days, at night, or in the tanneries during the winter season, under pain of severe penalties for any violations." These penalties included loss of the Indian's tribute for a period of three years for the first offense and permanent loss for a second violation. Employers were forbidden, moreover, to pay their workers with rations of wine, or to give them wine in exchange for anything "because of the great harm that results from such transactions." Encomenderos who transgressed this regulation would have to forfeit the Indian's tribute for two years for the first offense, and sacrifice the privilege of hiring his services if the violation were repeated. Violators who were not encomenderos were subject to a fine of two hundred pesos and of two years' service in the army at a private's pay. If the offender was physically incapacitated for army life, he would have to pay the salary of one of the soldiers for the duration of his fine. Culprits who ran taverns would be punished with two hundred lashes of the whip. The enforcement of these penalties was entrusted to the district judge and corregidores who were warned that they would have to give a strict account of their stewardship at the time of residencia. Finally, all natives who had been removed from their homes in the south were to be registered with the authorities within ten days after the publication of the tasa, so that arrangements could be made to send them back home where their services would be useful in defending the frontier. Failure to comply with this injunction involved a fine of two hundred pesos and a year's service in the army.

All provisions of the royal tasa of 1622 that did not conflict with the new regulations were to remain in force. The judges of the audiencia were charged with the duty of checking up annually on the manner in which the laws were being observed, but how this was to be done was not spelled out in detail.[37]

Despite the severe penalties prescribed, the tasa of 1635 was incapable of curing the evils of the encomienda system in Chile. As was frequently the case with Spanish colonial legislation, there were too many loopholes in the law, and there was no adequate machinery for enforcement. With many local officials themselves encomenderos or allied with the encomendero interests, the opportunities for graft and evasion were numerous. Another deficiency of the tasa was its failure to improve the economic status of the mapuches. Although it abolished the servicio personal and the mita as legal institutions, it left the Indians economically high and dry. Still obliged to pay taxes, the only way they could was by working for others, and "others" meant the encomenderos. The law freed the Indian, but circumstances did not. The system was thus a vicious circle in which the Indian was doomed to remain until the government made it possible for him to learn a trade and thus achieve a modicum of financial independence.[38]

The opposition that the tasa aroused was a reliable index of its future effectiveness. On the very day the tasa appeared, the cabildo of Santiago petitioned the governor to postpone sending a copy of it to Spain until the members of the council had had an opportunity to study its provisions in greater detail. Three days later, on April 19, the cabildo decided to appeal the governor's enactment.[39]

The cabildo of Concepción took a similar stand, enumerating fourteen reasons for not abolishing the servicio personal, of which the following were typical: (1) The encomienda Indians were so few in number that it would be impossible for the encomenderos to live on the tribute they received from them if it were paid in coin or kind. (2) The servicio personal benefited not only the landed proprietors but also the army, since the frontier garrisons obtained their supplies from the haciendas around Concepción. (3) Two reales per day was an excessive wage. The encomenderos could not pay even a portion of it because money was scarce, especially in the south. (4) Allowing the natives to live in their own villages would mean the ruination of the haciendas because there would not be enough workers left on the farms to cultivate the fields and to care for other necessities. (5) It was a mistake to forbid the sale of wine to the Indians, because it was the commodity they prized most of all, and was the one they used as a medium of exchange. It was also one of the reasons they were willing to live among the Spaniards. To deprive them of it would result in their going over en masse to the side of the enemy. (6) It would be impossible for the designated officials to be present at the payment of salaries because the distances between haciendas were too great. (7) Enforcing the tasa would put an end to trade and commerce, disturb the public weal, and greatly diminish the royal and ecclesiastical rents, all of which depended on the continued prosperity of the haciendas. (8) The natives were already well paid and were satisfied with the treatment they were receiving from their encomenderos.[40] (One wonders, then, why the encomenderos were perpetually afraid of an uprising among their own workers whenever there was talk of rebellion on the southern frontier!)

The unfavorable reaction of the two cabildos was a sufficient warning to Governor Lazo de la Vega, who knew very well that without the support of the town councils the projected reform would certainly fail. He therefore refrained from attempting to enforce it. The tasa of 1635 remained on the books, but in practice it accomplished no more than its predecessors. Pedro Gutiérrez de Lugo, oidor of the audiencia of

Chile, evaluated it when he informed the Crown in 1639 that "the only people who observe some [of its prescriptions] belong to the poorer class of citizens, for among the rich and powerful the *servicio personal* is as much in evidence now as before. Most of the latter (for there are a few who fear the judgments of God and who have a sense of justice) make use of the unfortunate natives as if they were slaves, treating them woefully and without paying them the small price of their labor and their sweat."[41] Among the injustices Gutiérrez noted was the "intolerable labor" to which the natives were subjected day and night in the tanneries and copper mines of La Serena.[42]

Given these circumstances, it is not surprising that Santiago de Tesillo, *maestre de campo* (company commander) under Lazo de la Vega, gloomily predicted that a solution to the problem would never be found. The roots of the evil, he declared, had grown too deep. It was no longer possible to reconcile the king's wishes with public interest (by which he meant encomendero interest).[43] These opposing forces were destined to remain apart until the final dissolution of the encomiendas a century and a half later.

In the meantime, however, as the uproar over Lazo de la Vega's tasa subsided, the focus of attention centered once more on the defiant Araucanians. The first decisive break in the seasaw struggle between Spaniards and Indians occurred in 1641, when the Marquis of Baides, Francisco López de Zúñiga, was governor of Chile.[44] Like his predecessors Baides was a professional soldier, a veteran of fifteen years' campaigning in Germany and Flanders. But he was at bottom a peaceful man who was willing to use other means than force to gain an objective. He was also a great admirer of Luis de Valdivia and a close friend of two other Jesuits in Chile: Diego de Rosales, whose help and advice he frequently enlisted, and Francisco de Vargas, who acted as his confessor and spiritual guide.[45] Their views on peaceful conquest very likely helped shape his own.[46] As he explained to the king in one of his early reports:

> This war should not be conducted in the manner in which it has been up to now through military incursions and malocas, because of the many horses lost in the process and because of the danger that, while pillaging

the farms [of the enemy], the raiders will capture piezas [for use as slaves].... These seizures are impeding the peace we seek with these rebels, for when they see themselves despoiled of what they love most, namely, their wives, children, and relatives, and see them snatched from their homes and carried off to other kingdoms and strange lands the name of Christian becomes odious to them and they grow more obstinate and obdurate in their rebellion and refuse to make peace, just as they have done in all the time that these malocas have been practiced.[47]

The conciliatory policy Baides adopted paid early dividends. During his first swing through the rebel provinces in January 1640, several chiefs from the district of Culacura, led by their principal toqui, Lincopichón, offered to make peace with the Spaniards.[48] Their example and the governor's benevolent response encouraged other tribes to send emissaries to Concepción in the months that followed. Baides received the envoys kindly, assured them of his friendship, and gave them gifts of clothing, silver-tipped canes, beads, and other baubles that they prized highly.[49] The governor was ably assisted on these occasions by Diego de Rosales and the inspector general of the army, Francisco de la Fuente Villalobos, who invited the visiting ambassadors to his home and feasted them at his own board. These courtesies made a profound impression on the envoys, who returned to their native provinces with glowing reports of the fine treatment they had received and of the advantages that would accrue from peaceful coexistence.

The general peace congress following the months of preliminary talks took place early in 1641. On January 6 of that year several thousand Spanish soldiers, officials, frontier settlers, Indian allies, missionaries, and representatives of the unpacified tribes met in the valley of the Quillín River to decide on the basis for a lasting peace between the Araucanians and the whites. The result of this conclave was the celebrated Pact of Quillín, the main provisions of which were as follows: (1) Spanish recognition of Araucanian independence; (2) acceptance of the Araucanians as allies of Spain; (3) cessation of military raids, malocas, and forced labor; (4) establishment of the Biobío River as the permanent frontier between Indians and whites, with the understanding that no armed member of either nation be permitted to cross the line; (5) release of all Spaniards held captive by the Araucanians; (6) acceptance of a defensive alliance between Indians and Spaniards to protect the colony against foreign attacks by the English and the Dutch; (7) return of the rebels to their respective provinces within six months; (8) guarantees of safety for Spanish settlements in Indian territory; (9) admission of missionaries into Araucania to evangelize the natives and teach them how to live as Christians; and (10) the giving of hostages to the whites for a period of six months as a surety for the exact observance of the terms of the treaty.[50] These terms, which met with the approval of all the assembled toquis, were solemnly ratified under oath by the representatives of the two nations, and in the weeks that followed scores of Spaniards were released from captivity by the Araucanians in proof of their readiness to honor the compact.[51]

As the provisions outlined above make clear, the Pact of Quillín was an important milestone in the history of Spanish-Indian relations in Chile. For the first time in more than a hundred years the antagonists had met on terms of political equality and agreed on a settlement that was mutually honorable and beneficial. The significance of this achievement can scarcely be exaggerated. It was a great diplomatic revolution whose potentialities for the future were incalculable. All that still remained to ensure success was confirmation by Madrid and observance of the treaty stipulations by both sides.

The first of these requirements presented no problem. Philip IV formally approved the Pact on April 29, 1643, in a decree commending the Marquis for his prudence and judgment and instructing him to continue treating the Indians "with all kindness, benevolence, and consideration" so that they might experience the benefits that flowed from accepting his rule.[52]

The second requirement proved more difficult, although the Araucanians demonstrated more than once that they were prepared to abide by their solemn engagements. When the toquis of the mountain districts of the interior who had not subscribed to the treaty attempted to disrupt the peace by staging an uprising, they were promptly quelled by the caciques of Arauco, Purén, Elicura, and Imperial. And when Dutch corsairs under Henry Brouwer tried to invade southern Chile in 1643, it was primarily the Araucanians who repelled the attack.[53] Had the Spaniards been equally sincere, the history of Chile after 1641 would have been different. But following the departure of Baides in 1646 the situation began to deteriorate rapidly. The Pact of Quillín was officially renewed by Governor Martín de Mujica in 1647, but by that time it had already begun to lose its force.[54] The frontier garrisons continued to indulge in malocas, despite the treaty agreement. Encina, who is by no means favorable to the Araucanians, frankly admits that the war in Chile had by this time degenerated into a scramble for personal gain; he attributes this circumstance to the influence of Valdivia's theory of peaceful conquest, which, he says, robbed the Spanish army of the last vestiges of dignity, honor, and devotion to duty, and sowed the seeds of egoism, avarice, and rapacity.[55] The explanation ignores the fact that the greed for piezas was not a new phenomenon in the 1630's and 1640's; it had been operative in Chile long before the establishment of defensive warfare. Even while defensive warfare was in progress the army had engaged in occasional malocas. They simply stepped up the practice when the system was revoked.

Encina might have argued more convincingly had he considered the personnel of the army when seeking a reason for the shocking immorality that he condemns. The military guardians of the southern frontier were, for the most part, a motley group of provincial levies and lower-class mestizos who had little interest in fighting a patriotic war. Most of the mestizos were Peruvian recruits, who deserted at any opportunity, and roamed the countryside, preying on anyone who came along. They had all the vices but none of the virtues of mercenary soldiers.[56] Many of the officers were little better. There was scant military glory to be gained in Chile, but the prospect of loot was an attractive inducement. Diego de Vibanco, himself an officer in the king's cavalry, stated the case baldly when he said that "prompt elimination of the abuses connected with the enslavement of the Indians would contribute greatly [to ending the war]. These abuses are the main cause of its duration, and are the principal reason why the officers in charge, namely, the governor, the general of the army, and the *sargento mayor* (sergeant major) are desirous of continuing it."[57] Vibanco added that the greed for piezas was very pronounced because of the price they commanded. A male Indian sold for one hundred pesos, each adult female and boys over ten years of age for over two hundred pesos, while those under ten were worth one hundred or more pesos. The governor, the maestre de campo, and the sargento mayor all received a share of the proceeds. It was not strange, therefore, Vibanco concluded, that they wanted the war to continue.[58]

The corruption and inefficiency that characterized the army during this dismal period were vividly shown in the infamous exploits of Juan and José Salazar, the favorite kin of their sister Juana, who was the comely wife of Antonio de Acuña y Cabrera, the soldier-politician who governed Chile from 1650 to 1656. Besides being beautiful, young, and very ambitious, Juanita completely dominated her elderly spouse, who hesitated to deny her any whim. The childless Juanita sought diversion by dabbling in statecraft and accumulating wealth, two interests that her influence over Don Antonio and the situation in Chile enabled her to satisfy easily.

Both of Juana's brothers were married but poor. Like her they were ambitious for personal fortune, and they quickly found a way of realizing their desire. Needing only a position of authority in the army to carry out their plans, they obtained it through Juana. She smiled a little, cajoled a little, and "papa" Antonio cheerfully capitulated. Juan received a marshal's baton, while José was appointed sargento mayor. The Salazar brothers were on their way, with two of the top commissions in the army!

The frontier garrisons were accustomed to large-scale grafters, but the Salazars were in a class by themselves. They started by quietly taking over the provisioning of the troops and pocketing the profits. Prices began to soar while the quality of the supplies became worse and worse. The soldiers grumbled, the Salazars rejoiced, and the money continued to roll in. Next, the brothers looked around for another easy mark and found what they wanted without much trouble—a rich slave trade ripe for the picking. The local encomenderos needed slaves badly, for the number of pacified Indians available for labor was steadily diminishing. The Peruvian landowners were in a similar predicament, since the Portuguese rebellion had put a crimp in the African slave trade.[59] Under the circumstances, the price of slaves could be boosted up and up for a limited time. The opportunity was too good to miss.

When the Salazars stepped into the picture, no eyebrows were raised, because an interest in slaves was common. But the scope of their activities was astounding. The whole of Araucania was converted into a source of supply. Men, women, and children were considered equal prey. They were acquired through exchange, by deceit, and by any other means that came to hand, and they were sold for a profit. The *plaza* (fortified town) of Boroa, where the elder Salazar was in command, became a huge depot of dark-skinned humans waiting to be shipped to their deaths in the north. It was a piteous spectacle such as the frontier had never before witnessed.[60]

The pressure of outraged public opinion finally forced Governor Acuña y Cabrera to take action against his in-laws, but, since he contented himself with a few mild reprimands no improvement resulted. The situation became worse instead of better. Other officials emulated the Salazars, and a profitable trade in "certified" slaves sprang up overnight in the Spanish outposts. Since peaceful Indians could not legally be sold as slaves, the commandants of the frontier forts would certify, for a fee, that the victims had been captured in legitimate raids on the rebel tribes.[61] The audiencia protested vigorously against this miscarriage of justice, but its protests had no immediate effect.[62]

Meanwhile, a combination of events provided the Salazars with an unexpected opportunity to expand their operations. On March 26, 1651, a Spanish vessel carrying, among other things, the army payroll and a large contingent of passengers, was shipwrecked off the coast of Arauco. The passengers and crew reached shore safely only to meet death at the hands of some Cunco Indians who lived in that region.[63]

As soon as news of the two-fold disaster reached Spanish headquarters, Governor Acuña y Cabrera proposed to the members of the audiencia that a punitive expedition be sent into the territory. The audiencia acquiesced, but with the qualification that the Indians captured in the maloca were not to be considered slaves until an investigation had established whether or not they had been implicated in the massacre of the ship's survivors. Acuña y Cabrera agreed to this reservation and instructed the military governor of Chiloé, Ignacio de la Carrera Iturgoyen, to carry out the administration's decision.

The reprisals that followed were bloody and swift. Scores of Cuncos, including numerous women and children, were indiscriminately rounded up by the troops and shipped off to Santiago to be sold as slaves. The presence of women and children among the captives made the audiencia skeptical as to the thoroughness of the investigation, and one of the oidores, Nicolás Polanco de Santillana, voiced the opinion of his associates when he roundly condemned military officials who were content with only the word of their interpreter to prove that the Indians brought before them for certification as legal slaves had been seized in legitimate malocas. Polanco insisted that such dubious testimony was insufficient to warrant application of the royal decree of May 26, 1608, regarding rebel slaves. He added that it was clearly contrary to the intention of that decree that male children under ten and a half years of age and females under nine and a half be enslaved.[64]

All efforts of the audiencia to protect the rights of the Indians proved ineffectual, however. The slave hunts continued, as did the illegal seizure of piezas, particularly women and children, regardless of whether they were members of pacified tribes or not.

As for the Cuncos, they were made an object of special attention. Using their murder of his countrymen as a pretext, Juan de Salazar organized one of his infamous expeditions against them. He set out in December 1653, with a force of nine hundred Spaniards and fifteen hundred native auxiliaries ostensibly to chastize the Cuncos further. Núñez de Pineda y Bascuñán, a contemporary witness, candidly admits that "the greed for piezas and the desire to enslave these people (which is what most disturbs the peace, prolongs the war, and is and has been the origin of all the disastrous events that have befallen and continue to befall this realm) was the reason behind this expedition."[65] Córdoba y Figueroa, another chronicler of the period, similarly notes that "the most powerful incentive for this entrada was the prospect of taking prisoners who could be sold as slaves either inside or outside the realm. As slaves they were the source of a very profitable trade, and many volunteers signed up for the expedition because of their desire for some of this booty."[66] So convinced was Salazar that the enterprise would be a complete and easy success that he took his wife along, dressed as a man.[67]

By January 11, 1654, the expedition had arrived without incident at the Río Bueno, some one hundred and thirty leagues south of Concepción. It was here that contact with the "enemy" was finally made. Half hidden among the underbrush and trees that lined the opposite bank was a large body of Cunco warriors, some on horses, others on foot, together with the women and children who had accompanied them to avoid falling into the hands of the Spaniards. The sight of so many potential slaves quickened the spirits of the soldiers, who scurried around looking for ways and means of crossing the river and bringing the hunt to a profitable conclusion before the prey had a chance to escape. Since there were no fords in the vicinity, Salazar decided, over the protests of some of his companions, to construct a makeshift pontoon bridge.

The crossing resulted in a humiliating fiasco. The bridge broke up quickly, drowning some of the troops and incapacitating others. Those who had succeeded in reaching the opposite side were promptly attacked by the embittered Cuncos, thrown back into the river by superior numbers, wounded and killed. Approximately one hundred Spaniards and more than thirty Indian auxiliaries lost their lives in the ill-starred attempt. Recognizing the futility of the situation, Salazar angrily turned tail and headed back to Concepción to lick his wounds. He reached that town without further mishap, but without a single pieza to show for his efforts.[68] Public indignation over this untoward event was so profound that Salazar was forced to undergo an official enquiry into the particulars of the expedition, but the enquiry proved to be little more than a formality intended to allay public opinion; Salazar was officially acquitted, and the case was closed for the time being.

One of the people particularly incensed over Salazar's entrada was Diego de Rosales, who was in charge of the Jesuit mission of Boroa at the time. Rosales, knowing the temper of the Indians, warned the governor that an uprising would occur if the injustices continued.[69] Acuña y Cabrera not only dismissed the warning as being without serious foundation, but also allowed Salazar to embark on a second expedition into the same area. On February 6, 1655, Salazar, planning revenge, set out, accompanied by four hundred Spaniards and a large number of Indian auxiliaries. He was joined on the way by Núñez de Pineda y Bascuñán, commander of the plaza of Boroa, and a member of the garrison of that fort.

Reports of an impending insurrection started reaching Governor Acuña y Cabrera in the days that followed. Apparently disturbed by their growing frequency and urgency, he moved his base of operations temporarily from Concepción to the fort at Buena Esperanza where he would be in a position to cope more directly with any emergency. He arrived there on February 12, bringing with him a detachment of infantry reinforcements. Two days later, during the night of the fourteenth, the possible uprising became a horrible reality.[70]

The rebellion of 1655 was widespread, rapid, and well coordinated. Within a few hours not only the entire frontier but also the more settled territory between the Biobío and the Maule rivers was in flames. All the Spanish posts in Araucania were attacked simultaneously, and practically all of them had to be abandoned sooner or later after a resistance of varying duration. Three hundred and ninety-six farms and haciendas were completely destroyed,[71] while property damage was estimated at eight million pesos.[72] More deplorable, however, was the loss of life, liberty, and honor. According to Pedro de Córdoba y Figueroa, "many persons of both sexes were taken prisoner by the rebels, including some of distinguished birth whose names I could mention; but since there is no reason to recall their shame, suffice it to say that the illegitimate progeny living amongst us today is a product of that disgrace."[73]

Personal tragedy stalked many other Spaniards also, including the Salazars and their relative Governor Acuña y Cabrera. José de Salazar, who as sargento mayor commanded the garrison at Nacimiento (at the confluence of the Biobío and the Vergara rivers) was the least fortunate of the three. Following a series of attacks that dangerously reduced the limited supplies of stores and ammunition, he evacuated the fort and took to the river in an effort to reach Concepción. As many of the garrison pointed out, this move was unwise, for the few available boats were in poor repair, the low level of the river would interfere with the movement of the craft, and the presence of the troopers' women and children would be an additional impediment. Nevertheless, Salazar stubbornly insisted on having his way. As had been predicted, the overloaded boats repeatedly ran aground, exposing their occupants to harassment from the hundreds of hostiles on both sides of the stream. Faced with the prospect of complete annihilation, Salazar coldheartedly ordered the women and children cast ashore in a desperate effort to lighten the craft and escape. But shortly thereafter, in the vicinity of Santa Juana, the boats ran aground for the last time, and the Indians moved in for the kill. A hand-to-hand struggle ensued that did not end until the entire group of two hundred and forty Spaniards had been killed. Salazar himself, badly wounded, leaped into the river in a final effort to save his life, and quickly drowned.[74]

Juan de Salazar was luckier than his brother. News of the rebellion reached him while he was on the march against the Cuncos. From that moment on he lost all interest in tracking down slaves. His primary concern was to save his skin. Instead of returning overland to Concepción and thus relieving the pressure on the Spanish outposts along the way as some of his subordinates urged, he pushed forward rapidly to Valdivia, where he ordered the horses to be destroyed to prevent their falling into the hands of the enemy,[75] embarked his troops, and headed back to Concepción, secure in the safety that the sea afforded.

Governor Acuña y Cabrera's conduct was no more admirable than that of his brothers-in-law. When the uprising occurred, he abruptly left the garrison at Buena Esperanza and hurried back to Concepción, where the chances of survival were considerably greater. There he learned to his dismay that his troubles were only beginning. The entire populace was up in arms over this latest outburst of the Araucanians, which they attributed to the ineptitude and irresponsibility of the governor and his relatives. Their animosity increased by leaps and bounds as further evidence of the disaster began to accumulate. On Saturday, February 20, a mob of angry citizens, headed by the corregidor Francisco de Gaete and the cabildo, demonstrated before the governor's house. Cries of "Long live the king! Death to the bad governor!" filled the air. Acuña y Cabrera, now thoroughly frightened, took to his heels once again and sought refuge in the college of the Jesuit Fathers. Here he lost no time in writing out his resignation and submitting it to the mob.[76]

Encouraged by this sudden capitulation, the townspeople took another revolutionary step. Without waiting for directions from superior authorities, they proceeded to elect a new governor on their own initiative. Two candidates were nominated for the position: the maestre de campo, Juan Fernández de Rebolledo, who had achieved a certain reputation for ability and merit among the vecinos, and the *veedor general* (inspector general), Francisco de la Fuente Villalobos, a man of advanced age[77] but a great friend of the Indians and a former disciple of Luis de Valdivia. After considerable haggling, the choice narrowed to De la Fuente in the hope that his personal prestige among the Araucanians would suffice to bring the rebellion to an end. De la Fuente was reluctant to accept the honor, claiming that it was illegal in origin, but he ultimately yielded to popular demand. Letters were thereupon dispatched to the rebellious chiefs informing them of the change in administration, and measures were taken to improve the military situation. The new governor appointed Antonio de Urra and Jerónimo de Molina, both of whom had been influential in securing his election, to the important posts of maestre de campo and sargento mayor respectively.[78] In doing so he aroused the enmity of Fernández de Rebolledo, who had been maestre de campo under Acuña y Cabrera and whom some of the townspeople had favored as a possible governor.

Word of the revolutionary developments in Concepción reached Santiago on the morning of March 2 via special courier letters from Acuña y Cabrera to the audiencia of Chile and Nicolás Polanco de Santillana, the senior oidor. Polanco's astonishment when he read the news was extreme. Nothing like this had ever happened before in the history of the colony. Unless corrected speedily it could undermine the entire structure of royal control in Chile. Realizing the need for acting circumspectly, Polanco first commanded the courier, under pain of dire penalties, to preserve secrecy in the matter. He also ordered him to postpone delivery of any other letters that he carried. He then summoned the members of the audiencia to an extraordinary session to be held that same afternoon.

The meeting began promptly at three thirty o'clock. One of the first items on the agenda concerned the advisability of inviting the cabildo of Santiago and the junta de guerra, which had been formed following the outbreak of hostilities, to join the audiencia in secret session. After prolonged discussion it was decided to do so, even though this increased the danger of a security leak. The advantages to be gained from a broader spectrum of opinion made the risk worthwhile.[79]

The details of the deliberations held on this day and the next need not concern us. The military element was divided in its counsels, some advocating the use of force to restore the governor to his office, others favoring a more conciliatory approach. The majority were agreed, however, that the governor could accomplish little by remaining in Concepción and recommended that he come to Santiago as he himself had suggested in his letter to the audiencia.[80]

The cabildo viewed the situation with greater sympathy for the local authorities and vecinos in Concepción. While agreeing with the junta that Acuña y Cabrera's authority should be restored and that he should leave the south, the town fathers nevertheless recommended that nothing be done that might imply a lack of confidence in the city of Concepción or the military officials there. Rather, they advised that every possible effort be made to assist them in the crisis.[81] One member of the cabildo, Diego de Aguilar y Maqueda, argued unsuccessfully that since Acuña y Cabrera had been responsible for the "loss of the realm" and since he had already abdicated his position, his resignation should be honored and the audiencia should take charge and appoint someone else to serve as temporary governor.[82]

After all opinions had been thoroughly aired, the audiencia drafted an auto on March 3 summarizing its thinking on the subject. It is an amazing document. It labeled as seditious the civil disturbance that had forced the governor's abdication, yet it also affirmed the audiencia's faith in the loyalty of the guilty parties, noting that in times of public distress it was not unusual for citizens to blame administrators for misfortunes. But the choice of a close friend of the Indians as a replacement for Governor Acuña y Cabrera had been a mistake, for the rebels would interpret it as a sign of cowardly fear and would exploit it as much as they could. An experienced soldier, a man who was ready to use fire and the sword in dealing with the insurrectionists, would have been a better choice.

The document recognized the necessity of extricating Acuña y Cabrera from his perilous position, but rejected the use of force to restore law and order in Concepción. It also noted that failure to remove De la Fuente from power would be tantamount to approving the changeover that had occurred. This could not be tolerated, since it would minimize the authority of the audiencia and the viceroy and would encourage future malcontents to depose public officials whenever the spirit moved them. Unfortunately, no means were at hand to rectify the situation immediately. It would be necessary, therefore, to play a waiting game. Perhaps in the meantime the ill-advised culprits would come to their senses.[83]

The month of March passed while the stalemate continued. On April 1 the audiencia finally came to life and addressed two decrees to the dissidents in the south. The first of these provided for the safe departure of Governor Acuña y Cabrera to Santiago. The second appointed Juan Fernández de Rebolledo military commander of Concepción and ordered him to arrest De la Fuente and send him, under armed guard if necessary, to the capital for questioning. Anyone who refused to accept Fernández's authority would be considered a traitor to the king and would forfeit his property to the Crown.[84] This display of strength, plus the recent arrival of Juan de Salazar and his troops from Valdivia, did much to resolve the situation in Concepción.

Acuña y Cabrera reached Santiago in May 1655 and began to function once again as governor. Several weeks later a decree arrived from the viceroy of Peru, the Count of Alba, ordering him and his family to proceed to Lima on the first available boat. Acuña y Cabrera decided to ignore the summons, arguing that the unsettled state of affairs in the colony obliged him to remain where he was. The viceroy countered by appointing a new governor for Chile. On New Year's Day 1656, Admiral Pedro Porter Casanate landed at Talcahuano to assume command of the colony and to insure his predecessor's departure for Peru.[85]

The official investigation to which Acuña y Cabrera and the luckless Francisco de la Fuente Villalobos were subjected was a tedious, drawn-out affair that produced 13,373 pages of written records and little else before it was over. De la Fuente escaped the final ignominy of an adverse verdict by dying in a *limeño* prison while the enquiry was still in progress. Acuña y Cabrera avoided the consequences of his official misdeeds through family influence and the refusal of the audiencia of Chile to open its secret records to examination by a special agent of the viceroy. Not content with this negative victory, he sought more positive vindication by appealing to Madrid for reinstatement as governor of Chile.[86] Philip IV, who may have had his fill of the exasperating situation by then, was in no hurry to respond to the request. When he finally did on June 28, 1660, his reply gave little consolation to either side. Acuña y Cabrera was politely informed (through the viceroy to whom the communication was addressed) that his request had been denied because his term of office had already expired. Besides, there were "other considerations that indicated that no advantage would be gained from returning him to his former post."[87] The document went on to reprimand the Count of Alba for his temerity in removing a royal appointee from office without first consulting Madrid on the matter. Both he and his successors were reminded sharply that they had no authority to make such decisions. Even when the gravity of the case allowed no delay, they were not to act without first obtaining the consent and approval of the audiencia of Lima. This precaution was considered necessary to avoid possible embarrassing complications.[88]

The decree of June 28 closed the book on what should have been a most enlightening experience for the Spanish Crown. The shouts of "Long live the king! Death to the bad governor!" that had sparked the *tumulto* of February 20, 1655, were a portent for anyone who had the wisdom to interpret them. Practically the same cries of "Long live the king! Down with bad government!" were to be heard a century and a half later during the independence movement of the early nineteenth century.

EMANCIPATION: DECREED AND DEFERRED

THE REBELLION OF 1655 convinced the authorities in Madrid that something was still radically wrong in the government of Chile. Even before the start of the uprising, the king, alarmed by numerous critical reports, had begun to think seriously of more equitable treatment for the Indians. Thus he had exhorted Fray Dionisio Cimbrón, the newly appointed bishop of Concepción, to make the care of the mapuches his first concern.[1] The disastrous effects of the rebellion helped strengthen his resolution.[2] In a decree of July 5, 1658, Philip IV ordered the viceroy of Peru to administer "justice and equality" in Chile, and to secure the punishment of Spanish offenders and the good treatment of the Indians, because "failure to do so had been responsible for the general uprising that had occurred."[3] It seemed that the Crown was preparing for a showdown.

Subsequent developments confirmed this view. The reports that Bishop Cimbrón sent back to Spain made it clear that the enslavement policy initiated in 1608 and reaffirmed in 1625 had been a dismal failure. Instead of persuading the rebels to lay down their arms, it had merely afforded the military an opportunity to enrich themselves.[4] To remedy this situation, Philip IV issued a series of decrees on April 9, 1662, striking at the roots of the problem: future slave raids were prohibited; so were military excursions into hostile territory unless approved in advance by a special committee set up for the purpose.[5] More importantly, the governor of Chile was instructed to summon a council of clergy to consider the advisability of abolishing the law on slavery. Results of their deliberations were to be sent to Spain for final decision, but in the meantime the majority opinion of the council was to prevail. Under no circumstances were any more rebels to be sold as slaves or transported outside the realm. All Indians who had been sold into slavery outside of Chile were to be returned to their home provinces without delay* and were to be assigned to encomiendas to cultivate the land and to "restore to these provinces the fertility and abundance of fruits and other products that they had formerly possessed."[6]

Not content with these measures, Philip IV went a step further. In another decree of the same date he announced that he was pardoning all Indians who had participated either directly or indirectly in past uprisings. Those who pledged obedience to the Crown would be absolved of all past guilt and would enjoy the same liberty and privileges as other royal vassals. This meant that they could not be punished or molested in any way because of their previous offenses, could not be deprived of their possessions and lands, and could not be made the object of legal suits. All other provisions to the contrary were nullified.[7]

To ensure compliance with the decrees, Philip appointed a cleric, in this case Bishop Cimbrón, to serve as temporary governor of Chile.[8] This move, however, went for naught, for unbeknownst to Madrid, Cimbrón had already died.[9] Anjel de Peredo, whom the viceroy named provisional governor in 1662, was thus saddled with the responsibility of implementing the royal commands.[10]

Peredo lost no time in forming a council composed of the bishop of Santiago and the superiors of the major religious Orders in the capital, the Dominicans, Franciscans, and Jesuits. The diocese of Concepción was not formally represented, because a successor to Bishop Cimbrón had not yet arrived. Rosales, who assisted at the meeting in his new capacity as vice-provincial of the Jesuits in Chile,[11] recorded the results of the conference in these words: "Most of the members of the council were of the opinion that the Indians should be free not only because the motives that prompted the insurrection [of 1655] were different from those that had prompted the other one [of 1598], but also for many other reasons."[12] Rosales added that even though the king had ordered the majority view enforced, enactment of the opinion was, nevertheless, suspended. The fault lay not with Peredo but with the viceroy who appealed against the decrees of April 9 forbidding the sale of

---

* How this was to be done was not explained. The decree also stated that owners of slaves could recover their purchase price from the sellers, but how this was to be carried out was also not stated.

Chilean slaves and ordering the return to Chile of all Indians who had been transported as slaves to Peru.[13] His reason for doing so is clear: Peru was experiencing a shortage of slave labor; a halt in the flow of slaves from the south and the return of those already in Peru would have produced a serious economic crisis. The viceroy's appeal was like a last-minute reprieve to the racketeers in Chile, who immediately stepped up their operations.

Their efforts were facilitated by the appearance of a new royal governor, a military man, Francisco de Meneses, better known as "Barrabas" to his contemporaries, whose overt abuse of power made the excesses of Acuña y Cabrera seem mild.[14] Meneses governed the colony as though it were a personal fief during the four years of his administration (1664–68).[15] He quarreled with almost everyone, including the audiencia, the cabildo, the clergy,[16] and the citizens of Santiago.[17] He shocked the sedate aristocrats of the capital with his predilection for commoners, bullfights, and gay dances, obstructed the impartial administration of justice,[18] fined, imprisoned, exiled, or executed those who opposed him, maintained a bodyguard of military toughs who preyed on the defenseless vecinos, established his own business enterprises,[19] monopolized the export of strategic goods,[20] diverted military supplies into other channels for personal profit, distributed favors for a price. In short, he used almost every public office and service to his own advantage. Events finally reached such a pass that the inspector general of the army, Manuel de Mendoza, decided to take matters into his own hands and attempted publicly to assassinate the tyrant. The plan miscarried. Although wounded, Meneses defended himself with such vigor that Mendoza was forced to seek sanctuary in a nearby church. The governor had him forcibly removed, paraded him through the streets in the garb of a fool, with his eyebrows, head, and beard shaven, and had him tried by a kangaroo court and sentenced to death.[21] Meneses and his accomplices were, in turn, excommunicated by Francisco Ramírez de León, commissary of the Holy Office, for having violated the right of sanctuary. The battle continued with great recrimination on both sides until the audiencia finally persuaded Ramírez to lift the ban lest the commonweal suffer irreparable harm and the natives be encouraged to stage another uprising.[22] (The audiencia's mention of possible Indian trouble, as a reason for restoring a semblance of harmony between public and ecclesiastical authorities, shows how pervasive was the fear that civil unrest might at any time infect the native element of the population and incite even the pacified tribes to rebel.)

Angry letters were meanwhile making their way to Lima and Madrid castigating the governor and petitioning relief from his autocratic rule. Meneses succeeded in intercepting some of the correspondence, but enough got through to convince the Crown that a change was necessary. He was removed from office in 1668, sought safety in flight, was apprehended, arrested, tried and convicted, and ended his turbulent career behind prison bars.[23]

The administration of Francisco de Meneses was a time of trial for the conservative, law-abiding elements in the colony, but it was especially difficult for the encomienda Indians. Existing grants were extended for two or three lifetimes, while other grants were declared vacant and were awarded again, for a substantial fee that the governor pocketed.[24] Indians from Peru who had wandered into Chile were not spared either; if they failed to report to the magistrates for assignment to encomiendas they were punished with two hundred strokes of the lash, enough to kill a man on the spot.[25]

The inhabitants of Araucania fared no better than their countrymen farther north. The practice of conducting malocas reached unprecedented proportions during Meneses' term of office. Expeditions against the pacified tribes were particularly frequent because they involved less risk and brought more lucrative returns. A single raid into the provinces of Paicaví, Cayucupil, and Tucapel, for example, yielded four hundred piezas who were later sold as slaves. Twenty tribal chieftains who courageously spoke out against the raid were summarily put to death "viciously and in cold blood."[26]

The Indians protested vigorously and were ignored. They took up arms in self-defense,[27] but this gave the army a better excuse for running them down. Their only hope lay in flight, and even then they were not safe, for the military pursued them relentlessly. Lope Antonio Munive, who had been sent as visitor to Chile to investigate reports of military misdeeds, epitomized the situation accurately when he exclaimed in amazement: "What are we coming to? Is this the way we remedy past wrongs, by committing others just as bad and even worse?"[28]

Neither the governor of Chile nor the viceroy of Peru, the Count of Santistéban, was interested in suppressing the slave trade. The viceroy was more concerned about keeping the trade alive for the benefit of the Peruvian capitalists and encomenderos. He consequently devoted all his efforts to convincing the Crown that the abolition of Indian slavery in Chile would be harmful. Prior to his death in 1668, the Count dispatched two lengthy memorials to Madrid outlining the reasons for his stand.[29] In the first of these documents the viceroy proposed six arguments for keeping the Araucanians in bondage: (1) They captured Spaniards and killed them during their drunken celebrations; those whom they spared they used as slaves. (2) The king had condemned the rebels to slavery on several occasions. (3) Subjects who had once rebelled against the Crown deserved to remain enslaved thereafter. (4) Unless the Araucanians were punished with enslavement they would rebel again very quickly. (5) The gradual extermination of the Araucanians was a salutary goal. (6) If the hostiles captured in the war were not assigned to encomiendas they would again take up arms against the whites; therefore he recommended that all rebel prisoners, including women and children, be shipped to Peru for employment in the quicksilver mines of Huancavelica.[30] The second memorial repeated the arguments of the first with incidental variations and additions. Once again the viceroy urged that all captive rebels be removed to Peru where they would, as he put it, receive good religious instruction.[31]

The viceroy's suggestions and recommendations caused considerable perplexity in Madrid because they were directly opposed to the views of the council of ecclesiastics in Santiago. In the hope of arriving at some conclusion, the queen mother, Mariana of Austria, who was serving as regent during the minority of her son, the future Charles II,[32] instructed the governor of Chile, Juan Henríquez,[33] to call another meeting of religious superiors to study the question anew.

The new council convened in October 1671. Among the participants were the bishop of Santiago, Fray Diego de Humanzoro, and the superiors of all the religious houses in the capital, with the exception of the Jesuit vice-provincial, Diego de Rosales, who was in Concepción preparing for a missionary excursion to the island of Mocha.[34]

Contrary to expectation, the group unanimously approved the decrees of 1608 and 1625 that condemned to slavery all rebels over ten years of age, including females, who were captured in the war. The influence of the two memorials favoring slavery by the Count of Santistéban was apparently the decisive factor in this surprising approval.[35]

Because of the prestige Rosales enjoyed, the governor decided it would be advisable to secure his opinion also before submitting a report to the queen. He accordingly sent a copy of the proceedings, together with the viceroy's memorials, to Concepción for examination. The Jesuit's reply was contained in a rather extensive treatise dated March 20, 1672, divided into four chapters of which the first two, concerned with proving that the Indians could not justly be enslaved, were the most important from a doctrinal standpoint.[36]

Following a few introductory remarks summarizing the events preceding the writing of the treatise, Rosales took up the question of the justice involved in enslaving the *indios amigos*, the pacified natives of Arauco, San Cristóbal, Talcamávida, and Santa Juana who had assisted the Spaniards in their campaigns against the hostile tribes. Both the viceroy and the junta had favored their enslavement because they had participated in the rebellion of 1655 and thus fell into the category of *indios de guerra* (unpacified Indians). This type of reasoning, Rosales affirmed, displayed a complete ignorance of the historical facts, for these warriors had accompanied the Spanish army on its march against the Cuncos.[37] During their absence the indios de guerra had pillaged their villages and carried off the women and children who had been left behind. Discovering their loss, the indios amigos had gone on the warpath to recover their families. While engaged in this business many of them were captured by the Spaniards and sold as slaves as if they were rebels. This action, Rosales asserted, was unjust, for the indios amigos were *not* rebels. Their only "crime" consisted in entering rebel territory in search of their loved ones as they had a perfect right to do. When they had completed the search, they had returned home, reaffirmed their friendship for the Spaniards, and remained loyal ever since. Even if they had been guilty of rebellion, only the king, not the governor, had the authority to condemn them to slavery. The slavery decrees of 1608 and 1625 did not apply to the indios amigos, for these decrees had been directed against the rebels and not against the native allies. The king had specifically stated in his decree of 1625 that "it is my will and my command that if the rebellious natives of Chile accept the [Catholic] Faith their enslavement is to cease, as well as the permission to sell them as slaves." This condition was fulfilled by the peace treaty that the Marquis of Baides negotiated with the rebels in 1641. As a consequence of that agreement the enslavement of the rebels was *ipso facto* abolished. Moreover, if it was abolished for them, it was certainly abolished for the indios amigos. Therefore, any enslavement of the Indians, hostiles or allies, for any reason whatsoever, was illegal so long as the king did not issue a new decree making it legal. In his decree of April 9, 1662, the king had expressly forbidden the sale of all Indian captives, regardless of age or sex. The present practice of selling them as slaves therefore was unjust, contrary to the will of His Majesty, and a violation of all natural rights.[38]

Rosales next took up the defense of the hostiles. Examining the reasons the viceroy and the council gave for enslavement,[39] Rosales discovered that ignorance of the facts had once again led to a false conclusion. The viceroy and the junta had erroneously assumed that the indios de guerra were *de jure* rebels and that war against them was, consequently, justified. But this was not the case, for the indios de guerra had made peace with the Spaniards in 1641, had remained at peace for fourteen years, had permitted missionaries to enter their territory, and had received instructions in the Faith.[40] The only difference between them and the indios amigos during this time was that the latter were military allies of the Spaniards and the former were not. Why, then, had they again resorted to arms? What was the cause of their so-called rebellion? It was the crimes of which the Spaniards themselves had been guilty: "So great were the evils they endured, so grievous the crimes that the Spaniards committed against them, so unjust the malocas to which they were subjected . . . that when their pleas for justice and relief went unheard, they finally resolved to rise up in a desperate attempt to escape the heavy yoke oppressing them, saying, as they said to me many times: We are not rebelling against the Faith or against the things of God, but only against the vicious treatment we receive from the Spaniards, and because the governor refuses to provide us with any justice."[41] This being the case, Rosales continued, the rebels were clearly justified in taking up arms in self-defense. Despite this fact, the viceroy recommended their enslavement, arguing that they had been captured in a just war and implying thereby that a just war was all that was required to sanction the enslavement of the enemy, "a fallacy that is held by many." Yet the viceroy had himself admitted in his first memorial that the Indians had been justified in rebelling because of the grievances they suffered, thus conceding that the war was unjust on the part of the Spaniards and that the Indians captured in it could not be enslaved.

There was, however, a more weighty reason for condemning enslavement even if the war were just. This was the famous declaration of 1537 of Pope Paul III, which had decided the question once and for all as far as Catholic nations were concerned. In that pronouncement the Pontiff had forbidden, under pain of excommunication, the enslavement of the Indians of the New World even though they resisted the Faith. What more was there to say?[42]

Before concluding his treatise Rosales warned the Crown that the strife in Araucania would never cease unless "this root of slavery, which is the principal cause of the war," were eradicated. As long as gross injustices continued, the war itself would be unjust, the enslavement of the Indians would be unjust, and the conquest of Araucania would never be accomplished. All of this could be changed, he insisted, if only the Crown would effectively abolish the cause of it all: Indian slavery.[43]

The prospect of the Crown doing so, however, seemed rather remote at the time. Of all the people whose opinions had been solicited, Rosales alone had come out in defense of the embattled Araucanians. His was truly the voice of one crying in the wilderness of greed, injustice, suffering, and fear. Lined up against him were the viceroy of Peru, the governor of Chile,[44] the bishop of Santiago,[45] and the heads of other religious corporations in the colony. What chance would one man's views have against so many? The outlook for the mapuches was bleak, indeed.

Nevertheless, on December 20, 1674, Queen Regent Mariana issued the decree that abolished all forms of Indian slavery in Chile,

declared the Indians to be free human beings, ordered all natives held
in bondage to be set free, and commanded the governor of the colony
to implement these decisions without any further discussions or appeals.[46]

What was the cause of this unexpected development? Who was responsible for persuading the Queen Regent to enact a law that went
counter to the advice of the most exalted officials and ecclesiastics in
Chile and Peru? The wording of the decree gives a clue to the answer.
After enumerating the legal precedents for the decision, the document
continues:

> And now in this present time the Papal Nuncio has informed me that there
> have come to the attention of His Holiness the sighs of the Indians of this
> realm who have been reduced to a miserable form of slavery by political
> and military officials, under various pretexts and contrary to the repeated
> commands of my predecessors as well as the dispositions of the Holy See
> and the bull of Pope Paul III . . . and although His Holiness is acquainted
> with the directions that have been given in this matter, he cannot refrain
> from wishing that these dispositions be reaffirmed in all severity so that
> the ministers of these provinces may know them and treat the Indians as
> free beings, not only as regards their persons but also as regards their
> possessions.[47]

It seems clear from the preceding that the intervention of the Holy
See played an important part in the final outcome. The role of the
parecer that Rosales submitted is open to conjecture,[48] but regardless
of the influence it may have had, the legislation he urged was approved, and Indian slavery in Chile was legally dead.

The decree of 1674, which reached Santiago on January 10, 1676,[49]
marked the end of legal slavery in Chile but not the end of *de facto*
servitude. Significant developments that followed the emancipation
legislation not only underscore the problems inherent in the slave-
labor issue, but also the ingenuity of the colonials in circumventing the
law. The arrival of the emancipation decree touched off a storm of
protest throughout the colony, much of which could have been avoided
had the measure been more realistic. As it was, the new legislation
failed to specify the procedures to be followed in liberating the slaves,

and said nothing about compensation for the slaveholders, many of whom had invested considerable capital in their holdings. It provided no transitional period in which to adjust to the demands of a wage economy, thus ignoring a problem of paramount concern to the business community: how to stave off economic collapse in case the former slaves refused to work for the whites. Except for exhorting the ecclesiastical and civil officials to care for the spiritual and physical well-being of the natives, it completely ignored the social and psychological effects of immediate emancipation on the slave population. These were problems that had to be solved before the new law could go into effect; otherwise the colony would be faced with social and economic chaos. The failure of the home government to anticipate these problems is truly amazing. Small wonder that the Chileans refused to abide by the Crown's decision.

Fortunately for all concerned, Governor Henríquez was more realistic than his superiors in Madrid. His position, however, was extremely precarious: as chief representative of the Crown he was expected to enforce the decree unreservedly, but he knew full well that any attempt to do so would arouse the determined opposition of the propertied class and conceivably result in revolution. To make matters worse, he himself had profited handsomely from the sale of Indian slaves in the past,[50] thus providing the hacendados with a reason for assuming that his office would be sympathetic to their cause in the crisis. To please both sides without compromising himself would not be easy.

Henríquez reacted to the challenge in a masterly fashion. On receipt of the decree he dutifully ordered the frontier garrisons to desist from enslaving any more Indians, under pain of forfeiting their property and their lives, and to prevent the native auxiliaries from doing so also.[51] In this way he demonstrated a willingness to enforce the law and protected himself against subsequent charges of having been remiss in his duties. He next enlisted the aid of the audiencia in determining the steps to be followed in freeing the slaves. This clever move served to provide additional proof of a desire to implement the Crown's command, to make the oidores partially responsible for what followed by involving them in the decision-making process, and to enable the governor to propose a compromise arrangement that would reassure the hacendados. The decree, Henríquez reminded the judges, had instructed the colonial officials to ensure the spiritual and material welfare of the slaves after their emancipation. This, he maintained, would be impossible if they were freed unconditionally, for he was personally convinced that they would straightway return to their native provinces, resume their former barbarous ways, and end up by apostatizing. To prevent this he suggested assigning them temporarily to trustworthy persons (namely, their current owners or encomenderos) who would agree to treat them as freemen and watch over their spiritual and material wants until the Crown decided differently.[52]

Two of the judges, Juan de la Peña Salazar and José de Meneses, expressed approval of the governor's proposal. The third, Diego de Portales, objected to it on the grounds that it did not differ essentially from the system of repartimientos and personal service that had been prohibited on numerous occasions. His own solution, however, was not much better. In order to guard against the danger of apostasy, he recommended that the emancipated adult males be organized into special encomiendas under the care of reputable citizens and assigned to live in separate reductions of their own. This would free them from control by their former masters and enable them to live together in more congenial surroundings. Similarly, female slaves and male children who were too young to be included in the encomiendas were to be entrusted to the care of a designated person in each district or reduction and allowed to work freely without being forced to go outside the district. Meneses and De la Peña refused to go along with this recommendation, arguing that it failed to prevent the newly freed slaves from wandering off on their own, giving up the Faith, and reverting to barbarism. Once that happened the problems confronting the government and the army would be multiplied endlessly.

Since two of the judges supported his plan, Henríquez decided to put it into operation. On September 28, 1676, he ordered the corregidores of the individual *corregimientos* (administrative units) to begin drawing up registers of all the Indian slaves living in their districts, noting the name, age, place of origin or birth of each, and the legal title under which they were being held. After this was done the corregidores were to reassign the now "emancipated" slaves to their former masters with the understanding that the latter would deal with them kindly and in a Christian manner, providing for their education and religious training. The Indians, for their part, were to abide by this arrangement or be punished.[53]

The governor's compromise met with general approval from the interested groups in the colony, for it enabled the slaveholders and encomenderos to evade the objectionable provisions of the emancipation act by retaining control of their encomienda workers and slaves. Theoretically and legally the slaves were now free; actually they were as closely tied to their Spanish overlords as before.

Henríquez still had the unpleasant task of informing both the viceroy, the Count of Medellín, and King Charles II of what he had done. To convince them that all was for the best, he directed separate letters to them in October 1676, explaining why it had been judged impractical to give the Indian slaves their unrestricted freedom immediately. He emphasized, first of all, the serious economic loss the slaveowners would have suffered if they had suddenly been deprived of their valuable and costly investment. He then pointed out that, because of the numerical superiority of the Indian slaves, there was a very real danger that the liberated slaves would have been tempted to turn upon their former masters had they been granted their unconditional release. The need to forestall such a catastrophe was self-evident. There was also the danger that the emancipated mapuches would have refused to continue working for the Spaniards, thus stripping the farms and haciendas of the laborers needed to keep them functioning and thereby destroying the economy of the colony.

The governor's reasoning presented Charles II with an embarrassing dilemma, for approving the compromise would be equivalent to revoking the emancipation declaration. But insisting that the original declaration be enforced would apparently expose the colony to very grave disorders. Neither of these alternatives was acceptable, but how could he avoid both of them without losing face?

The answer that Charles II devised surprised everybody. In a move reminiscent of the shortsighted policies of some of his predecessors, he proposed to solve the difficulty by transferring it to a different locale. On June 12, 1679, he issued an unexpected decree in which he solemnly reaffirmed the emancipation legislation of 1674 and then calmly negated its effects by ordering the initiation of a comprehensive program to transport all liberated male slaves from Chile to Peru, where they

were to become members of encomiendas under the care of reliable
Christians. The removal was to be accomplished gradually over a period
of years without straining the financial resources of the government,
by making use of the fleet that carried the annual military subsidy
(*situado*) to Chile.

This program, the king confidently asserted, would keep the Indians
from reverting to their ancient pagan practices, would eliminate the
possibility of an unfavorable alliance between the ex-slaves and anti-
Spanish intruders in Chile, and would benefit the Indians themselves
by settling them in a more favorable climate.[54]

The royal edict caused rejoicing in Peru and consternation in Chile.
The Peruvian capitalists, always on the lookout for cheap labor to
replenish the decimated ranks of their native workers, were particularly
happy at the prospect of obtaining a steady supply at no cost to themselves. The Chileans, whose need was equally great, understandably
resented a measure that threatened to deprive them of their principal
source of wealth.[55] As Governor Henríquez hastened to impress on
the king in a letter of December 6, 1680, the proposed expatriation
could only result in the complete annihilation of the deportees. The
Peruvian climate was so radically different that the Chilean mapuches
would be unable to adjust sufficiently well to survive the change.[56] He
was convinced that if the Indians were given a choice between freedom
in Peru or bondage in Chile they would unhesitatingly opt to stay.
Furthermore, the Indians in question were married men whose wives
and families would also have to be included in the transfer; otherwise
the government would be guilty of breaking up homes, destroying
family life, and violating the sacred bonds of matrimony. Added to
this was the fact that the government would have to pay for the cargo
space it preempted in the situado fleet. Thus the cost of implementing
the entire program would be far greater than the Crown had originally
estimated, and would make the plan unfeasible, because there were
no funds available in the colonial coffers to underwrite the operation.
There were other considerations, too, Henríquez noted. Chile needed
all the help it could get to maintain itself, to wage the internal struggle
against the defiant Araucanians, and to defend its shores against the
inroads of aggressive European powers. If the king's plan were put
into effect the colony would before long become depopulated, the

fields would remain idle, and a strategic outpost of Spanish empire in the New World would wither away and die.[57]

The governor's plea had the desired effect. By a decree dated in Madrid on May 19, 1683, Charles II reversed his earlier decision, cancelled the deportation project, allowed the emancipated slaves to remain in Chile, and magnanimously exempted them from the obligation of paying tribute for a period of ten years dating from 1679. A like exemption, starting with the year of their capitulation, was extended to all hostiles who voluntarily made peace with the Spaniards and accepted Spanish rule. After the periods of grace were up both groups were to begin paying tribute to the Crown like other royal subjects.[58]

The decree of May 19 was too generous for the colonials' acquisitive tastes. The only clause that was scrupulously observed was the one forbidding the transfer of emancipated slaves to Peru. In all other respects the "liberated" slaves were no better off. Though free in the eyes of the law, they still had no real freedom of choice, no personal independence, and no social mobility.

Likewise, the decrees of 1674 and 1683 did not put an end to the exploitation of Indian hostiles captured in the war, although they did mitigate to some extent the hardships and indignities to which they had formerly been subjected. Since they could no longer be sold as slaves, they were spared the ignominy of being auctioned off like cattle on the open market, but they still had to pay the penalty for participating in an alleged conspiracy against the State. After 1674 this penalty invariably took the form of being "deposited," that is, placed in the custody of some hacendado who agreed to keep an eye on the prisoners in exchange for the privilege of profiting from their labor. Although he was to compensate them for their work, in practice this amounted to keeping them alive and well by feeding, housing, and clothing them, and controlling their tendencies to vice. It did not include a salary that might have enabled them to become economically independent at some future date. In effect, therefore, the custodial system was little more than a variation of the familiar servicio personal, but with the important distinction that the prisoners assigned to the Spanish hacendado did not belong to him in the sense that his encomienda Indians did. Theoretically at least, they were merely entrusted to him until the Crown would either approve the system or order some other disposition to be made of hostiles seized in the war. Nor was his control over his charges as absolute as that which he exercised over his encomienda workers, since there was always the possibility that he might be deprived of their services if they complained to the corregidors of mistreatment and the complaint proved, on investigation, to be true. This built-in control tended to keep the hacendado in line, thus lessening the possible grievances of the prisoners. It did not, of course, rectify the intrinsic inequity of a system that assumed guilt without proof.

Besides satisfying the hacendados, the custody arrangement could be justified by politicians. As Governor Garro explained to the king in a letter of January 18, 1684, the system was both just and necessary. The Indians included in the "deposits" benefited from the good treatment and training they received, and the peace and security of the realm were measurably enhanced "because if left without any supervisory control [the captured Araucanians] would, as a result of their natural instability, repeat the same crimes of which they had been guilty on previous occasions."[59] Significantly, no mention was made in the letter of the economic advantages of the system.

Shortly after Garro had dispatched his letter of January 18 to Spain, the royal cédula of May 19, 1683, revoking the idea of deporting the ex-slaves to Peru and exempting them from paying tribute for a period of ten years, finally reached Chile. Concern lest the king be persuaded to extend the same privilege to the prisoners of war already assigned to deposits prompted the governor to direct another appeal to the Crown on July 28, 1684, repeating at greater length the reasons why such a move would be unwise. Were the prisoners to be freed, he contended, they would return to Araucania and become hostile, thus losing the healthy effects of their contact with Spanish civilization. The lives of the deposit Indians and of their families would be disrupted. Furthermore, without the workers, the fields would become sterile, seriously affecting not only the food supply of Chile but also that of Peru.[60] The governor reiterated the precautions he had taken to ensure the proper treatment of the war prisoners and the payment of their *jornales* (daily wages), concluding his remarks with a summary of the practical difficulties that impeded an early application of the royal decree.[61]

As had been the case when Henríquez was governor, so on this occasion the views of the local administration proved decisive. In an edict of November 19, 1686, Charles II provisionally approved the depository system that Garro advocated.[62] Two other decrees on the same subject dated March 18 and April 18, 1688, reminded the colonials that prisoners of war were not to be incorporated into existing encomiendas under any circumstances but were to remain in the custody of those to whom they had been assigned for a period of ten years, during which time the tribute they paid was to go only to the royal treasury.[63] Even though the Chilenos had not gained all they wanted, their primary goal had been achieved: approval of the custody plan and with it the opportunity to capitalize on the labor potential of the Araucanians.

José de Garro was less successful, however, in his efforts to obtain royal approval of his plan for the subjugation of the Araucanians. Disturbed by the humiliating inability of the Spaniards to conquer Arauco, Garro came up with what he considered a surefire scheme for solving the problem. The plan was simple and direct, with duplicity as its main ingredient. Garro proposed—first to the viceroy of Peru, the Duke of La Palata, and later to the king—to invite all the enemy chiefs and tribal fathers to a massive peace conference, during which the Spanish troops would capture the unsuspecting guests and lock them up in the guardhouses of the frontier forts. Once deprived of their headmen, he reasoned, the rest of the hostiles would quickly capitulate. The army could then move unmolested through rebel territory, round up the families and herds of the various tribes, and resettle them in areas under Spanish control where the job of keeping them in line and teaching them how to live like civilized beings would be immensely simplified. In this way the long-attempted pacification of Araucania could be brought to a bloodless and orderly conclusion.[64]

Both the viceroy and the king indignantly rejected Garro's proposal. In a strongly worded cédula of November 19, 1686, Charles II expressed amazement at the governor's audacity in thinking that the Crown would consent to such treachery, lectured Garro about the immorality of employing deceit to gain a good end, and forbade him to do anything that might upset the good relations then existing between the Indians and the whites. He reminded the governor that the troops on the frontier were to treat the Indians well, "dealing peaceably with them without using force and seeking to instruct them in the Faith and in the knowledge of letters." Furthermore, they were not to deprive the hostiles of their horses for precautionary reasons, as Garro had suggested, because the natives needed the animals to work their fields, and taking them away would only aggravate the owners and result in unpleasant complications.[65]

With the failure of his pet project, Garro resigned himself to maintaining the status quo and devoting his energies to other problems of state during the remainder of his term as governor.[66]

The administration of Tomás Marín de Poveda, who succeeded Garro as governor of Chile on January 6, 1692, was in sharp contrast to that of his energetic predecessor.[67] An Andalusian by birth, a member of the aristocracy by marriage and descent, and a connoisseur of gracious living, Marín de Poveda brought to the rough frontier society of Santiago a touch of elegance and refinement it sorely lacked. His marriage shortly thereafter to Doña Juana de Urnadegui, daughter of the Marquis de Villafuerte and a prominent figure in the social life of Lima, was the occasion for lavish feasting and public display. According to one contemporary account, the entertainment that saluted the newlyweds included, besides numerous sports events and kindred demonstrations "such as had never before been seen in Chile," the presentation of fourteen comedies that added novelty and variety to the general gaiety[68] and signalized the beginning of the legitimate theatre in Chile. It was, in a sense, the most enduring contribution of Marín de Poveda's administration.

As a society leader, Marín de Poveda was a smashing success, but as a political administrator, he was less spectacular. Although well-intentioned, generous, and sincere, he lacked the experience, firmness, insight, and tact needed to unify the colony and to guide its energies into productive channels. His handling of the Araucanian problem was a case in point.

Marín had taken office with orders from the Crown to put an end to the frustrating war in Araucania. The method he chose for carrying out this order was essentially the same as that which Luis de Valdivia had advocated eighty years earlier and Bartolomé de las Casas had urged so consistently in the sixteenth century: peaceful conquest through the ministry of the Word. The program began well enough, with the pacified tribes eager to cooperate. They appreciated the benefits—especially the newly established practice of government largesse[69] —that peace had brought, so they raised no objections to the influx of missionaries that followed. Nine new mission centers were established at Boroa, La Imperial, Repocura, Tucapel, Peñuela, Virquén, Mulchén y Renaico, Quecheregua, and Maquegua. The first three were assigned to the Jesuits; Tucapel, Peñuela, and Maquegua were staffed by Franciscans, and the remaining three were run in the beginning by members of the diocesan clergy.[70] A school for the training of the sons of caciques was another feature of the expansionist movement. Its establishment was formally approved and financed by the governor's *junta de hacienda* (committee on finances) in an *acuerdo* (resolution) of February 23, 1693, and a site not far from the old Spanish town of La Imperial was chosen for the purpose, with administration of the school entrusted to the Jesuits.[71]

For the first two years all went well. The natives were friendly and helpful, the missionaries busy and content.[72] But some of the pagan tribes were not. They resented the efforts of the padres to wean them away from their tribal customs, especially their adherence to polygamy. Misunderstandings occurred, tensions developed, and talk of war began again. A crisis might have been averted, thanks to the intervention of friendly caciques, had not the governor made a colossal blunder. Encouraged by the success of the mission program and unmindful of the resentment in the air, he decided to go a step further in bringing the hostiles to heel, by ordering the natives of Maquegua to leave their fortified mountain homes, take up residence in the plains country where they could more easily be Christianized and controlled, and get rid of their tribal *machis* (medicine men). This the Indians resolutely refused to do, saying that they were "happy in their mountain habitations and wanted no other; and just as the Spaniards had doctors of their own to cure them, so they had their medicine men to take care of them and to guard their tribal secrets. For these reasons they were determined to defend their liberty and their national customs."[73]

A wiser man than Marín de Poveda would have moved slowly in

the matter. But the governor was determined to enforce his will on the defiant mountaineers. The final break came when Nunguepanqui, a disgruntled chieftain of the frontier district of Virgüenco, killed a Spanish captain in charge of native allies, Miguel de Quiroga, and raised the standard of revolt.[74]

Marín, who happened to be in Concepción at the time, sought the advice of theologians and military men on the matter. All of them, so he informed the king in a letter of April 18, 1695, favored sending the army to punish the insurgents and, by a show of force, to prevent the friendly (but wavering) tribes from joining the uprising. To accomplish both of these objectives creditably, however, the assistance of the militia of Santiago, Chillán, and Concepción was considered necessary. "These militia," he explained to the king, "enlist for the defense of their own district. They serve without pay and they live by their work in cultivating the fields, on which their subsistence and that of their families depends. Consequently, they suffer great losses when drafted for service with the [regular] army" on the frontier.[75]

Financial loss was a favorite excuse of the vecinos in the more pacified areas north of the Biobío to justify not responding to the call to arms. To get around this difficulty and persuade them to sign up voluntarily, Marín de Poveda suggested allowing all citizens who participated in the fighting to retain for use on their own farms and haciendas, as part of the official custody system, all the rebels they captured during the campaign.[76]

The offer could not have been more tempting. As colonial society grew more refined the size of a householder's domestic staff had become a mark of distinction, especially in the capital city where social life was more active than in the provincial towns. Apart from this, there was always the demand for new blood to strengthen the labor forces in the rural areas. The response to Marín de Poveda's offer exceeded his most sanguine hopes. The vecinos of Santiago, spurred by the prospect of acquiring cheap labor, eagerly provided the government with financial loans to underwrite the military effort until the situado arrived from Peru, sold supplies on credit, and personally enlisted for active duty. The only disagreeable note in the preparations was the reaction of the audiencia, which interpreted the governor's enlistment bonus as a license to reestablish the forbidden institution of Indian slavery and brought pressure to bear on him to withdraw the offer.[77] This unexpected complication failed to stifle the enthusiasm of the people, however, for, since the deposit system was still in effect, they were confident that they would not miss out on a share of the spoils as originally planned.

Ironically, however, no spoils were forthcoming. The impressive combination of provincial militia, regular frontier troops, and Indian auxiliaries that Marín de Poveda was able to put into the field quickly cooled the rebels' zest for battle and caused them straightway to sue for peace. The governor would have preferred to teach them a lesson before coming to terms, but the necessity of defending the coast against the renewed threat of piracy dictated a quick cessation of hostilities.[78] The crisis passed without further bloodshed, and the situation reverted to the status quo ante bellum.[79]

The audiencia's opposition to the governor's enlistment ploy was a harbinger of other disappointments for the colonial officials. On June 21, 1693, Charles II had issued a general decree applicable to all the American colonies, confirming the right of the Indians to pay their tribute in money or in produce, rather than in personal service. If they chose to make payment in kind, the retail prices in effect in that particular locality were to be the basis for computing its cash value. The agents in charge of tribute collections were authorized, nevertheless, to demand payment in kind when circumstances warranted it, as in times of poor harvests or when the consumer price of the produce in question was excessive. Payment in kind was also recommended as a remedial device for forcing slothful Indians to develop sound work habits.[80] The provisions of the decree clearly show that the Crown was using the tribute payments as another way of combating the institution of personal service.

The decree had no perceptible effect on existing conditions in Chile, for the encomenderos successfully opposed every effort to substitute tribute payments in money or in kind for payment in manual labor. The fiscal of the audiencia of Chile, Gonzalo Ramírez Baquedano, exposed their economic motive clearly in a report to the king on April 25, 1696, when he said that "the encomenderos reap very ample benefits from the servicio personal throughout the entire year, because by his work in tilling the soil, breeding and butchering cattle and sheep, manufacturing linen cloth, and tanning leather, each Indian produces more than two hundred pesos' worth of products for his master."[81] No encomendero in his right mind was going to sacrifice this annual revenue for only a share of the eight and a half pesos that the ordinance of July 17, 1622, had fixed as the amount of tribute to be paid each year. Not only had the encomenderos blithely ignored the law, but the audiencia itself had violated the ordinance by approving a payment of ten pesos instead of only eight and a half for the jurisdictions of La Serena, Santiago, Chillán, and Concepción.[82]

Acting on the information supplied by Baquedano, the king issued a supplementary decree on July 16, 1700, in which he again ordered that the annual tribute was not to exceed eight and a half pesos. He also expressed displeasure that the servicio personal was flourishing despite the numerous instructions to the contrary, and informed the governor that he was that same day investing Alvaro Bernardo de Quirós, judge of the audiencia of Chile, with authority to enforce the tribute regulation strictly.[83] There is no record that Quirós was any more successful in carrying out his commission than the officials who had preceded him. Personal service was so closely linked with the encomiendas that as long as the latter remained intact the former was bound to continue also. Not until the appointment of Don Ambrosio O'Higgins as governor of Chile in 1788 was any permanent change effected in the status of Indian labor. Under his enlightened guidance the encomienda system was finally abolished in 1791, and with it the regime of forced labor that had been the reason for so much misery and strife in the past. By that date, however, the racial complexion of the colony had changed to such an extent that the Araucanian was no longer considered a menace to the future of Spanish supremacy in the land. Miscegenation had quietly accomplished what military force and peaceful persuasion had failed to achieve earlier: a stifling of the will to resist on the part of the once indomitable Araucanians.

BALANCING THE BOOKS

ONE REASON WHY the struggle for social justice in Chile was so long and so complicated was that the Spaniards were unable to bring the war in Araucania to a favorable conclusion. As we have seen, success in terminating the war was largely dependent on success in finding an equitable, viable solution to the problems of Indian slavery and forced labor. But other factors—most of which have already been mentioned— also played a part. The purpose of this final chapter is to examine these factors in greater detail to see what effect they had on the war and its continuance. To do so it will be necessary to turn the clock back to the early years of the colony when Pedro de Valdivia was governor of Chile, for it was his plan of conquest that was partly responsible for many of the difficulties that followed.

There seems to be little doubt that Valdivia's primary aim in conquering Chile was to civilize the country, not merely to exploit it. Admirable as this aim was, its realization was impeded from the start by his other overriding ambition to extend Spanish hegemony southward from Santiago to the Strait during his own lifetime.[1] In his letters to Emperor Charles V, Valdivia speaks repeatedly of the Strait as the chosen limit of his prospective conquests, and his actions following the founding of Santiago attest to the strength of this preoccupation.[2] Not content with establishing a center for future expansion on the Río Mapocho and consolidating his position before advancing further into enemy territory, he embarked on a program of optimistic settlement and exploration that ended in tragedy for himself and three centuries of racial strife and misunderstanding for Chile. The method he chose, erecting a cluster of small towns several hundred miles south of Santiago and close to the heart of the Araucanian homeland, was hazardous. The first of these, Concepción, was established in 1550, less than a decade after the founding of Santiago. La Imperial (modern Carahue) came into existence in 1551, followed by Valdivia and Villarrica[3] in 1552 and Los Confines[4] in 1553. Each of these municipalities was dignified with the allocation of land among the vecinos, the assignment of Indian encomiendas, and the appointment of secular cabildos. In addition to these political entities, Valdivia built three military posts in the same territory: Fort Arauco on the seacoast below Concepción, and Forts Tucapel and Purén farther inland on the western and eastern slopes, respectively, of the Nahuelbuta cordillera.

By giving the name La Imperial to one of the new frontier villages, Valdivia unwittingly revealed a hitherto unsuspected part of his plan— that this southern outpost, rather than Santiago, might become the political center of his territory. Mariño de Lovera, who fought at his side and who by chance escaped being killed with him at Tucapel, says that, upon arriving at the confluence of the Cautin and the Río de las Damas, Valdivia "decided to build a city there that would be the head of the realm."[5] In view of his preoccupation with the southern Strait and his avowed desire to bring all the intervening territory under Spanish rule, Valdivia's interest in transferring the capital of the colony to this area is understandable. An administrative center near the geographical heart of the country would certainly have been preferable to one situated much farther north. But fate (and the Araucanians) intervened, the project failed, and its author met an untimely end.

In choosing frontier towns as the most effective instrument of permanent occupation and control, Valdivia erred in attempting too much in too short a time with too few resources. Concepción was started with only forty vecinos. La Imperial had eighty, Valdivia, one hundred, and Villarrica, fifty.[6] The number of settlers located at Los Confines is uncertain, but it could not have been large. In all, some three hundred householders had the responsibility of developing an area of several hundred square miles, and this in the face of the ever-present danger of Indian attack. Valdivia apparently believed that the Indians no longer constituted a threat to Spanish designs in the region, a belief proven false by the uprising that occurred shortly thereafter, which resulted in his death.

By spreading his forces too thin, by widening the gap between the southern outposts and the pacified territory farther north, and by failing to protect the lines of communication between the two regions, Valdivia seriously weakened his defensive position and exposed the frontier to easy attack. Unfortunately many of his successors followed the same failing course thus unconsciously encouraging the Araucanians in their defiance and aiding their periodic raids and insurrections. As Miguel Amunátegui has observed: "The multiplication and isolation of the [frontier] towns, without sufficient settlers to populate them, was one of the gravest blunders the Spaniards committed in the conquest of Arauco."[7]

Failure to people adequately the frontier settlements affected the military situation in a number of other important ways. Besides facilitating hostile attack, it made defense of the region appreciably more difficult. It meant, for instance, that the army had to rely on outside supplies to maintain itself, instead of being able to live off the land as the enemy did. When these supplies were delayed or lost, as sometimes happened, the garrisons found themselves in desperate straits, being forced on more than one occasion to butcher their horses (a costly sacrifice for fighting men who depended upon the animals for offensive mobility while in the field), mules, and other animals, even cats and dogs, in order to survive. The suffering that accompanied these crises was often severe, as the following personalized account of the plight of one Spanish garrison near the confluence of the Laja and Biobío rivers vividly illustrates.

> After the scanty rations of wheat and barley were exhausted, I first assigned one of the two companies under my command the task of going out daily into the barren and unproductive countryside to gather thistles, of the kind that in Spain are customarily fed green to the horses, because this was the most nutritious "food" available. . . . Once the supply of these had given out we began collecting other unfamiliar plants, some of which made the men ill. . . . So extreme was the hunger the men endured that it was necessary to use force to restrain them while these "rations" were being distributed. The situation finally became so bad that no shield or other article made of leather was left untouched. The very palisades of the fort were torn apart to get at the leather thongs, rotted by exposure to sun and rain, which held the timbers together.[8]

The threat of starvation was only one of the many problems of the frontier garrisons. Another, perhaps more serious because of its origin and demoralizing effects, was the exploitation the troops experienced at the hands of greedy merchants and dishonest officials, exploitation often directly related to the administration of the military subsidy (situado), which the Crown began to appropriate at the beginning of the seventeenth century in a more determined effort to put an end to the struggle in Araucania. But instead of shortening the war, the subsidy actually prolonged it.

As initially introduced in 1600 the situado provided for the expenditure of 60,000 ducats a year (supplied from the royal treasury in Peru) to finance the military program in Chile. Within a few years this sum was increased to 212,000 ducats, a figure that remained more or less constant for the next century and a half. Had the bulk of this money been transferred intact to Chile and used for military salaries, as the Crown intended, the army would have had little trouble in attracting more capable recruits into its ranks, and the war might conceivably have been shortened. Prior to 1685, however, most of these funds were converted into merchandise and other matériel purchased in Peru and transported by boat to Concepción for sale to the troops on the frontier. This unwieldy system, a result of viceregal opposition to the flow of specie from Peru to Chile, provided numerous opportunities for large-scale graft. Instances of such irregularities began to crop up within a few years and became more common and notorious as the century advanced. Two of the prime offenders were the procurator general in Lima and the *situadista*, the special agent in charge of military buying, who worked through the procurator general's office. Both of these administrators profited handsomely from the kickbacks they received from merchants and speculators eager to secure military contracts.[9] Goods were often bought at inflated prices, with the difference being split between merchant and agent. Large sums were squandered carelessly on shoddy materials and luxury items of little or no value on the frontier, where guns and ammunition meant the difference between life and death and finding enough to eat was of more interest to the soldiers than wearing fine clothes.[10]

The allocation of contracts for transporting the situado from Callao to Concepción was the occasion for more profiteering. The shipowners, attracted by the prospect of making money out of the government, vied eagerly for the chance to carry the cargo, much to the delight of the government factors. Freight charges for each shipment usually ran as high as 8,500 pesos.[11]

The irregularities did not end with delivery of the goods at their destination. If anything, they increased. Mention has already been made in an earlier chapter of the scandalous activities of the Salazar brothers, who took over control of the quartermaster's office during the administration of Governor Acuña y Cabrera. Scores of other army officers apparently had been guilty of similar illicit practices long before the Salazars appeared on the scene, as is evident from a letter that Gabriel de Celada, one of the oidores of the audiencia of Chile, sent to the king in 1610.[12] The abuses he cited were repeated at length in the official report of the audiencia to the Crown one year later, part of which read as follows.

> The soldiers are extremely discouraged, for . . . the subsidy Your Majesty has provided is delivered almost entirely in goods from Peru on which they have to pay a tax of twenty-five to thirty per cent, and seldom less than twenty. Furthermore, the prices they are required to pay for food are excessive . . . and although the government operates two royal estates for the benefit of the garrisons and forts in the war zone, which concentrate on the production of wheat, barley, and beef[13] . . . which Your Majesty has commanded be made available to the soldiers at moderate prices, these products are being sold at more than double their original cost. . . . Another regrettable fact . . . is that most of the army captains and officers have adopted the trade of commercial wholesalers and retailers. The zeal that they ought to exercise in taking care of their troops they devote to figuring out ways and means of despoiling them of their pay by charging them exorbitant prices for supplies . . . with the result that the troops are left in a state of misery without shoes or stockings and with only a blanket or an animal skin with which to cover themselves in some fashion. Thus it is that not a few of them, driven by necessity and want, have defected to the enemy. Conditions are so bad that a mutiny of the troops such as was attempted in 1607 is more to be feared than the enemy.[14]

Merchants and military commanders were not the only ones who sought to make money out of the war. Prominent politicians and administrators, including several governors, also displayed a talent for black market dealings. Acuña y Cabrera, for example, condoned and abetted the misdeeds of his relatives in the service; Henríquez left the governorship in 1681 with a fortune estimated at one million pesos accumulated during his eleven years in office;[15] but the corruption associated with the name of Francisco de Meneses was decidedly worse. "During the four years of [his] administration," the audiencia of Chile reported to the king, "the troops were poorly clothed, without coverings for their feet and legs, ill-provisioned, and disgruntled. What little clothing they possessed was of inferior quality. They had no swords and were insufficiently supplied with other weapons." It is not surprising, the audiencia concluded, that many of the soldiers went "over the hill" and that many others engaged in petty thievery and crime.[16]

Abuses in the handling of the situado continued even after Meneses' dismissal from office. According to one official account of the period, profits of sixty and one hundred percent on the sale of goods to the soldiers were not unusual.[17] The situado was, in effect, as one writer has observed, "an open money bag into which everybody dug with both hands, except those for whose benefit the subsidy had originally been established."[18]

The situation improved temporarily during the 1680's following the loss of practically the entire annual shipment in the wreck of the *San Juan de Dios* some twenty-six leagues out of Concepción on November 26, 1683. This disaster enabled Governor Garro to convince the Crown that the situado should be delivered in specie rather than in goods, and that it should be transported overland from Potosí to avoid the dual hazard of the sea and piratical attack. Charles II approved the request on January 16, 1685. Chilean merchants and military personnel welcomed the change, for it meant cash salaries for the soldiers and officers and an increase in the supply of hard money circulating in the colony. The arbitrary suspension of situado payments during the 1690's, however, forced the army into debt amounting to more than two million pesos as a result of buying food and supplies on credit from local merchants and producers. Before the decade was out it had become extremely difficult to obtain further extensions of credit, and the army was once again faced with a crisis. Many of the troops deserted; others took to pillaging the farms and homes of private citizens in order to survive. "Conditions are so bad," Governor Marín de Poveda exclaimed, "that something that has never before happened has now become common: army officers are resigning their commissions because they are suffering from the same misery and destitution that the rest of the soldiers are undergoing. Garrison commanders are forced to allow their troops to scatter among the [private] estancias in search of something with which to cover their nakedness. The forts are left completely abandoned, because the garrisons simply leave whether they have permission to do so or not. It is impossible to bring them back to their posts as long as military order, discipline, and all other necessary resources are lacking."[19]

The privation and suffering that characterized military life on the frontier had such a demoralizing effect on officers and men alike that the army began to seek compensation wherever it could be found. One solution that quickly gained favor was the institution of slave hunts (described in an earlier chapter), a practice that was one of the principal reasons the Araucanians refused to make peace.

Another cause of the war's long duration was the inferior quality of the Spanish troops. During the early stages of the conquest, most of the fighting was done by the conquistadores and their followers, the original encomenderos who profited most directly from the distribution of lands and Indians. This was in keeping with an established custom whereby the recipient of a royal *merced* or grant of Indians assumed the obligation to bear arms in defense of the king's interests, not only in his own province but also in others as occasion demanded.[20] As long as this arrangement lasted, the Spaniards retained the upper hand despite the numerical superiority of the enemy, but with the pacification of the northern territory and the shift of military concentration to the south the situation changed radically. The encomenderos who had borne the brunt of the fighting earlier began to lose interest in the war, and stubbornly resisted all attempts by the government to keep them personally involved in the struggle. The colony, forced to rely more and more on outside help, had to use troops sent out from Peru and, less frequently, from Spain.[21] That these reinforcements were at best second-rate is evident from the documents of the period, which make frequent reference to their military and moral shortcomings. This was particularly true of the Peruvian recruits, an unsavory lot of idlers, thieves, restless mestizos, unruly Indians, troublesome politicos, and unwelcome foreigners, many of whom were pressed into service on the Chilean frontier as a penalty for crimes.[22] The reinforcements that Monroy, Villagra, and Valdivia himself brought back from Lima during the first decade of the conquest, for example, included many who had been condemned to exile from Peru because of their part in the separatist movement led by Gonzalo Pizarro. Similarly, the regiment that accompanied Hurtado de Mendoza to Chile in 1557 was composed mainly of rebels from the Jirón and Contreras uprisings.[23]

The value and reliability of such troops was clearly suspect. They had no feel for the country and no desire to remain there. As one army officer expressed it in 1594: "The name of Chile is becoming more hated every day," so much so that "not a single one of the men serving there at the present time who is not also a settler would remain if he were given permission to leave."[24] The situation did not improve with the passing of time. García Ramón reported to the king in 1607 that "the confidence we can have in people of this kind, who are so dissatisfied with their lot, is so slight that I assure Your Majesty that no ship on which they travel nor any that is anchored in our ports feels secure for fear that they will seize it and flee away in it."[25] Governor Jara Quemada repeated this complaint a few years later when he said: "There has not been a port in this kingdom through which they could leave that they have not tried to do so," and he urged the Crown to refrain from sending any more of these "low types and condemned criminals" to Chile.[26] Their lack of discipline and military esprit made them more of a liability than an asset in the struggle. Núñez de Pineda y Bascuñán, himself a veteran of numerous clashes, voiced the opinion of most of his contemporaries when he asserted that "four Chileans are worth more than a hundred of the troops sent down from Lima who usually arrive without clothes or arms, so that instead of filling the hearts of the enemy with fear and caution, they become for them an object of contempt, derision, and scorn."[27] Even the officers commanded little respect, since the majority of them were callow youths and mestizos with no military experience. The presence of Indians among these levies was a further disadvantage, Governor Jara Quemada noted, because it tended to revive past hatreds by "continuing the war of conquest that Yupangui, the Inca ruler of Cuzco, had initiated a century before the entry of the Spaniards [into Chile]."²⁸

In 1613 Governor Alonso de Ribera recommended that salaries in the Chilean army be increased in order to attract more reliable and honorable men into the service "because good soldiers are the best defense against mutinies and other disservices to Your Majesty." The prevention of mutinies was important, he explained, "for if the garrisons here were to attempt some change, as happened in the time of Alonso de Sotomayor and of Governor Alonso García Ramón, it would mean the end of this kingdom, because the rebels would leave their posts [on the frontier] and retire to Santiago . . . and everything would be lost, and that city itself would not be safe."²⁹ Unfortunately the recommendation was made at a time when the court of Philip III was faced with a widespread demand for economy and fiscal reform, leaving little time for attention to Chilean affairs.³⁰ The recommendation was accordingly ignored.

The low caliber of the frontier troops was clearly evidenced in their disgraceful treatment of the natives, allies and hostiles alike. Rape, theft, violations of property rights, and kidnapping were common occurrences. "The grievances that the unhappy Indians suffered [at the hands of the Spaniards]," Mariño de Lovera wrote in his *Chronicle*, "were truly deplorable. The soldiers raided their homes and haciendas, seized their stock and grain, kidnapped the Indians for use as servants and, what is worse, carried off the women for more shameful purposes, as is proved by the fact that in one encampment where there were soldiers recently arrived from Spain, together with others whom the maestre de campo had under his command, sixty of these women gave birth to illegitimate offspring in a single week. So justified was the anger of the Indians that their deep-seated spirit of rebellion is not at all amazing; what is amazing is that so many of them agreed to peace despite so much injury and evil inflicted upon them by the Spaniards."³¹

Such behavior by the troops was not confined to the war zone. The inhabitants of Santiago and the intervening territory had to put up with similar conduct whenever the soliders were allowed to go north for the winter. The audiencia of Chile commented on the disorders in its *informe* (report) of 1611:

This city of Santiago and the kingdom of Chile suffer serious loss every year from the governors' practice of allowing large numbers of soldiers to spend the winters in the towns of the pacified provinces. . . . Besides disturbing the peace with their licentious habits and quarrels, they commit many robberies and other crimes. Worst of all, when they depart to continue the war, each one takes with him four or six male and female Indians (the latter for use as concubines) whom he has stolen [from their masters], under the pretext of needing them for servants. In this manner they take away three or four hundred Indians every year, separating wives from husbands in many cases, and in others carrying off the sons and daughters, as a result of which the Indians living at peace with the Spaniards are constantly growing fewer and dying out.[32]

Sporadic efforts were made to improve the quality of the Chilean army, but these efforts had little effect. Thus on April 9, 1662, Philip IV informed the viceroy of Peru, the Count of Santistéban, that he was sending a contingent of 1,000 reinforcements to Chile by way of Buenos Aires as soon as the war with Portugal permitted. Philip also stated that he had understood from Santistéban's predecessor that "the companies of mestizos and mulattoes collected in Lima for service in Chile were of no help whatsoever, since they did not persevere in the king's service." He therefore instructed the viceroy to recruit instead Spaniards and other people who had migrated to the viceroyalty without official permission or whose period of legal residence had run out, as well as unemployed people or troublemakers. He suggested, furthermore, that some inducement be offered to swell the ranks of volunteers and urged the viceroy to use every available means to persuade members of the regular Spanish army in Peru to sign up for a tour of duty in Chile.[33]

Philip's proposals changed nothing. Criticism of the military continued and became particularly bitter during Meneses' governorship (1664–68). Despite his misuse of the situado, Meneses succeeded in keeping a powerful segment of the army favorably disposed by allowing them to indulge their weakness for lawlessness and violence. Three hundred of the best troops remained stationed in the capital and its environs during the four years of his administration where, in the words of one contemporary account, they committed "outrageous crimes of robbery, murder, assault, rape, brawling, fornication and such-like excesses without ever being punished and without performing any services of benefit to Your Majesty. . . . If any citizens took offense at these actions and went to register a complaint with the captain in charge, they soon regretted having done so because of the verbal abuse to which they were subjected."[34]

The frequency and regularity with which these charges of military crimes and misconduct recur in the documents of the seventeenth century suggest that the quality of the Chilean army did not appreciably improve as long as the Hapsburgs remained on the throne. This lack of improvement was a major psychological and military factor in the continued duration of the war. A better-disciplined, better-trained, better-led army would have refrained from the excesses that strengthened existing hostilities and created new ones, would have constituted a more effective fighting force, would have elicited more support from the civilian population, and, by inspiring more respect for Spanish power on the part of the enemy, would have prepared the way for a settlement of differences.

Opposition to the war on the part of the property owners in Santiago was another significant factor in its duration. This opposition began to manifest itself early in the struggle. The many demands made on the capital for men and supplies prompted the cabildo to send Juan Godinez as procurator to Lima in 1567 to petition the viceroy for relief from these burdens. According to the brief Godinez presented, the Santiagoans had already contributed more than 400,000 pesos to the military effort, thereby impoverishing themselves to such an extent that every house and hacienda was mortgaged or sold to meet the demands. "Since we have nothing further with which to bear the costs of this war except our immortal souls," Godinez exclaimed, "we wish to return them to the God from whom we received them, for it is certain that of the conquistadores who live in this city as vecinos, not three remain who are still capable of bearing arms, because they are so old, so maimed and reduced to such extreme poverty."[35] Bravo de Saravia, who was governor at the time (1567–75), substantiated Godinez's claim in a letter to the king some months later in which he urged the sending of reinforcements to Chile because the few Spaniards left in the colony were so "poor and worn-out."[36]

If any advantages accrued to the residents of Santiago from the Godinez mission they were only temporary at best. The hated requisitions continued and the resentment of the vecinos grew in proportion. The arbitrary methods employed by some government officials did nothing to improve relations. When sufficient quantities of horses, cattle, grain, and other supplies were not forthcoming from the local citizenry, the governor or his agents simply commandeered what was needed in exchange for promises of compensation from the royal treasury at some future date. In practice, as Mariño de Lovera remarked, what this amounted to was a forced gift from the colonists, since money to repay the "loans" was seldom found.[37]

A similar crisis occurred in 1581, when Governor Gamboa levied an extraordinary tax of 20,000 pesos on the capital to finance the war. The cabildo of Santiago once again dispatched procurators to Lima to protest this "tribute." The protest, seconded by Dr. Azocar, Gamboa's locum tenens in Santiago, did not pay off immediately, but it had its effect some years later when the audiencia of Lima exempted the Santiagoans from the obligation of providing men and supplies for the military campaigns.[38] The vecinos put the exemption to good use in 1596 and 1597, citing it as a justification for refusing to comply with the demands of Governor Oñez de Loyola for fresh contributions of money, horses, and supplies.

The establishment, by royal decree of January 1603, and March 1604, of a permanent standing army in Chile absolved the encomenderos of their legal responsibility to serve in the war, but it did not free them of their moral obligations. As the war dragged on, however, these obligations tended to be ignored in favor of more personal concerns. Thus when Governor Lazo de la Vega issued a call for new recruits in June 1630, following the setbacks at Picolhué and Los Robles earlier that year, not a single vecino volunteered his services. The audiencia of Chile had recourse to a manpower draft to raise the necessary troops,[39] but the draft produced only meager results: thirty encomenderos from Santiago and some 150 other volunteers (including a number of tramps).[40] The expenditure of two military situados at one time was eventually required before Lazo de la Vega succeeded in raising what Carvallo y Goyeneche termed "a mediocre force of 800 Spaniards and 500 auxiliaries"[41] with which he won the famous victory of La Albarrada on January 13, 1631, a victory that was wrongly heralded throughout the Americas and Spain as marking the end of the war in Arauco.

Santiago's opposition to the war was based on more than a reluctance to sacrifice its human and material resources for the benefit of the frontier provinces, and on more than a resentment of the uncouth soldiers who wintered in the capital. Civic pride also played an important part. Valdivia's predilection for the south had aroused the resentment of the Santiagoans during his own lifetime, and the preference that most of his successors displayed for Concepción during the sixteenth and seventeenth centuries kept this feeling alive. Prior to 1655 Concepción was the favorite residence of the governors, and Bravo de Saravia went so far as to urge that it be designated the capital of the colony, arguing that it was the most wealthy city in the kingdom.[42] As a possible seat of government, Concepción enjoyed a number of advantages over its rival: it was close to the scene of military action, it was a port town, and it contained a governor's house.[43] For much of this time Santiago was, in truth, as one writer has expressed it, "little more than a pasture for horses, a hospital for invalids, a lodging house for troops on leave, and a place of retirement and approaching death for worn-out soldiers."[44] After 1655 it became customary for the chief executives to divide their time between Concepción and Santiago, spending six months of the year in each locality. But it was not until the beginning of the eighteenth century and the administration of Governor Ibáñez de Peralta (1700–1708) that Santiago became the *de facto* as well as *de jure* political center of Chile.

The possibility of an uprising of encomienda Indians and slaves was a recurrent and not unfounded fear in the seventeenth century also influencing the attitude of the northern settlers toward the war. The prolonged Araucanian resistance and the occasional rebel victories undoubtedly had a disquieting effect on the pacified mapuches, especially those who had been captured in the fighting and sold as slaves to the Spanish hacendados. Alonso de Ribera called attention to this danger in a letter of 1613 in which he declared that "all the Indians are of one mind and one will with regard to us, as can be seen daily, for whenever there is a lack of Spaniards they begin circulating the skulls [of whites slain in battle] and the arrows [which are a summons to rebellion] throughout the pacified provinces all the way to Santiago."[45] Santiago de Tesillo, writing at a later date, expressed a similar view: "The pacified Indians, whom we call allies and who serve as soldiers in the war, are weak in their loyalty [to us] and their intentions are uncertain."[46]

Rumors of impending insurrections threw the capital into an uproar on more than one occasion. In March 1630, for example, two dispatches from Governor Lazo de la Vega reached Santiago from the south warning the audiencia of a band of three thousand hostiles moving north along the eastern side of the cordillera with a view to crossing over and launching a surprise attack upon the capital. Believing that the crossing would take place at Rancagua, the militia hurriedly left Santiago to take up a defensive position along the banks of the Cachapoal River,[47] leaving the city unprotected.

Anxieties increased in the days that followed as fresh reports of a suspected uprising of Negro slaves and encomienda workers began to filter in to Santiago from the outlying districts, notably Ligua, Colina, and Quillota. The audiencia met in special session on March 13 and 14 to consider ways of coping with this new threat. The oidores, concluding that their first responsibility was to the resident vecinos, decided to recall the militia from Rancagua, leaving only a token force of thirty men at the river to guard the pass and keep an eye on enemy movements. They also decided to distribute arms and ammunition to all able-bodied monks and ecclesiastics for additional support in case of attack.[48]

The expected rebellion and attack never occurred. The prospect of encountering organized resistance from the Santiagoans may have caused the hostiles to change their minds. As for the uprising of domestic slaves and workers, the opinion expressed by the oidor, Pedro Machado de Cháves, was probably the most accurate: the rumored insurrection was precisely that, nothing more than a rumor.[49]

Regardless of the outcome, the inhabitants of Santiago had profited from the incident, for they promptly set to work devising means of discouraging future insurrections. On April 30 of that year Francisco Alvarez Berrío, an influential official in the *hermandad* (police force), requested the enactment of a law forbidding Indians to use horses for travel. Of all the oidores on the audiencia, only Machado de Cháves opposed the recommendation arguing that it would be contrary to the king's wishes regarding equal treatment for his vassals to enforce such a law. Machado recommended, therefore, that the Crown's advice be sought in the matter before taking any action, but his colleagues disagreed and ordered the prohibition to be promulgated and enforced.[50] An additional effort to avoid domestic uprisings was Lazo de la Vega's order to the cabildo of Santiago to distribute firearms to all the vecinos, in exchange for funds to buy grain for the frontier garrisons.[51]

Another incident occurred in 1647 in connection with the great earthquake of May 13, which devastated the city of Santiago and much of the surrounding area for a distance of 100 leagues.[52] The uncertainty accompanying this disaster fed a fear that the hacienda workers would take advantage of the widespread confusion to seek revenge for past cruelties. The audiencia later informed the king:

> The rumor spread, not without some foundation, that the Indian slaves were conspiring with the Negroes to stage an uprising. . . . Since tumults among desperate-minded idlers and malcontents are dangerous at such times, and since the Indian workers are bellicose by nature, resent the detestable servitude under which they live, and have armed support close at hand in the persons of the hostiles, and since the houses [of the city] were in a defenseless condition because of the damage [caused by the earthquake], it was decided to . . . publicly play down the rumors . . . [while] secretly making diligent inquiries to ascertain the truth in order to forestall any mischief. One Negro who had foolishly amused himself by going around making wild boasts, was hanged on the pretext that he had accidentally killed a Negro woman (for which reason a lawsuit had already been brought against him), had been convicted of attacking his master with a lance, and had claimed to be a son of the ruler of Guinea. By means of this execution and by doubling the amount of work required of the slaves, by keeping them separated at night, by alerting the night patrols to be on the lookout for suspicious activity, by locking up the firearms in the guardroom, and by taking other precautions the authorities succeeded in stifling the rumors and allaying the terror they had caused.[53]

Even though the rumors of projected insurrections were usually false, the panic they caused was real. The incentive to rebel was constantly present in the exploitation to which the Indians were subjected, and the vecinos knew this. Living with it was the price they had to pay for the slavery and injustice they favored and condoned. But it was also an excuse for abstaining from the war.

The scarcity of Spanish manpower during the sixteenth and seventeenth centuries was clearly a significant handicap from a military as well as a social and economic standpoint. No doubt this scarcity of resources prolonged the war. Prior to 1600 the statistical information on this point is quite reliable, because the bulk of the white population was composed almost entirely of military personnel whose arrival in the colony was duly noted in the official records. Encina, who has examined the pertinent data in some detail, estimates that the population of Chile at the end of the sixteenth century included, roughly speaking, 2,400 Spaniards (principally soldiers), 480,000 Indians (the great majority of whom lived south of the Biobío), 16,000 mestizos, and 5,000 Negroes, mulattoes, and *zambos*.[54]

Population figures for the seventeenth century, on the other hand, are too fragmentary, confused, and contradictory to be reliable. According to a census compiled in 1613 by the oidor Hernando de Machado, there were 1,717 Spaniards, 8,600 Indians, and 300 Negroes living in Santiago and the adjacent districts at that time.[55] Statistics for the decade of the 1630's suggest progress but are more confusing. In 1633, for example, Bishop Salcedo informed the Crown that there were 4,000 Spaniards living in Chile.[56] A memorial of the following year drawn up by Lorenzo de Arbieto, secretary to Governor Lazo de la Vega, stated that Santiago had 500 vecinos, from which Encina estimates a total population of 3,500 Spaniards and "Spanish" mestizos on the basis of the average size of families in those days. Concepción reportedly had more than 500 Spanish settlers; Chillán had approximately 200, and La Serena a similar number.[57] Five years later the audiencia of Chile asserted that "the Spaniards in the whole of this kingdom, including the provinces of Cuyo [in modern Argentina], number between 700 and 800 souls distributed among eight towns."[58] Besides not matching each other, these estimates are at variance with documentary evidence from other sources, which lists more than 500 clergy and religious and more than 2,000 soldiers resident in the colony during these years.[59] The discrepancies are explained in part by the fact that some documents patently refer only to the number of adult Spaniards capable of performing military service, while others apparently include all the vecinos and their families, and still others concentrate only on the civilian population without taking into account the military, the clergy, and the members of religious convents and monasteries. Thus the audiencia's informe of 1639 evidently refers only to the civilian population of military age and says nothing about the army, the ecclesiastics, the religious, and the women and children, whose number was usually several times greater than that of the adult males in the urban areas. Bishop Salcedo's estimate apparently includes the military, but the context indicates that he is referring only to adult males.

Another reason for the discrepancies is the application of the term "Spaniards." This concept, which was very clear in the sixteenth century when it referred only to the *peninsulares* and *criollos*, had already become blurred by the third decade of the seventeenth, by which time a mestizo race had developed and the colony's social structure had begun to change. In the most restricted sense, "Spaniard" referred to the peninsulares, their pureblood offspring, and the grandchildren of mestizo mothers who belonged to the upper class of society. A broader use of the term included all mestizos with Spanish blood who were accepted as being capable of living like Spaniards. In this sense, the concept excluded the "people," the mass of mestizos who made up the artisan class, the city workers, the farm hands, and so forth. When it was a question of computing the men of military age, however, it was customary, at least later on in the century, to count as Spaniards or white anyone who spoke Spanish, who was a Christian, and who followed a way of life that was more European than indigenous. In this wider meaning of the term, upper-, middle-, and lower-class groups were included as Spaniards, in contrast to the encomienda workers, the Indian slaves, the Negroes, and the multiple mixed breeds resulting from the union of these latter blood types.

Using the second definition of the term, which predominated during the first half of the seventeenth century, as the basis for comparison, the known statistics suggest that the "Spanish" population in the 1630's fluctuated between ten and eleven thousand.[60] A comparison with totals cited earlier for the end of the sixteenth century reveals only a small increase in the Spanish population during the thirty-two years between the disaster of 1598 and 1630. It must be remembered, however, that the destruction of the southern towns in the uprising of 1598 resulted not only in the capture or death of more than 1,000 "white" inhabitants of the northern zone, but also in the loss of numerous mestizos who, cut off from the influence of the Spaniards, reverted to Indian ways. Epidemics and disease took a further toll of life during this period, especially among the mestizos.

The same problems of interpretation complicate an accurate estimate of Spanish population at the end of the century. In 1671 Governor Henríquez observed that there were in Santiago 739 men of military age, and twice that number if the outlying rural districts of the capital were included.[61] In 1702 Governor Ibáñez reported that "as a result of the musters that I have caused to be made among the vecinos, business men, and common people [of Santiago], I have ascertained that there are in this city more than 800 men qualified to bear arms, including the cavalry companies of the agricultural districts of Calera and Tango."[62] Thus while the population of the colony doubled during the last four decades of the century, the number of men of military age had seemingly diminished by fifty percent. The apparent contradiction is resolved by noting that Henríquez was referring to all adults of military age while Ibáñez was speaking only of trained militia.[63] Encina accordingly concludes that by the end of the seventeenth century the total population of Chile in the territory between Copiapó in the north and the Biobío in the south was 152,000, of whom 110,000 were Spaniards and "Spanish" mestizos, 20,000 were Indians and native half-breeds, approximately 15,000 were Negroes, mulattoes, and zambos, and some 7,000 were pacified Indians in Chiloé.[64]

These statistics, interpretive as they are, nevertheless suggest that the manpower resources of the colony during the period under consideration were insufficient to meet the demands of the war in Arauco. In any event, help from outside was a priority need throughout the seventeenth century. At the same time it became increasingly difficult for the Spanish government to ease this need with reinforcements from the Peninsula because of the many pressures, internal and external, under which the Empire was laboring at home. International rivalries weakened the Spanish position in Europe, dictated the diversion of men and money to other areas to deal with these crises, and thus prevented the dispatch of necessary aid to Chile. Without an army of adequate size with which to challenge the Araucanians effectively, it was impossible to bring the war to a successful conclusion.

THE DEATH OF THE RACHITIC and mentally incompetent Charles II on November 1, 1700, is a convenient point at which to terminate this discussion of the struggle for social justice in Chile. With his demise, the Age of the Hapsburgs came to an end, and the conflict between Araucanians and whites also began to acquire a new dimension. By the beginning of the eighteenth century the unpacified tribes south of the Biobío had lost much of their earlier aggressiveness and were clearly on the defensive. A hundred and fifty years of bloody, inconclusive strife had taken their toll, and the hostiles were now more interested in preserving their liberty and defending their lands than in seeking revenge for real or imagined wrongs. Native uprisings still occurred,[65] but they were few and far between and did not seriously threaten the white man's position in the land. The colonists, too, had had their fill of war by this time and were ready to direct their energies into more productive channels—such as the establishment of new towns[66]—to consolidate their resources instead of expending them on military campaigns. Most important of all, however, was the gradual evolution taking place in the economic and social structure of the colony. With the emergence of a mestizo laboring class, a product of the miscegenation of the preceding century, the demand for Indian slaves began to decline and with it one of the principal sources of friction between the two races. The social and administrative reforms that Charles III introduced during the second half of the century accelerated this trend by giving the Indian more legal and social freedom, finally bringing about the permanent abolition of the encomienda system and forced labor in 1791. Although the still unconquered Araucanians refused to capitulate for another ninety years, they ceased to be a significant influence in Chilean life.

As the discussion in the foregoing pages has tried to make clear, the struggle for justice in Chile during the sixteenth and seventeenth centuries was a complex undertaking affecting practically every sector of colonial activity—political, economic, social, military, and religious. The origins of the movement and the reasons for its continuance were likewise numerous and complex. The abuses connected with the encomienda system, the vicissitudes of official Spanish policy on the subject, the unwillingness or inability of local administrators to enforce the law, the scarcity of Spanish manpower that led to the introduction of Indian slavery, the greed of landed proprietors and city merchants, the corruption of military officers and colonial bureaucrats, the numerous changes in administrative control, the lack of a coordinated military program, the inferior quality of many Spanish troops, the difficult terrain, the success of the Araucanians in adapting to new methods of fighting,[67] their ability to live off the land and to wage guerrilla warfare[68]—all of these circumstances made the struggle for justice by the Chilean Indians a prolonged and a unique experience for the Spanish conquerors. To single out any one of them to the exclusion of the others would be rash indeed. Yet the weight of evidence points to the conclusion that some were more important than others and that disregard of the rights of the natives was the most important of all.

That the Spaniards themselves were of this opinion is clear from the frequent attempts at corrective legislation during the first century and a half of the colony's existence. But the refusal of the encomenderos to support measures that threatened their interests doomed these efforts to failure from the start. From a moral and legal standpoint, the emancipation decree of 1674 was a major triumph for the proponents of racial justice, but the decree proved to be intrinsically defective, and its enforcement was easily circumvented. Despite the efforts of sincere legislators and zealous ecclesiastics, basic attitudes changed little between 1540 and 1700, and the abuses that fostered antipathy between Indians and whites continued to prevent a rapprochement.

To fault the people of the sixteenth and seventeenth centuries for not being more conscientious in the observance of interracial justice would be unfair, especially when our own generation, three hundred years later, is encountering difficulty in wrestling satisfactorily with similar problems, for some of the same reasons. Legislation that was designed to correct injustices failed at that time because it went counter to the interests of the propertied class and lacked the support of public officials who controlled its enforcement and who profited, directly or indirectly, from maintaining the status quo. A recognition of this fact—and its implications—by men of goodwill may, in the long run, prove to be the most significant result of the unhappy strife between Indians and whites in the Long Land.

NOTES

Complete authors' names, titles, and publication data are given in the Bibliography, pp. 301–13.

Chapter 1

1. López de Gómara, p. 156.
2. The report, which was intended for official eyes only, was entitled *Discurso y Reflexiones Políticas sobre el estado presente de los Reynos del Perú*. It was the work of Jorge Juan y Santacilia and Antonio de Ulloa, two young officers from the aristocratic Guardia Marina, who had been designated by Philip V to accompany an expedition of French scientists to South America in 1735. Based upon the authors' personal observations and experiences during the period between 1736 and 1744, the document was a scathing account of the social and political scandals and abuses existing in the viceroyalty of Peru at the time. Because of its damaging character it remained hidden in the secret archives of the Spanish government until 1826 when David Barry, an English merchant in Cádiz, succeeded in acquiring a copy of it which he published in London, with certain uncomplimentary interpolations of his own, under the propagandistic title of *Noticias secretas de América*. For a critical evaluation of the ecclesiastical aspects of the report as well as of associated historiographical problems, especially the reliability of the Barry edition, see Merino. Regarding the authenticity of the report and its historical veracity, see Hanke, "Dos Palabras," and the articles by Arthur P. Whitaker listed in the Bibliography.
3. Las Casas, *Historia*, II, 71. For a shorter version, see Herrera y Tordesillas, II, 310. For a discussion of the evolution of the terms encomienda and repartimiento, see Simpson, *Encomienda*; Kirkpatrick; and Zavala, *La encomienda*. The introduction of forced labor was a by-product of the first serious uprising of Indians against whites in the history of America. The uprising, which broke out in 1494 while Columbus was absent in Spain, had been occasioned by the intolerable demands for food by the colonists on the natives. On his return Columbus tried to regularize the situation by levying a small tribute of gold or cotton payable four times a year by all Indians over fourteen years of age. Labor service was later substituted to accommodate those who could not afford payment in kind. For a list of the Spaniards killed in the uprising, see Navarrete, II, 18–20.

4. For an account of this episode as reported by an interested party, see Ferdinand Columbus's biography of his father as translated and annotated by Benjamin Keen (Keen, pp. 191–211).

5. Cédula of Queen Isabella to Nicolás de Ovando, December 20, 1503, in Pacheco *et al.*, XXXI, 209–12. Italics added.

6. Letter of Ferdinand to Diego Columbus, March 20, 1512, in Chacón y Calvo, p. 429.

7. The encomienda in Chile, for example, was not effectively abolished until 1791.

8. Simpson, *Encomienda*, pp. 16–28; Zavala, *La encomienda*, pp. 5–11. For the contract between Ferdinand and Pinzón, see Pacheco *et al.*, XXXI, 309–17.

9. Simpson, *Encomienda*, p. 20. Typical of Ferdinand's attitude were his instructions to Diego Columbus following the latter's appointment as governor of the Indies, October 21, 1508. This document includes a number of passages that admirably express the king's ideas on the Indians. The opening admonition concerning the converison and charitable treatment of the natives is effectively countermanded in later clauses. The king complains of the high price of slaves and instructs Columbus to arrange for the procurement of cheaper ones from the "useless" (because lacking in gold) Bahama islands. He also suggests that it would simplify matters if some pretext could be found for depriving these new Indians of their free status and making them outright slaves. See Instruction of Ferdinand to Diego Columbus, August 14, 1509, in Pacheco *et al.*, XXXI, 436–39. Another cédula of the same date granted kidnapping patents to various Spanish adventurers on the condition that half of the captured Indians were to become the property of the Crown. The others the kidnappers could keep for themselves by paying the king half a peso per head. The need for more workers in Hispaniola was assigned as the reason for this license. Cédula of Ferdinand to Diego Columbus, August 14, 1509, in *ibid.*, XXXI, 449–52. The colonists, of course, needed little encouragement to engage in such activities. By 1510 the supply of Indians in the Bahamas had been well-nigh exhausted, and covetous eyes were looking in the direction of Cuba, Jamaica, and points farther west. Letter of Ferdinand to Diego Columbus and the royal officials, June 15, 1510, in *ibid.*, XXXII, 79–95; Zavala, *La encomienda*, pp. 5–7.

10. For a résumé of the memorial of abuses that the Dominican friar Antonio de Montesinos presented to the king, see Las Casas, *Historia*, II, 450–51.

11. Heredia, *Un precursor*, p. 5. Heredia thus disagrees with Las Casas, who located Paz at the University of Salamanca in 1512 (Las Casas, *Historia*, II, 453). Since he considers Paz a forerunner of Vitoria, he finds evidences of similarity in their thought. However, he hastens to note that Paz fell into two capital errors that Vitoria later refuted: the denial of true sovereignty or dominion among the infidels, and the supposition that the Pope, as vicar of Christ on earth, has direct temporal jurisdiction over the entire world. Heredia traces these limitations to the excessive respect Paz had for the opinions of canonists, to his deficient knowledge of Thomistic doctrine, and to his failure to assimilate the distinctions that the Dominican Cardi-

nal Torquemada had introduced a half century earlier into the dispute over the temporal jurisdiction of the papacy.

12. Other members of the Council were Bishop Juan Rodríguez de Fonseca, the Crown minister in charge of Indian affairs; Hernando de Vega, "a most prudent man esteemed as such throughout Castile"; Luis Zapata, a prominent Licentiate whose influence with the king was so great that he was called *regulus*, "little king"; the Licentiate Santiago; the Licentiate Móxica, a learned and virtuous man; the Licentiate de Sosa, who later became bishop of Almería, a man of much virtue who was partial to the Indians; the Licentiate Gregorio, a theologian and court preacher; Fray Bernardo de Mesa, another court preacher; and the Dominican scholars Tomás Durán and Pedro de Covarrubias. Las Casas, *Historia*, II, 452–53.

13. Zavala and Millares Carlo, p. xxx; Heredia, *Un precursor*, p. 8; Las Casas, *Historia*, II, 458.

14. This looks very much like the ideological germ of the notorious *requerimiento* (requirement) by which Spanish *adelantados* attempted to dignify their conquests with a semblance of legality. For a brief discussion of this "most remarkable document," see Hanke, *The Spanish Struggle for Justice*, pp. 31–36.

15. Paz, pp. 222–23.

16. John Major, a Scottish professor at the University of Paris, was one of the first of the sixteenth-century theoreticians to apply Aristotle's idea to the American scene. See Leturia; Hanke, *Aristotle*, p. 14.

17. Paz, pp. 220–22.

18. For some interesting facts concerning the circumstances and date of composition of this document, see Zavala and Millares Carlo, pp. xiii–xvii.

19. Las Casas, *Historia*, II, 452; III, 28, 112.

20. Zavala and Millares Carlo, pp. 30–32.

21. This principle was regularly observed in the Spanish administration of the Americas, "for it fitted into the Spanish scheme of things to exempt the ruling class (*caciques*) from debasing labor, as well as from certain taxes, services, and restrictions. The cacique class, in fact, was early incorporated into the Spanish system of government. It supplied the local governors, mayors, police, councilmen, tax collectors, overseers, and petty magistrates the country over, and its oppression of the *macehuales* [Indian working class] was, if anything, worse than that of the Spaniards." Simpson, *Studies*, p. 4.

22. Palacios Rubios, p. 36.

23. *Ibid.*, pp. 37–38. Zavala believes that Palacios Rubios was here thinking of the encomienda as the concrete institution for bringing the Indians under the control of wiser and more experienced men without depriving them of their liberty. His opinion is supported by a passage in the treatise that reads as follows: "First of all, we must admit that these islanders [namely, the Indians] are obliged to perform the same services and duties as are incumbent on the subjects of this realm with whom they have been incorporated. If they are unable to perform them, then they should be given others that are the equivalent, provided always that these latter do

not encroach upon their personal freedom. These tributes and services Your Majesty may freely assign to whomsoever you please, as a consequence of which the tributary is now obliged to pay his tax to the king's delegate, just as if he were paying it to the king himself." *Ibid.*, p. 149. If Zavala's interpretation is correct, Palacios Rubios was one of the first to apply the doctrine of natural servitude to the encomienda as an institution for the government of the Indians. See Zavala, *Servidumbre*, p. 34.

24. Palacios Rubios, p. 39.

25. *Ibid.*, pp. 42–43, 45.

26. Fray Pedro de Córdoba, the Dominican superior in Hispaniola, who had come to Spain to clear up certain charges resulting from the inflammatory sermons that one of his subjects, Antonio de Montesinos, had preached against the encomenderos on the Island in 1511, was the prime mover behind the revision. Ferdinand offered him an opportunity to do the revising personally, but Córdoba prudently refrained from assuming the responsibility. The king thereupon entrusted the task to a junta. Of the five additional regulations proposed by the junta, four were duly proclaimed at Valladolid on July 28, 1513, as the "Clarifications of the Ordinances of Burgos." See Hussey, pp. 305–6; and Getino, pp. 32–42.

27. Article 17 entrusted the education of the young sons of caciques to the Franciscans for a period of four years. In granting this privilege to a rival Order, the Crown may have been subtly reprimanding the Dominicans for their embarrassing agitation regarding the Indian problem.

28. For one of the strongest indictments of the status quo in the Indies during these years, see the report, dated Dec. 4, 1519, that the Dominicans in Hispaniola submitted to Cardinal Chievres. It is reproduced in Pacheco *et al.*, XXXV, 239–50.

29. For a detailed account of this episode in the struggle for justice, see Hanke, *First Social Experiments*. The reports that the Jeronymites sent back to Spain are given in Pacheco *et al.*, I, 264–81; XXXIV, 199–201, 279–86. The interrogatory that they conducted to determine whether or not the Indians were capable of self-government and of living like Spaniards is in *ibid.*, XXXIV, 201–29.

30. Las Casas is the only available source for this information on Quevedo. See his *Historia*, III, 336–51, for the pertinent facts related in typical Las Casas fashion. The remarks must be accepted cautiously in view of the known bias of the writer.

31. Typical of those who refuse to recognize Las Casas as a historian is Agustín Yáñez, who concludes: "It is necessary to repeat it many times. Las Casas was not an historian, but an apologist." (Yáñez, p. 33.) For other opinions on the same subject, see Lewis Hanke, "Interpretaciones de la obra y significación de Bartolomé de las Casas, desde el siglo XVI hasta el presente," *Latinoamérica*, I (July 1949).

32. This fact, taken for granted today, does not seem to have been equally apparent in the sixteenth century. At all events, Felix de Azara, the Spanish naturalist, stated flatly some two hundred years later that the early Spaniards looked on the Indians as an intermediate species between animals and men. See Barras de Aragón, II, 86. A useful bibliography on the nature of the American Indian is contained in Hanke, *First Social Experiments*, pp. 74–81.

33. Las Casas, *Apologética historia,* pp. 103–29.
34. *Ibid.,* p. 494.
35. *Ibid.,* pp. 580–83.
36. *Ibid.,* pp. 86–92.
37. *Ibid.,* pp. 131–45.
38. *Ibid.,* "Prologue," p. 1. Las Casas was not the first to observe that the irrationality of the Indians would reflect on the wisdom of God. In an opinion that he submitted to the Council of Burgos in 1512, Bernardo de Mesa, later bishop-elect of Cuba, noted that one of the main objections to the Aristotelian theory of natural slavery was the imperfection it postulated in the Creator: "The defenders of the Indians say that the incapacity we posit in the Indians contradicts the goodness and power of their Maker, for it is certain that when the cause produces an effect that is incapable of attaining its end, then there is some deficiency in the cause, and thus there would be a lack of something in God if He created human beings who did not have sufficient capacity to receive the faith and to be saved. Consequently, I hold that no one of right mind can say that these Indians do not have the capacity to receive our faith and sufficient ability to save themselves and to arrive at the goal of final beatitude." *Parecer* of Fray Bernardo de Mesa as reported in Las Casas, *Historia,* II, 461–62. Las Casas is the only source for Mesa's opinion.
39. Las Casas, *Apologética historia,* pp. 396–97.
40. *Ibid.,* "Prologue," p. 15.
41. *Ibid.,* pp. 127–28.
42. This treatise on the proper method of Christianizing the Indians is one of the works that give glory to the name of Las Casas in the drama of the Spanish conquest. (The others are his *Historia,* the *Apologética historia,* and the refutation of Sepúlveda's position, which he formulated in Valladolid in 1550–51. The last, still in manuscript form in the National Library of Paris, numbers some 500 folio pages. A photostatic copy of it, obtained through the agency of the Carnegie Institution, is on deposit in the Library of Congress in Washington.) The principal ideas of the *Del único modo* were for a long time known only through the excellent summary made by Antonio Remesal in the second decade of the seventeenth century in his *Historia general de las Indias Occidentales.* The manuscript itself had been considered lost. Joaquín García Icazbalceta subscribed to this view, as appears from his *Don Juan de Zumárraga,* p. 186. Thanks to the singular efforts of another erudite Mexican scholar of the past century, Nicolás León, a fragment of the manuscript was discovered and saved for posterity. This fragment was published for the first time in 1942 by the Fondo de Cultura Económica in Mexico under the editorship of Agustín Millares Carlo in a Latin-Spanish edition. The published copy, while apparently including all the essential ideas of the original treatise, actually contains only the fifth, sixth, and seventh chapters of Book I. Excerpts from these chapters in French translation are available in Mahn-Lot, *Barthélemy de Las Casas.*
43. For a Spanish reprint of this bull, *Sublimis Deus,* see Cuevas, pp. 84–86. A reproduction in Latin appears in Millares Carlo, *Bartolomé de las Casas, Del único*

modo, pp. 364–66. The document in both Cuevas and Las Casas carries the date of June 2, 1537. An informative article on the circumstances relating to the issuance of the bull is Hanke's "Pope Paul III and the American Indians."

44. Ricardo Levene, pp. 56–57.

45. See Honorio Múñoz, p. 25. I have slightly modified Múñoz's translation.

46. The *Relecciones* were special two-hour discourses on timely problems of public interest, which the University of Salamanca required its professor of theology to deliver each year in addition to the regular course of lectures. Only twelve of Vitoria's *Relecciones* have survived; if the requirements of the University had been fulfilled, there would have been twenty to correspond to the twenty years he spent as professor of theology at that institution. See Honorio Múñoz, p. 10.

47. Vitoria, *Relecciones*, p. 24. The edition I have used, published in Madrid in 1928, contains the original Latin text with a Spanish translation.

48. *Ibid.*, p. 50. It is interesting to note that Vitoria's arguments closely parallel those of Las Casas on this point.

49. *Ibid.*, pp. 50, 52. Commenting on the atrocities committed during the conquest of Peru, Vitoria wrote in November, 1534: "Truly, if the Indians are not human beings but monkeys, they are not capable of suffering injustices. But if they are men and our neighbors and, as they [the Spaniards in America] assert, vassals of the emperor, I do not see how it is possible to excuse these conquistadores of the grossest impiety and tyranny, nor do I see how they are peforming any great service to his Majesty by causing him to lose his vassals." Letter of Vitoria to Fray Miguel de Arcos, November 8, 1534, in Pirotto, p. 25.

50. Vitoria, *Relecciones*, pp. 52–54.

51. *Ibid.*, pp. 182–84.

52. *Ibid.*, p. 186. The reservation contained in the phrase "in part" suggests that Vitoria, too, may have been thinking of a type of tutelage similar to the encomienda system or to the more modern form of mandate government.

53. A convenient summary of the circumstances and issues relating to this debate is in Hanke, *Aristotle*, pp. 38–73.

54. The treatise was so named because of the *Demócrates Primus*, which Sepúlveda had composed in 1533 to justify the European wars of Charles V. Owing in part to the determined opposition of Las Casas, the *Demócrates Secundus* remained unpublished during the author's lifetime and for many years after; it first appeared in print in 1892. Loaysa was president of the Council of the Indies at the time and a firm critic of the New Laws of 1542. Sepúlveda's public support of the wars against the Indians prompted the cardinal to encourage him to write the work.

55. Whether or not Sepúlveda was advocating the type of slavery envisioned by Aristotle is still an open question. At least one present-day scholar, Robert E. Quirk, does not think so. Quirk believes that *natura servi* at Valladolid really referred to serfs in the medieval sense and not to slaves in the classical sense, either natural or legal. The philological data he adduces to bolster his contention are interesting but not always convincing. He says, for instance, that in "describing the Indians as

natura servi, he [Sepúlveda] used words such as *stipendiarii* and *vectigales*," which "clearly do not refer to slavery but rather to a condition of serflike dependency." Quirk, p. 360. The implication is that Sepúlveda never used *servi* when referring to the Indians. This is not true; see, for example, Sepúlveda, pp. 20, 84, 119, 120.

56. Sepúlveda, pp. 22, 42, 47, 61–62.

57. *Ibid.*, pp. 27, 118.

58. *Ibid.*, pp. 28–29.

59. *Ibid.*, p. 33.

60. *Ibid.*, p. 120.

61. *Ibid.*, pp. 122–24.

Chapter 2

1. Alonso de Ercilla y Zúñiga, a participant in the conquest of Chile, immortalized the Araucanians' defense of their homeland in a stirring epic poem, *La Araucana*, the first part of which appeared in Madrid in 1569 and the second part in 1578. Pedro de Oña published an inferior poem on the same theme, the *Arauco domado*, in 1596, and Fernando Alvarez de Toledo followed with his *Purén indómito* in 1599. The *Arauco domado* of Lope de Vega is definitely mediocre in quality. José Toribio Medina, the great Chilean bibliographer, published an excellent critical edition of Ercilla's work under the title *La Araucana de d. Alonso de Ercilla y Zúñiga*. A useful English translation is Walter Owen's *La Araucana: the Epic of Chile*.

2. Commenting on this point, Molina says: "They never form towns, but live in scattered villages or hamlets, on the banks of rivers, or in plains that are easily irrigated. Their local attachments are strong, each family preferring to live upon the land inherited from its ancestors, which they cultivate sufficiently for their subsistence. The genius of this haughty people, in which the savage still predominates, will not permit them to live in walled cities, which they consider a mark of servitude." Molina, II, 59.

3. "Each soldier is obliged to bring from home not only his arms but his supply of provisions. . . . The provision consists in a small sack of parched meal for each, which diluted with water furnishes sufficient food for them until they are enabled to live at free quarters upon the enemy. By adopting this mode, the troops, being free and unincumbered with baggage, move with greater celerity, and never lose an opportunity of attacking the enemy with advantage, or of making, when necessary, a rapid retreat." *Ibid.*, p. 74.

4. "They are enthusiastic lovers of liberty, which they consider as an essential constituent of their existence." *Ibid.*, p. 56.

5. The encomienda was really the nucleus of effective colonization in Chile. Its feudal character contributed greatly to a merging of the indigenous element with the European that was the basis for the later Chilean nation. See Latcham. Domingo

Amunátegui Solar has a fine discussion of this point also in his *Las encomiendas,* I, 59–76.

6. Pedro de Valdivia's army, for example, included only some 150 Spaniards. The rest were Peruvian *yanaconas* (or *anaconas*), Indians whose function it was to serve others. Juan de Solórzano Pereira, the most authoritative of the commentators on the laws of the Indies, gives this definition of yanaconas: "In the language of that country [Peru] it signifies Indians who are servitors. They and their descendants have been and continue to be servants, and they are assigned as such to the homes and possessions of the conquistadores." Solórzano Pereira, I, 67. Encina calls them a kind of modern inquilino. As used in Chile the term also included, later on, the Araucanians who were captured in the war and assigned to individual Spaniards for profitable safekeeping. Encina, IV, 71.

7. "Ordenanzas para el buen tratamiento de los naturales" issued by Charles V on December 4, 1528. A copy of these ordinances is included in *Colección de documentos inéditos relativos al descubrimiento,* IX, 386.

8. "Leyes y ordenanzas nuevamente hechas por S.M. para la governación de las Indias y buen tratamiento y conservación de los Indios," in Pacheco *et al.,* XVI, 376–406.

9. Encinas, *Libro de provisiones,* IV, 259.

10. *Recopilación,* libro 6, tit. 12, ley 15; and *Actas,* July 1, 1552, I, 298.

11. Encinas, *Libro de provisiones,* IV, 259–62.

12. Almagro started out from Cuzco in March 1535. His retinue included Paullu, the brother of Manco Inca, many Indian nobles, and several thousand native servitors who carried the arms and baggage of the army. Garcilaso de la Vega, I, 160.

13. The men in question had apparently been acting as scouts in advance of Almagro's forces. The anonymous author of the *Conquista y población del Pirú* attributed their death to "their desire for booty, their wicked deeds and the cruel way they treated the natives." See DI, VII, 469; Molina, p. 59.

14. DI, VII, 469–70; Molina, pp. 60–61. The author was a member of the Almagro expedition and an eyewitness to the cruelties his companions committed. His account is the only reliable firsthand source for the expedition. The information contained in Oviedo y Valdés, *Historia general de las Indias,* is based on Almagro's reports to the king and paints a more favorable picture of the journey.

15. "Información de Rodrigo de Quiroga," 1560, p. 150. See also Errázuriz, *Pedro de Valdivia,* I, 137.

16. Letter of Valdivia to Charles V, Sept. 4, 1545, in DI, VIII, 98–118.

17. Among these obligations was one calling for active participation in the war against the Araucanians. In an edict of July 26, 1546, Valdivia reminded the encomenderos that they were expected to furnish arms and horses for the defense of the colony, and to accompany the governor on future campaigns. Those who could not equip themselves for cavalry service within five months were to serve in the infantry. *Ibid.,* pp. 130–31. The five-month stipulation by Valdivia was a special concession, since the royal cédulas allowed only four. See *Recopilación,* libro 6, tit. 9, ley 8.

Those who refused to serve were to be deprived of their Indians. *Ibid.*, libro 6, tit. 9, ley 4. With the passing of the years the encomenderos became more and more reluctant to comply with this obligation, and their negligence was the subject of frequent complaints to the Crown. Some of the later governors even introduced the practice of requiring the recipients of encomiendas to take an oath, very similar in tone to the one medieval lords exacted of their vassals, to perform faithfully all the services incumbent upon them as encomenderos. Amunátegui Solar has published a specimen of this oath in his *Las encomiendas*, I, 70.

18. For the subsequent history of these thirty-two encomiendas, see Amunátegui Solar, *Las encomiendas*, II, "Apuntaciones y documentos," pp. 3–140. Among those who retained their titles were Valdivia's mistress, Doña Inés Suárez, and Gonzalo de los Ríos, the grandfather of Doña Catalina de los Ríos y Lisperguer, the notorious "La Quintrala" of Chilean history and one of the worst oppressors of the Indians.

19. Letter of Valdivia to Charles V, Sept. 4, 1545, in DI, VIII, 98. Although Valdivia already possessed the faculty of granting encomiendas, he was expressly authorized to do so on April 18, 1548, when he received confirmation of his position as governor of Chile. Until then he regularly qualified titles of encomienda as "deposits" of Indians instead of making them outright grants, thus reserving to himself the right of annulling or modifying the concessions at a later date. See Amunátegui Solar, *Las encomiendas*, I, 67–68.

20. "Relación de los agravios que los indios de las provincias de Chile padecen, dado por el padre Gil González de la Orden de Predicadores," in *Historiadores*, XXIX, 463.

21. Santillán, "Relación," 1559.

22. *Actas*, July 1, 1552, I, 298.

23. Writ of encomienda in favor of Juan Jufré, Nov. 1, 1552, in DI, XV, 17.

24. Cédula of Aug. 10, 1529, in Encinas, *Cedulario indiano*, II, 215–16.

25. "Testamento de Doña Marina Ortiz de Gaete," p. 338. The document contains other clauses of similar import.

26. Encinas, *Cedulario indiano*, IV, 280–81.

27. *Actas*, Aug. 4, 1553, I, 357.

28. "Los oficiales reales y el fiscal de S.M.," 1561, pp. 413–14.

29. *Ibid.*, p. 406.

30. "Información de Antonio Tarabajano," 1555, p. 289.

31. "Testamento de Doña Agueda de Flores," p. 255.

32. Amunátegui Solar, *Las encomiendas*, I, 143.

33. "Pleito de Diego García de Villalón," p. 185.

34. There are many versions of Valdivia's death; but since no Spaniard survived the catastrophe at Tucapel to furnish historians with an accurate account, it is necessary to rely on the reports of the Indians themselves. Alonso de Góngora Marmolejo, the soldier-chronicler who narrowly escaped being included in the ill-fated expedition, summed up the accounts that were current at the time in his *Historia de*

Chile, pp. 38–39. Valdivia was captured on December 25, 1553, but he was probably not put to death until several days later. See Vernon, p. 178.

35. The system of panning gold in these *lavaderos de oro* (places where gold is washed) was similar to that used by miners in the old American West. For a detailed description of the process, see Oviedo y Valdés, II, 24–25.

36. Letter of Valdivia to Charles V, Sept. 1545, in *Historiadores*, I, 5. Operation of the mines was under the direction of Pedro de Herrera and Diego Delgado, two experienced Spanish miners who had accompanied Valdivia to Chile as soldiers in his army. Lovera, pp. 54–55.

37. "Información de servicios de Rodrigo de Quiroga," 1560, pp. 147–53. Some of the other conquistadores had gangs of yanaconas working at Malgamalga before the end of 1541 also. DI, XVI, 129, 138, 144, 155, 205.

38. Lovera, p. 53.

39. The rebellion of Michimalongo occurred shortly after the founding of Santiago (February 1541). There is some question about the exact date of the founding. The *Actas*, I, 67, give February 12 as the date. Valdivia, in two of his letters to Charles V (Sept. 4, 1545, and Oct. 15, 1550), mentions February 24. Tomás Thayer Ojeda, writing in the *Diario Ilustrado* of Santiago on February 24, 1910, suggested as a reason for the discrepancy that whereas the designation of the town site and the preliminary arrangements of streets and lots may have begun on February 12, the "raising of the tree of justice"—always the final act in the founding of a town—may have been delayed until February 24. See Errázuriz, *Pedro de Valdivia*, I, 152, note 2. A simpler explanation postulates an error in the rewriting of the *Actas* in 1544, following the destruction of the originals during the Indian attack on the town in Sept. 1541.

40. Cited in Barros Arana, I, 412.

41. Lovera, p. 75.

42. "Claúsula testamentaria de Bartolomé Flores, Santiago, noviembre 11, 1585," in Vicuña Mackenna, *Los Lisperguer*, p. 253.

43. Licentiates were men who had taken their first university degree. Also included in Mendoza's entourage were several other men who were destined to become famous in the annals of Chile and of Spanish America: Alonso de Ercilla y Zúñiga, the author of *La Araucana*; a German subject of Charles V, Don Pedro Lisperguer, and Don Francisco de Irarrázaval, gentlemen of the highest quality, who became founders of the leading families in colonial Chile; and the Dominican friar Gil González de San Nicolás, whose heated defense of the Indians made him the center of more than one controversy. At the time of his appointment Mendoza was a youth of twenty-two, full of high resolve and desirous of acquiring fame in the war against the Araucanians.

44. Santillán, "Relación."

45. *Ibid.*, pp. 285–86.

46. Suárez de Figueroa, p. 20.

47. Santillán, "Relación," p. 286.

48. "In regard to levying taxes they are to observe the rules we have prescribed, namely, that the tribute is not to include personal service, and that the encomenderos are not to send their Indians to work in the mines." *Recopilación*, libro 6, tit. 5, ley 21.

49. Santillán, "Relación," p. 287.

50. This was in compliance with the king's instructions calling for a computation of the tribute on the basis of individual encomiendas, so that the Indians concerned would know precisely what their obligations to their own encomendero were. *Recopilación*, libro 6, tit. 5, ley 21.

51. During his previous stay in La Serena, Santillán had not had time to do more than prepare a number of regulations for the encomiendas of that district. Consequently, the tasa he promulgated in Santiago was made applicable to La Serena also. The text of the Santiago tasa has not survived, but a summary of it appears in Santillán's "Relación." Briefer résumés are included in Rosales, *Historia general*, II, 88–90, and Suárez de Figueroa, p. 20.

52. Santillán, "Relación," pp. 286–88; Rosales, *Historia general*, II, 89.

53. Santillán, "Relación," p. 289.

54. In effect, women and those under eighteen and over fifty did not have to pay tribute. Rosales, *Historia general*, II, 89.

55. According to Rosales, the encomenderos were supposed to construct hospitals in the native villages, to provide medicine and gifts for the patients, and to plant crops for the use of the communities. *Ibid.*

56. Santillán, "Relación," p. 289.

57. The complete text of the ordinance has survived. Medina published it in his *Documentos inéditos*, XXVIII, 297–302, as "Ordenanzas para la Concepción, Imperial, Cañete, Valdivia, Villarrica y Osorno."

58. *Ibid.*, pp. 297–98.

59. *Ibid.*, p. 298; Rosales, *Historia general*, II, 89.

60. The cabildo of Santiago had made sporadic efforts to regulate the demora for several years before the arrival of Santillán. In its session of December 10, 1548, it decided that Indians could be sent to the mines for a period lasting from January 15, 1549, until the beginning of the spring planting season in September. In 1555 the demora ended officially with the beginning of October, and the cabildo by a vote on September 30 threatened all who failed to observe this limit with a fine of five hundred pesos. One offender, Gonzalo de los Ríos, escaped by paying only one hundred pesos. *Actas*, Dec. 10, 1548, and Sept. 30, 1549, I, 495, 497.

61. Santillán, "Ordenanzas," p. 299.

62. *Ibid.*, p. 300.

63. *Ibid.*, pp. 298–99.

64. *Ibid.*, pp. 300–301.

65. *Ibid.*, pp. 300–302.

66. Since Santillán left Chile sometime during June 1559, the royal cédula recalling him to Lima, which was issued in March of that year, could not possibly

have been the reason for his departure. Cédula of Philip II to Santillán, March 15, 1559, in DI, XXVIII, 376–77.

67. Santillán, "Ordenanzas," p. 302. Hurtado de Mendoza arranged for the execution of the ordinances, as he reported to the Council of the Indies some three months later: "I have promulgated the aforesaid provisions and have made it clear that they are to go into effect immediately. I shall continue to enforce them *in a way that is useful and that results in no detriment to the colony.* And I shall be most diligent in the undertaking as befits a good servant who wishes to succeed in the task at hand." Letter of Governor García Hurtado de Mendoza to the President of the Council of the Indies, Aug. 30, 1559, in DI, XXVIII, 319–24. My italics.

68. Santillán, "Relación," p. 290.

69. Letter of Santillán to the Council of the Indies, March 18, 1560, DI, XXVIII, 359–60. Some of the measures he had already initiated to protect the Indians were enumerated in his "Relación" of June 4, 1559, a copy of which apparently accompanied the letter.

70. In its session of Aug. 12, 1558, at which Santillán presided, the cabildo of Santiago chose Juan Godinez, the *alcalde ordinario,* for the position, and Santillán appointed Francisco Pérez de Valenzuela. *Actas,* Aug. 12, 1558, II, 41.

71. The document reads "por escritura pública." Santillán, "Relación," p. 289.

72. *Ibid.,* pp. 290–91.

73. *Ibid.,* pp. 291–92.

74. According to Encina, this part of Santillán's letter to the Council of the Indies is unreliable. For one thing, it was based on hearsay. For another, "it lacked veracity and suffered from the exaggerations inherent in all documents of the sixteenth and seventeenth centuries, when written by men who were motivated by sentimentality or self-interest." Encina, IV, 70. Encina conveniently forgets in his discussion that the opponents of reform were equally influenced, if not more so, by group prejudices and self-interest.

75. Before his appointment as governor of Chile, Villagra had distinguished himself in a number of minor capacities, including that of *corregidor* of Santiago. An ambitious man, he had hoped to succeed Valdivia as political leader of the colony after the latter's death, but was forced to wait for that honor until 1561.

76. Galvez, "Relación." The document cited carries no date, but we know that Galvez arrived in Chile in 1550 and remained for more than thirty years.

77. See Reisse González, pp. 834–35.

78. Rosales, *Historia general,* I, 89.

Chapter 3

1. Jorge Ferrada says he was born in 1527 "probably in Ciudad-Real in Spain." See Ferrada, p. 16. Crescente Errázuriz in *Los orígenes,* p. 98, note 2, and Amunátegui Solar in *Las encomiendas,* I, 156, both believe that he came from Ávila. The

variant form of his name, Gil González de Ávila, found in some of the chronicles of the period, lends credence to this second opinion. See Suárez de Figueroa, p. 42; Lovera, p. 205; and Góngora Marmolejo, p. 94. The confusion in names presents no real difficulty. "Ávila" refers to his town of origin, while "San Nicolás" is the name he adopted while in religion. The practice is still common in many religious Orders and congregations.

2. This was in obedience to a royal cédula of September 4, 1551, that instructed the superior of the Dominicans in Peru "to send three religious of your Order to the kingdom of Chile to protect the Indians and to instruct them in our most holy faith." See Juan Meléndez, I, 159, 335.

3. Silva Cotapos, p. 9. Crescente Errázuriz is mistaken when he says that González arrived in Chile in 1552, and founded a convent in the capital under the patronage of Our Lady of the Rosary on a tract of land donated for the purpose by Juan de Esquivel, a resident of Santiago. See Errázuriz, *Los orígenes*, p. 98.

4. Errázuriz, *García de Mendoza*, p. 6.

5. "Información de los méritos del capitán Riberos," pp. 116, 144, 163, 174, 197, 210. "Título de encomienda de indios dado por Pedro de Villagra a Francisco de Irarrázaval y Real Cédula y poder sobre el mismo título," in DI, Second Series, I, 19–20.

6. Errázuriz, *García de Mendoza*, p. 7. The mines were located in the territory of La Serena, some distance north of Santiago.

7. Commenting on the incident, Pedro de Miranda testified that Captain Francisco de Riberos had counseled the governor "with sufficient reasons not to establish the proposed pueblo, because it would be of no value, and so the governor did not do so." "Información de los méritos del capitán Riberos," p. 210.

8. Santillán, "Relación," p. 285. My italics. Francisco de Villagra and Francisco de Aguirre were both former lieutenants of Valdivia. Villagra was elected first regidor (alderman) of the cabildo of Santiago on March 7, 1541; Aguirre functioned as governor of La Serena and Barco.

9. Lautaro had planned the strategy that resulted in the death of Valdivia. R. B. Cunninghame Graham credits him with being the military genius behind the Araucanian resistance in the beginning: "Owing to him, the warfare that lasted down to the middle of the last century in Chile was initiated. Before his time the Araucanians had developed no special fighting powers, and might easily have been crushed." Graham, p. 115.

10. According to Miguel de Olivares, Gallegos was "a skilled theologian, an excellent jurist, and an accomplished linguist who was versed in many languages; in addition to various European tongues, he knew Latin, Greek, Hebrew, and Chaldean." Olivares, *Historia militar*, pp. 178–79. He was a formidable adversary, to say the least.

11. Letter of González to the President of the Council of the Indies, April 26, 1559, in DI, XXVIII, 276–83.

12. Ercilla fixes the date in his *La araucana*, canto XV. See Medina, *La araucana*.

It coincides with the information contained in the letter of the cabildo of Concepción to the king, May 12, 1558. See Morla Vicuña, p. 140, for the letter.

13. Mendoza brought some 450 fighting men with him from Peru. Among them was the heroic Pedro Cortés, whose military exploits made him worthy of being considered one of the founders of the colony. See Amunátegui Solar, *Las encomiendas*, I, 155.

14. "I reproved him in secret," he wrote in his letter to the President of the Council of the Indies, in DI, XXVIII, 277.

15. *Ibid.*

16. Included in these instructions was the notorious "Requirement," which the conquistadores were obliged to read to the Indians before hostilities against them were considered legal. The patent insufficiency of the document as a means of justifying armed conquest made it an object of derision to historians then and now. Even Las Casas confessed that on reading it, it was difficult to decide whether to laugh or to weep. Las Casas, *Historia*, III, 31. The requerimiento technically remained in effect until it was replaced on July 13, 1573, by an ordinance of Philip II, which improved on the terms of the earlier document by providing more humane consideration for the Indians. This ordinance regulated all future conquests as long as Spain governed her colonies in America. See Hanke, *Spanish Struggle for Justice*, pp. 130–31.

17. Letter of González to the President of the Council of the Indies, in DI, XXVIII, 277. Unless otherwise indicated, the details of the González-Gallegos controversy described in these pages are taken from this letter.

18. See Errázuriz, *García de Mendoza*, p. 103.

19. Errázuriz, *Los orígenes*, pp. 150–51.

20. "Documentos relativos a la fundación de una casa y convento para la Orden de Santo Domingo en Santiago," in DI, Second Series, I, 74.

21. Ghigliazza, I, 128–31.

22. Errázuriz, *García de Mendoza*, p. 115.

23. "Declaración de Rodrigo de Quiroga e Inés Suárez sobre los fines que persiguen con la fundación de la ermita y casa de Nuestra Señora de Monserrate," in DI, Second Series, I, 1–5.

24. Letter of González to the President of the Council of the Indies, in DI, XXVIII, 277.

25. *Ibid.*

26. For an account of this incident see Errázuriz, *García de Mendoza*, pp. 119–32.

27. Amunátegui Solar, *Las encomiendas*, I, 168.

28. Theoretically the communal lands of the Indians were inalienable. For the protest that the cacique Don Jerónimo registered with the officials of Santiago on this point, see DI, Second Series, I, 5.

29. Ghigliazza, I, 151, 157.

30. Amunátegui Solar suggests another reason for the friar's visit to Peru: the

Dominican provincial had recalled him at the request of the viceroy because his presence in Chile was interfering with the government of his son, Don García. This is an interesting suggestion, but it lacks documentary proof. Amunátegui Solar, *Las encomiendas*, I, 169.

31. Ghigliazza, I, 152–55.

32. Mendoza had incurred the enmity of Villagra when, shortly after arriving in Chile, he had ordered the arrest of Villagra and had him confined under guard on board a ship in Valparaíso.

33. Ronquillo, p. 257; Ghigliazza, I, 205.

34. Ronquillo, p. 258. Some of the army captains strongly opposed the presence of Fray González. They would have preferred a Franciscan with less extreme opinions. See Hanke and Millares Carlo, p. lxii.

35. Góngora Marmolejo, p. 95. Juan de Herrera, the *teniente general* (lieutenant general), testified that Fray González was the one who aroused the most scruples in the minds of the officers, soldiers, and judges by telling them that they were going to hell for their deeds against the Indians. See Juan de Herrera. The statement implies that there were other ecclesiastics attached to the army who condemned the waging of the war, but who did so with less acidity and greater circumspection.

36. Villagra succumbed to his infirmities in Concepción on June 22, 1563. He was succeeded as governor by his cousin, Pedro de Villagra. "Carta del licenciado Herrera a S.M. sobre la muerte de Francisco de Villagra, 29 de junio de 1563," in DI, Second Series, I, 5–6; "Carta del Conde de Nieva, virrey del Perú, a S.M., avisando de la muerte del gobernador de Chile Francisco de Villagra y de haberle substituido su primo Pedro de Villagra, 19 de octubre de 1563," in *ibid.*, pp. 7–8.

37. Juan de Herrera, pp. 253–54.

38. *Ibid.*, p. 254.

39. *Ibid.*

40. *Ibid.*

41. Letter of Herrera to the Council of the Indies, April 30, 1562, in DI, XXIX, 146.

42. Medina, *La inquisición*, I, 21–37.

43. Errázuriz, *Los orígenes*, p. 158, and Barros Arana, II, 323, following Góngora Marmolejo, erroneously call him Cristóbal de Molina.

44. Medina, *La inquisición*, I, 51–106; Letter of Antonio de Molina to the king, Aug. 24, 1564, in AAS, XXI, 2–4.

45. *Ibid.*, pp. 8–10.

46. Ghigliazza, I, 334.

47. The *Brevísima relación* of Las Casas, a searing denunciation of Spanish mistreatment of the Indians, was translated into all the major European languages within a few years after its publication in 1552 and rapidly became a best seller. Its pointed account of Spanish cruelty and oppression, described with lurid scenes of massacre and torture, provided Spain's political enemies with a very effective propa-

ganda instrument and contributed greatly to the formulation of the Black Legend (an exaggerated idea of Spanish cruelty toward the Indians) from which Spanish pride has suffered ever since.

48. González de San Nicolás, *Relación*.

49. *Ibid*.

50. On December 12, 1563, for instance, the new governor of Chile, Pedro de Villagra, promulgated a series of ordinances that were to complete the work begun by Santillán and to provide the Indians with a greater measure of relief from their woes. Unfortunately, for reasons which will be noted later, these regulations also soon became inoperative. "Ordenanzas que hizo Pedro de Villagra."

51. Santiago was designated the seat of a new ecclesiastical diocese by Pope Paul IV on June 27, 1561, and González Marmolejo, already more than seventy years of age, was named its first prelate that day. Born in the Spanish village of Constantina in 1490, he had come to Chile with Pedro de Valdivia in 1540. He so impressed that warrior with his wisdom and virtue that Valdivia urged the king to secure his appointment as bishop of Santiago. Almost a year and a half intervened, however, following the appointment before González Marmolejo was able to take possession of his see. During the interim the diocese was administered by a representative of the bishop of Charcas in Upper Peru (modern Bolivia), to whose jurisdiction the territory of Chile had previously been attached. Silva Cotapos, p. 5; Letter of Pedro de Valdivia to the king, Oct. 15, 1550, in *Historiadores*, I, 19–53.

52. The formal installation and transferral of powers seem to have occurred on this date. Errázuriz, *Pedro de Villagra*, pp. 79–80. Silva Cotapos (p. 5) gives June 18, 1563, as the date. This probably refers to the private ceremony following his arrival in Chile during which Bishop González Marmolejo recorded acceptance of his new office for civil purposes before the notary public Juan Hurtado.

53. Errázuriz, *Pedro de Villagra*, pp. 232–33.

54. Errázuriz believes that Fray Gil González also submitted a written parecer before departing for Peru, and that it was this document, now lost, that was cited a half century later in Lima by proponents of defensive warfare. *Ibid.*, p. 233.

55. Paredes.

Chapter 4

1. The exact date of Bishop González Marmolejo's death is uncertain. Eyzaguirre (I, 51) gives 1565, but this is obviously a mistake. Probably he died in September or October 1564, for in a petition that Juan Gómez, *regidor* of Santiago, presented to the audiencia of Lima dated December 10, 1564, he referred to the episcopal see of Santiago as being vacant. Yet the bishop was still very much alive on August 30, 1564, for on that day Nicolás de Garnica and Juan de la Peña, notary publics, attested to the authenticity of his signature on a letter to the king. Allowing

a minimum of five to six weeks for Gómez's trip from Santiago to Lima, it follows that Bishop González must have died between September 1 and November 1, 1564. See Errázuriz, *Los orígenes,* pp. 520–22, 525–26.

2. "Consulta del Consejo de Indias a S.M. sobre que se nombre para el obispado de Santiago de Chile a fray Hernando de Barrionuevo, 5 de julio de 1566," in DI, Second Series, I, 68. Barrionuevo had been consecrated bishop in Spain some three years earlier, but ill health and other complications prevented him from proceeding immediately to America. In one of his letters to the king (apparently the only one that has survived) dated from Lima on February 6, 1570, he mentions that he is preparing to depart for Chile. Errázuriz, *Los orígenes,* p. 214. Carvallo y Goyeneche (p. 166) and Eyzaguirre (I, 53) are accordingly both wrong in asserting that he arrived in Chile in 1567.

3. Letter of Fray Antonio de San Miguel to the king, Oct. 25, 1566, in DI, Second Series, I, 81–82.

4. Errázuriz, *Los orígenes,* pp. 205–6.

5. Letter of Fray Antonio de San Miguel to the Council of the Indies, April 4, 1568, in DI, Second Series, I, 113–14.

6. Olivares erroneously reports that San Miguel took possession of his see in 1574. Olivares, *Historia militar,* p. 129.

7. In relating this chapter in Chilean history Encina says: "Like many of the ecclesiastics who came to America, Bishop San Miguel was one whom the mystical sense completely deprived of a feeling for reality. . . . As far as he was concerned, there were latent within the American Indian the same intellectual and moral aptitudes that the Spanish conqueror possessed; the only problem was how, by means of Christian teaching, education, and baptism, these dispositions that lay dormant because of ignorance were to be awakened. According to San Miguel forced labor, the war, and the cruelties inflicted on prisoners were the real causes of the Indian's rebellion and of his resistance to accepting Christianity and adopting European customs and ways of life." Encina, II, 24–25. To Encina, of course, the conquistador was eminently superior to the aborigine, and it was only the "mystical feelings that addled the brains" (*ibid.,* I, 378) of the churchmen that blinded them to the necessity of forced labor and the impossibility of large-scale conversion of the Araucanians except through a lengthy process of miscegenation.

8. The first members of the audiencia were Melchor Bravo de Saravia, oidor of the audiencia of Lima, whom the king appointed president of the new tribunal, Juan Torres de Vera y Aragón, Egas Venegas, Diego Núñez de Peralta, and the Licentiate Navia. The audiencia was installed with unusual public solemnities on August 10, 1567, and continued to function with indifferent success until June 1575.

9. Letter of San Miguel to Philip II, Oct. 24, 1571, in Errázuriz, *Los orígenes,* p. 535.

10. The 150,000 figure is given in *ibid.* According to a letter of Lorenzo Bernal

de Mercado to the viceroy of Peru, Francisco de Toledo, dated June 25, 1571, the fines imposed on the vecinos of Valdivia alone totaled 170,000 pesos. DI, Second Series, I, 376.

11. Cited in Barros Arana, II, 410.

12. Letter of the Licentiate Juan Torres de Vera and of Dr. Peralta to the king, Feb. 25, 1571, in DI, Second Series, I, 353–56.

13. Letter of Governor García Oñez de Loyola to the king, Jan. 12, 1598, in Amunátegui Solar, *Las encomiendas*, II, "Documentos," pp. 141–58.

14. Errázuriz, *Los orígenes*, p. 224.

15. Córdoba y Figueroa, p. 59; Olivares, *Historia militar*, p. 130. Both of these authors cite the public document that was preserved in the files of the ecclesiastical cabildo of Concepción.

16. Diego de Gaete was the brother-in-law of Pedro de Valdivia. He had received a large encomienda in Osorno from the ex-governor Hurtado de Mendoza. In addition to the sum mentioned, he also set aside 54,000 pesos for other pious works; these munificent benefactions did not prevent him from leaving a sizable fortune to his son, Francisco Ortiz de Gaete. See Olivares, *Historia militar*, p. 201, and Córdoba y Figueroa, p. 109.

17. Córdoba y Figueroa, p. 60; Olivares, *Historia militar*, p. 130.

18. Cédula of Philip II to the audiencia of Chile, July 17, 1572, in AAS, XLIII, 237–38.

19. Cédula of Philip II to the bishop of La Imperial, July 17, 1572, in *ibid.*, pp. 238–39.

20. Encinas, *Cedulario indiano*, IV, 294–96.

21. Góngora Marmolejo, p. 199. Two residents in each of the towns visited were to assist them in their work.

22. Errázuriz, *Los orígenes*, p. 306.

23. Letter of San Miguel to the king, Oct. 26, 1575, in Amunátegui Solar, *Las encomiendas*, I, 228. Rodrigo de Quiroga, who assumed political leadership in the government of Chile after the abolition of the audiencia, was more lenient in his judgment of that body's conduct. Writing to the king in 1576, he declared: "The royal audiencia drew up a schedule of the tribute that the Indians of the more important cities of the diocese of La Imperial ought to pay; but since the natives are a destitute people and so barbarous that they do not live in pueblos or show obedience to their cacique, or are possessed of any orderly existence or resources whereby they might support themselves and pay their taxes, the audiencia concluded that the tasa was impractical for the time being and so suspended it." Letter of Rodrigo de Quiroga to Philip II, Feb. 2, 1576, in Gay, II, 109.

24. Quiroga, the legitimate son of Fernando Camba de Quiroga and María López de Ulloa, was born in San Juan de Boime in 1512. Medina, *Diccionario*, pp. 716–19.

25. Letter of Rodrigo de Quiroga to the king, Jan. 2, 1577, in Gay, II, 112–18.

26. For the cédula of Aug. 5, 1577, see AAS, XLI, 108–9.

27. *Actas*, Feb. 11, 1577, and Jan. 26, 1580, II, 494–95, and III, 185–88. The alcalde of the mines was a judge of first appeal in cases affecting the Indian workers. He enjoyed the prerogatives and salary of a judge, and his principal function was to guarantee the faithful observance of the Tasa de Santillán. In matters involving grave civil or criminal charges he was obliged to refer the case to the corregidor of Santiago for a definitive sentence.

28. *Ibid.*, March 23, 1579, III, 103–6. This document mentions the Huarpe and Huilliche Indians as working in the mines. The Huarpes were a tribe from the province of Cuyo on the other side of the Andes. The Huilliches were natives of Chile whose habitat varied from time to time. In the sixteenth century and later, the term was applied to the mapuches who lived south of the Biobío River. The use of Indians from other parts of the country and from across the cordillera is an enlightening commentary on the killing effects of labor in the mines.

29. Encina, II, 53. Theoretically, "disabling" was used only in the case of legal slaves, but evidence exists that some private encomenderos were also guilty of the practice. One notorious offender during the seventeenth century was Doña Catalina de los Ríos y Lisperguer, more commonly referred to as "La Quintrala." For a review of the fact and fiction in her career, consult Vicuña Mackenna, *Los Lisperguer*.

30. Cited in Barros Arana, II, 448.

31. Cited in Amunátegui Solar, *Las encomiendas*, I, 236. The removal of captive Araucanians had given rise several years earlier to resounding protests from Doña Marina Ortiz de Gaete and other encomenderos of the south, who claimed a right to the victims as belonging to their encomiendas. See the "Expediente de Doña Marina Ortiz de Gaete, 1571."

32. Cited in Amunátegui Solar, *Las encomiendas*, I, 237. The caciques were, perhaps, more fortunate. They were handed over to the viceroy of Peru. Letter of Quiroga to the king, Jan. 26, 1578, in Barros Arana, II, 449–53.

33. Medellín was the first priest to receive the doctorate degree from the University of San Marcos in Lima. Carvallo y Goyeneche, p. 180.

34. *Ibid.*, p. 181.

35. Errázuriz was the first historian to fix the approximate date of Medellín's arrival. Carvallo y Goyeneche, Gay, Eyzaguirre, and others merely mention the year in which the papal bulls were issued. For the evidence on which his conclusion is based, see Errázuriz, *Los orígenes*, p. 255, note 1.

36. Letter of Medellín to Philip II, Jan. 6, 1577, in AAS, XX, 31–33.

37. Letter of Medellín to Philip II, April 15, 1580, in AAS, XX, 39–45.

38. *Ibid.*, pp. 44–45. Governor Oñez de Loyola later complained of similar corruption by officials in his letter to the king of Jan. 12, 1598. It was a common complaint throughout most of the colonial period.

39. Rosales, *Historia general*, II, 206; Letter of Elmo Gallegos to the king, Oct. 23, 1566, in DI, Second Series, I, 80–81, identifies Gamboa as Quiroga's son-in-law. On October 28, 1573, Philip II granted Quiroga the privilege of choosing a temporary successor until the Crown or the viceroy of Peru should appoint someone

else; he used this power to name Gamboa as provisional governor on February 16, 1577. See Encina, II, 67.

40. Letter of Medellín to Philip II, June 4, 1580, in AAS, XX, 46–48. The reasoning behind Medellín's action was clearly that he believed a confessor should not absolve penitents who gave no signs of true repentance other than a verbal promise that experience had often shown to be devoid of sincerity.

41. Letter of Martín Ruiz de Gamboa to the king, March 31, 1580, in Encina, II, 70.

42. Amunátegui Solar, *Las encomiendas*, I, 239.

43. Encina, II, 71. Characteristically, Encina fails to mention that most of the "hundreds of thousands of lives" lost were Indians', and a large percentage were not battle casualties. For an evaluation of Encina's views, see Griffin. A less detached critique by a Chilean author is the pamphlet by Almeyda Arroyo. Both serve to document the inaccuracy, dogmatism, prejudice, and racist conviction that characterize Encina's interpretation of the colonial period.

44. Rosales, *Historia general*, II, 207–8. See also the letter of Oñez de Loyola to the king, Jan. 12, 1598, in Amunátegui Solar, *Las encomiendas*, II, "Documentos," pp. 142–43.

45. Rosales, *Historia general*, II, 208. The corregidores were Captain Juan Vásquez de Acuña, Marcos de Barrueta, Francisco Alvarez de Toledo, and Gerónimo de Benavides.

46. *Ibid*. For a detailed analysis of the tasa see Gligo Viel.

47. Gamboa credited the tasa with being the main reason that some of the Indians came to terms with the Spaniards, adding that without it they would have preferred to die than to accept obedience to the king. Letter of Gamboa to Philip II, Feb. 15, 1585, in Errázuriz, *Los orígenes*, pp. 340–41. In referring to Gamboa's work on behalf of the Indians, Errázuriz says: "We are familiar with the efforts made by Gamboa in favor of the natives, efforts that by themselves ought to suffice to make his name immortal and to present him to us as one of the most illustrious conquistadores in Chile." *Ibid*., p. 339. See also Gligo Viel, pp. 201–9.

48. Letter of Gamboa to the king, Feb. 15, 1585, in Errázuriz, *Los orígenes*, p. 341; Feliú Cruz and Monje Alfaro, pp. 114–15.

49. Letter of Gamboa to the king, Feb. 15, 1585, in Errázuriz, *Los orígenes*, p. 341.

50. Escobedo resigned his commission and was replaced on April 6, 1581, by Lorenzo Bernal de Mercado, one time maestre de campo general under Quiroga. *Actas*, April 6, 1581, III, 284.

51. Becerril.

52. Memorial of Cristóbal Núñez to the viceroy of Peru, in DI, Second Series, III, 127–29.

53. Barros Arana, III, 36. The *patronato real* was a series of papal grants and concessions that gave the Spanish Crown virtual control over practically every phase of ecclesiastical and religious activity in the Indies.

54. *Actas*, Oct. 12, 1582, IV, 49; Letter of Governor Oñez de Loyola to the king, Jan. 12, 1598, in Amunátegui Solar, *Las encomiendas*, II, "Documentos," p. 153.

55. Sotomayor was a member of a noble family of Estremadura and the son of Gutiérrez de Sotomayor, one of the outstanding captains in the army of Flanders. He left San Lucar de Barrameda on September 27, 1581, with a contingent of 600 men. Desertions in Cádiz reduced this number to 520.

56. Reisse González, pp. 847–52; Feliú Cruz and Monje Alfaro, pp. 116–17.

57. Lovera, pp. 413–14.

58. In addition, the encomendero was entitled to a chicken and a fanega of wheat and corn yearly from each of his Indians. Letter of Governor Oñez de Loyola to the king, Jan. 12, 1598, in Amunátegui Solar, *Las encomiendas*, II, "Documentos," p. 153. This letter is a detailed account of the tasas, tributes, encomiendas, and Indians of the various geographical zones constituting the kingdom of Chile in the sixteenth century, from La Serena in the north to Castro in the south.

59. *Ibid.*, pp. 153–55.

60. Letter of Medellín to the king, Feb. 18, 1585, in Errázuriz, *Los orígenes*, pp. 361–66.

61. *Actas*, Sept. 19, 1583, April 7, 1589, and Nov. 22, 1583, IV, 127–30; V, 204.

62. *Ibid.*, Aug. 1, 1588, and May 26, 1589, V, 167, 213.

63. *Ibid.*, Feb. 5, 1590, V, 244.

64. *Ibid.*, Feb. 5 and 9, 1590, V, 243–50.

65. Letter of Oñez de Loyola to the king, Jan. 12, 1598, in Amunátegui Solar, *Las encomiendas*, II, "Documentos," p. 157.

66. Instructions of Governor Oñez de Loyola to Jerónimo de Benavides, corregidor of Santiago and alcalde mayor of the mines in that area, Feb. 24, 1593, in *Actas*, March 5, 1593, V, 440.

67. *Ibid.*, pp. 446–51, 516, 522.

68. Góngora Marmolejo, p. 31.

69. Cited in Amunátegui, *Los precursores*, II, 82.

70. Letter of Cisneros to Philip II, Dec. 17, 1590, in Amunátegui Solar, *Las encomiendas*, I, 285–86.

71. Letter of Governor Oñez de Loyola to the king, Jan. 12, 1598, in *ibid.*, II, "Documentos," p. 149.

72. *Ibid.*, pp. 149–50.

73. Amunátegui Solar, *Las encomiendas*, I, 286.

74. *Ibid.*, p. 287.

75. *Actas*, July 28, 1594, V, 619–21.

76. Letter of Luis de Vizcarra to the king, Feb. 20, 1599, in Pastells, LXXXI, 172.

77. Encina, II, 154.

Chapter 5

1. Ovalle, XIII, 212. Ovalle's account is particularly valuable because it was based on the *Cartas ánuas* of the period, the official reports that Jesuit superiors in missionary enterprises sent to the General of the Order in Rome. A manuscript copy of a history of the Jesuit college in Santiago gives April 12 as the date of arrival at Coquimbo, but all authorities are agreed that April 12 is the date of the party's arrival in Santiago. "Historia del Colegio Máximo," p. 4.

2. The passage from Callao to Coquimbo in northern Chile had required thirty-nine days partly because of a violent storm that had threatened to capsize the vessel. According to the early chroniclers, the ship had been saved through the timely intercession of St. Matthew the Apostle, whose protection the passengers had confidently invoked. Ovalle, XIII, 212; Olivares, *Historia militar*, p. 275; Rosales, "Varones ilustres," p. 1.

3. Rosales reports that the humility the travelers demonstrated by entering the town barefoot greatly impressed the people. Rosales, "Varones ilustres," p. 1.

4. Lozano, I, 117.

5. Letter of Atienza to Claude Aquaviva, General of the Order, August 7, 1585, in Astrain, IV, 669.

6. Miguel de Olivares, *Historia de la Compañía*, p. 9.

7. Lozano, I, 119.

8. *Ibid.* The original documents, dated Sept. 12, Sept. 19, and Oct. 3, 1590, are preserved in the National Library of Lima, *Sección Manuscritos*, XXXVI, folio 22 ff. The *pase real* is reproduced in Olivares, *Historia de la Compañía*, p. 12.

9. De la Parra is sometimes referred to as Parricio because of the latinized equivalent of his name, *Parricius*. Alteration of surnames was quite common among the early writers. For instance, the French Jesuit Nicolas du Toict, author of a well-known history of the Jesuits in Paraguay, is cited almost exclusively under the Spanish form of his name, Nicolás del Techo.

10. Olivares, *Historia de la Compañía*, pp. 12, 14.

11. An interesting biographical account of him is in Lozano, I, 172–93.

12. Cartas de obediencia were the credentials that major superiors issued to their subjects when assigning them to foreign missionary service. The letters identified the bearers, stated the nature of their mission, and noted that it was being undertaken with the approval of the Order. The document Piñas carried as superior of the group traveling to Chile read as follows: "Juan Sebastián, Provincial of the Company of Jesus in these dominions of Peru, to all who may inspect these letters: Health everlasting in the Lord. Since it is the custom of this least Company of Jesus that all of its members sent to any part of the world should take with them a testimonial of their religious affiliation, I do accordingly declare that the Fathers Baltasar Piñas, Luis de Valdivia, Hernando de Aguilera, and Gabriel de la Vega, as well as the temporal coadjutors Miguel Teleña and Fabian Martínez of the Company of Jesus are being

sent by their Order to the kingdom of Chile to labor for the welfare of their neighbor in the ministries that the Company is accustomed to exercise, and that the superior of the group is Father Baltasar Piñas. We pray the Almighty that they may fulfill this task accepted under obedience to the greater glory of God and the greater satisfaction of their neighbor. Given in Los Reyes on the 28th day of January 1593. *Juan Sebastián.*" The text of the foregoing letter is reproduced in Enrich, *Historia*, I, 14. The original is preserved in the national archives of Chile, *Archivo del Interior*. At the foot of the page that contains the text there appears the permission of the Holy Office phrased briefly: "The individuals named in this document are traveling with permission of the Inquisition. Dated in Los Reyes on January 29, 1593. Cerms of the Inquisition." On the reverse side of the same page is an order signed by the viceroy of Peru directing that the Jesuits listed in the letter be given passage on board the first boat en route to Chile. Although the name of Juan de Olivares is not included in the carta de obediencia, he was regularly regarded by all the early Jesuit chroniclers as one of the founders of the Chilean mission. Olivares was living in the Jesuit college of Potosí at the time and did not reach Callao in time to embark for Chile with the rest of the group; he left Peru on another vessel shortly thereafter.

13. There is some dispute concerning the actual date of departure from Peru. Olivares, *Historia militar*, p. 275, mentions Feb. 2, while Gay, II, 330, gives Feb. 12. Lozano, I, 121, and Ovalle, II, 212, both say it was Feb. 9. Enrich, *Historia*, I, 15, note 3, agrees, pointing out that Feb. 9 coincides better with the date of the viceroy's pase and of the arrival at Coquimbo.

14. Olivares, *Historia militar*, p. 277.

15. Olivares, *Historia de la Compañía*, p. 16.

16. *Ibid.*, p. 17.

17. Rosales, "Varones ilustres," p. 1; Olivares, *Historia de la Compañía*, p. 18.

18. Olivares, *Historia de la Compañía*, p. 18; Ovalle, II, 212; Rosales, "Varones ilustres," p. 1.

19. Ovalle, II, 213; Olivares, *Historia de la Compañía*, p. 18.

20. Lozano, I, 160–61.

21. *Ibid.*, I, 159; "Historia del Colegio Máximo," pp. 4–5.

22. Lozano, I, 159–60; Ovalle, II, 215.

23. The ease with which Valdivia acquired a working knowledge of the intricate Araucanian language impressed all of his associates. Lozano records that "after thirteen days he was able to hear confesssions satisfactorily in that language, and after twenty-eight days he began to preach in it with singular success to the great astonishment of all who heard him." Lozano, I, 160. This achievement seems less remarkable, however, when one learns that during the lengthy sea voyage from Callao he studied under the direction of Hernando de Aguilera, who spoke the language fluently. In referring to Valdivia, the author of an anonymous history of the early Jesuits in Peru says expressly: "Such was his intellectual capacity . . . that while on board ship he learned the language of Chile during the forty days that the voyage

lasted, with such results that on the day of his arrival in that kingdom he commenced preaching in that language." Mateos, I, 387–88.

24. Lozano, I, 166–67; Ovalle, II, 213.

25. Enrich, *Historia*, I, 46.

26. *Ibid.*, p. 56.

27. *Ibid.*, p. 58.

28. "Oratory is particularly held in high estimation by them, and, as among the ancient Romans, is the high road to honour, and the management of public affairs. The eldest son of an Ulmen [chieftain] who is deficient in this talent is, for that sole reason excluded from the right of succession, and one of his younger brothers, or the nearest relation that he has, who is an able speaker, substituted in his place. Their parents, therefore, accustom them from their childhood to speak in public, and carry them to their national assemblies, where the best orators of the country display their eloquence." Molina, II, 101.

29. Lozano, I, 334–35; Hernando de Aguilera, "Account of the missionary journey to Araucania, November 1, 1595, to March 1, 1597," in *Carta ánua del Perú, 1598*, pp. 3–12.

30. *Ibid.*, p. 3.

31. Lozano, I, 169.

32. Aguilera, "Account of the missionary journey to Araucania," in *Carta ánua del Perú, 1598*, p. 11.

33. For a contemporary account of the disastrous effects of the uprising, see Domingo de Eraso, "Información hecha en Santiago sobre los grandes trabajos y perdidas que ha sufrido aquella provincia con motivo de la guerra de 1599, 25 dias del mes de Enero de 1599," in BNC, *Archivo Vicuña Mackenna*, CCLXXVI, 120–43. Another account on the same subject is the "Información hecha en la Concepción de Chile a 8 de Noviembre [1599] por el Governador Don Francisco de Quiñones," in *ibid.*, pp. 1–101.

34. For the Spanish text of this treatise, see Medina, *Biblioteca*, II, 5–20. Medina suggests 1601 as the date of its composition, but it must have been written early in 1599 because Viceroy Velasco enclosed a copy of it with the letter he sent to the king on May 2, 1599. "Carta del Virrey del Perú D. Luis de Velasco a S.M. sobre el estado de las cosas del Reino de Chile, después de la muerte del Gobernador Martín García de Loyola . . . y pretensiones de los vezinos de Chile sobre que se hagan esclavos los indios que se prendieren en la guerra. Mayo 2, 1599," Pastells, LXXI (Peru 2), 174–75.

35. Medina, *Biblioteca*, II, 20.

36. *Ibid.*, p. 6.

37. Calderón remarked that the reason for submitting his proposal in writing to the viceroy of Peru was to enable "the letrados of Lima, who are removed from the passion and justifiable resentment that we here feel against these Indians who have been the cause of so much spiritual and temporal damage, freely to submit their

opinion in the matter." Calderón did not mention his advisers by name. He merely stated that "availing himself of the advice of some learned persons of this city of Santiago, he put together in writing all the important reasons that presented themselves . . . from among the intelligentsia here in Chile." *Ibid.* His gesture in requesting Valdivia to do the public reading of the tract lends credence to the theory that the Jesuit was one of the "learned" consultants.

38. *Ibid.,* pp. 6–7.

39. *Ibid.,* p. 7.

40. *Ibid.*

41. *Ibid.,* pp.8–9.

42. Among those who criticized Oñez de Loyola for his friendliness to the Araucanians was the cabildo of Santiago. In a letter of April 30, 1599, to the king, the cabildo complained bitterly that during the six years of Loyola's administration the Araucanians had astutely taken advantage of the governor's gullibility to stockpile their resources with government matériel prior to revolting. The same criticism has been leveled against Loyola by some modern historians; Encina, a good example, comments: "Loyola's policies not only achieved the destruction of the seven southern towns, but also put into the hands of the Indians the knife with which they cut his throat together with those of the Spaniards living south of the Biobío River. The Indians converted into lances all the iron that he gave them; and, as if this were not enough, he distributed knives and weapons to those who gave the peace, in order that they might defend themselves against their neighbors who were warring with the Spaniards. In his naiveté he believed that he could count on their support in effecting the pacification of Arauco in the same way Lazo de la Vega accomplished it years later under very dissimilar circumstances. He supplied arms to all those who deceitfully presented themselves as friends, and by his conduct he facilitated their organization [for war]." Encina, II, 151.

43. This was probably a reference to the welcome that the natives had tendered the Hawkins expedition of 1594, when the English buccaneer had stopped for provisions at the island of Mocha before proceeding to attack Valparaíso.

44. Calderón, pp. 9–10.

45. Reference here is especially to the Peruvian recruits who proved to be very inept and unreliable; many of them deserted at the first opportunity.

46. This was a hyperbole that none of Calderón's contemporaries would have taken literally. There were too many Spaniards who had survived captivity among the Indians to lend more than rhetorical emphasis to the charge, and in some cases captivity was not a tremendous hardship, as Pineda y Bascuñán testified in his *El cautiverio feliz.*

47. Calderón, pp. 11–13.

48. *Ibid.,* p. 14.

49. *Ibid.,* pp. 14–17.

50. *Ibid.,* pp. 17–20.

51. The document containing this questionnaire is entitled "La relación que se ha de dar al señor arzobispo y a los demás religiosos en lo que ponen a los que fueron al socorro de Chile sobre si la guerra ha sido justa o injusta." It is preserved in the National Library of Madrid, MS. 3044, No. 25, folios 243–45. See Hanke and Millares Carlo, p. lxv, note 184.

52. See Lizárraga. The original is listed as MS. 2010 in the National Library of Madrid.

53. Hanke and Millares Carlo, p. 296.

54. Lizárraga, pp. 296–97.

55. *Ibid.*, p. 297.

56. *Ibid.*, pp. 297–98.

57. *Ibid.*, p. 299.

58. *Ibid.*, pp. 299–300.

59. *Ibid.*, p. 300.

60. *Ibid.*

61. Alonso de Ribera, a veteran of distinguished service in the military campaigns in Flanders, arrived at Concepción on February 9, 1601. His tactical plan called for the establishment of a fortified frontier and the gradual reduction and occupation, through successive stages, of the enemy territory. Speaking of Ribera, Agustín Edwards says: "By his capacity for organization and by his zeal in introducing certain standards of administration Ribera marks in the history of the Araucanian War the period of transition from conquest to colony. . . . During his period of office [1601–4] he worked hard to obtain fixed revenues for Santiago and the other towns, to provide the hospitals and monasteries with resources, to bring about the exemption from military service of the citizens of Santiago and La Serena in order that they might devote themselves to the cultivation of the fields, and to suppress cruelty on the part of the encomenderos toward the Indians. One of the tasks causing the greatest irritation among the natives was that of 'bearing sedan-chairs in which the women went to Mass or to make visits'; Ribera prohibited their doing this 'unless they did so of their own free will and were paid for it.' " Edwards, pp. 126, 265.

62. Eraso, L, 221.

63. *Ibid.*, pp. 229–31. For a summary of the war in Chile, 1598–1607, together with a parecer aimed at inducing the Council of the Indies to declare the war just, see González de Nájera.

64. Juan de Vascones, p. 310.

65. *Ibid.*, p. 311.

66. Cédula of Philip III to the governor of Chile, Aug. 16, 1604, in Lizana and Maulén, II, 304.

67. Cédula of Philip III to the governor of Chile, May 26, 1608, in AAS, LVII, 151.

68. "The publication of this cédula was greeted with delight by the soldiers because of the profit that they would realize from the sale of slaves." Rosales, *Historia general*, II, 478.

Chapter 6

1. Lozano, II, 51–52. The Jesuit residences in Córdoba and Santiago del Estero on the other side of the mountains had received similar but smaller benefactions.

2. The details of the Torres-Salazar encounter are related in *ibid.*, pp. 50–51.

3. *Ibid.*, p. 51. In referring to Salazar, Lozano adds: "He spent his entire fortune in the achievement of this end, but he was completely happy to employ it in such a just cause, as he personally informed Father Diego de Torres in Panama when Torres was returning to Lima to lay the foundations of the province of Paraguay."

4. Letter of Claude Aquaviva to Diego de Torres Bollo, April 28, 1609, in Astrain, IV, 649–50.

5. Lozano, II, 52–53. Lozano notes that they were all "competent, learned men, and that almost all of them had taught theology with distinction."

6. *Ibid.*, p. 52.

7. *Ibid.*, p. 53. See also Torres Bollo, *Carta ánua de 1609.* An excellent critical edition of this and other annual reports of the period is contained in Leonhardt, *Documentos.*

8. Lozano, II, 54.

9. Report of Diego de Torres Bollo to the members of the provincial congregation in Santiago, in *ibid.*, p. 54.

10. Resolution of the provincial congregation, April 28, 1608, in *ibid.*, pp. 53–54. Lozano copied the document verbatim from the original manuscript preserved in the archives of the Jesuit college in Córdoba. Muñoz is in error when he identifies this resolution with the regulations Torres promulgated on June 19, 1608. See Humberto Muñoz, p. 74.

11. Resolution of the provincial congregation, Lozano, II, 53–55.

12. Copies of this document are in the archives of the Colegio San Ignacio in Santiago, A-II-35, 11–14, and the National Library of Chile, *Archivo Medina, Documentos,* CCLXXIII, No. 8,071. It has been reproduced in printed form in Ferrada Ibáñez, pp. 163–66, and in Amunátegui Solar, *Las encomiendas,* I, 338–45.

13. Amunátegui Solar, *Historia social,* p. 59.

14. Encina, IV, 77–78. Encina claims that the main reason the Jesuits were willing to free their Indian employees of the burden of compulsory personal service was because "they understood from the very beginning that the labor of Negro slaves was much more economical than that of either free Indians or encomienda Indians. Negro slaves did not have to pay tribute and produced a high return on the money invested in them, while the profit realized from the labor of Indian workers was only average and irregular; Indian labor was also the source of excessively frequent difficulties with the administrators in charge of Indian towns, with the protectors of the Indians, the parish priests, the encomenderos and the ordinary vecinos." *Ibid.*, p. 75. While it is true that by the time of their expulsion from the Spanish American domains in 1767 the Jesuits in Chile had become one of the largest corporate

employers of Negro slaves in the colony, it is also true that this development did not occur until long after 1608, at which date the total number of Negro slaves in Chile was too small to figure as a significant force in the labor economy. Nor is there any indication that the Jesuits were planning to replace their native workers with Negro slaves at that time. As will be pointed out in a subsequent chapter, the high price of Negro slaves on the Chilean market was in itself a prohibitive consideration that made the employment of contented Indian labor more economical.

15. Lozano, II, 56–57. There were some Spaniards, however, who reacted favorably to the situation. On the very day Torres issued his proclamation, one of the merchants of Santiago, Juan de Sigordia, sent an alms of 1,200 patacones to the Jesuit college. The will that another vecino drew up at this time included a bequest of 6,000 pesos to the college. Torres Bollo, *Carta ánua de 1609*, p. 11; Lozano, II, 57.

16. For the text of the cédula, see Lozano, II, 57.

17. *Ibid.*, p. 58.

18. Torres Bollo, *Carta ánua de 1609*, p. 12. Espinosa's support was particularly gratifying, since he was not considered a friend of the Jesuits.

19. García Ramón replaced Ribera as governor of Chile in April 1605. Rosales describes him as being "a handsome man with a cheerful countenance, a large moustache and a full beard ... throughout his tenure of office he displayed excellent qualities in the administration of business, dealing personally with all requests submitted to him and replying in all cases very tactfully so as to make denials more acceptable and to lessen the disappointment of refusals in cases in which he was unable to accede to the request." Rosales, *Historia general*, II, 490.

20. The text of the petition, composed by Torres Bollo, is included in the *Carta ánua de 1609*. The governor was absent from Santiago at the time, being engaged in campaigns against the rebels.

21. The reaction of the viceroy of Peru, the Marquis of Montesclaros, and of the Council of the Indies, to whom copies of the petition were also sent, was reportedly more encouraging. Lozano claims that the petition influenced them in their determination to correct the injustices of obligatory personal service. Lozano, II, 60.

22. *Ibid.*, p. 61. More serious opposition was felt in Córdoba, Santiago del Estero, and Asunción when Torres put his policy into effect in the Jesuit houses in those areas. Virtual persecution of the Order developed under the leadership of the encomenderos who refused to sacrifice what they considered their rightful profits, and even certain ecclesiastics allied themselves with the opposition. In Santiago del Estero the vicious attack on the padres forced them to leave town until December 1611. The Jesuits in Córdoba were reduced for a time to a state of virtual siege within their residence. *Ibid.*, pp. 87–103. Reports of such events make it difficult to understand why Amunátegui Solar says: "The liberty conceded to the yanaconas of the Colegio San Miguel [in Santiago] was purely nominal, and had no more binding force than that of a solemn promise made by the provincial of the Order in the presence of the public authorities to treat the Indians in a paternal manner and

to remunerate their services equitably. . . . The unpopularity the Jesuits in Chile experienced was transitory, and the principal reason why the disaffection did not spread or endure is to be found in the fact that the liberty granted to the yanaconas was merely illusory. The encomenderos knew from experience that the natives did not know how to make use of their liberty and would refuse to work voluntarily in any case." Amunátegui Solar, *Las encomiendas*, I, 346–47. If the Chilean scholar is correct, why did the encomenderos react so vehemently to a situation that, according to him, in no way endangered their position? Organized opposition lasting for more than two years, and shortened only in one instance by the intervention of extrinsic causes, surely should not be termed "a passing thing." In practice, not just in theory, the Jesuits gave the Indians freedom to choose employers, to accept or reject the terms of a contract, to quit their jobs, and to hire out to someone else. Amunátegui Solar does not seem to accept that people may refuse to work voluntarily for an unjust employer but may willingly work for one who treats them fairly.

23. "Aviso de la audiencia." Miguel Luis Amunátegui has published this document in his *Los precursores*, I, 132–36.

24. The legislators were careful to note that they had been "unable to find the text of the ordinances the Licentiate Santillán prepared during the administration of the Marquis of Cañete." This temporizing attitude of the audiencia was directly contrary to the explicit orders of the Crown and the viceroy regarding the abolition of personal service.

25. This is a reference to the decree of May 26, 1608, which reached Chile on May 5, 1609.

26. Feliú Cruz and Monje Alfaro, p. 158. Although Cajal signed the document he continued to oppose the servicio personal.

27. Letter of Gabriel de Celada to the king, Jan. 6, 1610, in Gay, II, 194–203.

28. Letter of the cabildo of Santiago to the king, Oct. 25, 1666, cited in the royal cédula of Sept. 11, 1670, to the audiencia of Chile, AAS, XLII, 137–40.

29. Notably Amunátegui Solar, *Las encomiendas*, I, 346. See note 22, above.

30. The decree enslaving the rebel Araucanians was issued on May 26, 1608, with a companion decree authorizing the governor of Chile to postpone its enactment for as long as he deemed prudent. García Ramón invoked this authorization to prevent publication of the document until after his death, which occurred on August 5, 1610. Amunátegui Solar explains the inconsistency between García Ramón's bloody campaigns against the Araucanians and his refusal to enforce the legal penalty against them by citing the influence of the Jesuits and especially that of Diego de Torres Bollo. In a letter to the king dated in Santiago on February 17, 1609, Torres wrote: "I am informed that the Royal Audiencia brings orders from Your Majesty for the abolition of obligatory personal service and the enslavement of the warring tribes. The first of these orders is most just. . . . The second involves great moral difficulties, for up until now the peace and pardon of Your Majesty has not been made known to a twentieth part of these Indians, many of whom are not Christians. Others who rebelled did so because the Spaniards persecuted them.

Finally, all of them are fighting to free themselves of the servicio personal and of other evils such as the oldest and most loyal Christian subjects would not endure. Furthermore, even if offers of peace and pardon had been made to all of them, they could scarcely be blamed for refusing to accept them at face value in view of the innumerable times similar promises have been made and broken. And if, prior to being declared slaves by order of Your Majesty and while legally free in virtue of your decrees and laws, not only all rebel Indians but many who are living in peace are being sold into slavery together with their wives and children, Your Majesty can well imagine what will happen in the future if they are condemned to slavery." Quoted in Amunátegui Solar, *Las encomiendas*, I, 364–65. Whatever may have been the reasons that influenced García Ramón, the decree of 1608 was not promulgated in Chile until August 20, 1610, when his successor, Luis Merlo de la Fuente, published it in an effort to stimulate interest among the vecinos of Santiago in his projected campaign against the Araucanians. *Actas*, IX, 188–89.

31. Alfaro was a relative of Diego Alfaro, a Jesuit who attained considerable reputation in the Río de la Plata region. See Furlong, p. 22.

32. For a reliable discussion of this episode, see Lozano, II, 285–89, 297–306, and Astrain, IV, 654–66. The reasons preventing Maldonado from making the visit are not known. Torres Bollo reports in his *Carta ánua* of 1611 that it was only after four years of arguing that a successor was finally appointed to the task around the end of 1610. *Ibid.*, p. 654.

33. Astrain, IV, 661. Two copies of the ordinances are preserved in Seville, *Archivo General de Indias*, Audiencia de Charcas, 74, 4, 4, one of which was dated in Asunción on Oct. 12, 1611. This earlier text was very likely the first draft Alfaro submitted to the judgment of the experts whom he mentioned in the definitive document. It is reproduced in Hernández, II, 661–77.

34. Torres, *Carta ánua de 1613*, p. 192.

35. "Decisión real en el Consejo de Indias, 1618."

36. The Prince's father was Don Juan de Borja, third son of Francisco Borja, the Duke of Gandia, who later became a Jesuit and served as General of the Order from 1567 to 1572. Briseño, p. 403.

37. Ulloa y Lemos arrived in Peru in 1604 in the company of the Count of Monterrey. He later married a prominent, wealthy matron of Lima. Encina asserts that he was a very close friend of the Jesuits and that he accepted the appointment as governor of Chile solely for career reasons. Encina, III, 122. His arrival in Chile was accompanied by a display of wealth that was unusual. He and his wife brought with them expensive furniture, clothing, and jewels, and one of the first complaints that Ulloa made to the king was that his salary was inadequate to enable him to "live with the integrity and honor" to which he was accustomed. Edwards says of him: "During the period of nearly three years for which he governed, Ulloa y Lemos accomplished nothing useful. The most durable memory he left behind him was that of his arrogance, based upon the noble pedigree of which he boasted." Edwards, p. 275. During his term as governor, Ulloa attempted without success to induce the

Crown to establish the African slave trade in Chile as a substitute for the personal service of the Indians. Barros Arana, IV, 139.

38. Encina, III, 122.

39. Letter of Hernando Machado to the king, March 5, 1618, in Amunátegui Solar, *Las encomiendas*, I, 393.

40. *Actas*, April 18, 1618, VIII, 253.

41. *Ibid.*, April 23, 1618, VIII, 254–55.

42. *Ibid.*, Sept. 7, 1618, IX, 74. The documents referring to Lisperguer's commission are in *ibid.*, X, 281–356.

43. *Ibid.*, IX, 74; Silva y Molina, p. 22.

44. *Actas*, Nov. 6, 1619, X, 281.

45. Valdivia, "Memorial al rey, 1622." A more personal reason for Valdivia's sudden trip to Peru will be treated in a later chapter.

46. Barros Arana, IV, 142. Valdivia also carried with him an enthusiastic recommendation from Governor Ulloa to be given to the king in the event that he were to continue on to Spain after concluding the business with the viceroy in Lima. Rosales, *Historia general*, II, 643–44. This recommendation was tangible evidence of the support Ulloa consistently gave the Jesuits in their fight against Indian oppression. His proposal that Negroes be imported to free the mapuches from the onus of slavery and to provide agricultural workers for the colony was characteristic of his feelings in the matter. The proposal had been made repeatedly by different individuals following the insurrection of 1598. The Augustinian friar Vascones included it in his memorial to the king in 1601, as did González de Najera in his *Desengaño i reparo de la guerra de Chile*, and various Jesuits, including Diego de Torres Bollo and Luis de Valdivia.

47. Valdivia, "Memorial al rey, 1622," p. 220.

48. For the complete text of the tasa, see Medina, *Biblioteca*, I, 134–51, or Gay, II, 317–46.

49. *Actas*, Dec. 11, 1620, X, 409.

50. Ulloa died in Concepción on Dec. 8, 1620. Encina, III, 142.

51. Barros Arana, IV, 168.

52. *Auto de Osores de Ulloa*, 1622, pp. 154–55. Osores de Ulloa governed efficiently for two and a half years, despite his advanced age.

53. To guard against possible abuses, Esquilache had suppressed the Spanish administrators of Indian pueblos, and had replaced them with native alcaldes chosen by the Indians themselves. According to numerous documents of the period, some of these Spanish administrators were veritable tyrants. In a letter to the king dated Feb. 20, 1625, Adaro y San Martín castigated these officials because "instead of being concerned about the well-being of the Indians and the preservation of their property, they exploit them for their own profit, treating them worse than slaves and doing them a thousand wrongs, depriving them of their women and children, contrary to all instincts of justice, and uprooting them from their homes by transporting them to wherever they please; and regardless of how much or how little the

victims own, the administrators take a share of it for themselves, so much so that today not even 800 head of cattle remain out of herds that previously had numbered 30,000." BNC, *Archivo Medina, Documentos*, CXXVI, 195–97.

54. Medina, *Biblioteca*, I, 166–67. Among the signers was the Augustinian friar Juan de Toro Mazote, who years later had a change of heart and became an ardent defender of the mapuches.

55. *Ibid.*, pp. 165–66.

56. Of the eight and a half pesos, the encomendero received six, the doctrina one and a half, and the corregidor and protector of the Indians one-half each. The salaries that the corregidores of Concepción and Chillán received from the government as army captains were reduced in an amount corresponding to the tribute they collected. Since the corregidores in the districts of Santiago and La Serena held no military offices, no adjustment was made, but any previous salary they had derived from Indian property was canceled. The tribute for the province of Cuyo was eight pesos, of which the encomendero received five and one-half. The other allotments were the same as those in the territory west of the cordillera and north of the Biobío. The inhabitants of Chiloé paid seven pesos two reales in tribute each year, of which the encomendero received five and one-half pesos.

57. "Ordenanzas sobre el servicio personal." Gay, II, 317–46.

58. Astrain, IV, 666.

Chapter 7

1. Crescente Errázuriz calls it the "idea más importante" and the "sistema más notable del siglo XVII en Chile." Errázuriz, *Estudios históricos*, II, 11.

2. Torres Saldamando, p. 84. Gaspar de Zúñiga y Acevedo, the Count of Monterrey, succeeded Luis de Velasco, Marquis of Salinas, as viceroy of Peru in 1604. He had served a term as viceroy of New Spain before being transferred to Peru.

3. Valdivia was in Lima at the time teaching theology in the Jesuit college of San Pablo. He had returned to Peru in 1603 after serving as rector of the college in Santiago for four years.

4. One of these periti was Luis de Torres Minensa, protector of the Indians in Chile, who had come to Lima for the express purpose of securing justice for his charges. According to Torres, obligatory personal service was the underlying cause of the war and the reason for its continuance. Although it had been abolished twenty times in the past by royal decree, it still functioned as vigorously as ever without respect to age or sex. The encomenderos, Torres asserted, were concerned only with their own economic advantage and had no regard for the welfare of the Indians. Letter of Valdivia to the Count of Lemos, president of the Council of the Indies, Jan. 4, 1607, ACSI, A-II-63, part I, 249; Tribaldos de Toledo, p. 95; Errázuriz, *Estudios históricos*, II, 13–14.

5. The reception, not long before, of a royal cédula dated in Valladolid on Nov.

24, 1601, in which the king prohibited the practice of converting the payment of tribute into personal service very likely had a suasive effect on the viceroy. See Amunátegui, *Los precursores*, II, 121–22. The junta included Luis de Velasco, former viceroy of Peru; Luis de Torres, protector of the mapuches; García Ramón, the new governor-elect of Chile; Juan de Villela, judge of the audiencia of Lima; Doctor Acuña, an alcalde de corte; Francisco de Coello, S.J., a theologian who had been one of the viceroy's asesores and an alcalde de corte before becoming a Jesuit; and Valdivia. Letter of Valdivia to the Count of Lemos, Jan. 4, 1607, ACSI, A-II-63, part I, 249–50.

6. *Ibid.*, pp. 249–51. Errázuriz believes Valdivia was the guiding spirit in this junta and that the decisions reached were principally due to him. *Estudios históricos*, II, 18.

7. The party reached Penco on March 19, 1605. García Ramón took over the government of the colony from Alonso de Ribera in nearby Concepción on March 21. Errázuriz, *Estudios históricos*, II, 18, 20; Enrich, *Historia*, I, 103.

8. Two hundred well-equipped reinforcements had accompanied García Ramón to Chile from Peru. An additional thousand arrived from Spain shortly thereafter under the command of Antonio de Mosquera, and another two hundred and fifty came from New Spain with Captain Villaroel. These, plus those already in Chile and the native allies, raised the total number of troops to more than two thousand.

9. García Ramón's conduct prompts the conclusion that his earlier endorsement of Valdivia's report on the status of the war had been only a piece of political chicanery designed to insure his appointment as governor of Chile. Miguel Luis Amunátegui suggests that he changed his views after arriving in Chile in order to curry favor with the encomenderos and the military. *Los precursores*, II, 123.

10. Indicative of García Ramón's "get tough" policy was his edict of July 27, 1605, which relieved Torres Minensa, an outspoken critic of obligatory service, of his position as protector of the Indians. It appeared ten days after he had taken the oath of office before the cabildo of Santiago and sworn to "protect the interests of God and His Majesty, and to obey the king's commands." Juan Venegas, son of Francisco de Toledo and half brother of Fernando Alvarez de Toledo, the author of *Purén indómito*, succeeded Torres.

11. Letter of Valdivia to the Count of Lemos, ACSI, A-II-63, part I, 258.

12. *Ibid.*, p. 259.

13. Astrain, IV, 693. Valdivia made use of the months following his return to Lima to prepare a number of publications that would be helpful to others in the conversion of the Araucanians. These included a grammar of the Araucanian language, two catechisms, directions for confessors, and a dictionary. Amunátegui, *Los precursores*, II, 125.

14. A letter of Dec. 8, 1609, from the General of the Order congratulating him on his safe crossing supports this conclusion. Allowing two months for the passage of mail from Seville to Rome and back again, this would put Valdivia in Spain at the time suggested. See Astrain, IV, 697, note 1.

15. Lozano, II, 455.

16. Valdivia, "Tratado," 1610.

17. The plan envisioned the rebuilding of Concepción and Chillán, which had been destroyed in the uprising of 1598, the erection of a new town farther to the northeast, and the construction of four additional forts in strategic spots along the north bank of the river. These last would be defended by some 400 or 500 soldiers, mostly cavalry, who would serve for a period of three years at the king's expense. A minimum of 150 vecinos were to settle each town and were to provide their own protection. Soldiers could become *pobladores* (settlers) if they wished. The Crown was to supply them with the means of building houses and working the fields.

18. Valdivia, "Tratado," 1610, p. 84.

19. García Ramón, through Salto, had asked the viceroy for 1,000 troops on Aug. 9, 1608. It is logical to assume that Salto repeated the request in Spain. Astrain, IV, 699, note 1.

20. "Puntos para contestar," 1610.

21. The junta must have been toying with the idea as early as Feb. 20, 1610, for on that date Valdivia applied to Rome for instructions governing his conduct in case he were to be offered certain dignities not consistent with his religious profession. The General of the Order, Claude Aquaviva, contented himself with replying: "In your letter of Feb. 20 you ask what you should do in case the Council does not order you to return [to Chile], or does so under some condition that is incompatible with your religious profession. In the first instance you may retire to the province of Castile and occupy yourself in keeping with your many talents. Since the answer to the second possibility depends on a more precise knowledge of the Council's intentions, we can do no more than advise you that if they order you to return to Chile with one of the dignities that you have mentioned, you ought to excuse yourself with good reasons as the circumstances may require, giving an account of the matter to the rector of the college and following his directions in everything." Letter of Claude Aquaviva to Luis de Valdivia, March 30, 1610, ACSI, A-II-63, part II, print 1.

22. Letter of Aquaviva to Bartholomé Pérez, April 27, 1610, ACSI, A-II-63, part II, print 4.

23. Letter of Aquaviva to Valdivia, April 27, 1610, ACSI, A-II-63, part II, print 5.

24. Letter of Aquaviva to Valdivia, June 22, 1610, ACSI, A-II-63, part II, print 6. Since Valdivia's letter was dated May 7, Aquaviva's instructions of April 27 to the provincial of Toledo could not possibly have reached Spain by that time. It is clear, therefore, that the Jesuit superiors in Madrid had acted on their own initiative without waiting for word from Rome.

25. Letter of Viceroy Mendoza to the king, April 30, 1610, in Astrain, IV, 701.

26. The complete text of this letter, dated in Madrid on Dec. 8, 1610, is reproduced in Errázuriz, *Estudios históricos*, II, 68–69. For a detailed study of the con-

troversy involving the question of the episcopacy, see *ibid.*, pp. 101–29, 181–227.

27. Undated manuscript, BNC, *Archivo Morla Vicuña*, XXIV, No. 7.

28. The document carries neither signature nor date, but Valdivia was evidently the writer. It is addressed to someone he calls "Most Reverend Paternity," very likely the king's confessor, for in a letter to Diego de Torres, Valdivia speaks of the "Father confessor of His Majesty" in referring to this matter. Astrain, IV, 704, note 1.

29. Undated and untitled manuscript, BNC, *Archivo Jesuítas*, XCIII, 190. The letter was probably written in Nov. 1610, judging from other documents on the subject.

30. Letter of Valdivia to Pedro de Ledesma, Madrid, Nov. 28, 1610, ACSI, A-II-55, 5–6.

31. Valdivia, "Memorial al rey," 1610.

32. "Consulta de la junta de guerra," 1610. This is a pivotal document in the still unsettled controversy over Valdivia and the episcopacy. Barros Arana cites it incorrectly in his *Historia jeneral de Chile*, II, 34: "In its session of Dec. 9 it [the junta de guerra] decided that it was not expedient to give Father Valdivia the office of bishop because this would embarrass him in the performance of his duties." This statement is directly contrary to the fact. The junta not only did *not* decide that it was not expedient to give the episcopacy to Valdivia, but positively recommended that it be conferred on the ground that it would "contribute very much" to the mission he was about to undertake. Barros Arana asserts that the junta said it was not useful ("no convenía") for Valdivia to receive the episcopacy; the consulta of the junta states the exact opposite in very emphatic language ("que sería muy conveniente"). There is no doubt that the Chilean historian was referring to this particular document, for he cites it in his reference in note 41, p. 34: "Memoriales del P. Valdivia de 28 de Noviembre de 1610 y acuerdo del Consejo de Indias de 9 de Diciembre del mismo año." The only memorials and acuerdos on this point are the ones mentioned in the text of this chapter. That Barros Arana's error was not the result of inadvertence is evident from his note 38 on p. 32 of the same volume, in which he says: "The Archive of the Indies possesses all the documents referring to these negotiations, including the rough drafts of the acuerdos. In our discussion we have limited ourselves to epitomizing these documents, but we have been forced to do so with considerable prolixity and by entering into details and accidental issues that will perhaps seem unnecessary." On p. 34, note 41, the reason for this diligence is revealed: "As we have said in an earlier note, we are obliged to enter into details in order to reestablish the truth that has been distorted by the Jesuit chroniclers." It is regrettable, indeed, that his concern did not enable Barros Arana to present the facts more accurately. Besides the one already noted, he was guilty of several lesser errors. He asserts, for example, that the king, acting upon the advice of the junta, resolutely refused to sponsor the episcopacy for Valdivia; this statement would suggest that all members objected to the episcopacy of Valdivia. In fact, the majority opinion of the junta favored petitioning the Pope to confer the dignity upon the

Jesuit, but the king acted on the advice of the minority. Similarly, it is not correct to say, as Barros Arana does, that Valdivia's letter was addressed to the president of the Council of the Indies; it was addressed to the king's secretary, Pedro de Ledesma. The assertion that Valdivia's memorial carried the date of Nov. 28, 1610, is also faulty; the document was not dated. Furthermore, it is not true, as Barros Arana claims, that Ovalle was the first to mention "this fictitious offer [of the episcopacy] that the king made to Valdivia." The offer was reported as real, not fictitious, by the Jesuits Alegambe and Nieremberg prior to Ovalle.

33. The following words, written in the king's hand, appear on the back of the junta's consulta: "Let the minority opinion of the Council of the Indies be followed and order him [Valdivia] to leave immediately." The cédula informing Bishop Pérez de Espinosa of the king's wishes was dated Dec. 8, 1610. AAS, XLI, 115.

34. Lozano, II, 460.

35. Cédula of Philip III to the audiencia of Chile, March 3, 1611, ACSI, A-II-63, part I, 223–24.

36. Rosales, *Historia general*, II, 510.

37. Lozano, II, 465.

38. Enrich, *Historia*, I, 236.

39. Letter of Aquaviva to Valdivia, April 27, 1610, in Astrain, IV, 707.

40. Letter of Aquaviva to Valdivia, July 20, 1610, in *ibid.*

41. Letter of Aquaviva to Valdivia, Feb. 28, 1612, in *ibid.*

42. Letter of Aquaviva to Valdivia, Feb. 26, 1613, in *ibid.*

43. Lozano's faulty interpretation may have been due to a copyist's mistake. Aquaviva's letter to Diego de Torres was written on Feb. 26, 1613, as was the one to Valdivia cited above. Lozano's reproduction gives Feb. 26, 1612, as the date of composition.

44. Letter of Valdivia to the king, Sept. 7, 1613, ACSI, A-II-55, No. 4. Complaining of Ribera's refusal to cooperate, Valdivia recalls "the favor Your Majesty showed him *at my request* by sending him to this government." Emphasis added. During his first term as governor of Chile Ribera had incurred the wrath of Bishop Pérez de Espinosa because of his scandalous private life and lack of respect for the clergy. Errázuriz believes that Ribera's reappointment for a second term, for which Valdivia admits he was primarily responsible, was the main reason the Jesuit feared that the bishop would try to hamstring his efforts to implement the system of defensive warfare. *Estudios históricos*, II, 152–53.

45. Olivares, *Historia militar*, p. 320.

46. "All the members of the Royal Audiencia and the other consultors agreed by a unanimous vote of 20–0 that the war should be curtailed by making it defensive and that personal service in Chile should conform to the norms of justice. His Excellency decided the issue on this basis." "Compendio," 1611.

47. *Ibid.*

48. "Provisión del Marques de Montes Claros," 1612. It is interesting to note that Valdivia resisted being appointed to this office. In a memorial addressed to the

viceroy on March 1, 1612, he said: "Although His Majesty ordered me in a letter of Dec. 8, 1610, to attend to the affairs of his royal service, which Your Excellency might commit to me in connection with this experiment in the kingdom of Chile, and although I have received similar instructions from Father Claude Aquaviva, General of the Society of Jesus, to whom His Majesty had written in support of this arrangement, I must, nevertheless, inform Your Excellency that the visita which you are entrusting to me is not conformable to my religious profession nor to the spiritual purpose for which I am being sent. I therefore entreat Your Excellency to excuse me from this task (if it be possible) lest I fail in my service to the king, and to entrust it to some other person who is better qualified for executing it. Your Excellency will thus be doing me a great favor." Valdivia, "Memorial que dió al virrey del Perú," 1612. The viceroy's reply was contained in a *decreto* (decree) of March 28 that read as follows: "Since the concerns of this visita are so bound up with the principal end for which Father Luis de Valdivia was sent by order of His Majesty, and since it is of such importance that care be exercised in choosing the person for this purpose, it is impossible to relieve him of this duty. Rather, we affectionately enjoin him with it once again. Lima, March 28, 1610. The Marquis, Gaspar Rodríguez de Castra." *Ibid.*

49. "Provisión y placarte," 1612.

50. "Capítulos y ordenanzas," 1612.

51. Valdivia, "Relación," 1612.

52. Astrain, IV, 714.

53. "Información de las cosas de Chile," 1612. This is an important document because it contains the sworn testimony of men who had years of experience in Chile and who were eyewitnesses to the events. See also the memorial of Gaspar Sobrino to the king in 1614, BNC, *Archivo Vicuña Mackenna*, CCXCII, 208–54. Valdivia notes that the reason for the uprising was the "insults and oppression that the Indians suffered at the hands of the encomenderos and others who made use of their services, together with some military setbacks on our part." Valdivia, "Relación," 1612, p. 94.

54. Letter of Valdivia to the king, Sept. 30, 1612, ACSI, A-II-55, No. 3.

55. "Información de las cosas de Chile," p. 263.

56. "Governor Juan Xara, predecessor of Governor [Ribera], was in Concepción when Father Luis de Valdivia arrived, and he [and] many other inhabitants of the town who held a contrary opinion tried with many cogent arguments to dissuade the Father from putting his program into effect because they considered it a horrendous plan, the product of sinister reports to His Majesty." *Ibid.*, p. 262.

57. Other chiefs came to the Spanish fort in Paicaví for the same purpose. *Ibid.*, p. 264.

58. Before sending messengers to Catiray, Valdivia had consulted the military officials of the fort about its propriety, since the governor had not yet arrived at Concepción and the missionary had no way of knowing whether the dispatches he had forwarded to Santiago had reached him. "All the members of the council unani-

mously agreed that it would result in great service to God and His Majesty to send the said messengers, and that even though Father Luis de Valdivia did not possess full authority for such matters, he should apply the principle of *epieikeia* in the present case, because the state of affairs demanded it for many reasons." Valdivia, "Relación," 1612, p. 96.

59. Letter of Valdivia to the king, Sept. 30, 1612, ACSI, A-II-55, No. 3.

60. Letter of Valdivia to Diego de Torres, Sept. 3, 1613, in Astrain, IV, 717.

61. Barros Arana sees in these peaceful overtures of the natives another proof of their innate hypocrisy. He believes that they feigned friendship temporarily solely for the purpose of securing the liberation of some of their tribesmen who were held captive by the Spaniards. Barros Arana, IV, 50.

62. "Información de las cosas de Chile." The process began on Sept. 17 and ended on Oct. 18.

63. "Información del Padre Luis de Valdivia," 1612.

64. Concerning these records Barros Arana says: "These informaciones, in which the interrogations were artfully worded in favor of the subject, and in which witnesses were called who were disposed to answer them satisfactorily, were a favorite device of the period and undoubtedly enjoyed great influence in governmental councils." Barros Arana, IV, 53.

65. Letter of Ribera to the king, Oct. 25, 1613, in Gay, II, 295–96.

66. Letter of Fr. Pedro Torrelas to Fr. Juan Pastor, Dec. 22, 1612, BNC, *Archivo Morla Vicuña*, XXIV, No. 25.

67. Letter of Martín Aranda and Horacio Vecchi to Alonso de Ribera, Elicura, Dec. 10, 1612, in Barros Arana, IV, 65.

68. Letter of Valdivia to Diego de Torres, Dec. 24, 1612, in Medina, *Biblioteca*, II, 118.

Chapter 8

1. Letter of Alonso de Ribera to the king, April 17, 1613, in Barros Arana, IV, 74–75; Encina, III, 104.

2. The first news of the massacre was obtained from Cayumari, a faithful Araucanian whom Valdivia had sent to Elicura with additional instructions for the missionaries. On returning to Lebu, where Valdivia had gone from Paicaví, Cayumari reported that he had discovered the bodies of the Jesuits, "naked and covered with wounds," and that the Indians whom he met there had told him the story of the tragedy. He added that many of the natives of Purén regretted the evil deed and were prepared to join the Spaniards in tracking down the assassins who had treacherously deceived the people of Elicura. Letter of Valdivia to Ribera, Dec. 16, 1612, ACSI, A-II-63, part I, 385–87. Barros Arana's interpretation is: "Cayumari's story was artfully designed to justify not only the Indians of Elicura but also those of Purén, and to incite the Spaniards to penetrate into the valleys of the interior where

they were assured of meeting their most deadly enemies." Barros Arana, IV, 67. Encina (III, 107) holds the same opinion.

3. "Información que se hizo," 1613; Letter of eleven army captains to the king, April 9, 1614, ACSI, A-II-63, part II, 641–45; Letter of Diego de Villarroel to the king, April 10, 1614, *ibid.*, 645–48; Letter of Gaspar Viera Alderete to the king, April 18, 1614, *ibid.*, 669–74; Declaration of Fray Juan Falcón de los Angeles, April 18, 1614, *ibid.*, 677–701; Letter of Alonso de Ribera to the king, Sept. 18, 1613, *ibid.*, 589–609; Barros Arana, IV, 75; Encina, III, 107–9.

4. Letter of Valdivia to the provincial, Diego de Torres, Dec. 24, 1612, in Medina, *Biblioteca*, II, 118. Emphasis added.

5. Letter of Valdivia to the king, Fort of La Esperanza, Feb. 20, 1613, ACSI, A-II-63, part I, 437–50.

6. Letter of Pedro Torrelas to Fr. Juan Pastor, Dec. 22, 1612, BNC, *Archivo Morla Vicuña*, XXIV, No. 25.

7. Diego de Torres, *Carta ánua* of 1613, in Leonhardt, *Documentos*, pp. 244–47. The report is dated Feb. 13, 1613. See also Valdivia's letter to the king, Feb. 20, 1613, ACSI, A-II-63, part I, 443.

8. Sobrino. Valdivia notes that the casualties included two leading caciques killed and more than 100 tribesmen taken prisoner. Letter to Valdivia to the king, Feb. 20, 1613, ACSI, A-II-63, part I, 443. Córdoba y Figueroa says nothing about the number of captives, but mentions (p. 299) that Anganamón showed no mercy "to those of his own nation, killing forty" of the Elicureans. Carvallo y Goyeneche (p. 299) reports that Anganamón "killed almost all the inhabitants of that district, and carried off ninety-two female captives." Miguel de Olivares reports the name of at least one of the slain caciques: "They likewise killed Utablame, toqui general of the districts of Elicura and Cayucupil, and many Indians of Elicura who valiantly tried to defend the padres; and although none of the historical writings and manuscripts definitely confirm this fact of Utablame's death, I found it so declared in the informaciones that were compiled on the glorious death of these padres by the vicar general of the city of Santiago." *Historia militar*, p. 342.

9. Torres Bollo, *Carta ánua* of 1613, p. 244.

10. *Ibid.*

11. Sobrino. See also the Memorial of Francisco de Figueroa to the king in favor of Valdivia and defensive warfare, BNC, *Archivo Vicuña Mackenna*, CCLXXXIX, 108–17, and Rodrigo Vásquez's defense of Valdivia against charges made by Ribera (1616), BNC, *Archivo Jesuítas*, XCIII, 65–70.

12. The treatise is part of Rosales' *Historia general*, II, 513–669.

13. *Ibid.*, 571–73. Emphasis added.

14. Anganamón blamed the Jesuit for the loss of his wives, saying that they never would have deserted him but for the treacherous influence of Valdivia's envoy Pedro de Meléndez (who was actually the governor's envoy). Encina passes over in silence the part Meléndez played in the affair of Anganamón's wives.

15. Anganamón's relatives had accused him of being responsible for the flight of

their daughters, arguing that he had planned to use their departure as an excuse for following them and taking up residence among the Spaniards. This charge is indirect proof of the cacique's favorable feeling toward the whites prior to this event.

16. Pineda y Bascuñán, pp. 128–31.

17. "Everything makes me believe that the author of this book has done nothing more than narrate a naive tradition that is more or less true, and that the account of his conference with Anganamón is a literary device intended to make his story interesting." Barros Arana, IV, 74, note 39.

18. Another purpose was to provide juridical proof of the alleged phenomena that accompanied the tragedy, such as Aranda's prophecy of his impending death, the appearance of three suns in the sky over Elicura on the day of the mishap, the revelations experienced by two Jesuit priests in Córdoba del Tucumán and Santiago —all alleged events that were common knowledge at the time and were duly recorded in the documents of the period. Barros Arana notes that the Jesuit provincial Diego de Torres sent a summary of these singular events to the famous Jesuit theologian in Spain, Francisco Suárez, who, after examining the evidence, declared that the three missionaries were undoubtedly martyrs in the technical sense of the term. The Chilean historian was not impressed by these reports, however, implying that they were a deus ex machina with which Valdivia and his confreres attempted to counteract the unfavorable impression that the murders had produced among the populace. He accordingly concluded that the movement in favor of their canonization soon died out: "I believe that that was the end of the matter, and that after a short time no one any longer spoke of canonizing those unfortunate victims of the *natural ferocity* of the savages." Barros Arana, IV, 75–76, note 47. Emphasis added. Apparently Barros Arana was not acquainted with the official investigations of 1665, or else he omitted mentioning them. In any case, a summary of the Santiago *Información*, together with the names of the deponents, is included in Olivares, *Historia militar*, pp. 345–46, with which Barros Arana must have been familiar.

19. The original documents are preserved in the State Archives in Rome, *Fondo Gesuítico, cajón* 15, *Canonizaciones*, No. 2, "Información del glorioso martirio." A similar title identifies the "información" compiled in Concepción. A complete transcript of these documents is available in Blanco, pp. 359–432. The witnesses at Concepción were Fray Francisco Rubio, military chaplain at the fort in Monterrey at the time of the massacre; Reverend Juan del Pozo, S.J.; Reverend Antonio Félix Sarmiento, commissary of the Holy Office in Concepción; Reverend Juan de Losada, S.J.; General Fernando de Mieres y Arce, alcalde ordinario of Concepción; General Santiago Tesillo; Captain Francisco Jiménez Lobillo; Captain Jerónimo de Mejia Reinoso, "vecino feudatario" of Concepción; Reverend Diego Centeno de Cháves; Francisco Jiménez de Herrera, who was with the soldiers in Paicaví on the eve of the tragedy; Sergeant Domingo de Romay; Sergeant Andrés de Meneses; Doña Luisa de Sierra Carrillo, widow of Captain Juan de Fontalba Angulo, "vecina feudataria" of Concepción; Captain Alonso Sánchez Conejero; Don Domingo Gullipangue, "cacique y gobernador principal, que se sucedió en el gobierno al cacique y

gobernador Anganamón"; the commissary general, Domingo de la Parra; Captain Juan de Uturiay; and Don Agustín de Celantara, "gobernador de los indios de guerra." Those at Santiago were Reverend Juan de Álvarez, vice-provincial of the Jesuits in Chile and commissary of the Holy Office in Concepción; Brother Pedro del Castillo, S.J.; Reverend Hernando de Mendoza, S.J.; Sergeant Juan de Mendoza Monteagudo; Captain Juan Ferres; General Juan Velázquez de Cobarrubias; Fray Miguel Crispo, religious of the Order of San Juan de Dios; and Reverend Alonso Venegas.

20. "Información del glorioso martirio," pp. 323–24.

21. "Información del glorioso martirio," p. 331.

22. "Declaración del cacique Gullipangue," in Blanco, p. 419.

23. "Declaración del cacique Llancagueni," in *ibid.*, pp. 429–30.

24. Córdoba y Figueroa, p. 200.

25. Carvallo y Goyeneche, pp. 299–300.

26. After giving a sketchy account of the murders, Barros Arana (IV, 66), for instance, states: "History cannot provide more details concerning the manner in which this iniquitous deed was carried out. It was not witnessed by any person who had any desire or interest in telling the truth."

27. "Letter of the cabildo of Concepción to Pope Alexander VII, March 2, 1665," in Blanco, pp. 642–43. The document carries the signatures of Juan Carretero, Fernando de Mieres, Juan de la Barra, Fernando de la Cea, Domingo Losa, and Pedro del Campo. For similar letters from the ecclesiastical cabildo of Santiago and the governor of Chile, Francisco Meneses, see *ibid.*, pp. 644–48.

28. Encina (II, 103) reports that Valdivia, mentally upset (so he claims) by the widespread opposition in the colony to the idea of defensive warfare, prevailed upon Governor Ribera to issue an edict forbidding the citizens of the capital to speak against the king's commands regarding defensive war, under penalty of being fined and being forced to serve for a year in one of the frontier forts.

29. Barros Arana, IV, 77.

30. Letter of the cabildo of Santiago to the king, April 13, 1613, ACSI, A-II-63, part II, 517–21.

31. "Memorial del procurador de Chile, maestre de campo Pedro Cortés, al rey, Mayo 18, 1614," ACSI, A-II-63, part II, 721–27. Captain Pedro de Lisperguer had originally been selected for the task because he was sufficiently wealthy to pay for the trip out of his own pocket, but Ribera favored the appointment of Cortés and his preference won out. Letter of Pedro de Lisperguer to Alonso de Ribera, April 3, 1613, *ibid.*, 505–7.

32. Letter of Diego de Torres to Alonso de Ribera, Jan. 30, 1613, BNC, *Archivo Morla Vicuña*, XXIV, No. 30.

33. Letter of Valdivia to the rector of the Jesuit college in Madrid, Aug. 30, 1613, *ibid.*, No. 31.

34. Letter of eleven army captains to the king, April 9, 1614, ACSI, A-II-63, part II, 641–45. The letter was signed by Tomás Durán, Juan Ortiz de Azayas,

Juan de Barrios, Juan de Araya Berio, Juan Fernández de Córdoba, Gaspar Calderón, Francisco Hernández Aredondo, Andrés Fernández de la Serna, Juan Guerea de Salazar, Diego de Guartenilla Gutiérrez, and Alvaro de Naxa y Roenes.

35. For an anonymous account of the sermon Sosa delivered before the audiencia and other leading citizens of Santiago, see the "Relación de lo que el Padre Guardián predicó."

36. *Ibid.*

37. Letter of Ribera to the king, April 17, 1613, in Blanco, pp. 245–49. The capture of the women and children shows that this was more than a punitive expedition.

38. *Ibid.*, p. 246.

39. Letter of Valdivia to the king, Feb. 20, 1613, ACSI, A-II-63, part I, 437–50.

40. Barros Arana, IV, 71, note 37.

41. Letter of Valdivia to the king, Feb. 20, 1614, ACSI, A-II-63, part II, 617–22. Barros Arana does not mention this later epistle.

42. Letter of the viceroy of Peru to Alonso de Ribera, Feb. 25, 1613, ACSI, A-II-63, part I, 471–76.

43. Letter of Ribera to the king, Oct. 30, 1613, in Barros Arana, IV, 85.

44. Gay, I, 269–72.

45. "The purpose of this discourse is to make clear the utility of the means that Your Majesty has applied to the affairs in Chile." Sobrino, p. 756.

46. *Ibid.*, pp. 756–59.

47. "It is clear from the governor's own letters, the originals of which I possess, that in the beginning while he was still well disposed to this plan he credited it—not offensive war—with these happy results." *Ibid.*, pp. 758–59. Like a good advocate, Sobrino based his arguments on documentary evidence throughout.

48. *Ibid.*, p. 760.

49. Sobrino, p. 763.

50. Letter of Ribera to the superiors of religious houses in Santiago, in *ibid.*, pp. 763–64.

51. Letter of Ribera to Diego de Torres, Aug. 31, 1612, in *ibid.*, p. 764.

52. *Ibid.*

53. *Ibid.*, pp. 764–65.

54. Letter of Ribera to Valdivia, Feb. 9, 1614, in *ibid.*, pp. 761–62. Barros Arana (IV, 85, note 4) incorrectly gives Feb. 6 as the date of this letter.

55. Sobrino, pp. 765–70.

56. In his report of March 8, 1614, the Marquis of Montes Claros warned the king to look with suspicion on information from Chile that originated with people who had personal reasons for urging the abolition of defensive war. Barros Arana, IV, 97.

57. The king's decision was anticipated in his instructions to Don Francisco de Borja y Aragón, Prince of Esquilache, who was appointed viceroy of Peru in Feb-

ruary 1614. Referring to the request of Pedro Cortés for 3,000 additional troops for the pacification of Araucania, Philip remarked: "Having considered the whole question in my junta de guerra, and seeing that it is impossible at the present time to send the reinforcements that they [in Chile] desire, I have decided to order you to enforce the instructions given in this matter to the Marquis of Montes Claros, your predecessor. . . . And I command you to carry out without fail the decree concerning the personal service of the Indians, and those that the aforementioned Marquis of Montes Claros issued in this regard." Cédula of Philip III to Francisco de Borja y Aragón, March 4, 1615, in Amunátegui, *La cuestión de límites,* II, 306–9.

58. Cédula of Philip III to Alonso de Ribera, Jan. 3, 1616, in Olivares, *Historia de la Compañía,* pp. 187–88. See also the cédulas of Nov. 21, 1615, directed to Ribera, the viceroy of Peru, the audiencia of Chile, and the bishop of Santiago, AAS, LVII, 162–64, XLI, 120.

59. Cédula of Philip III to Luis de Valdivia, Jan. 3, 1616, AAS, II, 515.

60. Delivery of the document had been entrusted to Gaspar Sobrino, who reached Concepción later in the month of Ribera's death. Medina, *Biblioteca,* I, 186.

61. Letter of Valdivia to Philip III, March 15, 1617, in Astrain, V, 629.

62. Letter of Luis Merlo de la Fuente to the king, April 19, 1620, in Barros Arana, IV, 122, note 6.

63. Gallegos had been appointed interim governor by Ribera who mistakenly believed he had the power to appoint by virtue of a decree of Philip III dated Sept. 2, 1607, which authorized García Ramón to name a successor. But this concession was a personal one that was not communicable. Still, the audiencia of Santiago confirmed Ribera's action, and Gallegos took the oath of office on March 16. A few days later he headed south to assume command of the army on the frontier.

64. See Errázuriz, *Continuación,* II, 358–61; Amunátegui Solar, *Las encomiendas,* I, 391.

65. Barros Arana, IV, 131.

66. Letter of Valdivia to Mutius Vitelleschi, General of the Society of Jesus, Feb. 3, 1618, in Astrain, V, 629.

67. The viceroy's special instructions to Ulloa covered fourteen points, all of them referring to the business of defensive war. Sections 11, 13, and 14 dealt directly with the problem of forced labor. "Instruction of the viceroy of Peru."

68. Letter of the viceroy of Peru to the audiencia of Chile, Dec. 1, 1617, ACSI, A-II-63, part II, 885–87.

69. Letter of the viceroy of Peru to Luis de Valdivia, Dec. 1, 1617, *ibid.,* pp. 887–91.

70. Letters of the viceroy of Peru to the bishop of Santiago and the army officials in Chile, Dec. 1, 1617, *ibid.,* pp. 891–94.

71. Barros Arana, IV, 142. The Chilean historian erred in supposing that Valdivia was still visitor general of the colony; the appointment of Machado had released him of this responsibility.

72. Encina, III, 82, 125.

73. "I have resolved to abandon everything in order to escape Your Reverence's jurisdiction because of your imprudent way of governing." Letter of Valdivia to Pedro de Oñate, Lima, April 20, 1620, in Astrain, V, 697–701. In a second letter of April 30, which refers to the viceroy's desire that he return to Chile, he remarked: "I was forced to tell him that under no circumstances would I return to Chile if it meant being subject to Your Reverence." Toward the end of the same letter he exclaimed bitterly: "Your Reverence has accused me, insulted me, and wronged me." *Ibid.*, p. 704.

74. The exact date of his departure is unknown, but it must have been around the end of November, for in one of his communications to Oñate he remarks that he had arrived in Lima five months before.

75. Cédula of Philip IV to the viceroy of Peru, April 13, 1625, AAS, LVII, pp. 182–83.

76. *Actas*, Jan. 30, 1626, IX, 342–43.

Chapter 9

1. Torres Saldamando and Frontaura Arana, p. 3. The date is deducible also from a declaration that Rosales made in 1672 in connection with an ecclesiastical lawsuit between Luis Chacón Rojas, rector of the Jesuit college in Concepción, and Captain Francisco de Torres y Añazco. In reply to one of the questions asked of him, Rosales stated under oath that he was then sixty-nine years of age. "Expediente sobre derecho al patronato de una capellanía fundada por Doña Juana Jiménez, Concepción, Noviembre, 4, 1672," BNC, *Archivo Jesuítas*, XLIII, 190–272. Medina is consequently in error when he says that Rosales was born in 1601 (*Diccionario*, p. 764). So, too, is Astrain (V, 664), who places the event in 1605. Enrich refrains from committing himself on this point, stating simply that Rosales was a native of Madrid (*Historia*, I, 768). Both he and Vicuña Mackenna were apparently unaware of Ferreira's sketch (see Torres Saldamando and Frontaura Arana), for neither refers to it in his biography of the Jesuit. Mackenna says categorically in his introduction to the printed edition of Rosales' *Historia general*: "Thanks to the title page of his work we know at least the place of his birth. But the same lucky chance has not brought to light one single trace of either his family or the date of his birth." *Ibid.*, I, xi.

2. One of Rosales' nephews, Don Pedro de Echaburu, later became a member of the Royal Council of Spain. The Echaburu family likewise prided itself on its blue-blooded lineage. An American descendant on the distaff side, Doña Sinforosa López de Echaburu y Cívico, daughter of General Juan López de Echaburu, was the wife of General Luis Antonio de Oviedo y Herrera, corregidor of Potosí, whom Charles II rewarded with the title of Count of La Granja on February 20, 1690, in recognition of his many services. His name is more familiar to students of Latin American literary history as the author of two poetical works, *Santa Rosa de Lima* and *La Pasión de Cristo*. Torres Saldamando and Frontaura Arana, p. 65, note 4.

3. The exact date of his entry into the Order is uncertain. Enrich says that it took place in Lima on October 14, 1620 (Enrich, *Historia*, I, 768). This is clearly an error, for Rosales did not come to America until several years later. Ferreira, who wrote his account shortly after Rosales' death in 1677, states that the latter had been a Jesuit for fifty-eight years and that Father Francisco Aguado had received him into the Society in Madrid. The best evidence, therefore, indicates the end of 1618 or the beginning of 1619 as the proper date. This coincides with the fact that Aguado was instructor for novices for the Toledo province during the period extending from 1618 to 1622. Torres Saldamando and Frontaura Arana, p. 3.

4. Enrich, *Historia*, I, 768. Medina for some reason claims that he was ordained in Santiago. *Diccionario*, p. 764.

5. Torres Saldamando and Frontaura Arana, p. 7.

6. Ferreira records that his mastery of the Indian tongue was so perfect that not even the Araucanians themselves could surpass him in eloquence at public functions. *Ibid.*

7. Cédula of Philip IV to the viceroy of Peru, April 13, 1625, AAS, LVII, 182–83.

8. Letter of Luis Fernández de Córdoba to Philip IV, Jan. 10, 1628, in Barros Arana, IV, 207–8.

9. Cédula of Philip IV to the audiencia of Chile, March 16, 1628, in *Actas*, June 25, 1629, X, 103.

10. Royal ordinance of Philip IV, Sept. 12, 1626, AAS, XXI, 153.

11. Letter of Bishop Salcedo to the king, Jan. 20, 1630, Pastells, LXXIII (Peru 4), 1–4. The branding was done with a hot iron applied to the cheek, forehead, or shoulder of the victim. The practice was not, of course, peculiar to the Spaniards. It was a common form of punishment in some countries of Europe even in relatively modern times. In England, for example, during Edward VI's reign, vagabonds and slaves were socially ostracized by having a V or an S burned into their bodies. Rosales writes of such mutilation in a well-reasoned passage in which he tries to show that the practice was morally unjust and contrary to all natural right, positive and divine. Rosales, *Historia general*, III, 40–42.

12. *Ibid.*, III, 37.

13. The administration of Lazo de la Vega (1629–39) was a decade of unremitting campaigns against the Araucanians, the details of which Tesillo recorded in his military history, *Guerras de Chile*, first published in Madrid in 1647. Lazo de la Vega's plan for populating the war zone with military garrisons and towns and terrorizing the enemy into surrender failed for want of men and money. Encina (III, 184–86) considers him one of the outstanding governors of Chile during the 17th century.

14. Letter of Nicolás Polanco de Santillana to the viceroy of Peru, May 7, 1633, Pastells, LXXXIX, 423–25; Minutes of the junta de guerra of the Council of the Indies for April 24, 1635, in Amunátegui Solar, *Las encomiendas*, I, 471–76; Torres Saldamando, p. 262.

15. Since God is pure spirit, nothing material can serve as the terminus for a physical comparison. The image or likeness referred to pertains rather to man's spiritual faculty, his intellect, which is an infinitesimal reflection of the Divine intellect.

16. Minutes of the junta de guerra, p. 472; Rosales, *Historia general*, III, 40–42.

17. Letter of Polanco to the viceroy of Peru, May 7, 1633, p. 424; Minutes of the junta de guerra, pp. 472–73.

18. *Ibid.*, p. 473; Letter of Polanco to the viceroy of Peru, May 7, 1633, p. 424.

19. The Jesuit superior Diego de Torres was one of these consultors. He was acting as the viceroy's confessor at the time. *Ibid.*, p. 425.

20. Letter of the viceroy of Peru, the Count of Chinchón, to the king, April 6, 1633, Pastells, LXXXIX, 419–20.

21. Minutes of the junta de guerra, pp. 474–75.

22. *Ibid.*, pp. 475–76.

23. Cédula of Philip IV to the governor of Chile, May 5, 1635, AAS, LVII, 184.

24. Rosales, *Historia general*, III, 41.

25. Although there is no positive evidence on the point, it is reasonable to suppose that Rosales, who was a close companion of the governor, probably influenced his thinking in the matter. Lazo de la Vega's tasa reflected many of the social principles underlying the ordinances that Diego de Torres Bollo issued in 1608.

26. Letter of Governor Francisco de Córdoba to the king, Feb. 1, 1628, in Gay, II, 351–52.

27. *Actas*, Aug. 19, 1628, X, 39–40.

28. Cédula of Philip IV to Governor Lazo de la Vega, April 14, 1633, in Rosales, *Historia general*, III, 114.

29. Tesillo, p. 80; Rosales, *Historia general*, III, 114.

30. The audiencia included only three other members besides the governor at that time: Pedro Machado de Cháves, who acted as fiscal, and the oidores, Jacobo de Adaro y Samartín and Cristóbal de la Cerda.

31. *Acuerdo* of the audiencia of Chile, 1634.

32. *Actas*, March 10, 1635, XI, 87.

33. *Ibid.*, March 24, 1635, XI, 90.

34. *Dictámen* of Pedro Machado de Cháves, fiscal of the audiencia of Santiago, concerning the execution of the decree of 1633, April 6, 1635, in Amunátegui Solar, *Las encomiendas*, II, 15–17.

35. *Actas*, April 16, 1635, XI, 95.

36. This concession was included in the tasa at the instigation of the cabildo of Santiago. See *ibid.*, March 10 and 24, 1635, XI, 87 and 90.

37. Ordinances of Governor Francisco Lazo de la Vega, Santiago, April 16, 1635, in Rosales, *Historia general*, III, 115–20; BNC, *Archivo Medina: Documentos manuscritos*, CXXXIII, No. 2, 411.

38. Encina disagrees with this evaluation. He considers Lazo de la Vega's tasa a significant step forward "which made possible the transition from obligatory labor to voluntary labor, thus introducing an intermediate stage of development. . . . The ordinances of Lazo de la Vega thus mark the end of personal service and the beginning of the institution of tenant farming (*inquilinato*), which Father Torres Bollo had tried to initiate in the properties belonging to the Company of Jesus twenty-six years earlier." Encina, IV, 82–83. The only trouble with this statement is its lack of historical accuracy. Lazo de la Vega's tasa did *not* put an end to the servicio personal.

39. *Actas*, April 16 and 19, 1635, XI, 94 and 96.

40. Rosales, *Historia general*, III, 121–22. Rosales concludes his discussion of the cabildo's protest with these words: "As a result no action was taken, and although the legislation was good it accomplished nothing."

41. Letter of Pedro Gutiérrez de Lugo to Philip IV, March 19, 1639, in Amunátegui Solar, *Las encomiendas*, II, 23–24.

42. *Ibid.*, p. 23.

43. Tesillo, p. 81.

44. Baides, as he was commonly called, took the oath of office before the cabildo of Concepción on the night of May 1, 1639, "while fireworks burst in the square outside, and the flashes from discharged muskets and artillery turned the night into day" (Tesillo, p. 109). He reluctantly remained in the post until May 8, 1646. Following a favorable residencia, he retired to Peru, where he lived for the next ten years. While journeying to Spain in 1656 he and his family lost their lives when their ship was attacked by the English. Baides was not a forceful administrator, but his record of relations with the Indians was considerably better than that of most governors assigned to Chile during the seventeenth century.

45. Like most Spanish noblemen of the period, Baides had strong religious convictions. Rosales relates that "his personal standard was beautifully embroidered with an image of Our Lady on one side and on the reverse that of St. Francis Xavier, the Apostle of the East Indies, whom he adopted as the patron of his undertaking in order that he might obtain from God the conversion of the Indians of the West." Rosales, *Historia general*, III, 152.

46. Encina, who has a very low opinion of Baides, accuses him of gross self-interest in his peace campaign. He asserts that, prior to his arrival in Chile, Baides had already made up his mind to come to terms with the Indians at any cost so that he might be free to devote himself to commerce and thus amass a private fortune, which was his real reason for coming to America. Encina, III, 189, 191.

47. "Informe de la real audiencia sobre el estado de Chile, Santiago, Noviembre 14, 1639," in Gay, II, 410–16. The document carries the signatures of Baides and the audiencia judges.

48. For an eyewitness account of the details of the meeting between Baides and these Araucanian leaders, see Rosales, *Historia general*, III, 153–64. Rosales, who was present as Baides' interpreter and expert adviser, recorded part of the toqui's

discourse in the following words: "Do not be surprised, O great Marquis, that our nation has so resolutely and gallantly opposed the superior Spanish forces. . . . The defense of one's homeland, offspring, wives, and liberty is so natural that even the wild beasts act this way. . . . The grievances we have endured have made us valiant and proud; taking away our women and children has made us brave and ferocious in defending them; oppression and cruel servitude have made us rise up to break the bonds and escape the yoke that held us. . . . But just as wild beasts are more easily tamed by kindness than by harshness . . . so your graciousness is more effective in overcoming our resistance than your sternness would be. . . . Our forefathers depicted the Spaniards as being so cruel and fierce (in order that we might hate them) that we considered it better to die gloriously at their hands in war than to live with them in peace, and even though we promised peace to other governors, they refused it because they thirsted for our blood; we thus became convinced that they were cruel and greedy men who did not want peace because of their passion for plunder and slaves; by their wicked and tyrannical conduct and by refusing to make peace they kept the war alive." *Ibid.*, III, 158–59.

49. *Ibid.*, III, 167–71.

50. *Ibid.*, III, 184–85; Gómez de Vidaurre, XV, 240.

51. Gómez de Vidaurre, XV, 242.

52. *Ibid.*, p. 243; Edwards, p. 281. The Pact of Quillín was the only treaty of its kind to merit the distinction of being included in the *Gran colección de tratados, 1598–1700*, which José A. Abreu y Bertodano, Marquis of La Regalía, published in Madrid from 1740 to 1752. See Briseño, p. 414.

53. Gómez de Vidaurre, XV, 243; Rosales, *Historia general*, III, 194–98, 237.

54. *Ibid.*, III, 299–300.

55. Encina, IV, 103.

56. Letter of Pedro Gutiérrez to the king, March 19, 1639, in Amunátegui Solar, *Las encomiendas*, II, 23–24.

57. Letter of Diego Vibanco, captain of cavalry, to the king, Oct. 18, 1656, in Gay, II, 417–21.

58. *Ibid.*

59. Amunátegui, *Los precursores*, II, 287.

60. Rosales, *Historia general*, III, 383, 431–38; Enrich, "Vida," pp. 27–30. The reference to death is not a rhetorical exaggeration but a plain statement of fact. The sudden change in climate and the debilitating effects of constant and unaccustomed labor seriously shortened the life expectancy of the Araucanians.

61. Letter of Philip IV to Governor Acuña y Cabrera, April 18, 1656, AAS, LVII, 185–86.

62. *Ibid.* The king later issued a decree on April 18, 1656, condemning the practice, but by that time the damage had been done. Rosales, *Historia general*, III, 431; *Libro de votos de la audiencia de Santiago de Chile*, acuerdo of Nov. 22, 1651, in Amunátegui, *Los precursores*, II, 291–92.

63. The Cuncos inhabited the coastal district between Valdivia and Chiloé. Córdoba y Figueroa, p. 251.

64. *Libro de votos de la audiencia de Santiago,* acuerdo of Nov. 22, 1651, in Amunátegui, *Los precursores,* II, 291–92.

65. Pineda y Bascuñán, p. 343.

66. Córdoba y Figueroa, p. 251.

67. Quiroga, *Compendio histórico de los más principales sucesos de la conquista y guerra del reino de Chile hasta el año 1656,* in Amunátegui, *Los precursores,* II, 294.

68. Córdoba y Figueroa, p. 251.

69. Enrich, "Vida," p. 33.

70. Córdoba y Figueroa, p. 255.

71. Carvallo y Goyeneche, II, 85. The exact number is uncertain. Some reports put the figure as high as 462.

72. *Ibid.*

73. Córdoba y Figueroa, p. 256.

74. *Ibid.,* p. 258.

75. According to one estimate, as many as 6,000 horses were killed on this occasion. See Amunátegui, *Los precursores,* II, 301. The figure is probably exaggerated since no more than four hundred Spaniards participated in this entrada. Nevertheless, the economic—as well as military—loss was great in view of the high price and relative scarcity of the animals throughout the seventeenth century.

76. Letter of Philip IV to Governor Acuña y Cabrera, Nov. 12, 1656, reproduced in *ibid.,* pp. 338–41; *Libro de votos de la audiencia de Santiago,* acuerdo of March 3, 1655, in *ibid.,* pp. 315–20.

77. Quiroga in his *Compendio histórico* remarks that De la Fuente was ninety years old when elected. *Ibid.,* p. 309.

78. *Libro de votos de la audiencia de Santiago,* acuerdo of March 3, 1655, in *ibid.,* pp. 315–20.

79. *Ibid.;* acuerdo of March 2, 1655, in *ibid.,* pp. 310–11. This was an intelligent move since only three members of the audiencia were present in Santiago at the time. A fourth, Juan de Huerta Gutiérrez, had left some weeks earlier to begin an investigation of government activities and personnel in Concepción. His enquiries offended some local sensibilities, thus making him a secondary target of attack in the demonstrations of February 20. Like Acuña y Cabrera, he, too, was forced to find asylum behind the walls of a religious convent.

80. *Ibid.,* pp. 312–13. The members of the military junta were Diego González Montero, former military governor of Valdivia, Francisco de Carrasco, Juan Polanco de Guzmán, Juan Rodulfo de Lisperguer, General Bernardo de Amasa, General Ignacio de la Carrera Iturgoyen, who had served as military governor of Chiloé, and Captains Gaspar Calderón and Pedro de Figueroa.

81. *Ibid.,* pp. 313–14. The members who supported this view were Francisco

Arévalo Briceño, Gregorio Hurtado de Mendoza Quiroga, Jerónimo Hurtado de Mendoza, Antonio de Barambio, Francisco de Erazo, Gaspar de Ahumada Maldonado, Pedro de Salinas y Córdoba, Martín Ruiz de Gamboa, José de Guzmán, Francisco Cortés de Navarro, and Francisco Maldonado.

82. *Ibid.*

83. *Ibid.*, acuerdo of March 3, 1655, 315–20.

84. *Ibid.*, acuerdo of April 1, 1655, 321–22.

85. Porter Casanate had enjoyed a varied career before coming to Chile. Following a course of brilliant studies he was named a "Captain of the Sea" in 1634 while still a young man of twenty-two years. He was the author of an important treatise entitled "Reparos y Errores de la Navegación Española," which won him the reputation of being an intelligent and experienced mariner. His previous exploits in America included command of an exploring expedition to the Gulf of California, an adventure that brought him to the attention of the Count of Alba, who was then serving as viceroy of New Spain. When the Count went to Lima to take up his appointment as viceroy of Peru in 1654, Porter accompanied him and later served energetically and well as governor of Chile from 1656 to 1662. His administration was beset by many trials, including a serious Indian uprising under the astute leadership of a deserter from the Spanish army, a half-breed named Alejo, who successfully challenged the Spanish troops for a number of years; a fearful earthquake and tidal wave that hit the southern provinces on March 15, 1657, killing more than forty persons and destroying the city of Concepción; a series of violent epidemics that took their toll of Spaniards and Indians alike; and the ineptitude of local officials. Encina, III, 261–80.

86. Acuña y Cabrera had originally been appointed provisional governor in 1650 by the viceroy of Peru. This appointment was confirmed by the king some two years later, at which time his term of office was extended to eight years. He thus had some time remaining when he was recalled to Peru for the second time in January 1656.

87. Cédula of Philip IV to the viceroy of Peru, June 28, 1660. A reprint of this document apppears in Amunátegui, *Los precursores*, II, 346–48. The king's decision made no difference to Acuña y Cabrera. He was already dead by the time the document reached Lima.

88. *Ibid.*

Chapter 10

1. Cimbrón was still in Spain at the time of the uprising. He arrived in Concepción in 1656 and found his diocese in ruins.

2. According to the statistics recorded in Carvallo y Goyeneche, the rebellion of 1655 resulted in the death or capture of 1,300 whites and an unspecified number of Indian auxiliaries, the destruction of 396 estancias, and the loss of 400,000 head

of cattle, horses, sheep, and goats. The plazas and forts of Arauco, San Pedro, Colcura, Buena Esperanza, Nacimiento, Talcamávida, San Rosendo, Boroa, and Chillán were either abandoned or destroyed, thus depriving the colony of half of its military stores and equipment. Carvallo y Goyeneche, II, 85. To these calamities were added those of the earthquake of March 15, 1657, which devastated further the territory between the Cautín and Maule rivers.

3. Cédula of Philip IV to the viceroy of Peru, July 5, 1658, in Amunátegui, *Los precursores*, II, 350.

4. Cédula of Philip IV to the governor of Chile, April 9, 1662, AAS, LVII, 191–92.

5. *Ibid.* Included on the committee were the governor of Chile, the bishops of Santiago and Concepción, the senior judge of the audiencia, the commander-in-chief of the frontier army, the inspector general, the sergeant major, and the commissary of the cavalry.

6. Cédula of Philip IV to the governor of Chile, April 9, 1662. Notice of these instructions was given to the audiencia of Chile and the viceroy of Peru, the Count of Santistéban, in companion documents of the same date. See Lizana and Maulén, III, 119–24.

7. The principal provisions of this decree are reproduced in Amunátegui, *Los precursores*, II, 373–75.

8. Execution of the decrees was clearly the motive behind Cimbrón's appointment. The king had initially chosen an army man, Juan de Balboa Mogrovejo, to replace Porter Casanate as governor of Chile. The latter's lack of familiarity with land operations may have dictated the change. See Amunátegui, *La cuestión de límites*, III, 37.

9. Cimbrón passed away in 1661 long before the decree was even drafted. See Silva Cotapos, p. 93.

10. Balboa Mogrovejo died before assuming his post. This led to the viceroy's choice of Peredo as provisional governor of the colony. Contemporary records imply that he was highly religious, reporting that he spent seven hours a day in prayer. Rosales says of him: "He had no interest in malocas or slaves but only in the right service of the king." Rosales, "Tratado," p. 221.

11. Rosales served two terms as vice-provincial: 1661–66 and 1670–72.

12. Rosales, "Tratado," p. 230. He did not mention which members held a different view or what the "many other reasons" were.

13. *Ibid.* As Rosales correctly noted, even if the decision had been that the rebels deserved to be considered slaves, they still could not have been sold as such because this would have been contrary to the express will of the king. *Ibid.*, p. 231.

14. Meneses held the rank of a general of artillery at the time, a position to which he had been promoted by the king in order to give him greater prestige. He was a veteran soldier of twenty-five years of service in Milan, Flanders, Portugal, and Spain but was better known for his contentious nature, uncertain judgment, and skill as a horseman and a bullfighter.

15. Meneses was appointed governor in 1663 but did not reach Chile until the following year.

16. Shortly after his arrival in the colony he became embroiled in an acrimonious dispute with the bishop of Santiago, Diego de Humanzoro, over a point of official etiquette and procedure. Humanzoro, a strong believer in ecclesiastical rights, promptly excommunicated him. Meneses retaliated by attempting, unsuccessfully, to exile the prelate. He used the same tactic to discourage opposition from lesser clerics, many of whom feared to ascend the pulpit lest their sermons incur the displeasure of the governor.

17. Meneses did not spare even his predecessor, Anjel de Peredo, whom he accused of misappropriating public funds while in office. Peredo was completely cleared of the charge in the investigation that followed and was subsequently appointed governor of Tucumán. Edwards, p. 284.

18. In order to control the judicial decisions of the audiencia, Meneses removed the royal seal from the high court's chambers and hid it in his own residence.

19. Most notorious of his enterprises was the merchandise mart in Santiago that Francisco Martínez de Argomedo managed in his name and that was popularly known as "Del Gobernador," the governor's store. Amunátegui, *Los precursores*, II, 378. Many of the army supplies Meneses expropriated were brought to the capital with the royal stamp still on them and sold to private buyers through this store.

20. His most notable monopoly was on tallow, a principal article of export to Peru.

21. Córdoba y Figueroa, p. 287; *Libro de votos de la audiencia de Santiago*, acuerdo of Oct. 22, 1667, in Amunátegui, *Los precursores*, II, 384–86.

22. *Ibid.*

23. The Medina Collection in the National Library of Chile includes sixteen volumes of documents pertaining to Meneses and his administration, most of which deal with complaints and charges leveled against him.

24. Manuel Múñoz de Cuéllar, oidor of the audiencia of Chile, reported to the king on Feb. 1, 1665, that Meneses received large sums of money for these new grants, not a peso of which was passed on to the treasury officials. See Barros Arana, V, 62.

25. Letter of Bishop Humanzoro to the king, Nov. 15, 1664, in Amunátegui Solar, *Las encomiendas*, II, 217.

26. Rosales, "Tratado," p. 190.

27. Rosales defended their action as being perfectly legitimate. It was not rebellion, he declared, but a salutary caution. They were not making war on the Spaniards but were simply trying to protect themselves against unjust aggression, and there is no guilt in justifiable self-defense. "But the Indians' defense," he wryly added, "is always considered unjust." *Ibid.*

28. *Ibid.*, p. 192.

29. Rosales, "Dictámen," pp. 253–54. A somewhat shorter version of the docu-

ment dated July 25, 1672, is contained in Pastells, LXXIII, 131–42. This is, no doubt, the second draft which was sent to Spain by a different boat to insure delivery in case the original was lost in transit.

30. *Ibid.*, pp. 259–60.

31. Barros Arana, V, 193.

32. Philip IV had died on Sept. 17, 1665, while Charles II was still only four years old.

33. Henríquez was a native-born Peruvian, the son of a limeño judge. He was taken to Spain at an early age, studied law at the University of Salamanca, and spent several years in the army, serving with merit in Italy and France and on the Portuguese frontier. He was appointed governor of Chile by the Queen Mother Mariana in January 1670, replacing the Marquis of Navamorquende who had administered the colony as provisional governor during the interim following the dismissal of Meneses in 1668.

34. Rosales, "Dictámen," p. 254. His absence undoubtedly facilitated the council's decision.

35. *Ibid.*

36. The treatise is dedicated to Charles II. It is, in effect, a compendium of the views the author had expressed in his "Tratado" of 1670.

37. This was the second "punitive" expedition of Juan de Salazar against the Cuncos that precipitated the uprising of 1655.

38. Rosales gives four other arguments that are similar to the ones already cited. See "Dictámen," pp. 255–59.

39. These are the same arguments that were discussed previously in connection with the Count of Santistéban's memorials.

40. Rosales notes that he himself had baptized "more than 12,000 of them," and that there were numerous others who had been preparing to receive the sacrament. "Dictámen," p. 261.

41. *Ibid.*

42. *Ibid.*, pp. 263–66.

43. *Ibid.*, pp. 266–72.

44. Under date of Nov. 12, 1672, Governor Henríquez submitted an *informe* of his own to the Queen Mother urging the acceptance of the recommendations in favor of slavery but objecting to the removal of any more slaves to Peru. In the report he divided the mapuches into seven distinct categories: (1) Encomienda Indians of Santiago and the surrounding area who had been baptized and instructed in the Faith. (2) The yanaconas of Concepción and its environs who were also baptized Christians. (3) Frontier Indians attached to the outposts of Arauco, Nacimiento, San Cristóbal, Tucapel, Boroa, Santa Juana, etc., who participated in military campaigns against the hostiles, the greater part of whom had never belonged to an encomienda. (4) Unpacified natives living in the interior who had not received baptism and did not desire it, and who were the object of special efforts by the Jesuit missionaries. (5) Native boys and girls under ten and a half and nine

and a half years of age respectively who had been captured in the war and who served the Spaniards as domestic slaves (*indios de servidumbre*) until they were twenty years old. They received education and instruction in Christian doctrine from their Spanish masters during these years. (6) Indians whose parents or relatives had sold them to the Spaniards for a specified amount (usually paid in kind) with the understanding that if the purchase price was later refunded the Spaniard had to surrender the Indians acquired in this fashion (*indios de la usanza*). (7) Indians born in Spanish territory who were the offspring of female slaves captured in the war. Henríquez believed that the enslavement of the natives included in the third and fourth categories was perfectly justified because otherwise they would be better off than the encomienda Indians. He also believed that those in the last group should be treated the same as the ones in the fifth category. See Amunátegui Solar, *Las encomiendas*, II, 179–80; Barros Arana, V, 194.

45. It is important to note that Bishop Humanzoro's stand on this issue was not indicative of his overall attitude toward the mapuches. As head of the diocese of Santiago from 1661 to 1676 he repeatedly spoke out in defense of the pacified tribes. Thus he informed the king on July 15, 1662, that "the principal reason for their lack of religious formation is the constant labor to which they are subjected by the encomenderos who work them to death on their estates and treat them more cruelly than they do their [purchased] slaves; the latter receive better care because their death represents a financial loss." Similarly, on Oct. 5, 1666, he wrote as follows: "The personal service of the Indians continues to be an open scandal; Your Majesty's decrees [on this point] have effected no change." Amunátegui Solar, *Las encomiendas*, II, 216, 218.

46. Cédula of the Queen Mother Mariana to Governor Henríquez, Dec. 20, 1674, AAS, LVII, 203–8. The decision was communicated to the viceroy of Peru, the bishop of Santiago, and the audiencia of Chile in companion decrees of the same date.

47. *Ibid.*, p. 206.

48. Amunátegui Solar has the following on this point: "It seems that some religious in Chile requested the Holy See to intervene in the matter with the Spanish Crown. Probably the Jesuit Rosales, who had taken over Father Luis de Valdivia's vigorous defense of the mapuches, was one of those who brought the doleful supplications [of the Indians] to the attention of the Supreme Pontiff." *Las encomiendas*, II, 181. Encina (III, 338–39) expresses a like opinion.

49. *Ibid.*, p. 339.

50. "In the frequent campaigns or incursions into Arauco, [Henríquez] took some eight hundred Indians prisoner; and these he later sold as slaves to several agricultural encomenderos, the buyers paying for them at the rate he himself set—five hundred fanegas of wheat per Indian, each fanega being valued at fifty centavos only. In this way he gathered four hundred thousand fanegas of wheat, all of which he sold to the contractors of his own army at two pesos per fanega, and was paid from the royal treasury. Thus he gained eight hundred thousand pesos." Galdames, p. 90.

This traffic in slaves was one of numerous charges of dishonesty brought against Henríquez during his residencia. Córdoba y Figueroa, pp. 304–5; Barros Arana, V, 178, 219.

51. Alonso del Castillo y Rueda, "Relación de los autos hechos por el gobernador y capitán jeneral del reino de Chile en ejecución de la cédula de 20 de diciembre de 1674, en quese mandó que los indios dél se pongan en su libertad," Madrid, July 5, 1678, in Amunátegui Solar, *Las encomiendas*, II, 183. Castillo was fiscal of the Council of the Indies at the time.

52. *Ibid.*, p. 185.

53. *Ibid.*, pp. 185–86. The originals of the registers prepared by the corregidores were to be filed with the government authorities.

54. This decree of June 12, 1679, was included in the *Recopilación de Leyes de los Reynos de las Indias* as Law 16 of Book VI, Title II, "On the Liberty of the Indians."

55. Expressive of the physical value of the Indians was the phrase popularly used in Chile, "dar de comer," or "to provide the means of sustenance," which was synonymous with the idea of distributing Indians to someone for his advantage.

56. Henríquez illustrated this point by arguing that, since experiments had demonstrated that plants indigenous to Peru died when transplanted to Chile, it was evident that the physical differences of the two countries were very great. To compare plant life with human life was tenuous, but his point had its merits; the climate in Peru was hard on the Chileans. Letter of Governor Henríquez to the king, Dec. 6, 1680, in Amunátegui, *Los precursores*, II, 389.

57. *Ibid.*, pp. 389–90.

58. *Ibid.*, p. 390. Encina claims (III, 358) that the influence of the Jesuits was responsible for the tribute exemptions.

59. Letter of Governor Garro to the king, Jan. 18, 1684, in Amunátegui, *Los precursores*, II, 421–22. Garro governed Chile from 1682 to 1692. His exemplary public life and the zeal with which he strove to curb the licentious practices of some of his subordinates, notably two judges of the audiencia, Sancho García Salazar and Juan de la Cueva y Lugo, whom he exiled to Quillota and Valdivia respectively to do penance for their sins, won him the sobriquet of "El Santo" from the Chilenos. His administration was decisive and firm, as illustrated most dramatically in his successful defense of the colony against the repeated attacks of English pirates (Davis, Swan, Knight, and Strong).

60. Chile exported substantial quantities of wheat, jerked beef, lard, peppers, vegetables, dried fruits, anise, and other agricultural products to Peru during much of the colonial period.

61. Encina, III, 358–59. Encina considers Garro's letters of Jan. 18 and July 28, 1684, the highest expression of a realistic approach to the problem of personal service. They reveal in the governor, he maintains, a judiciousness, prudence, and a lofty sense of justice that would of themselves be sufficient to warrant including him among the outstanding colonial administrators. *Ibid.*, p. 359.

62. Cédula of Philip V to the bishop of Santiago, Francisco de la Puebla González, April 26, 1703, AAS, XC, 243–44.

63. *Ibid.*

64. Letter of Governor Garro to the king, Jan. 7, 1684, in Amunátegui, *Los precursores*, II, 391–92.

65. See *ibid.*, pp. 392–93, for a copy of this decree.

66. After leaving Chile, Garro served as governor of Gibraltar and later as captain general of Guipúzcoa. He died in this post on Oct. 15, 1720.

67. Marín de Poveda was the son of Tomás López Marín and María González de Poveda. He was born in Granada on Feb. 26, 1650, and came to America for the first time in 1667 with his uncle, Bartolomé González de Poveda, who served for a time as president of the audiencia of Charcas and later as archbishop of that diocese. Following a brief and undistinguished tour of duty in the colonial army, first in Peru and later (1670) in Chile, Marín de Poveda returned to Spain, where he purchased a commission as lieutenant general of cavalry. According to some reports he also purchased his appointment as governor of Chile. He arrived in Santiago on Jan. 5, 1692, with 306 military reinforcements who had accompanied him from Spain, and took the oath of office before the cabildo of that city the following day. Medina, *Diccionario*, pp. 500–502.

68. Carvallo y Goyeneche, II, 193. Among the comedies was one entitled "El Hercules Chileno," which Córdoba y Figueroa says was the work of two native-born Chileans.

69. The practice had its origin in the distribution of gifts that new governors made as a token of friendship during their first visit to the Araucanian frontier. It soon degenerated into a polite form of blackmail, with the Indians threatening to break the peace unless they were given presents to repay them for real or fictitious injuries received. The practice became so widespread during the eighteenth century that a separate branch of the treasury, called the *ramo de agasajos*, had to be established to handle the details. Governor Guill y Gonzaga (1761–68) ironically called it a form of tribute levied by the conquered on their conquerors. Letter of Guill y Gonzaga to the king, May 1, 1767, in Amunátegui, *Los precursores*, II, 467–68.

70. Encina, III, 378.

71. Olivares, *Historia de la Compañía*, p. 485; cédula of Charles II to the governor of Chile, Madrid, May 11, 1697, reproduced in *ibid.*, pp. 472–76; Enrich, *Historia*, II, 20–21.

72. Carvallo y Goyeneche, II, 198.

73. Olivares, *Historia de la Compañía*, pp. 481–82; Enrich, *Historia*, II, 21.

74. Oilvares, *Historia de la Compañía*, p. 482.

75. Letter of Marín de Poveda to the king, April 18, 1695, in Amunátegui, *Los precursores*, II, 422–23.

76. *Ibid.*, pp. 423–24.

77. *Ibid.*, p. 424.

78. The buccaneers in question seem to have been survivors of earlier expeditions that had their headquarters in the islands off the coast of Peru and in Juan Fernández, and made their living by preying on Spanish ships and settlements in the Pacific south of Panama.

79. Encina, III, 382–83.

80. Amunátegui, *Los precursores*, II, 394.

81. Letter of Gonzalo Ramírez Baquedano to the king, April 25, 1696, in *ibid.*, p. 396.

82. *Ibid.*, pp. 396–97.

83. Cédula of Charles II to the governor of Chile, July 16, 1700, in *ibid.*, p. 397.

Chapter 11

1. Letter of Valdivia to Emperor Charles V, La Serena, Sept. 4, 1545, in Medina, *Cartas*, p. 13.

2. In the letter of Sept. 4, 1545, for instance, he refers to the Strait on no less than four separate occasions.

3. Villarrica was actually founded by Captain Jerónimo de Alderete, one of Valdivia's lieutenants. It was called Villarrica, or Rich City, because of the gold and silver mines that the Indians claimed were nearby. Despite its euphemistic name, Villarrica turned out to be the poorest town in the whole of Chile.

4. Located at the confluence of the Malleco and Huequén rivers near present-day Angol, Los Confines derived its name from its situation on the jurisdictional boundary between Concepción and La Imperial.

5. Lovera, p. 126.

6. Vicuña Mackenna, *Historia*, I, 70, note 1.

7. Amunátegui, *Los precursores*, II, 65–66.

8. González de Nájera, pp. 189–90.

9. In addition, the procurator general received an annual stipend of 1,500 pesos for the equivalent of a few days' work. Report of the viceroy of Peru, the Duke of La Palata, to the king, Nov. 28, 1682, in Vicuña Mackenna, *Historia*, I, 346.

10. According to an inventory dated in Concepción on June 17, 1653, for example, the funds earmarked for the garrison in Arauco were expended on the following impractical commodities: 6,000 yards of linen cloth for undergarments; 2,800 yards of flannel cloth; 200 yards of taffeta; 80 pairs of silk hose; 150 yards of damask from Seville; 10 jars of honey, 10 of olive oil, 10 of sugar, and 1,000 pounds of soap. With the exception of the last-named items and the flannel cloth, none of these articles was of much utility on the frontier. Cited in *ibid.*, p. 346, note 2.

11. *Ibid.*, p. 346 and 347, note 1.

12. Letter of Gabriel de Celada to the king, Jan. 6, 1610, in Gay, II, 194–203.

13. The estates referred to here were those established by Governors García Ramón and Ribera. The cattle ranch, known as Catentoa and located on the banks of the Longomilla, ran as many as 12,000 head at one time. The estancia of Buena Esperanza, devoted to the raising of grain, produced an average of 7,000 fanegas of wheat annually and provided pasture for some 18,000 sheep. Ribera also established a cordage factory in Quillota to capitalize on the excellent hemp produced in that area, and a textile mill in Melipilla for the manufacture of homespun clothes for the troops. All of these industries had practically disappeared through official mismanagement and neglect by the time Lazo de la Vega took over as governor in 1629. See Letter of Governor Ribera to the king, Sept. 18, 1613, in ACSI, A-II-63, part II, 589–609; letter of Governor Jara Quemada to the king, Jan. 29, 1611, in Gay, II, 245–53; Vicuña Mackenna, *Historia*, I, 161; Encina, II, 384–85.

14. Report of the audiencia of Santiago to the king, 1611, in Amunátegui, *Los precursores*, II, 109–11. The danger of an army revolt was not an idle threat, as the projected rebellion of a cadre of dissatisfied soldiers that was planned in 1587 (while Alonso de Sotomayor was governor) had already proved. The conspiracy had its origins in the frontier fortress of Purén. The commander of the fort at the time was Tiburcio de Heredia, who had fallen ill as a result of his activities in the war. Among the soldiers of the garrison were some whose morale had been completely shattered by the poverty, hunger, and difficulties to which they were exposed, as well as by the conviction that their efforts were not properly appreciated. These disaffected troops decided to take advantage of the commander's illness to raise the banner of revolt. Mariño de Lovera recorded the incident as follows: "In keeping with the pact that they made, they planned to seize the best arms and horses available, go to the towns of Los Infantes and Chillán and to the two forts along the Biobío and persuade some of their friends who were as desperate as themselves to join the movement; after this the entire group would march on Santiago, capture and sack the city, retire with their booty to the kingdom of Tucumán, take over the government there and establish themselves as absolute lords." (Lovera, p. 425.) Though confined to bed, Heredia was aware of what was being planned. Since he was unable to oppose the movement with force, he prepared to deal with it in a more subtle way, and accordingly assigned a number of the conspirators to a detachment that he sent to La Imperial, where the governor was at the time, under the pretext of looking for supplies. At the same time he sent a secret communiqué to Governor Sotomayor acquainting him with what was going on. The governor immediately set out for Purén at the head of a squadron, which included the aforementioned ringleaders, under the guise of paying a visit to his sick lieutenant and of protecting the supply train. At Angol he ordered the conspirators to be put to death by garroting. "In this way," Lovera piously concluded, "the greatest harm that could have befallen these realms had God our Lord not provided a remedy was prevented." (*Ibid.*, p. 425.) Philip III recognized the danger that existed in a letter of Dec. 5, 1606, to Governor García Ramón in which he instructed him to deal vigorously with anyone in the army suspected of feeling trea-

sonous or disloyal. "In case there are some restless and rebellious soldiers among the troops, it is fitting that you publicly and in a manner that will serve as a deterrent and example for the entire army, punish those who give cause; others who are guilty of disloyalty or whom you suspect of the same, you are to expel from that realm in a circumspect fashion without revealing the true reason, sending them with letters and dispatches to Peru or to these kingdoms [of Spain], or making use of other means and artifices that may be applicable, forestalling, if this be possible, their taking up permanent residence [in Peru] or in any other part of the Indies, because of the trouble and harm they could cause among men of similar character in those parts; and you must always be vigilant in this matter, exercising the care and prudence that I am sure you have." Cited in Amunátegui, *Los precursores*, II, 114.

15. Córdoba y Figueroa, pp. 294, 304–5.

16. Summary of the residencias of various governors of Chile compiled by two judges of the audiencia of Chile, Gaspar de Cuba y Arce and Juan de la Peña Salazar, and submitted to the king under date of Aug. 16, 1688, in Amunátegui, *Los precursores*, II, 378–79.

17. Report of the viceroy of Peru to the king, Nov. 28, 1682, in Vicuña Mackenna, *Historia*, I, 346–47.

18. *Ibid.*, p. 347.

19. Letter of Governor Marín de Poveda to the king, Aug. 22, 1697, in Encina, III, 387–88.

20. *Recopilación*, Book VI, Title IX, Law 4. For a detailed discussion of the military obligations of the encomenderos, see Jara, pp. 28–31.

21. No peninsular troops reached Chile until 1583, when Alonso de Sotomayor arrived with 600 soldiers from Spain to put an end to the war in Arauco. His failure, and that of his successors, led to the occasional dispatch of additional reinforcements from the mother country, but at no time during the sixteenth and seventeenth centuries did the frontier garrisons number more than two or three thousand men. More commonly, the total of available effectives was considerably less. Even when the companies were at full strength, the proportion of seasoned veterans was distressingly small.

22. González de Nájera, p. 73; "Memorial de guerra, remitido por el Virey don Francisco de Toledo, Lima, 1570," in Sancho Rayón and Zabálburu, XCIV, 255–98.

23. Vicuña Mackenna, *Historia*, I, 49, note 1.

24. Memorial of Miguel de Olaverría, Lima [?], 1594, in Gay, II, 53.

25. Letter of Governor García Ramón to the king, April 12, 1607, in Vicuña Mackenna, *Historia*, I, 162–63. Alonso de Ribera stressed the same idea when requesting that a thousand men be sent out from Spain to put an end to the war in Arauco "because those who come from Peru enter through one port and leave through another." Letter of Governor Ribera to the king, 1609, BNC, *Archivo Vicuña Mackenna*, CCLXXXVIII, 1–22.

26. Letter of Governor Jara Quemada to the king, Jan. 29, 1611, in Vicuña Mackenna, *Historia*, I, 163.

27. In Pineda y Bascuñán, p. 235.

28. Letter of Governor Jara Quemada to the king, Jan. 29, 1611, in Vicuña Mackenna, *Historia*, I, 163.

29. Cited in Amunátegui, *Los precursores*, II, 115. See also the letter of Governor Ribera to the king, Sept. 18, 1613, in ACSI, A-II-63, part II, 589–609. The first military regulations promulgated in 1608 assigned the following monthly salaries for officers and men: *maestre de campo*: 137 pesos, 4 reales; *sargento mayor*: 68 pesos, 6 reales; *auditor de guerra*: 33 pesos, 5 reales; *veedor general*: 165 pesos, 1 real; *capellán*: 34 pesos, 5 reales; *cirujano mayor*: 28 pesos, 5 reales; *cirujanos asistentes*: 20 pesos, 5 reales; *intérprete*: 17 pesos, 5 reales; *capitanes de infantería*: 68 pesos, 6 reales; *alférez*: 27 pesos, 4 reales; *sarjento*: 16 pesos, 4 reales; *tambor*: 11 pesos, 4 reales; *cabo de escuadra*: 11 pesos, 4 reales; *mosquetero*: 11 pesos, 4 reales; *soldado*: 8 pesos, 6 reales; *capitanes de caballería*: 80 pesos, 4 reales. Carvallo y Goyeneche, *Descripción histórico-jeográfica*, I, 257–58, 340, note 163.

30. Elliott, pp. 317–19.

31. Lovera, p. 396.

32. Report of the audiencia of Chile to the king, 1611, in Amunátegui, *Los precursores*, II, 113–14. See also the letter of Gabriel de Celada to the king, Jan. 6, 1610, in Gay, II, 194–203, for similar complaints.

33. Cédula of Philip IV to the viceroy of Peru, April 9, 1662, reproduced in Amunátegui, *Los precursores*, II, 368–70.

34. Summary of the residencias of various governors of Chile, Aug. 16, 1688, in *ibid.*, pp. 378–79.

35. *Reclamación* of Juan Godinez, August 30, 1567, in Gay, II, 237.

36. Letter of Governor Bravo de Saravia to the king, May 8, 1569, in Medina, DI, Second Series, I, 166.

37. Lovera, p. 408.

38. *Provisión real* of the audiencia of Lima, April 26, 1595, in Vicuña Mackenna, *Historia*, I, 137. Azocar's action in supporting the protest is significant, since it implies that the complaint was justified. As soon as Gamboa learned of what had happened, he hurried to Santiago personally at the head of forty men, arrested Azocar, deported him to Lima, and forced the merchants and householders of the capital to comply with his demands. His successor, Alonso de Sotomayor, followed the same policy of forced contributions. Lovera, pp. 408–12.

39. Carvallo y Goyeneche, II, 18–19; *Libro de votos de la audiencia de Chile*, acuerdo of Aug. 7, 1630, in Amunátegui, *Los precursores*, II, 222–23. When it became clear that Lazo de la Vega intended to embark upon an all-out military drive against the Araucanians, the audiencia hastened to disassociate itself in writing from the plan, prophesying that it would result in certain defeat for the Spaniards. Acuerdo of Nov. 20, 1630, in *ibid.*, pp. 224–26.

40. Carvallo y Goyeneche, II, 20; Encina, III, 170. Fifty encomenderos had

originally been designated by the local cabildo, but popular pressure forced reduction of the number to thirty. Tesillo, p. 34.

41. Carvallo y Goyeneche, II, 22. The enemy numbered 7,000. Tesillo, p. 38.

42. Letter of Governor Bravo de Saravia to the king, May 8, 1569, in Gay, II, 99.

43. Vicuña Mackenna, *Historia*, I, 110 and note 3. Only seven of the thirty-five royally appointed governors who ruled Chile from 1541 to 1810 died in Santiago. They were Rodrigo de Quiroga (1575–80), Martín de Mujica (1646–49), Andrés de Ustariz (1709–17), Gabriel Cano y Aponte (1717–33), Antonio de Guill y Gonzaga (1761–68), and Luis Muñoz de Guzmán (1802–8). This number does not include the thirty interim governors appointed by the viceroys, most of whom ruled for only brief periods until the appointment of a new *royal* governor. *Ibid.*, p. 435, note 1.

44. *Ibid.*, p. 135.

45. Letter of Governor Ribera to the king, April 17, 1613, in Amunátegui, *Los precursores*, II, 215.

46. Tesillo, p. 16.

47. Encina, III, 170.

48. *Libro de votos de la audiencia de Chile*, acuerdos of March 13 and 14, 1630, in Amunátegui, *Los precursores*, II, 217–19.

49. *Ibid.*, p. 218.

50. Audiencia's acuerdo of April 30, 1630, in *ibid.*, pp. 220–21.

51. Audiencia's acuerdo of May 15, 1630, in *ibid.*, p. 221.

52. For a detailed and vivid account of the disaster, see Vicuña Mackenna, *Historia*, I, 261–79.

53. Report of the audiencia of Chile to the king, July 12, 1648, in Amunátegui, *Los precursores*, II, 269–70.

54. Encina, II, 197–98. For further information on the number of Negroes in Chile during the sixteenth and seventeenth centuries, see Mellafe.

55. Vicuña Mackenna, *Historia*, I, 228, note 1. The city itself was little more than a rural village consisting of only 200 houses after almost seventy-five years of existence. The other towns were even less impressive. Concepción, the largest settlement in the south, had only 76 houses, 36 of which were thatched. Chillán had eight houses roofed with tile and 39 with thatch. La Serena in the north was equally humble with its 46 houses, of which only 11 had tile roofs. Castro, on the island of Chiloé, was the most wretched of all: 12 straw-covered huts. Letter of Gabriel de Celada to the king, Jan. 6, 1610, in Gay, II, 194–203.

56. Encina, IV, 108.

57. Arbieto, *Informe*, March 16, 1634, in Gay, II, 360–409.

58. Report of the audiencia of Chile to the king, Nov. 14, 1639, in *ibid.*, II, 410–16.

59. See Encina, IV, 109.

60. Encina breaks down the total population as follows: 1,800 to 2,050 soldiers,

500 to 600 clergy and religious of both sexes, and 7,000 to 8,000 civilians, men, women, and children, including in this category the families of the military, which were relatively large as were those of the civilian residents. These figures do not include the mass of low-class mestizos who, despite their Spanish blood, were not considered Spanish in the ordinary acceptance of the term at that time. Their number was probably not less than 6,000. Encina, IV, 109–10.

61. *Ibid.*, p. 111.

62. Letter of Governor Ibáñez to the king, May 17, 1702, in *ibid.*, p. 111.

63. *Ibid.*

64. *Ibid.*, pp. 117–18.

65. Notably those of 1723 and 1766.

66. The eighteenth century witnessed a great surge in urban development especially from 1740 on.

67. Like the Comanches and Apaches in North America, the Araucanians soon became expert horsemen once they had stolen or captured a supply of horses from the invaders. Much of their military success was due to the mobility they thus acquired. Alonso de Ribera lamented in one of his reports that "as many of the enemy as can, move on horseback and thus they enter and leave our territory with increasing ease and rapidity." Letter of Governor Ribera to the king, Concepción, Sept. 18, 1613, in ACSI, A-II-63, Part II, 589–609. According to one reliable estimate of the same period, the cavalry the Araucanians could put into the field by the second decade of the seventeenth century numbered as many as 6,000. Testimony of Fray Juan Falcón de los Angeles, Santiago, April 18, 1614, in *ibid.*, pp. 677–701. Their military prowess was further enhanced by the adoption of European weapons and tactics, particularly the art of fortification against attack, the use of trenches and camouflaged pits to disrupt cavalry charges and trap unwary horsemen, the introduction of mass attacks in organized waves to wear down the adversary without allowing him time to recoup his strength, the development of protective helmets and coats of mail, *a la español*, which reduced the effectiveness of the Spanish sword, and the introduction of siege techniques and psychological warfare to dishearten the enemy and hasten his capitulation. For a discussion of this aspect of the war, see Armond.

68. The enemy warriors were able to get along on very little. Their rations for an eight-day period consisted of two pounds of cornmeal and barley mixed with a little water to form a kind of gruel. Their clothing included little more than a *chupa*, a kind of jacket. A Spanish cavalryman, on the contrary, was accompanied by at least three servants and sometimes as many as six who catered to his needs by preparing his food, looking after his baggage, and taking care of his horses, which frequently numbered a dozen or more. This striking contrast between the two antagonists caused one observer to remark that "every time the [Spanish] army makes or breaks camp it seems as though a city were being founded or moved, and in this kind of activity the Spaniards spend most of their time, while the Indians, in contrast, travel very light." Letter of Governor Jara Quemada to the king, May 1, 1611, in Gay, II, 234–44.

CHRONOLOGY, 1496–1700

1583 Arrival of first peninsular troops
Reestablishment of personal service
1592–99 Administration of Governor Oñez de Loyola
1593 Arrival of Jesuits in Chile
1598 Beginning of Araucanian rebellion under Pelantaro
Death of Oñez de Loyola at Curabala
Death of Philip II
1599–1601 Interim administrations of Viscarra, Quiñones, and García Ramón
1599 Spaniards retreat to the Biobío; destruction of Valdivia
Calderón's treatise advocating enslavement of the rebels
1600 Spaniards abandon La Imperial and Angol
Beginning of the *situado real* to finance the war
1601–5 Administration of Governor Alonso de Ribera
1602 Abandonment of Villarrica and Osorno
1603 Philip III orders establishment of a permanent standing army in Chile
Transfer of the diocese of La Imperial to Concepción
1605–10 Administration of Governor García Ramón
1606 Council of the Indies advises Philip III to legalize Indian slavery in Chile
1608 Philip III authorizes enslavement of war captives
Torres Bollo promulgates ordinances abolishing personal service in Jesuit establishments
1609 Second audiencia installed in Santiago
Luis de Valdivia arrives in Spain to urge adoption of defensive warfare
1610–11 Interim administrations of Merlo de la Fuente and Jara Quemada
1612–17 Second administration of Governor Ribera
1612 Official beginning of defensive warfare; parlamento at Paicaví
Massacre of Jesuit missionaries at Elicura
1614 Governor Ribera resumes offensive warfare
1615 Philip III reaffirms defensive warfare as official policy
1617 Interim administration of Talaverano Gallegos
1618–24 Interim administrations of Ulloa y Lemos, Cerda y Sotomayor, Osores de Ulloa, and De Alaba
1619 Departure of Luis de Valdivia from Chile
1620 Tasa de Esquilache
1625–29 Administration of Governor Fernández de Córdoba
1625 Philip IV legalizes enslavement of rebels; end of defensive warfare
1629–39 Administration of Governor Lazo de la Vega
1631 Spanish victory over Araucanians at La Albarrada
1633 Philip IV "abolishes" personal service in Chile
1635 Tasa de Lazo de la Vega

1639–46   Administration of Governor Baides
1641   Pact of Quillín
1643   Araucanians help repel Brouwer's invasion of southern Chile
1646–49   Administration of Governor Martín de Mujica
1647   Santiago earthquake
Pact of Quillín renewed
1650–56   Administration of Governor Acuña y Cabrera
1655   Indian rebellion of 1655
Deposition of Governor Acuña y Cabrera
Concepción vecinos elect Francisco de la Fuente Villalobos as governor
1656–63   Interim administrations of Porter Casanate, González Montero, and Peredo
1657   Earthquake destroys Concepción
1662   Philip IV forbids slave raids and pardons participants in past rebellions
1664–68   Administration of Governor Meneses
1665   Ecclesiastical investigations of Elicura massacre
1668–70   Interim administrations of Navamorquenda and González Montero
1670–81   Administration of Governor Henríquez
1670   Rosales' *Tratado* on the evils of Indian slavery
1672   Rosales' *Dictamen* on Indian slavery
1674   Queen Regent Mariana issues decree abolishing Indian slavery in Chile
1676   Beginning of the deposit system
1682–92   Administration of Governor Garro
1683   Charles II exempts emancipated slaves from paying tribute for ten years
1688   Charles II approves the deposit system
1692–1700   Administration of Governor Marín de Poveda
1693   Royal decree authorizing Indians to pay tribute in money or kind rather than in personal service
1697   School for sons of Indian caciques founded in Chillán
1700   Santiago becomes de facto capital of Chile
Death of Charles II; end of the Hapsburg regime and beginning of the Enlightened Despotism of the Bourbons

GLOSSARY OF SPANISH AND INDIAN TERMS

Acuerdo. Resolution

Adelantado. Private individual who undertook to explore and conquer new lands at his own expense in return for political rights in the new territory

Alcalde. Town mayor; justice of the peace

Alcalde de corte. A judge with criminal jurisdiction in the area within five leagues of a town

Alcalde ordinario. Cabildo judge elected annually to exercise jurisdiction of first instance in the town

Alférez. Standard bearer

Alguacil mayor. Chief constable; bailiff

Arroba. Weight of about twenty-five pounds

Asesor. Consultant; official advisor

Asesor letrado. An advisory counselor or lawyer whom the governor consulted when making decisions or settling lawsuits in which he participated as judge

Asiento. Mining area and its population

Audiencia. Highest legal and administrative tribunal under the viceroy; the area subject to the court's jurisdiction

Auditor de guerra. Military legal advisor

Auto. Decree or edict

Aviso. A notice

Ayuntamiento. Same as cabildo

Cabildo. Town council; meeting of the council

Cabildo abierto. Open town meeting to which leading citizens were invited when matters of grave importance pended

Cabo de escuadra. Corporal in the army

Cacique. Indian chief; member of the Indian ruling class

Capellán. Chaplain

Capitán de caballería. Cavalry commander

Capitán de infantería. Infantry commander

Carta ánua. Annual report sent to major superior in Rome by Jesuit missionaries in the field

Carta de obediencia. Credential letter accrediting the bearer as a member in good standing of a specified religious order or community

Cátedra. University chair

Catedrático de prima. Senior professor who lectured during the more favored morning hours

Caudillo. Chief, leader; political boss

Cédula. Letters patent

Cédula real. Royal order, either general or addressed to individuals, issued by the Crown as an order-in-council

Chacra. Small farm

China. Servant girl of Indian or mestizo blood

Chupa. A kind of jacket worn by Araucanian warriors

Cirujano asistente. Assistant surgeon

Cirujano mayor. Chief surgeon

Conquistador. Spanish conqueror of the sixteenth century

Consulta. Considered written opinion of councillors on proposed legislation

Cordillera. Mountain range

Corregidor. Spanish official in charge of a district

Corregimiento. Office or jurisdiction of a corregidor

Criollo. Pure-blooded Spaniard born in America

Decreto. Decree, resolution; royal or official order

Demora. Period of eight months that the Indians were obliged to work in the mines

Derecho de gentes. Natural law common to all men

Dictámen. A considered opinion, frequently of the fiscal in a given case

Doctrina. A parish of recently converted Indians that did not yet have a resident pastor or curate

Doctrinero. Catechist; priest in charge of a doctrina

Encomendero. Person entrusted with the physical and spiritual welfare of a group of Indians from whom he had the right to collect tribute

Encomienda. Grant of Indians, mainly as tribute payers

Entrada. Entry into new territory for purposes of conquest; yearly military campaign

Escopetar. To excavate gold mines

Escribano. Notary public

Estancia. Large farm; hacienda

Fanega. A measure of grain (about 1.5 bushels)

Fiscal. Attorney general

Frijoles. Kidney beans

Guazábara. Cavalry clash

Hacendado. Owner of a hacienda; a wealthy man

Hacienda. Large landed estate; wealth

Hermandad. Brotherhood; local police force

Indigenista. An advocate of Indianism

Indios amigos. Pacified Indians who frequently served as military allies of the Spaniards

Indios de guerra. Unpacified Araucanians; rebels

Indios de la usanza. Indians sold with the understanding that they could later be redeemed if the purchase price were refunded; a custom practiced by the Araucanians

Indios de servicio. Domestic Indian slaves who worked on farms and in private homes

Informe. A report, frequently by special request of the Crown authorities

Inquilinaje. System of tenant farming that replaced the encomienda in Chile

Inquilino. Type of tenant farmer in Chile

Intérprete. Interpreter

Jornales. Daily wages paid to Indians for their work

Junta. Meeting or committee of persons designated to consult upon or resolve some problem

Junta de guerra. Committee on war

Junta de hacienda. Committee on finances

Justicia. A minister or court that dispenses justice

Justicia mayor. Presiding officer of a town council

Lavadero de oro. Placer mine

Letrado. An expert; frequently a lawyer

Licenciado. Licentiate, the basic higher degree in university faculties; title given to lawyers

Limeño. A resident of Lima

Macehuales. Indian working class

Machis. Araucanian medicine men

Maestre de campo. Superior military officer in charge of a specified number of troops

Maestre de campo general. Commanding general of an army

Maloca. Invasion of Indian lands for purpose of capturing and enslaving the natives; slave hunt

Manta. Blanket; man's shawl

Mapuches. Native Indians of Chile

Maravedí. Spanish coin worth approximately one-sixth of a cent

Merced. A grant of patronage—dignity, land, employment, or income—to a Crown subject

Mestizo. Offspring of a union between Indian and white

Mita. Compulsory labor service of Indians

Mitayo. Mita worker

Mitimaes. Colonies of conquered Indians assigned especially to frontier provinces for purposes of defense and political unification

Moreno. Dark-skinned; a mulatto

Mosquetero. Musketeer; foot soldier

Obraje. Workshop or factory for manufacture of textiles

Oidor. Judge of an audiencia

Oidor decano. Senior judge of an audiencia

Panque. Plant used in tanning leather

Parecer. An official opinion, especially of the fiscal

Parlamento. Peace conference

Pase real. Royal permit

Patacón. Copper coin worth about one penny

Patrón. Patron, protector; master, boss

Patronato real. Series of papal grants and concessions that gave the Spanish Crown virtual control of the Church in the Indies; royal patronage

Peninsular. Spaniard born in Spain but living in America

Pensador. An intellectual, frequently a social philosopher

Peso. Monetary unit of eight reales

Pieza. A piece or part of anything; in Chile, Indians who were hunted down and enslaved

Plaza. Fortified town

Poblador. Settler, founder of a town

Procurador. A solicitor or agent of the town council or of a religious organization

Provisor. Ecclesiastical judge appointed by the bishop with ex officio jurisdiction in ecclesiastical cases

Pueblo. Indian village

Quinto. Royal tax on minerals

Ramo de agasajos. Public funds used to provide gifts for the Indians

Ranchos. Huts

Real. Spanish coin containing 34 maravedís; one-eighth of a peso

Real acuerdo. Executive session of an audiencia with its president and fiscals

Real decreto. Royal law issued like a cédula

Reducciones de paz. Settlements of peaceful Indians converted to Christianity

Reencuentro. Skirmish

Regidor. Alderman of a cabildo

Relación de méritos y servicios. A formal listing of services and accomplishments for the purpose of gaining some royal concession

Relecciones. Special two-hour discourses on timely problems of public interest that the University of Salamanca required its professor of theology to deliver annually in addition to the regular course of lectures

Repartimiento. Allotment of Indians for specific purposes, usually labor

Requerimiento. Legal document that had to be read to the Indians urging them to accept Spanish overlordship before hostilities could be initiated

Residencia. Judicial review held at end of an official's term of office

Sargento mayor. Sergeant major

Servicio personal. Forced labor without compensation

Sesmo. Sixth part of mineral products due the Indians as wages

Situadista. Special agent in charge of buying military supplies for the army in Chile

Situado. Annual military subsidy from the Crown

Soldado. Soldier

Tambor. Drummer in the army (infantry)

Tasa. Tribute assessment

Teniente general. Lieutenant general

Toqui. Araucanian war chief

Tumulto. Riot; uprising

Vecino. Property owner who paid taxes

Vecino feudatario. Same as encomendero

Veedor general. Inspector general

Visita. Official tour of inspection

Visitador general. Royal agent who enjoyed powers that made him temporarily superior to all Crown officials in a given territory

Yanaconas. Indian servitors. In Chile the term frequently applied to war captives "deposited" with individual Spaniards for safekeeping

Zambo. Offspring of a union between Indian and Negro

BIBLIOGRAPHY

The following abbreviations are used in the Bibliography:

AAS	Archives of the Archdiocese of Santiago.
ACSI	Archives of the Colegio San Ignacio, Santiago.
BNC	Biblioteca Nacional de Chile (National Library of Chile).
DI	Short form for Medina, *Colección de documentos inéditos.*
Historiadores	Short form for Medina, *Colección de historiadores de Chile.*
Pastells	Colección Pastells, in the St. Louis University Microfilms.
SLUM	St. Louis University Microfilms.

Actas del cabildo de Santiago. Twenty-eight volumes of these Actas, covering the period from 1541 to 1814, are included in the Colección de historiadores de Chile y documentos relativos a la historia nacional published under the direction of José Toribio Medina *et al.* Santiago: Elzeviriana *et al.*, 1861–1953. 51 vols.

Acuerdo of the audiencia of Chile concerning the abolition of personal service, March 7, 1634. In Amunátegui, Los precursores, II, 231–34.

Almeyda Arroyo, Elías. La Historia de Chile de Don Francisco Antonio Encina. Santiago: "San Francisco," 1952.

Amunátegui, Miguel Luis. La cuestión de límites entre Chile y la república argentina. Santiago: Nacional, 1879–80. 3 vols.

——— Los precursores de la independencia de Chile. Santiago: Barcelona, 1910. 3 vols.

Amunátegui Solar, Domingo. Las encomiendas de indíjenas en Chile. Santiago: Cervantes, 1909. 2 vols.

——— Historia social de Chile. Santiago: Editorial Nascimento, 1932.

Arbieto, Lorenzo de. "Informe" on the administration of Governor Lazo de la Vega, March 16, 1634. In Gay, II, 360–409.

Armando de Ramón, José. El pensamiento Político Social del padre Luis de Valdivia. Santiago: Editorial Universidad Católica, 1961.

Armond, Louis de. "Frontier Warfare in Colonial Chile," *Pacific Historical Review*, XXIII (May 1954), 125–32.

Asiento que se tomó con Cristóbal Guerra, Alcalá de Henares, 12 de Julio de 1503. In Pacheco *et al.*, XXXI, 187–93.

Asiento y capitulación que se tomó con Vicente Yáñez Pinzón para ir a descubrir, Toro, 24 de Abril de 1505. In Pacheco *et al.*, XXXI, 309–17.

Astrain, Antonio. Historia de la Compañía de Jesús en la asistencia de España. Madrid: Razón y Fe, 1910–25. 7 vols.

Auto de don Pedro Osores de Ulloa, gobernador de Chile, sobre la tasa que hizo el Principe de Esquilache, virrey del Pirú, y lo que sobre admitirse se ofreció y remisión a Su Majestad, Santiago, 8 de Diciembre de 1622. In Medina, Biblioteca, I, 151–62.

Aviso de la audiencia informando quitar el servicio personal de las mujeres casadas y solteras indias, Santiago, 28 de Septiembre de 1609. In BNC, Archivo Medina: Manuscritos, CX, No. 1,838, folios 297–304. Also published in Amunátegui, Los precursores.

Bannon, John Francis, ed. Indian Labor in the Spanish Indies. Was There Another Solution? Boston: D. C. Heath, 1966.

Barras de Aragón, Francisco de las, ed. Viajes por la América Meridional. Madrid: Progreso Editorial, 1923. 2 vols.

Barros Arana, Diego. Historia jeneral de Chile. Santiago: Rafael Jover, Editor, 1884–1902. 16 vols.

Becerril, Bernardo de. "Apuntamientos sobre la tasa de Chile." In DI, Second Series, III, 121–24.

Blanco, José María. Historia documentada de la vida y gloriosa muerte de los padres Martín de Aranda Valdivia y Horacio Vecchi y del hermano Diego de Montalbán de la Compañía de Jesús mártires de Elicura en Arauco. Buenos Aires: Sebastián de Amorrortu, 1937.

Briseño, Ramón. Repertorio de antigüedades chilenas. Santiago: Gutenberg, 1889.

Bullón y Fernández, Eloy. El problema jurídico de la dominación española en América antes de las "Relecciones" de Francisco de Vitoria. Madrid: La Rafa, 1933.

Calderón, Melchor. "Treatise on the Importance and Utility of Enslaving the Rebellious Indians of Chile, Santiago, 1599." In Medina, Biblioteca, II, 5–20.

Capítulo de la ordenanza real por el cual se prohibe la expatriación de los indios de Cuyo para traerlos forzadamente a Chile, 12 de Septiembre de 1626. In AAS, XXI, 153.

Capítulos y ordenanzas que el virrey del Perú, Marques de Montes Claros, embió en nombre de Su Majestad para los indios del reino de Chile, Lima, 29 de Marzo de 1612. In Rosales, Historia general, II, 534–35.

Carta ánua del Perú, 1598. In ACSI, A-II-34.

Carvallo y Goyeneche, Vicente. Descripción histórico-jeográfica del reino de Chile. In Historiadores, VIII. Santiago: Librería del Mercurio, 1875.

Chacón y Calvo, José María. Cedulario cubano. Los orígenes de la colonización (1493–1512). Madrid: Ibero-americana de Publicaciones, n.d.

Chamberlain, Robert S. The Pre-Conquest Tribute and Service System of the Maya as Preparation for the Spanish Repartimiento-Encomienda in Yucatán. Miami: University of Miami Press, 1951.

Colección de documentos inéditos relativos al descubrimiento, conquista y organización de las antiguas posesiones españoles de Ultramar. Second Series. Madrid: Real Academia de la Historia, ed., 1885–1925.

Compendio de algunas de las muchas y graves razones en que se funda la prudente resolución que se ha tomado de cortar la guerra de Chile haciéndola defensiva, Lima, 1611. In ACSI, A-II-55, No. 5.

Consulta de la junta de guerra de Indias, Madrid, 9 de Diciembre de 1610. In *ibid.*, A-II-63, Part II, 939–43.

Córdoba y Figueroa, Pedro de. Historia de Chile. In Historiadores, IV. Santiago: Ferrocarril, 1862.

Cortés, Pedro. "Memorial al rey, 18 de Mayo de 1614." In ACSI, A-II-63, Part II, 721–27.

Cuevas, Mariano, ed. Documentos inéditos del siglo XVI para la historia de México. México: Museo Nacional de Arqueología, 1914.

Decisión real en el Consejo de Indias aprobatoria de las ordenanzas de Alfaro, con las modificaciones en ellas introducidas, 1618. In Hernández, II, 677–81.

Declaración de Fray Juan Falcón de los Angeles, Santiago, 18 de Abril de 1614. In ACSI, A-II-63, Part II, 677–701.

DI. See Medina, Colección de documentos inéditos para la historia de Chile.

Edwards, Agustín. Peoples of Old. London: Ernest Benn, 1929.

Elliott, J. H. Imperial Spain 1469–1716. New York: The New American Library, 1966.

Encina, Francisco Antonio. Historia de Chile desde la prehistoria hasta 1891. Santiago: Editorial Nascimento, 1940–52. 20 vols.

Encinas, Diego de, comp. Cedulario indiano. Madrid: Ediciones Cultura Hispánica, 1945. 4 vols.

——— Libro de provisiones, cédulas, capítulos, ordenanzas, instrucciones, y cartas libradas y despachadas en diferentes tiempos por Sus Magestades . . . tocantes al buen gobierno de las Indias y administración de la justicia en ellas. Madrid: Real, 1596. 4 vols.

Enrich, Francisco. Historia de la Compañía de Jesús en Chile. Barcelona: Francisco Rosal, 1891. 2 vols.

——— "Vida del Padre Diego de Rosales." In ACSI, A-II-3, No. 7.

Eraso, Domingo de. "Papel sobre la esclavitud de los indios de Chile." In Navarrete *et al.*, Colección de documentos inéditos para la historia de España (Madrid: Imprenta de la viuda de Calero, 1842–95, 112 vols.), L, 221–31.

Errázuriz, Crescente. Continuación de los seis años de la historia de Chile. Santiago: Cervantes, 1908.

——— Don García de Mendoza, 1557–61. Santiago: Universitaria, 1914.

——— Estudios históricos. See Silva Castro.

———— Los orígenes de la iglesia chilena, 1540–1603. Santiago: Correo, 1873.

———— Pedro de Valdivia. Santiago: Cervantes, 1911–12. 2 vols.

———— Pedro de Villagra, 1563–64. Santiago: Universitaria, 1916.

Expediente de Doña Marina Ortiz de Gaete, mujer del gobernador de Chile, Don Pedro de Valdivia, acerca de los repartimientos de indios que le fueron concedidos como pertenecientes a su marido, Concepción, 26 de Octubre de 1571. In DI, XXIX, 8–39.

Expediente sobre derecho al patronato de una capellanía fundada por Doña Juana Jiménez, Concepción, 4 de Noviembre de 1672. In BNC, Archivo Jesuítas, XLIII, 190–272.

Eyzaguirre, José Ignacio Victor. Historia eclesiástica, política y literaria de Chile. Valparaíso: Comercio, 1850. 3 vols.

Feliú Cruz, Guillermo, and Carlos Monje Alfaro. Las encomiendas según tasas y ordenanzas. Buenos Aires: Casa Jacobo Peuser, 1941.

Ferrada, Jorge. "Eclesiásticos que se distinguieron en el descubrimiento y conquista de Chile." *La revista católica*, XXXVII, No. 430, 16–102.

Ferrada Ibáñez, Miguel. Historia de Linares, 1541–1810. Santiago: Gráficos San Vicente, n.d.

Figueroa, Francisco de. "Memorial al Rey, 1616." In BNC, Archivo Vicuña Mackenna, CCLXXXIX, 108–17.

Furlong, Guillermo. Los jesuítas y la cultura ríoplatense. Montevideo: Urta y Curbel, 1933.

Galdames, Luis. A History of Chile. Chapel Hill: University of North Carolina Press, 1941.

Galvez, Francisco de. "Relación de la orden que en este reino de Chile se tiene, y de la labor de las minas de oro y cuento dello y otras cosas tocantes a la real hacienda." N.d. In DI, XXVIII, 355–59.

Garcilaso de la Vega. Historia general del Perú. Segunda parte de los comentarios reales de los Incas. Buenos Aires: Emecé Editores, 1944. 3 vols.

Gay, Claudio. Historia física y política de Chile. Documentos sobre la historia, la estadística y la geografía. Paris: En Casa del Autor, 1852. 2 vols.

Getino, Luis Alonso. Influencia de los Dominicos en las Leyes Nuevas. Sevilla: Consejo Superior de Investigaciones Científicas, 1945.

Ghigliazza, Raymundo. Historia de la provincia dominicana de Chile. Concepción: Universitaria, 1898. 2 vols.

Gligo Viel, Agata. La Tasa de Gamboa. Santiago: Editorial Universidad Católica, 1962.

Godinez, Juan. "Reclamación," August 30, 1567. In Gay, II, 237.

Gómez de Vidaurre, Felipe. Historia geográfica, natural y civil del reino de Chile. 2 vols. In Historiadores, XIV, XV. Santiago: Ercilla, 1889.

Góngora Marmolejo, Alonso de. Historia de Chile desde su descubrimiento hasta el año de 1575. In Historiadores, II. Santiago: Ferrocarril, 1862.

González de Nájera, Alonso. Desengaño y reparo de la guerra del reino de Chile. In Historiadores, XVI. Santiago: Ercilla, 1889.

González de San Nicolás, Fray Gil. "Relación de los agravios que los indios de las provincias de Chile padecen." N.d. In Historiadores, XXIX, 461–66.

Graham, R. B. Cunninghame. Pedro de Valdivia. London: Heinemann, 1926.

Griffin, Charles C. "Francisco Encina and Revisionism in Chilean History," *The Hispanic American Historical Review*, XXXVII (Feb. 1957), 1–28.

Hanke, Lewis. Aristotle and the American Indians. London: Hollis & Carter, 1959.

———— "Dos Palabras on Antonio de Ulloa and the *Noticias secretas*," *The Hispanic American Historical Review*, XVI (Nov. 1936), 479–514.

———— The First Social Experiments in America. Cambridge, Mass.: Harvard University Press, 1935.

———— "Pope Paul III and the American Indians," *The Harvard Theological Review*, XXX (April 1937), 65–102.

———— The Spanish Struggle for Justice in the Conquest of America. Philadelphia: University of Pennsylvania Press, 1949.

Hanke, Lewis, comp., and Millares Carlo, Agustín, ed. Cuerpo de documentos del siglo XVI sobre los derechos de España en las Indias y las Filipinas. México: Fondo de Cultura Económica, 1943.

Heredia, Beltrán de. Francisco de Vitoria. Barcelona: Editorial Labor, 1939.

———— Un precursor del maestro Vitoria, el P. Matías de Paz, O.P., y su tratado "De Dominio Regum Hispaniae super Indos." Salamanca: Establecimiento Tipográfico de Calatrava, 1929.

Hernández, Pablo. Organización social de las doctrinas guaraníes de la Compañía de Jesús. Barcelona: Gustavo Gili, Editor, 1913. 2 vols.

Herrera, Juan de. "Segunda relación de las cosas de Chile." N.d. In Historiadores, II, 253–54.

Herrera y Tordesillas, Antonio. Historia general de los hechos de los castellanos en las islas y tierra firme del Mar Océano. Madrid: Academia de la Historia, 1934–54. 13 vols.

Historia del Colegio Máximo de Santiago. N.d. In ACSI, A-II-6.

Historiadores. See Medina *et al.*, Colección de historiadores de Chile.

Huneeus Pérez, Andrés. Historia de las polémicas de Indias en Chile durante el siglo XVI: 1536–98. Santiago: Editorial Jurídica de Chile, 1956.

Hussey, Roland D. "Text of the Laws of Burgos (1512–13) Concerning the Treatment of the Indians," *The Hispanic American Historical Review*, XII (Aug. 1932), 301–26.

Icazbalceta, Joaquín García. Don Juan de Zumárraga. México: Andrade y Morales, 1881.

Información a pedimento del Padre Luis de Valdivia sobre el estado en que estaba el reino de Chile, Santiago, 29 de Octubre de 1612. In ACSI, A-II-63, Part I, 229–44.

Información de Antonio Tarabajano, Santiago, 23 de Julio de 1555. In DI, XV, 283–308.

Información de las cosas de Chile en orden a la paz a pedimento del Padre Luis de Valdivia, Concepción, 18 de Octubre de 1612. In ACSI, A-II-63, Part I, 260–371.

Información del glorioso martirio que padecieron a manos de los indios bárbaros de Chile los venerables Padres Horacio Vecchi y Martín de Aranda y Hermano Diego de Montalbán hecha en el obispado de Santiago de Chile siendo juez y gobernador de él el señor Provisor y Vicario General Don Alonso Fernández de Córdova, canónigo y maestro de esta Santa Iglesia, en el año de 1665. In Blanco, 359–432.

Información de los méritos y servicios del capitán Francisco de Riberos, Santiago, 1563–64. In DI, XVII, 95–243.

Información de servicios de Rodrigo de Quiroga. Declaración de Don Rodrigo González, Santiago, 31 de Octubre de 1560. In DI, XVI, 147–53.

Información que los reverendos padres de San Xerónimo tomaron ansi de los dichos testigos que rescebieron como de los paresceres que los frailes le dieron para lo que se a de determinar de los indios, 1517. In Pacheco *et al.*, XXXIV, 201–29.

Información que se hizo con los que estubieron en prisión acerca de lo que avian dicho a el Padre Luis de Valdivia sobre la guerra de Chile, Santiago, 1613. In ACSI, A-II-55, No. 8.

Instruction of the viceroy of Peru to the governor of Chile, Don Lope de Ulloa, Lima, November 7, 1617. In ACSI, A-II-63, Part II, 877–83.

Jara, Alvaro. Guerre et société au Chili: essai de sociologie coloniale; la transformación de la guerre d'Araucanie et l'esclavage des Indiens, du début de la conquête espagnole aux débuts de l'esclavage légal (1612). Paris: Université de Paris. Institut des Hautes Études de l'Amérique Latine, 1961.

Keen, Benjamin, ed. and trans. The Life of the Admiral Christopher Columbus by His Son Ferdinand. New Brunswick: Rutgers University Press, 1959.

Kirkpatrick, F. A. "Repartimiento-encomienda," *The Hispanic American Historical Review*, XIX (Nov. 1942), 372–97.

Las Casas, Bartolomé de. Apologética historia de las Indias. In Nueva Biblioteca de Autores Españoles, XIII. Madrid: Bailly-Bailliere e Hijos, Editores, 1909.

——— Brevísima relación de la destrucción de las Indias, 1552. In Rivadeneira, CX, 134–81.

——— Del único modo. See Millares Carlo.

——— Historia de las Indias. México: Fondo de Cultura Económica, 1951. 3 vols.

Latcham, Ricardo E. "Sintesis del espíritu de la colonización española," *La revista católica*, XLVI (Feb. 1924), 292–303.

Leonhardt, Carlos, ed. Cartas ánuas de la provincia del Paraguay, Chile y Tucumán de la Compañía de Jesús (1609–14). In Leonhardt, Documentos.

——— Documentos para la historia argentina, XIX. Buenos Aires: Casa Jacobo Peuser, 1927.

Leturia, Pedro. "Maior y Vitoria ante la conquista de América," *Estudios Eclesiásticos*, II (1932), 44–82.

Levene, Ricardo. Introducción a la historia del derecho indiano. Buenos Aires: Librería Nacional, 1924.

Lizana, Elías, and Pablo Maulén, eds. Colección de documentos históricos recopilados del archivo del arzobispado de Santiago. Santiago: San José, 1919–21. 4 vols.

Lizárraga, Reginaldo de. "Parecer acerca de si contra los indios de Arauco es justa la guerra que se les haze y si se pueden dar por esclavos, Lima, 16 de Julio de 1599." In Hanke and Millares Carlo, 295–300.

López de Gómara, Francisco. Hispania victrix. Primera y segunda parte de la historia general de Indias. In Rivadeneira, XXII, 1946.

Los oficiales reales y el fiscal de S.M. en el pleito contra Juan Gómez y otros sobre la posesión de los repartimientos de indios del valle de Quillota y Mapocho, Santiago, 6 de Marzo de 1561. In DI, XI, 311–419.

Lovera, Pedro Mariño de. Crónica del reino de Chile. In Historiadores, VI. Santiago: Ferrocarril, 1865.

Lozano, Pedro. Historia de la Compañía de Jesús en la provincia del Paraguay. Madrid: Imprenta de la viuda de M. Fernández y del Supremo Consejo de la Inquisición, 1754–55. 2 vols.

Machado de Cháves, Pedro. "Dictámen sobre la cédula real de 1633, 6 de Abril de 1635." In Amunátegui Solar, Las encomiendas, II, 15–17.

Mahn-Lot, Marianne, ed. Barthélemy de Las Casas. L'Évangile et la Force. Paris: Les Éditions du Cerf, 1964.

Mateos, F., ed. Historia general de la Compañía de Jesús en la provincia del Perú. Crónica anónima de 1600 que trata del establecimiento y misiones de la Compañía de Jesús en los paises de habla española en la América meridional. Madrid: Consejo Superior de Investigaciones Científicas, 1944. 2 vols.

Medina, José Toribio. La araucana de Don Alonso de Ercilla y Zúñiga. Santiago: Elzeviriana, 1910–18. 5 vols.

———— Biblioteca hispano-chilena (1523–1817). Santiago: En casa del autor, 1897–99. 3 vols.

———— Diccionario biográfico colonial de Chile. Santiago: Elzeviriana, 1906.

———— La inquisición en Chile. Santiago: En casa del autor, 1890. 2 vols.

Medina, José Toribio, ed. Cartas de Pedro de Valdivia que tratan del descubrimiento y conquista de Chile. Santiago: Universitaria: Fondo Histórico y Bibliográfico José Toribio Medina, 1953.

———— Colección de documentos inéditos para la historia de Chile desde el viaje de Magallanes hasta la batalla de Maipo, 1518–1818. Santiago: Ercilla, 1888–1902. 30 vols. Cited as DI.

———— Colección de documentos inéditos para la historia de Chile. Segunda Serie. Santiago: Fondo Histórico y Bibliográfico J. T. Medina, 1956– . 6 vols. Cited as DI, Second Series.

———— *et al.* Colección de historiadores de Chile y documentos relativos a la historia nacional. Santiago: Ferrocarril *et al.*, 1861–1953. 51 vols. Cited as Historiadores.

Meléndez, Juan. Tesoros verdaderos de las Indias. Rome: N. A. Tinassio, 1681–82. 3 vols.

Mellafe, Rolando. La introducción de la esclavitud negra en Chile. Tráfico y rutas. Santiago: Universitaria, 1959.

Memorial de guerra, remitido por el Virey don Francisco de Toledo, Lima, 1570. In Sancho Rayón and Zabálburu, XCIV, 255–98.

Merino, Luis. Estudio crítico sobre las "Noticias Secretas de América" y el Clero Colonial (1720–65). Madrid: Consejo Superior de Investigaciones Científicas. Instituto Santo Toribio de Mogrovejo, 1956.

Millares Carlo, Agustín, ed. Bartolomé de las Casas. Del único modo de atraer a todas las gentes a la religión de Cristo. México: Fondo de Cultura Económica, 1942.

Minutes of the junta de guerra of the Council of the Indies, session of April 24, 1635. In Amunátegui Solar, Las encomiendas, I, 471–76.

Molina, Abbe Don J. Ignatius. The Geographical, Natural, and Civil History of Chili. Translated from the Italian with notes from the Spanish and French versions by the English editor. London: Longman, Hurst, Rees and Orme, 1809. 2 vols.

Molina, Cristóbal de. Destrucción del Perú. Lima: Editorial D. Miranda, 1943.

Morla Vicuña, Carlos. Estudio histórico sobre el descubrimiento y conquista de la Patagonia y de la Tierra del Fuego. Leipzig: F. A. Brockhaus, 1903.

Múñoz, Honorio. Vitoria and the Conquest of America. Manila: Santo Tomás University Press, 1935.

Muñoz, Humberto. Movimientos sociales en el Chile colonial. Buenos Aires: Editorial Difusión, S.A., 1945.

Navarrete, Martín Fernández de. Colección de los viages y descubrimientos que hicieron por mar los españoles. Madrid: Real, 1825–37. 5 vols.

Navarrete, Martín Fernández de, Miguel Salva, and Pedro Sainz de Baranda, eds. Colección de documentos inéditos para la historia de España. Madrid: Imprenta de la viuda de Calero, 1842–95. 112 vols.

Núñez, Fray Cristóbal. Memorial to the viceroy of Peru, 1580. In DI, Second Series, III, 127–29.

Olaverría, Miguel de. "Informe sobre el Reyno de Chile, sus Indios y sus guerras, Lima [?], 1594." In Gay, II, 13–54.

Olivares, Miguel de. Historia de la Compañía de Jesús en Chile. In Historiadores, VII. Santiago: Andrés Bello, 1874.

———— Historia militar, civil y sagrada de Chile. In Historiadores, IV. Santiago: Ferrocarril, 1864.

Ordenanzas de Alfaro, 1611. In Hernández, II, 661–77.

Ordenanzas del gobernador de Chile, Francisco Lazo de la Vega, Santiago, 16 de Abril de 1635. In Rosales, Historia general, III, 115–20.

Ordenanzas que hizo Pedro de Villagra, gobernador de Chile, aprobando las del licenciado Hernando de Santillán en favor de los indios de Chile, Concepción, 12 de Diciembre de 1563. In DI, XXIX, 293–98.

Ordenanzas sobre el servicio personal de los indios, Madrid, 17 de Julio de 1622. In AAS, LVII, 126–62.

Ovalle, Alonso de. Histórica relación del reino de Chile. In Historiadores, XII, XIII. Santiago: Ercilla, 1888.

Oviedo y Valdés, Gonzalo Fernández de. Historia general y natural de las Indias, islas y tierra firme del Mar Océano. Asunción: Editorial Guaranía, 1944–45. 14 vols.

Owen, Walter, trans. La Araucana: the Epic of Chile, by Don Alonso de Ercilla y Zúñiga. Buenos Aires: W. Owen, 1945.

Pacheco, Joaquín, Francisco de Cárdenas, and Luis Torres de Mendoza, eds. Colección de documentos inéditos relativos al descubrimiento, conquista y organización de las antiguas posesiones españolas de América y Oceanía, sacados de los archivos del reino y muy especialmente del de Indias. Madrid: M. Bernaldo de Quirós, 1864–89. 42 vols.

Palacios Rubios, Juan López. De las Islas del mar Océano. Zavala and Millares Carlo, eds. México: Fondo de Cultura Económica, 1954.

Paredes, Francisco de. "Instrucción y orden que puede tener y guardar el señor gobernador acerca de la pacificación y allanamiento de los indios naturales que en la provincia de Tucapel y Arauco y sus comarcas hay rebelados, Santiago, 20 de Abril de 1564." In DI, XXV, 42–54.

Paz, Matías de. Del dominio de los reyes de España sobre los indios. Zavala and Millares Carlo, eds. México: Fondo de Cultura Económica, 1954.

Phillips, John, trans. The Tears of the Indians. Stanford: Academic Reprints, n.d.

Pineda y Bascuñán, Francisco Núñez de. Cautiverio feliz y razón de las guerras dilatadas de Chile. In Historiadores, III. Santiago: Ferrocarril, 1863.

Pirotto, Armando D., ed. Francisco de Vitoria. Relecciones sobre los indios y el derecho de guerra. Buenos Aires: Espasa-Calpe Argentina, 1946.

Pleito de Diego García de Villalón, alguacil mayor de la ciudad de la Paz, con el fiscal de S.M. sobre restitución de los indios de que fué despojado, en que constan sus servicios hechos en Chile en tiempo de Pedro de Valdivia, Lima, 1565. In DI, XII, 162–258.

Polanco de Santillana, Nicolás. "Relación a Su Magestad, Lima, 7 de Mayo de 1635." In SLUM: Pastells, LXXXIX, 423–25.

Provisión del gobernador Martín García de Loyola acerca del buen tratamiento que se ha de dar a los indios. In BNC, Archivo Medina, Manuscritos, XCV, No. 1436.

Provisión del Marques de Montes Claros, virrey del Perú, en que nombra por visitador de Chile al Padre Luis de Valdivia, Lima, 29 de Marzo de 1612. In ACSI, A-II-55, No. 5.

Provisión y placarte de las órdenes que se han de guardar después de las dichas treguas, Lima, 29 de Marzo de 1612. In Rosales, Historia general, II, 539–42.

Puntos para contestar a una carta del virrey Montes Claros, Madrid, 19 de Febrero de 1610. In ACSI, A-II-63, Part II, 929–35.

Quirk, Robert E. "Some Notes on a Controversial Controversy: Juan Ginés de Sepúlveda and Natural Servitude," *The Hispanic American Historical Review*, XXXIV (Aug. 1954), 357–64.

Recopilación de las leyes de los reinos de las Indias. Madrid: Consejo de la Hispanidad, 1943.

Reglamento sobre el trato y trabajo a que estaban sujetos los indios en las tierras de Longavi de la Orden de los Jesuítas, 19 de Junio de 1608. In Ferrada Ibáñez, I, 163–66.

Reisse González, Julio. "Las tasas y ordenanzas sobre el trabajo de los indios en Chile," *Anales de la Universidad de Chile*, VII (1st quarter 1929), 390–434, 797–859.

Relación de lo que el Padre Guardián de San Francisco predicó en Santiago contra las órdenes de Su Magestad que traxo el Padre Luis de Valdivia. N.d. In BNC, Archivo Morla Vicuña, XXIV, No. 32.

Relación escripta por los religiosos de Santo Domingo que estaban en la Isla Española acerca de las crueldades que hacian los españoles con los indios de Ygués, Xaragua, e otros, dirigida a Mr. Xeare. In Pacheco *et al.*, XXXV, 199–240.

Remesal, Antonio. Historia general de las Indias Occidentales, y particular de la gobernación de Chiapa y Guatemala. Guatemala: Tipografía nacional, 1932. 2 vols.

Resolución adopted by the Fathers of the Provincial Council of Santiago concerning the question of the servicio personal, March 19, 1608. In Lozano, I, 151–56.

Rivadeneira, Manuel, ed. Biblioteca de Autores Españoles desde la formación del lenguaje hasta nuestros días. Madrid: Real Academia Española, 1943–58. 110 vols.

Ronquillo, Diego. "Relación de lo ocurrido en Chile durante el tiempo que asistió en dicho reino, 1570." In Historiadores, II, 254–59.

Rosales, Diego de. "Dictámen sobre la esclavitud de los indígenas chilenos, Concepción, 20 de Marzo de 1672." In Amunátegui Solar, Las encomiendas, II, "Documentos," 253–72.

———— Historia general del reino de Chile. Valparaíso: Mercurio, 1877–78. 3 vols.

———— "Tratado de los daños de la esclavitud de los indios del reino de Chile, 1670." In Amunátegui Solar, Las encomiendas, II, "Documentos," 183–251.

———— "Varones ilustres de la Compañía de Jesús en Chile, 1600–63." In ACSI, A-I-1.

Sancho Rayón, José, and Francisco de Zabálburu, eds. Colección de documentos inéditos para la historia de España. Madrid: Imprenta de la viuda de Calero, 1842–95. 113 vols.

Santillán, Hernando de. "Ordenanzas para la Concepción, Imperial, Cañete, Valdivia, Villarrica y Osorno, Valparaíso, 4 de Junio de 1559." In DI, XXVIII, 297–302.

———— "Relación de lo que el licenciado Hernando de Santillán, oidor de la Audiencia de Lima, proveyó para el buen gobierno y pacificación y defensa del reino de Chile, 4 de junio de 1559." In DI, XXVIII, 284–97.

Sepúlveda, Juan Ginés de. Demócrates Segundo o De las justas causas de la guerra contra los indios. Madrid: Consejo Superior de Investigaciones Científicas, 1951.

Seville, Archivo General de Indias. Audiencia de Charcas, 74-4-4.

Silva Castro, Raúl, ed. Obras de Crescente Errázuriz. Santiago: Empresa Editora Zig-Zag, 1936. 2 vols.

Silva Cotapos, Carlos. Historia eclesiástica de Chile. Santiago: San José, 1925.

Silva y Molina, Abraham de. Oidores de la Audiencia de Santiago de Chile durante el siglo XVII. Santiago: Cervantes, 1902.

Simpson, Lesley Byrd. The Encomienda in New Spain. Berkeley: University of California Press, 1950.

———— Studies in the Administration of the Indians of New Spain: The Repartimiento System of Native Labor in New Spain and Guatemala. Ibero-Americana No. 13. Berkeley: University of California Press, 1938.

Sobrino, Gaspar. "Memorial al rey. Continuar la guerra defensiva, 1614." In ACSI, A-II-63, Part II, 755–84. In BNC, Archivo Vicuña Mackenna, CCXCII, 208–54.

Solórzano Pereira, Juan de. Política indiana. Madrid: M. Sacristan, 1736–39. 2 vols.

Solórzano y Velasco, Alonso de. "Informe sobre las cosas de Chile, 2 de Abril de 1657." In Gay, II, 422–48.

Suárez de Figueroa, Cristóbal. Hechos de Don García Hurtado de Mendoza cuarto marques de Cañete. In Historiadores, V. Santiago: Ferrocarril, 1864.

Tesillo, Santiago de. Guerras de Chile, causas de su duración y medios para su fin. In Historiadores, V. Santiago: Ferrocarril, 1864.

Testamento de Doña Agueda de Flores, Santiago, 19 de Mayo de 1595. In Vicuña Mackenna, Los Lisperguer, 255–57.

Testamento de Doña Marina Ortiz de Gaete, muger que fué de Pedro de Valdivia, Santiago, 15 de Diciembre de 1589. In DI, X, 332–34.

Torres Bollo, Diego de. Carta ánua de 1609. In Leonhardt, Documentos, 3–82.

———— Carta ánua de 1613. In Leonhardt, Documentos, 146–259.

Torres Saldamando, Enrique. Los antiguos jesuítas del Perú. Lima: Liberal, 1882.

Torres Saldamando, Enrique, and José M. Frontaura Arana, eds. Vida del P. Diego de Rosales, historiador de Chile, escríta en 1677 por el P. Francisco Ferreira. Santiago: Santiago, 1890.

Tribaldos de Toledo, Luis. Vista general de las continuadas guerras. Dificil conquista del gran reino, provincias de Chile. In Historiadores, IV. Santiago: Ferrocarril, 1864.

Valdivia, Luis de. "Memorial al rey, Madrid, 1610." In ACSI, A-II-55, 2–5.

———— "Memorial al rey, Madrid, 1622." In Medina, Biblioteca, II, 220–39.

———— "Memorial al rey sobre la guerra de Chile, Concepción, 7 de Septiembre de 1613." In ACSI, A-II-63, Part II, 585–89.

———— "Memorial que dió al excelentísimo señor Marques de Montes Claros, virrey del Perú, acerca de la dicha visita del reino de Chile, 1 de Marzo de 1612." In ACSI, A-II-55, No. 5.

———— "Relación de lo que sucedió en el reino de Chile después que el Padre Luis de Valdivia, de la Compañía de Jesús, entró en él con sus ocho compañeros sacerdotes de la misma Compañía el año de 1612." In Medina, Biblioteca, II, 94–109.

———— "Tratado de la importancia del medio que el virrey propone de cortar la guerra de Chile y hacerla solamente defensiva, 1610." In Medina, Biblioteca, II, 60–93.

Valdivia, Pedro de. Edict addressed to the encomenderos of Chile, Santiago, July 26, 1546. In DI, VIII, 127–31.

———— Writ of encomienda in favor of Juan Jufré, Santiago, November 1, 1552. In DI, XV, 17.

Vascones, Juan de. "Petición en derecho para el rey nuestro señor en su real consejo de las Indias, para que los rebeldos enemigos del reino de Chile sean declarados por esclavos del español que los hubiere a las manos. Propónese la justicia de aquella guerra y la que hay para mandar hacer la dicha declaración, 1599 [?]." In Hanke and Millares Carlo, 301–12.

Vásquez, Rodrigo. "Memorial al rey en favor del padre Luis de Valdivia, Concepción, 9 de Abril de 1616." In BNC, Archivo Jesuítas, XCIII, 65–70.

Vernon, Ida Stevenson Weldon. Pedro de Valdivia, Conquistador of Chile. Austin: University of Texas Press, 1946.

Vicuña Mackenna, Benjamin. Historia de Santiago. Santiago: Universidad de Chile, 1938. 2 vols.

———— Los Lisperguer y La Quintrala. Santiago: Empresa Editora Zig-Zag, 1950.

Vitoria, Francisco de. Relecciones de Indios y del derecho de la guerra. Madrid: Espasa-Calpe, 1928.

———— Carta dirigida al P. Miguel de Arcos, 1534. In Pirotto, 23–26.

Whitaker, Arthur P. "Antonio Ulloa," *The Hispanic American Historical Review*, XV (May 1935), 155–94.

———— "Jorge Juan and Antonio de Ulloa's Prologue to Their Secret Report of 1749 on Peru," *The Hispanic American Historical Review*, XVIII (Nov. 1938), 507–13.

Yáñez, Agustín. Fray Bartolomé de las Casas, el conquistador conquistado. México: Ediciones Xochitl, 1942.

Zavala, Silvio. La encomienda indiana. Madrid: Helénica, 1935.

———— Filosofía de la conquista. México: Fondo de Cultura Económica, 1947.

———— New Viewpoints on the Spanish Colonization of America. Philadelphia: University of Pennsylvania Press, 1943.

———— Servidumbre natural y libertad cristiana según los tratadistas españoles de los siglos XVI y XVII. Buenos Aires: Peuser, 1944.

Zavala, Silvio, and Agustín Millares Carlo, eds. De las Islas del mar Océano por Juan López de Palacios Rubios; Del dominio de los reyes de España sobre los indios por Fray Matías de Paz. México: Fondo de Cultura Económica, 1954. *See* Palacios Rubios *and* Paz.

INDEX

MODERN
CHILE

Geographical Extent
Placenames and Sites are of the Colonial Period

0   100   200

Miles

Pacific Ocean

Copiapó

LA SERENA

Coquimbo

Choapa

La Ligua

Quillota

MENDOZA

VALPARAÍSO

Mapocho R.

SANTIAGO

Maipo River

Melipilla

Maule River

Cauquenes

Itata

Quiriquina Is.

CHILLAN

Penco

Yumbel

CONCEPCIÓN

Sta. Juana

San Cristóbal

Colcura

Laxa River

ARAUCO

Est. Del Rey

Los Confines

Lebo

Cañete

ANGOL

Elicura

Tucapel

Paicaví

PUREN

Caulín R.

Mocha Island

Quillín R.

LA IMPERIAL

Boroa

Toltén R.

Spanish-Araucanian
Boundary, 1700

Biobío River

TOLTEN

Villarrica

VALDIVIA

Río Bueno

OSORNO

Island of
Chiloé

Castro

1657
1968

SANTIAGO

250 Miles